EC CONSUMER LAW

Dedication

From Geraint to Shirley Peacock

EC Consumer Law

GERAINT HOWELLS and THOMAS WILHELMSSON

Ashgate

DARTMOUTH

Aldershot • Brookfield USA • Singapore • Sydney

Published by
Dartmouth Publishing Company Limited
Ashgate Publishing Limited
Gower House
Croft Road
Aldershot
Hants GU11 3HR
England

Ashgate Publishing Company
Old Post Road
Brookfield
Vermont 05036
USA

British Library Cataloguing in Publication Data
Howells, Geraint G.
  EC consumer law. - (European business law library)
  1.Consumer protection - Law and legislation - European
  Union countries
  I.Title II.Wilhelmsson, Thomas
  343.4'071

Library of Congress Cataloging-in-Publication Data
Howells, Geraint G.
    EC consumer law / by Geraint Howells and Thomas Wilhelmsson.
      p.   cm.
    ISBN 1-85521-596-9 (hb). -- ISBN 1-85521-602-7 (pb)
      1. Consumer protection--Law and legislation--European Union
  countries. I. Wilhelmsson, Thomas, 1949-   . II. Title.
  KJE6577.H69   1997
  341.7'5'0614--dc21   97-7845
                                                                            CIP

ISBN 1 85521 596 9 (Hbk)
ISBN 1 85521 602 7 (Pbk)

Printed and bound in Great Britain by
Biddles Limited, Guildford and King's Lynn

Contents

Preface

Two of the most important legal developments in Western Europe in the second half of the twentieth century have been, on the one hand, the growth of EC law, and, on the other hand, the development of special rules to protect consumers. Therefore we hope our book on EC consumer law should be relevant and of interest to a wide audience of scholars and practitioners.

We believe the book is timely, because there is now a good deal of EC consumer legislation and case law of the European Court of Justice relating to consumer matters. Given that consumer protection has received a new place in the Community's constitution following the Maastricht Treaty, we believe it is an opportune time to analyse past and current trends and suggest future directions in which EC consumer policy might develop. Readers will see that we wish the EC to develop a more radical approach to consumer protection than has been the case to-date so that the benefits of EC consumer law are not restricted to a few active internal market consumers, but reach out to all Europe's citizens.

The book was a collaborative venture and the two authors had surprisingly few disagreements about the general role EC law (or law in general) should play in protecting consumers. Where minor differences of opinion did appear we hope to have dealt with these adequately in the text. We therefore feel able to put our joint names to the whole book. Readers may care to know that of the substantive chapters Wilhelmsson took the lead in drafting Chaps 3,4,5,7 and Howells was responsible for the first drafts of Chaps 2, 6 and 8. Of the introductory and concluding chapters Wilhelmsson made the first drafts of sections 1.1, 1.4, 9.1-3 and Howells of section 1.2-3, 9.4-6 and 10. However, electronic means of communication and a visit to the European Football Championship, as well as several conferences, provided many opportunities for discussion and correction and so the final effort can be viewed as a true joint venture.

Thanks must also be given to various bodies which have provided financial support which assisted in the preparation of this book. On Wilhelmsson's part the book forms part of a project on Welfare State expectations, privatisation and private law funded by the Academy of Finland. For Howells Chap. 2 represents, in part, the fruits of research sponsored by the British Academy and Nuffield Foundation into product safety regulation. These issues are covered in more detail in *Comparative Product Safety* also to be published by Dartmouth. Much of the thinking will be incorporated into a project entitled *The Modern Character of Consumer*

Protection Laws which is funded by the British Academy and the results of which will also be published by Dartmouth.

Thomas Wilhelmsson would like to thank the personnel at the Helsinki Institute for International and Economic Law and Tuuli Junkkari, as well as Satu Paasilehto for valuable comments concerning the discussion of legal cultures in Chap. 1. Geraint Howells would like to thank Shirley Peacock for the invaluable assistance she provided him. Both would like to thank Julie Prescott for converting our discs into camera-ready copy with her usual skill and patience. John Irwin and his staff at Dartmouth should also be thanked for their faith in this project and for producing a book in keeping with the high production quality which readers have come to expect from them.

We have tried to state the law as of 1 October 1996.

GERAINT HOWELLS
THOMAS WILHELMSSON

1 November 1996

1 Introduction

1. APPROACH AND SCOPE

A. What is Consumer Law?

Most societies have had rules protecting their citizens as consumers. From a functional perspective one could extend the history of consumer protection as far back as ancient rules on weights and measures. Legislation in areas such as food and insurance have also existed for a long time in many countries. Still, the concept of consumer law in the form it is used today is a relatively recent creation. Developing consumer protection only became important in the legal policy of Western European countries in the 1960s and 1970s. The concept of consumer law, as used in this book, should be understood against the background of modern consumer policy.

The new feature in this modern discourse (in addition to the obvious fact of the increased importance attached to this topic) is the general approach to 'consumption' problems which sets them within the framework of what one could call a 'consumer protection ideology'. This approach contains two basic features which may be used as criteria to define the sphere of modern consumer law. First, the role in which a person acts in the market has become relevant in legal policy. It has been recognised that a consumer buyer might require additional forms of protection to those offered to a commercial buyer. In law the concept of 'consumer', that is a person acquiring goods or services for private use, and the concept of private consumption have become relevant. Second, the problems of the consumer are seen to arise out of his or her relationship to the commercial party – 'the enterprise'. The relationship between consumer and enterprise is considered to be the basic legal relationship in consumer law.

In this book consumer law is understood in this limited sense, referring to the class of norms which are especially designated to protect the consumer in his or her dealings with an enterprise. This excludes some neighbouring branches of law, even though they may have an important impact on the position of consumers. Thus this book will not consider rules on general supervision of businesses, such as banking and insurance supervision,[1] and

---

[1]   The very few rules in EC law of relevance for consumer insurance contract law are also not analysed. However the rules on banking supervision are addressed briefly in the chapter on financial services, but mainly for the purpose of seeing how they fit alongside the consumer credit directives: see Chap. 6 section 1B.

comparable rules on the conduct of certain other businesses, as these rules are not specifically geared towards the protection of consumers. The law of competition – the rules against restriction of competition as well as against unfair competition – are similarly excluded, as their primary object is regulating relationships between enterprises and any advantages for consumers arise only indirectly.

The aims of consumer law are sometimes described with the help of the concept of 'market failure'. The consumer law norms purport to regulate or intervene in the market in order to put the consumer into a better position than he or she would be in without the regulation (and sometimes to place the consumer in the same position as he or she would have been in given a perfectly competitive market). Consumer law thus has an interventionist character.

In the field of consumer law, as well as in other fields of law, the approximation of the legal systems in the European Community takes place both through 'positive' and 'negative' harmonisation. By the latter is meant the removal of barriers of trade by requiring Member States to abolish national rules which are considered to create such obstacles. The European Court of Justice (hereafter ECJ) functions as the engine of this negative integration.[2] However, as these measures lead to deregulation by the removal of national interventionist norms, they are not the primary concern of this book, although they will be mentioned at appropriate places. Our main focus is on positive harmonisation, that is on the creation of new interventionist norms at the Community level. The fact that these norms may also have as their primary goal the creation of a coherent internal market, rather than the protection of consumers, does not take them outside the scope of our inquiry.

B.   The Consumer Concept

As mentioned in the previous section, consumer law deals with rules and principles specifically designed to protect the consumer in his/her relationship to the enterprise(s). The rules to be analysed in this book are rules the scope of which are delimited by the consumer concept. The content of this concept draws the boundaries around the subject of the book.

'Consumer' can mean various things in different contexts. Economics and sociology have developed their own consumer concepts. In law the definitions of 'consumer' certainly vary both from country to country and with regard to different sub-areas of consumer law.

---

2   An illustrative overview of court practice is given by Th. Bourgoignie and D. Trubek, *Consumer Law, Common Markets and Federalism*, (Walter de Gruyter, 1987) at 162 *et seq.*

The Community has developed its own consumer concept, which can be interpreted independently, without reference to national legal systems. The interpretation of the ECJ expressly refers to the objective of the rules, that is protecting the economically weaker and legally less experienced party to the contract.[3]

The consumer concept is used four times in the Treaty of Rome.[4] However, it has no distinct legal meaning in this context. The word 'consumer' in the competition law Articles (85–86) certainly also covers professionals. The Treaty itself offers no basis for the creation of a specific consumer law. This development first took place in secondary legislation, mainly by means of directives on consumer protection.

A definition of the consumer is included in several consumer protection directives[5] as well as in the 1980 Rome Convention on the Law Applicable to Contractual Obligations (art. 5) and the 1968 Brussels Convention on Jurisdiction and the Enforcement of Judgments in Civil and Commercial Matters (art. 13). The definition is fairly formal and given in a negative form, excluding business and professional activities. A consumer is a natural person, who is acting for purposes outside his or her trade or profession.[6] If the contract relates only partly to a trade or profession, the consumer protection directives should (according to some commentators) be applied if the person is acting 'primarily outside his trade or profession'.[7]

---

3 N. Reich, 'Zur Theorie des Europäischen Verbraucherrechtes' (1994) 2 *Zeitschrift für Europäisches Privatrecht* 381 at 387 and R. Plender (ed.), *The European Contracts Convention*, (Sweet & Maxwell, 1991) at 127.

4 L. Krämer, *EEC Consumer Law*, (Story Scientia, 1986) at 1.

5 However, for obvious reasons in a directive like the General Product Safety Directive the focus is not on the definition of 'consumer' but on the definition of 'product' as a consumer product.

6 Doorstep Selling Directive art. 2, Consumer Credit Directive art. 1(2)(a) and Unfair Contract Terms Directive art. 2(b). The Unfair Contract Terms Directive, however, uses the phrase 'outside his trade, business or profession', while the Rome Convention and the other Directives referred to do not expressly mention 'business'. However, no difference in content seems to be intended. The definition in the Timeshare Directive art. 2, which in fact uses the term 'purchaser' instead of 'consumer', is also somewhat different ('for purposes which may be regarded as being outwith his professional capacity'), but seems to have the same meaning. Full references to the Directives are given below, in section 3B.

7 See e.g. P. Duffy 'Unfair Contract Terms and the Draft E.C. Directive' (1993) 37 *J.B.L.* 67 at 73 and N. Misita, 'Towards "Consumer Law proper" – on some aspects of the Brussels and Rome Convention', in T. Wilhelmsson & K. Kaukonen (eds), *Euroopan integraatio ja sosiaalinen sopimusoikeus*, (Lakimiesliiton kustannus, 1993) 239 at 246.

There has been much discussion about whether the consumer protection provisions should be extended to protect small enterprises as well. The ECJ has expressly stated that the protection by the Doorstep Selling Directive does not extend its reach to beyond consumers proper.[8] In that case the Advocate–General of the Court had suggested that the consumer concept should be defined concretely, rather than in the abstract, and so whether a person was acting as a consumer would depend upon the activity being undertaken. The case involved a businessman who sold his undertaking. The Advocate–General considered that he could be compared to a consumer, because the transaction in question was not common to him and thus was outside his trade or profession. The Court, however, did not accept the view of the Advocate–General; it preferred a narrower reading of the Directive. Only 'real' consumers – in the sense of private individuals – are to be treated as consumers when applying most of the Community consumer protection directives concerned with contract law.

Community consumer law is not, however, completely consistent in the way it delineates its scope. The Package Travel Directive uses a broader consumer concept – a person who takes or agrees to take the package or any person on whose behalf the purchase of the package is made or to whom the package is transferred (art. 2(4)) – and thus also covers, for example, a businessman buying a business trip.[9] The scope of the Overbooking Regulation is equally broad.[10] Therefore it is only logical that the Regulation – in contrast to the Package Travel Directive – speaks about 'passengers' instead of 'consumers'. Strictly speaking, the Package Travel Directive and the Overbooking Regulation could therefore be said to fall outside the sphere of consumer law, as it has been defined above. However, as the aim of these measures certainly is the protection of consumers, they will be analysed in this book.

In other areas than contract law, the approach has sometimes been wider. The Misleading Advertising Directive protects consumers, as well as persons carrying on a trade or business or practising a craft or profession and the interests of the public in general (art. 1). Member States are required to have control systems in place to protect not only consumers, but also competitors and the general public, and actions may be brought by persons and organisations regarded under national law as having a legitimate interest in prohibiting misleading advertising. This is broader than merely giving standing to consumer organisations and could include trade associations (art. 4). The Products Liability Directive covers death and personal injury caused

---

8   *Criminal proceedings against Patrice di Pinto*, Case C–361/89 [1991] ECR I 1189.

9   S. Storm, 'Harmonization of the Legislation of EC Member States on Consumer Protection Regarding Package Holidays' (1992) *E.Consum.L.J.* 189 at 191.

10   See Chap. 7 section 3.

by a defective product, irrespective of whether the injured person used the
product or was confronted by it as a consumer and regardless of whether the
product was a consumer product or not. Recovery for property damaged is,
however, restricted to damage caused to consumer goods. Obviously these
Directives must be analysed in a treatise on EC consumer law, but the focus
of this analysis will of course be on the effects of the Directives on the
position of the consumer.

C. Our Approach and its Limitations

Since the start of a Community consumer policy in the mid–1970s a
considerable amount of positive Community consumer law has been
produced. As a consequence of this growing bulk of concrete legal material,
legal writing in this area has also been expanding. Community consumer law
has already been systematised and described in detail in legal literature. In
addition to a large amount of articles in legal periodicals even a few
comprehensive textbooks have been published.[11]

The approach of this book is, however, somewhat different from the
approaches of the existing textbooks. As opposed to the perspective of
Norbert Reich's book, the main focus is on the positive consumer law
measures within the EC and not so much on the general regulation of market
integration in the area of consumption and its effects on the position of
consumers. Again, contrary to the approach of Vivienne Kendall, the aim is
not to give a description of all the numerous legislative measures which, with
a very broad definition of the scope of consumer law, perhaps could be said
to belong to this area. Here we try instead to analyse the more important
details of Community consumer law in connection with a general discussion
of the aims and principles of this branch of Community law.

The concrete parts of the study therefore focus on the most important
directives in the area, analysing them both from a legal policy perspective
and from a black–letter law perspective. All the details of the large amount
of legislation that constitute European Community consumer law will not be
looked at, as one purpose of the analysis of these details is to present the
basic policies and approaches – from a legal perspective one could also
speak about the general principles – of Community consumer law. The

---

11   Krämer, *op. cit.*, N. Reich, *Europäisches Verbraucherrecht*, (3rd ed., Nomos, 1996)
      and V. Kendall, *EC Consumer Law*, (Chancery, 1994). An interesting introductory
      work is shortly to be published by S. Weatherill, *EC Consumer Law and Policy*,
      (Longman), although we were kindly allowed advanced sight of this work we have
      been unable to include references to it in the body of our work.

details are analysed in the light of some general questions which have been considered relevant in this context.[12]

As noted above, the book deals with consumer law proper, leaving aside areas like competition law as well as banking and insurance law. In order to avoid too much detail, and as these questions often are analysed in specific treatises, we have also excluded the law on food and cosmetics and related products, although this area of consumer law has been subject to a significant amount of European legislation. We have also more generally tried to avoid discussing the detail of product specific legislation.

2. LEGAL BASIS OF EC CONSUMER LAW

A. Pre–Maastricht

The original Treaty of Rome did not have consumer protection as a specific object and only made a few tangential references to the position of the consumer in the European legal order. Thus:

(i) the Preamble stated an objective of the six original signatories to be 'the constant improvement of the living and working conditions of their people';

(ii) Art. 2 provided that one of the Community's tasks was to promote 'an accelerated raising of the standard of living';

(iii) Art. 39(1)(e) specified one of the objectives of the Common Agricultural Policy as being 'to ensure that supplies reach consumers at reasonable prices';

(iv) Art. 85(3) exempted agreements which may be anti–competitive if they contribute 'to improving the production or distribution of goods or to promoting technical or economic progress, while allowing consumers a fair share of the resulting benefit', and;

(v) Art. 86(c) stated an abuse of a dominant position within the common market may consist in 'limiting production, markets or technical development to the prejudice of consumers'.

As shall be seen, the lack of an express reference to consumer protection policy as a specific objective of the Community was not to prevent the Community from interesting itself in consumer protection matters. The basis for legislation in this area was usually taken to be art. 100 of the Treaty which permits directives to be made to approximate matters which directly affect the establishment or functioning of the common market. This approach

---

[12] See below, section 4B.

was strengthened by the Single European Act 1986 which inserted art. 100a into the Treaty. This changed the voting procedures for matters relating to the establishment or functioning of the internal market to one of qualified majority rather than the previous unanimity rule. Particularly important was art. 100a(3) which provided that when making proposals relating to the internal market concerning, *inter alia*, consumer protection the Commission would take as a base a high level of protection.

Consumer policy therefore started life as an incident of internal market policy. However, it has always been more than simply a support for commercial policy. This seems to be implicitly recognised in the Single European Act: for why should a high base be taken for consumer protection if protection of the consumer was only necessary to the extent that consumer laws (or the lack of them) impeded community trade? The debate on whether there is/should be an autonomous Community consumer policy independent of internal market concerns will be returned to at several points in this book. For the moment it is sufficient to note that it has not been resolved by the Maastricht amendments to the Treaty of European Union, despite consumer protection being recognised as a legitimate Community activity.

B. Maastricht

Art. 3(s) of the Treaty of European Union now provides that the activities of the Community shall include, *inter alia*, 'a contribution to the strengthening of consumer protection'. The wording of this objective is perhaps significant, for the qualification that the Community should merely contribute to the goal of strengthening consumer protection was clearly made with one eye on the subsidiarity principle (see below).

Art. 129a is, however, the most important provision in the new Treaty with regard to consumer protection. It provides:

'(1) The Community shall contribute to the attainment of a high level of consumer protection through:
(a) measures adopted pursuant to art. 100a in the context of the completion of the internal market;
(b) specific action which supports and supplements the policy pursued by the Member States to protect the health, safety and economic interests of consumers and to provide adequate information to consumers.'[13]

---

13 See H.–W. Micklitz and S. Weatherill, 'Consumer Policy in the European Community: before and after Maastricht' (1993) 16 J.C.P. 285.

Art. 129a(1)(a) seems merely to confirm the pre–existing position where consumer protection is an element of internal market policy, although attaining a high level of protection has become an objective of the Community and not just a condition to be satisfied by internal market directives. Art. 129a(1)(b), however, recognises for the first time the Community's power to act to protect consumers independent of internal market concerns. This is balanced by the fact that additional specific actions are merely to be such as support and supplement policies pursued by Member States (although supplement can give considerable scope for activity!) and by the inclusion of the subsidiarity principle which has the potential to take away with one hand that which has been given by the other.[14]

This is not the place for a detailed analysis of the subsidiarity principle, however, it is important to stress that the principle is not intended to prevent the Community from acting, but rather should be used to determine when Community action is desirable. Whether Community action is required should be judged against the criteria of whether Member States are individually able to achieve sufficiently the objectives required and whether the scale and effects of the proposed action merits Community involvement. As goods, services and advertising are increasingly conducted on an inter–state basis a case can quite easily be made out for domestic law not being sufficient since consumers may still be injured by the activities of enterprises in Member States with less protective laws. Consumers may be harmed either in their own country by imported goods or services or when visiting other Member States. Furthermore Community action can be justified in reaching beyond inter–state trade, since it would be confusing and illogical to apply higher standards to inter–state consumer contracts than to domestic consumer contracts.

The European Parliament in its resolution of 19 January 1993 was keen to stress that subsidiarity should not weaken consumer protection.[15] It saw subsidiarity, not as a reason for lack of activity in the consumer field, but rather as a principle by which democratic involvement could be maximised in policy–making, implementation and enforcement and through which maximum consumer protection could be achieved by decisions being taken at the most local level. It considered that repatriation of consumer protection

---

14   Art. 3b provides that 'in areas which do not fall within its exclusive competence, the Community shall take action, in accordance with the principle of subsidiarity, only if and in so far as the objective of the proposed action cannot be sufficiently achieved by the Member States and can therefore, by reason of the scale or effects of the proposed action, be better achieved by the Community'.

15   Resolution on the application of the principle of subsidiarity to environment and consumer protection policy: OJ 1993 C42/40.

policy competence to Member States and the weakening of minimum harmonised Community–wide standards would directly undermine the Single Market. It insisted that in determining future competence's consumer protection should be the prime criterion and resisted any attempt to apply a retrospective subsidiarity principle to consumer protection legislation. This is a sensible interpretation of the subsidiarity principle. It should be used as a means for determining the most effective method of achieving consumer protection, rather than as simply a means of thwarting the development of consumer policy at the EC level. It should promote a constructive relationship between Europe, Member States and regions so that consumers can be protected by the most effective means. Thus, in keeping with the true spirit of the subsidiarity principle, we would favour EC legislation, wherever practicable, allowing Member States to use existing structures and techniques of consumer protection so long as these are adequate and effective to achieve the desired results. What we do not welcome is the subsidiarity argument being used as a bargaining counter to persuade the Commission to take out the most radical measures or to propose a non–binding act instead of a binding legislation. Unfortunately the impression is that subsidiarity is being used less as a rule of principle and more as a political tool to restrict the development of a protective framework of consumer protection measures for Europe's citizens.

3.　THE EVOLUTION OF EUROPEAN CONSUMER LAW AND POLICY

A.　Programmes of Activity

In 1975 the Council issued a preliminary programme for a consumer protection and information policy.[16] This, echoing President Kennedy, set out a statement of five basic consumer rights, namely:

(i)　the right to protection of health and safety;
(ii)　the right to protection of economic interests;
(iii)　the right of redress;
(iv)　the right to information and education;
(v)　the right of representation (the right to be heard).

These rights were to be given greater substance under specific community policies and the programme set out a series of principles under each of the headings and priorities for action. In 1981 a second programme for a

---

[16]　OJ 1975 C92/1.

consumer protection and information policy was resolved upon by the Council.[17] This second programme reasserted the five basic rights listed above, but also noted that because of the recessionary climate more attention than before should be paid to the price of goods and services and the quality of services which were accounting for a greater share of household expenditure. It called for greater dialogue with consumer groups, but perhaps ominously called on the consumer movement 'while continuing to voice its proper concerns ...[to] progressively take into account ... economic and social implications...'. Although reasonable enough on face value, this is perhaps the early signs of the deregulatory approach affecting Community consumer law and policy. It is perhaps no accident that in the same vein the Council suggested that in some areas voluntary solutions could be adopted instead of legislation. Deregulation and soft law are frequent bed fellows.

On the tenth anniversary of the first programme the Commission issued an internal communication to the Council entitled *A New Impetus for Consumer Protection Policy*. It was a response to the perceived lack of progress in consumer affairs at the Community level which was blamed on:

(i)   the deep economic recession (consumer protection was seen as a 'fair weather phenomenon');
(ii) a perception that consumer affairs were a matter for national governments (especially concerning economic interests);
(iii) the need for measures to be adopted unanimously (this was prior to the Single European Act), and;
(iv) too much concentration being placed on vertical harmonisation of a restricted range of goods rather than focusing on fewer proposals with general coverage.

This last point was in line with the new approach to technical harmonisation.[18]

The Commission argued for a new impetus based on viewing consumer protection both from the standpoint of citizen's welfare and efficiency of production. This was welcomed by the Council in their 1986 resolution concerning the future orientation of consumer policy.[19] Perhaps significantly for our thesis – which is that consumer protection should have an independent social justification – the Council characterised the new impetus's objectives (of providing consumers with a high level of safety and health protection and an increased ability to benefit from the Community market) as constituting important steps on the road to a 'People's Europe'. The Council's

---

[17]   OJ 1981 C133/1.
[18]   See OJ 1985 C136/1, discussed in Chap. 2 section 4C(i).
[19]   OJ 1986 C167/1.

support for the integration of consumer policies in other common policies was spelt out further in a subsequent Resolution on 15 December 1986.[20]

By the end of the 1980s the importance of consumer protection within the Community framework was becoming apparent. Certain trends in policy could be discerned. It was recognised that consumer protection had to be taken into account when formulating other policies. Consumer representation and dialogue were considered important. There was a trend to general horizontal rather than specific vertical regulation. There was an increasing reliance on soft law. Although Member States are always most at ease when dealing with Community legislation relating to safety, the need for protection of the consumer's economic interest was also increasingly being recognised. The Council Resolutions of 9 November 1989 on future priorities for relaunching consumer protection policy[21] and of 13 July 1992 on future priorities for the development of consumer protection policy[22] clearly attempted to underline the commitment of European law to protecting consumer economic interests and improving access to justice.

1989 saw the creation of an independent Consumer Policy Service, which in 1995 became D–G XXIV. This Service produced two three year action plans for 1990–93[23] and 1993–95.[24] These followed a now well established pattern of stressing the need to integrate consumer policies with other policies and the need for better information (both through labelling and through education initiatives such as comparative testing and advice centres in frontier regions), consumer representation or 'concertation' as it has become known and protection of the consumer's health and safety. As already noted, protection of the consumer's economic interests is a more difficult area for a consensus on Community activity to be achieved. The first three year plan had a section on consumer transactions, whilst the second three year plan highlighted access to justice and financial services as areas of concern.

The new D–G XXIV has issued a third three year plan for 1996–8.[25] This proposes reviewing and updating the framework needed to guarantee the single market works for consumers, but offers few new major legislative initiatives apart from follow up measures to Green Papers on Consumer Guarantees and Access to Justice. It has, nevertheless, been welcomed for

---

[20]   OJ 1987 C3/1.

[21]   OJ 1989 C294/1.

[22]   OJ 1992 C186/1.

[23]   COM(90) 98. This is sometimes referred to as the Third Action Programme, see Consumer Policy in the Single Market, (Office for Official Publications of the European Communities, 1991) at 33–47.

[24]   COM(93) 378.

[25]   COM(95) 519.

adopting, for the first time, a political approach to the problems of consumer rights.[26]

General consumer education and information is seen as a priority with the Commission which desires consumers to be able to operate independently on the market with full possession of the facts. One of the aims of this book is to explain why this concern to educate and inform consumers is a necessary, but not sufficient, condition for an effective consumer policy. In part the Commission seems to share some of our anxieties for it notes that the explosion of available information may actually cause problems for consumers who have to select appropriate and relevant information. Also it stresses the need to complement information with effective consumer education targeted at schoolchildren from an early age. However, some consumers will always have problems protecting themselves, however much information they have, whilst the average consumer cannot be expected to rely solely on information for protection. Stress is also placed on the need to ensure consumers benefit from the development of the Information Society. An attempt is also made to align consumer policy with the general thrust of Community policy by referring to the consumer perspective on European Monetary Union.

Other matters of particular concern cited include (i) financial services, (ii) public utilities (this is a relatively new area of EC activity and the policy involves supporting liberalisation whilst protecting the consumer interest as regards quality, efficiency and cost and ensuring adequate guarantees of universal service); (iii) encouraging the adoption of sustainable consumer habits; and (iv) increasing confidence in foodstuffs safety and marketing (a Green Paper of the future of EC food legislation is foreshadowed).

The Commission also wants to improve and increase consumer representation. This is something which we support and consider to be particularly vital in those sectors where self–regulatory approaches to regulation are being adopted. Interestingly the Commission notes that increasingly it uses market research on consumer opinions to supplement the formal channels of communication it has with consumer groups. As only four million of Europe's consumers are subscribers to consumer associations this can be seen as a useful way of ensuring their statements about the consumer interest coincide with the actual values of ordinary consumers. This should be welcomed by consumer groups as being a way of demonstrating that they do indeed represent the general consumer interest and not an unrepresentative minority.

The Commission is also internationalising its consumer policy agenda. It is seeking to promote consumer rights in Central and Eastern Europe as a prelude to those countries possibly joining an enlarged Union. It also

---

[26]   See A. Davis [1996] *Consum. L.J.* CS1.

suggests linking consumer policy with development policy in developing countries.

Increasingly the plans of D–G XXIV are becoming more limited and pragmatic. This perhaps reflects the fact that the easy measures have been adopted and the more contentious issues are now on the horizon. It is, perhaps, also an effect of the subsidiarity principle. Many of the issues currently on the Commission's agenda do not always suggest easy legislative solutions. The basic legislative structure of EC consumer law is perhaps seen by the Commission as being almost in place and in the future consumer concerns may require negotiation, education and information as much as legal rights. Nevertheless the need for a solid legislative framework should not be underestimated. Thus it is, perhaps, encouraging that the Commission is on the verge of seeing Directives on comparative advertising and distant selling being adopted and that it proposes to follow–up its Green Papers with directives on consumer guarantees and access to justice. However, the current deregulatory climate is likely to mean that the content of some of these measures will be far from satisfactory. One might also point to the lamentable lack of regulation of consumer services, in particular as regards safety, as a glaring gap in EC consumer protection.

One can, nevertheless, reflect that it is an opportune time for this book to be written as EC laws in most of the substantial areas of consumer protection have either been adopted or are being discussed at the moment. The Commission is therefore rightly stressing the need for the directives to be both implemented by Member States and effectively enforced. This is important if consumer law is to have substance as well as symbolism. Improving co–operation between national authorities is seen as an important function of the Commission. This is particularly important as the number of cross–border complaints rises. However, it is a theme of this book that EC consumer law should be seen as important not just because of how it can help resolve cross border disputes, but because of the rights it can assure for all Europe's citizens be they at home or abroad.

B.   Legislation

We have limited our study, in the main, to the general consumer protection measures and have not dealt in detail with legislation relating to specific products and services. The principal consumer protection measures in European Community law are directives concerning:

- product liability,[27]
- general product safety,[28]
- unfair contract terms,[29]
- misleading advertising,[30]
- price indications on foodstuffs,[31]
- price indications on non–food products,[32]
- contracts negotiated away from business premises,[33]
- consumer credit,[34]
- package travel, package holidays and package tours,[35] and
- timeshares.[36]

---

[27]   Council Directive 85/374/EEC on the approximation of the laws, regulations and administrative provisions of the Member States concerning liability for defective products: OJ 1985 L 210/29 (hereafter Product Liability Directive, Appendix 1).

[28]   Council Directive 92/59/EEC on general product safety: OJ 1992 L 228/24 (hereafter General Product Safety Directive, see Appendix 2).

[29]   Council Directive 93/13/EEC on unfair terms in consumer contracts: OJ 1993 L 95/29 (hereafter Unfair Contract Terms Directive, see Appendix 3).

[30]   Council Directive 84/450/EEC relating to the approximation of the laws, regulations and administrative provisions of the Member States concerning misleading advertising: OJ 1984 L 250/17 (hereafter Misleading Advertising Directive, see Appendix 4).

[31]   Council Directive 79/581/EEC on consumer protection in the indication of the prices of foodstuffs: OJ 1979 L 158/19 (as amended by Directive 88/315/EEC: OJ 1988 L142/23) (hereafter Foodstuffs Price Indication Directive, see Appendix 5).

[32]   Council Directive 88/314/EEC on consumer protection in the indication of the prices of non–food products: OJ 1988 L 142/19 (hereafter Non–food Price Indication Directive, see Appendix 6).

[33]   Council Directive 85/577/EEC to protect the consumer in respect of contracts negotiated away from business premises: OJ 1985 L 372/31 (hereafter Doorstep Selling Directive, see Appendix 7).

[34]   Council Directive 87/102/EEC for the approximation of the laws, regulations and administrative provisions of the Member States concerning consumer credit: OJ 1987 L 42/48 (as amended by Directive 90/88/EEC: OJ 1990 L 61/14) (hereafter Consumer Credit Directive, see Appendix 8).

[35]   Council Directive 90/314/EEC on package travel, package holidays and package tours: OJ 1990 L 158/59 (hereafter Package Travel Directive, see Appendix 9).

[36]   Council Directive 94/47/EC on the protection of purchasers in respect of certain aspects of contracts relating to the purchase of the right to use immovable properties on a timeshare basis: OJ 1994 L 280/83 (hereafter Timeshare Directive, see Appendix 10).

There are also non–binding Recommendations on distant selling,[37] electronic payment,[38] payment systems,[39] and cross–border financial transactions.[40] There was a draft directive on service liability,[41] but this has been withdrawn and is likely to be replaced by sectoral directives. Draft directives on comparative advertising,[42] amending the rules on unit pricing[43] and regulating distant selling[44] are likely to be enacted in the not too distant future. The Consumer Policy Service has recently given priority to the Green Papers on *Guarantees for Consumer Goods and After-Sales Services*[45] and *Access of Consumers to Justice and the Settlement of Consumer Disputes in the Single Market*.[46] Draft directives on the sale of consumer goods and associated guarantees[47] and on injunctions for the protection of the consumers' interests[48] have been published as well as an action plan on consumer access to justice and the settlement of consumer disputes in the internal market.[49]

C. Institutions

Prior to 1989 consumer affairs were dealt with by D–G XI which had responsibility for the environment, consumer protection and nuclear safety. In 1989 an independent Consumer Policy Service was established. Perhaps as a sign that consumer protection is really beginning to be taken seriously at the Community level the Service was given Directorate–General status in 1995 (D–G XXIV). Its first Director–General is Spyros Pappas. In April 1996 the D–G was restructured so that it had four units directly attached to the Director–General (legal matters, co–ordination of monitoring group with Member States, resources and development of consumer information and representation), with a Directorate A split into five units (consumer training

---

[37] OJ 1992 L 156/21.
[38] OJ 1987 L 365/72.
[39] OJ 1988 L 317/55.
[40] OJ 1990 L 67/39.
[41] OJ 1991 C 12/8.
[42] OJ 1991 C 180/14.
[43] COM(94) 431.
[44] Common position at OJ 1995 C 288/1.
[45] COM(93) 509.
[46] COM(93) 576.
[47] COM(95) 520.
[48] COM(95) 712.
[49] COM(96) 13.

and the information society; transactions; products; services and sustainable consumption).[50]

The Consumer Policy Service was until recently advised by a Consumers' Consultative Council (CCC).[51] This was comprised of 39 members (16 from European consumer organisations, 17 from national consumer organisations and institutions and six individuals qualified in consumer affairs). It was criticised by some consumer groups because some of the consumer bodies also represented interests other than the consumer (for example, EURO COOP also represents farmers and producers). It was also felt that CCC was not properly consulted by other Community Institutions. As the CCC only included consumer representatives it did not permit dialogue with other interested groups, such as producers. Therefore Christine Scrivener, the former Consumer Policy Commissioner, instituted a more broadly based Consumer Forum. The CCC has also been replaced by a Consumer Committee; this is more streamlined than its predecessor having just 20 members (15 from national consumer organisations and five from European and regional consumer bodies). In addition consumer organisations are also widely consulted on developments. The most significant European consumer organisation is BEUC (Bureau Européen des Unions Consommateurs) which is an umbrella organisation for national consumer organisations.

In the European Parliament consumer affairs are principally handled by the Committee on the Environment, Public Health and Consumer Protection. The Economic and Social Committee also has a section dealing with these topics. The impact of these committees on community policy is difficult to assess, but certainly the Commission has to take their views seriously. This is particularly true of the European Parliament which has gained increased powers in recent years and has a good track record of sponsoring the consumer cause. It is less obvious that the opinions of these committees have a significant effect upon the Council which exercises the legislative function.

4.   STRUCTURE AND GENERAL QUESTIONS

A.   Structure

The material outlined in the previous section will be analysed more closely in the following chapters. The concrete analysis starts with the area which so far seems to have attracted most attention from the Community legislator,

---

50   Info – C 1996/3

51   This replaced the Consumers' Consultative Committee in 1989 which in turn replaced the Contact Committee for Consumer Questions (1962–73).

that is the protection of the physical safety of the consumer (Chap. 2). Thereafter the attention is focused on the subject of most interest from the perspective of the theory of private law, the more general rules on consumer contracts (Chap. 3). The various pieces of Community marketing law, covering both advertising (Chap. 4) and trade practices (Chap. 5) are treated next.

The chapters mentioned so far are not limited to particular trade sectors, but have a relatively general scope. There are, however, more specific rules in Community consumer law which regulate only certain areas of life. We have chosen to concentrate on two areas which are of great importance to consumers, namely financial services (Chap. 6) and tourism (Chap. 7). The legislation discussed in these chapters contains rules on both contracts and marketing and therefore connects to the more general chapters mentioned before. However, we considered it to be clearer and more comprehensible to present the rules on credit and tourism as a whole in their own chapters, instead of splitting the content of the directives into the chapters on contracts and marketing.

Substantive rules alone are not sufficient to ensure the efficient protection of consumers. A functioning system of protection requires that attention also be paid to the question of the consumers' access to justice. The efforts of the Community in this area – and the related questions of private international law – are analysed in the last concrete chapter (Chap. 8).

The following chapter (Chap. 9) contains our general conclusions concerning the aims and principles of Community consumer law. As already mentioned the concrete analysis of the various pieces of law in the preceding chapters is made against the background of certain general questions or theses concerning Community consumer law. The observations made in these chapters are drawn together in the conclusion which seeks to present a general perspective on Community consumer law. In other words the general results of the research are presented in this chapter. Finally, in a short concluding chapter (Chap. 10), we attempt to make a personal assessment of the achievements of Community consumer law from the point of view of consumer protection.

B. General Questions

The general questions or theses which we try to address throughout the book are the following:

(i) As noted above, the legal basis for Community consumer policy was, at least before Maastricht, related to *internal market policy* and not to consumer protection. The question we pose here is, to what extent this focus on internal market policy is the real purpose of the measures and to what extent, if any, it is rather a window–dressing needed to provide the necessary legislative power for the Community. Has there, in other words, been room for an *autonomous Community consumer policy* with consumer protection as its primary purpose? In connection with this one may also discuss the more normative question, whether and to what extent there is a need for such an autonomous consumer policy of the EC and what kinds of principles or general approaches – both in a material and a procedural sense – should be guiding such a policy.

(ii)   A consumer protection system can be based on various kinds of strategies. Without claiming that the system is wholly consistent as to its goals and means one can often point to certain strategies as the dominant ones. Our thesis is that Community consumer law is strongly founded on a *strategy of choice and transparency*, which emphasises rules on consumer information. We attempt to show to what extent the ideology of consumer choice dominates Community consumer law, and to discuss the deficiencies in the protection resulting from the choice of this approach. Of course there is also room for a more positive normative outlook. We therefore consider whether there is a basis in the Community material for developing a more radical transparency strategy.

(iii) Closely related to the models guiding consumer policy are our perceptions of the behaviour and needs of consumers. Various consumer protection strategies emphasise different characteristics of consumers. They each work with a different consumer image. From the emphasis on a transparency strategy, at least in the form it is perceived in the Community today, it seems to follow that the dominating consumer image in Community law is of the rational information–seeking consumer. We will claim that the Community, as a consequence of this, is primarily interested in the *well–equipped and active internal–market–consumer*, and we will show that the instances where the special needs of weak and poor consumers are taken into account are very rare. This, again, gives inspiration to a normative discussion concerning collective measures for consumer protection as well as rules against discrimination as possible methods for assisting vulnerable consumers.

(iv)   Of course the needs and wants of at least some kind of average consumer have to be reflected in the legal rules. One could perhaps speak about *the legitimate expectations of consumers* as a basic concept of Community consumer law. We attempt to show the usefulness of this concept in the analysis of Community consumer law on various levels. On the one hand it can be seen as a perspective under which various more specific rules can be interpreted as parts of a system which at least to some extent seems consistent. It can also be used as a means by which a criticism of some measures can be given an internal legitimation. On the other hand the legitimate expectation test can be developed as an independent substantive principle of Community consumer law.

(v) A reflection of the strong internal–market–orientation of Community consumer law may perhaps be seen also in the choice of subjects to be regulated. At least in the first phases of integration, rules pertaining to the free flow of goods rather than services have been in the forefront of general Community law. This seems also to be reflected in Community consumer law. We will attempt to discuss to what extent the consumer law of the Community is characterised by rules on *goods rather than services* and what impact this has on the chosen strategies and regulatory techniques. From a legal policy point of view one may also question the adequateness of this attitude.

(vi). Finally certain observations regarding the *legal techniques* used in Community consumer law will be discussed. This requires an analysis of the development towards a more frequent use of various forms of soft law and a discussion of the need for having sufficient legal back–up for such new forms of law. One must also draw attention to the reluctance of Community law to regulate the remedies for breach of law – including both the substantive remedies and the procedural questions regarding access to justice – and to leave these, within certain limits, to national law. Finally one reaches the ultimate question from the point of view of legal technique: how far can one proceed with the help of the present scattered and unsystematic legal technique before one reaches a point where the need for a more systematic type of consumer code comes on to the agenda and what would be the advantages and drawbacks of such a more comprehensive perspective?

C. Problems of a Multinational Approach

This book is written by a lawyer trained in common law and a lawyer whose legal upbringing has taken place within a specific version of the continental legal system, that is Finnish, or more broadly Nordic, law. This has certain implications for the perspective and scope as well as for the methodology of the survey which should be made clear to the reader. It certainly poses problems, some of a very fundamental nature, but it also gives rise to new possibilities.

The main consequence of the different backgrounds of the authors is the impossibility to anchor the analysis of Community law in any specific national legal order. Of course many of our examples are taken from English and Nordic law – but not exclusively from these areas – but we have not adopted a national perspective when looking at the Community materials. The perspective of an English and a Finnish lawyer are so different that they cannot be combined in one coherent national platform. The book cannot therefore consistently look at Community law in its interplay with a certain national legal culture, but has to approach it as an autonomous multinational construct. In a way this seems like an impossible mission (although this is what the ECJ in fact requests European lawyers to do): law can never be deeply understood disconnected from its roots in a particular society and culture. However, as we have embarked on the mission, we at least have to mention the problems which lie ahead and some possible solutions.

First, a study of Community law without any national perspective is a study of law disconnected from society. Such a study can obviously give only a superficial and even misleading picture of the law, as there is an inseparable linkage between 'law' and 'society' and the divide between those two spheres is always to some extent artificial. Still there is much Community law research purporting to be able to cut the ties to (national) society – which is probably one reason why Community law doctrine often seems so lifeless. This problem of course affects this study as well. In the area of consumer law, however, the problem is perhaps not as acute as in some other fields of law. To some extent, even on a global scale, but certainly within the Western world, some convergence in the behaviour of the actors on the consumer market has certainly occurred. The same products are sold, same or similar advertising campaigns are used, the marketing methods are similar and the distribution systems (supermarkets etc.) become more alike the world over. This is especially true in Europe, and this tendency may have been enhanced, to some extent, following the creation of the internal market. A consumer abroad, in some other Member State of the Community, can in most situations connected with consumption feel more or less at home. Partly as a consequence of this one suspects that the consumption habits of consumers in different states are becoming more alike. Another strong influence in this direction is the multinational information and entertainment industry. The culture of consumption, produced and reproduced at an ever faster speed in the consumer society, is probably one area where European (or rather, Western) culture really has become more homogeneous[52] – for good and for bad. One could perhaps speak about a

---

52   This goes for the homogeneity between consumption patterns in the various Member States of the European Union. Probably there are greater differences between, say, a farmer and an urban white collar employee in the same country than between similar types of people in different countries within the Union. In general consumption patterns may have become more heterogeneous in the post–modern world. The

European consumer society emerging as a social substratum to Community consumer law.[53] At least this is what we have tried to bear in mind when assessing Community consumer law in relation to society. Of course inevitably to some extent our perception of this European consumer society is tainted with our British and Finnish experiences.

Second, and this seems to be a more crucial problem, a 'pure' Community law approach seems to disconnect the European rules from their natural base in a legal culture (the term here being used in the limited meaning of how law and its institutions are perceived in a certain community of legal actors). It is an obvious misconception if one looks at law only as a system of rules which can be seen in cases and statutes. This is only the surface level of law beneath (or depending on the metaphor we want to use, above) which the legal culture plays a crucial role. There is a close and constant interplay between the levels: the development of the concrete legal material of course affects and is a part of legal culture, but legal culture on the other hand has a decisive influence on the way one reads and uses the statutes, cases and other materials, and on how they are understood to be a part of 'the law'. A legal rule cannot be understood and used as a legal rule without the meaning given to it by its legal culture.

It is of course a general problem of European Community law that it issues materials on the surface level without having any – or at least any sufficiently developed – substratum of legal culture. Therefore the legislative measures of the Community always to some extent have to be read through the glasses of the national legal culture of the spectator. This is certainly also the case in this book. The legal cultures of the authors obviously to some extent steer the way in which the material is perceived.

As legal culture is something which lies beyond the details of a concrete and specific legal order, the influence of national legal culture would perhaps not be a very great problem if the authors belonged to fairly similar cultures. The perspective on the Community material would be, if not identical, at least relatively similar. However, the co–operation between a common lawyer and a civil lawyer has to meet more problems of this kind. It has even been claimed that 'the differences arising between the common law and civil law *mentalités* at the epistemological level are irreducible' which means that

___

differences, however, are not anymore tied so much to national cultures than to various subcultures which may reach across national boundaries.

53 By this we mean the idea of an at least partly common European consumer society as opposed to the concept of strictly separate national consumer cultures in the Member States. We do not want to claim that this European consumer society necessarily to any great extent differs from the more general Western consumer society or, at least concerning certain features, even from a global consumer society. For our purpose it is sufficient to note the convergence within the Community.

'the common law and civil law worlds cannot ... engage in an exchange that would lead one to an understanding of the other'.[54] Even though our experience would suggest that such a communication is not entirely impossible, and we will return to the reasons at the end of this section, it is obvious that there may be serious difficulties in co–ordinating our understanding of the law. These difficulties should be openly addressed. In the following we will mention some such problems inherent in our analysis.

Already on the ontological level one encounters the problem of what law is perceived to be. As is well known, the law for a civil lawyer is primarily a system, almost scientific as to its nature,[55] while the common lawyer tends to look at law as a (relatively unsystematic) collection of solutions to practical problems. This difference in perspective has created difficulties in reaching a common perception of the 'existence', role and status of general principles of Community consumer law (which is one of the central issues of this book). While a common lawyer rather would see such principles as pedagogical tools, perhaps useful for showing the similarities in approach in different rules, a civil lawyer in addition might render them the ontological status of norms which may be used as arguments in legal reasoning. This ambiguity undoubtedly to some extent affects the analysis of the general principles of Community consumer law in this book.[56] As already noted above, the principle of legitimate expectations has been understood in both senses, and some other principles developed here, such as the radical principle of transparency, certainly are meant by its author to function as a normative construct, but may of course be read otherwise by a common lawyer. As far as possible we have tried to make clear what we mean, but it seems unavoidable that there may remain passages of a systematical nature which will be perceived differently depending on the legal culture of the receiver.

Also on the epistemological level there obviously are ingrained differences in approach. The question, how to find knowledge of the law, receives different answers in common law and in civil law. As the positive harmonisation measures of Community law are made by legislation the difference between a statute–based and a precedent–based approach does not

---

54   P. Legrand, 'European Legal Systems are not Converging' (1996) 45 *I.C.L.Q.* 52, at 62 and 76. The article contains one of the best founded critiques of the rather commonly accepted thesis that Community law is causing the legal systems of the Member States to converge.

55   One should, however, note that Nordic law is not obsessed with the system so deeply as some continental legal cultures, but also has a strong strand of pragmatic legal engineering. This has probably made it easier for the authors to reach a common understanding.

56   This may also be one explanation for the difficulties encountered in common law in understanding the good faith principle in the Unfair Contract Terms Directive.

come very clearly to the fore in this context. Subtle differences may, however, be noted in relation to other sources, such as legal doctrine. Obviously the (normative) references to legal doctrine – and to legal doctrine in 'foreign' countries like Germany – were much more frequent in the versions written by the civil law author than the common lawyer. We have of course tried to harmonise our use of sources; although a careful reader may still probably be able to discern traces of these initial differences.

As statutes are not interpreted in exactly the same way in different countries there are obviously also differences in our attitudes towards the wording of the directives and other legislative materials presented here. An English lawyer would tend to emphasise the literal meaning of every word used in the legal text stronger than a Nordic lawyer who to a higher degree would subordinate this to the intention of the communication.[57] As this difference is a question of nuances rather than opposite approaches it has not, however, given us very great difficulties. It can probably be seen, for example, in the way one approaches words like 'significant imbalance' in the Unfair Contract Terms Directive. As we note later, while a Nordic lawyer would conceive the word 'significant' just as a signal that there is a hurdle and that not every imbalance in the contract may give the court the right to interfere, a common lawyer would also tend to try to give a concrete content to the level of the hurdle by analysing the literal meaning of that word when applying the rule.

Fundamental differences are not restricted to the ontological and epistemological levels. Perceptions of various legal institutions can also be very different. From the point of view of the present study, the way in which the institution of contract is understood clearly affects the understanding of some of the Community materials. Although the present authors have made comparative work together in this area before,[58] there has still been room for misunderstandings due to the basic differences between our legal cultures. As just one example one could mention the question of the relation between law and contract. When a civil lawyer seeks the solution to problems not regulated in the contract in (non–mandatory) law, which is perceived as being something outside the contract itself, a common lawyer would often experience a need to tie the solution more closely to the contract by speaking

---

57 In the UK the intention of the legislature is an accepted argument in interpreting statutes as well. However, the court tends to assume that the linguistic meaning of the words is the best indication of this intention and thus tends to resort much more to the exact wording of the statute, see R.S. Summers and M. Taruffo, 'Interpretation and Comparative Analysis' in D.N. MacCormick and R.S. Summers (eds), *Interpreting Statutes*, (Dartmouth, 1991) at 470.

58 See R. Brownsword, G. Howells and T. Wilhelmsson (eds), *Welfarism in Contract Law*, (Dartmouth, 1994).

of implied terms in the contract. Differences like this, which mirror fundamental differences in the perception of the status and role of contract, have required very careful phrasing of certain passages in the contractual parts of the book.

However, in spite of all these difficulties, we have not considered our mission to be impossible. The work as such should show that a meaningful communication between a civil[59] and a common lawyer is possible, especially when dealing with Community law. On the contrary, the combination of these two perspectives rather gives rise to contradictions which can prove fruitful for the deeper understanding of the Community materials. It counteracts the danger that one too quickly and without reflection chooses the interpretation of a Community enactment which is in harmony with the structures of one's own legal culture.

Still the problem is left unresolved as to how we imagine it possible to convey any deeper understanding of a set of legal rules if they are detached from a specific legal culture which is needed to give them meaning. This question could in fact be answered along two lines (which can only be hinted at in this context).

One could claim that it is a mistake to equate Community law with national law and believe that the methods of understanding are the same for both types of law. It could be argued that Community law is not law in the same sense as national law. National law has developed more or less organically with the history of the nation, but Community law is more of an artificial construct, a law *sui generis*. This is not to say that national law is not created by express and deliberate (political) decisions; in fact this is increasingly the case. However, these decisions are rooted in a legal tradition, a mode of thinking, some kind of a structure and a language; in contrast Community law is the outcome of, at least partly, deliberate decisions to create a new legal sphere. Created artificially Community law cannot be understood but artificially.

In fact many Community rules are not created to produce precise solutions but rather seek to show directions in which the law can develop. Therefore the way in which they are understood and interpreted has to differ from the methods of national law. In ascertaining the direction of development required by the Community rules, which set certain more or less vague frameworks for national law, it may suffice to read the rules in

---

59   It should be underlined once again that it is perhaps somewhat easier for a Nordic lawyer than a continental civil lawyer to approach common law. Nordic law, although clearly being civilian in both the ontological and epistemological sense as well as using civilian legal institutions, lacks a general civil code and seems to have a somewhat more pragmatic approach than the laws based on great – and almost sacred – codifications.

connection with the more vague notions inherent in the heritage of common Western legal culture.

On the other hand one should admit that the connection between legal culture and concrete legislation is not one–sided. Not only does the legal culture have an effect on the creation and understanding of the concrete norms; the concrete rules also influence the development of the legal culture. Elements of thinking from the surface of rules sink to deeper levels (or rise to higher levels) of culture. This naturally goes for Community law as well. One could claim that Community law has developed so far that traces of a specific Community legal culture is at least emerging. The bearers of this culture would be the ECJ, the expanding Community law doctrine and perhaps the legal élite in Brussels. In the national setting this Community legal culture surfaces in a pluralist mix[60] of national and Community law. The understanding of Community legislation and practice could at least to some extent take place in connection with this specific Community legal culture.

The two answers to our question are not necessarily conflicting. Community law can be regarded as an artificial construct which slowly may create traces of a legal culture of its own. The analysis of Community law therefore must oscillate between an artificial understanding directly related to the common Western legal heritage and a reflection of the certain modes of thinking traceable in an emerging Community legal culture. However, in addition, as one cannot (and should not) cut one's roots from a specific national legal tradition, one cannot avoid a reflection of the national legal cultures of the authors in their analysis. As mentioned before, we have at least tried to bring to the surface some of the differences in understanding which are due to our different backgrounds in this respect, whilst maintaining a generally consistent approach to the central questions posed by EC consumer law.

---

[60] The view of one of the authors on legal pluralism and Community law is expressed in T. Wilhelmsson, *Social Contract Law and European Integration*, (Dartmouth, 1995) at 13 *et seq.*

2   Consumer Safety

1.   COMMUNITY INVOLVEMENT WITH CONSUMER SAFETY MATTERS

The EC has been concerned with consumer safety issues for a long time. As far back as 1975 in the Council's preliminary programme for a consumer protection and information policy[1] the right to protection of health and safety interests was cited as one of the consumer's five basic rights and safety has since then been a dominant theme in EC consumer policy. Three broad areas of activity can be distinguished: the food sector, consumer products and consumer services. Food law is a highly technical specialist sector which is considered elsewhere in this series and so we will not look at it in detail.[2] Most activity has been undertaken in the product sphere. We shall see that there is a gamut of new approach technical harmonisation directives as well as horizontal directives on product liability and general product safety and a system for collecting data on home and leisure accidents. In comparison to the work undertaken in the product sector, Community activity in the service area has been disappointing. To highlight the weakness of EC policy in relation to service safety we will consider this topic first, before returning to the healthier picture with regard to products.

2.   SERVICE SAFETY

A.   Introduction

The EC is doubtless, to some extent, anxious that services provided within the Community are safe. Some EC legislation does affect the safety of services. For instance, the EC's work on mutual recognition of qualifications has as one of its objectives ensuring that consumer's safety is not threatened by the greater freedom of movement of professionals.[3] Equally safety is a

---

[1]   OJ 1975 C 92/1.

[2]   See K. de Winter, 'EC Food Law' in *European Business Law*, G. Howells (ed.), (Dartmouth, 1996) and his forthcoming book in this series.

[3]   See Council Directive 89/48/EEC on a general system for the recognition of higher education diplomas: OJ 1989 L 19/16; and Council Directive 92/51 on a second general system for the recognition of professional education and training to supplement Directive 89/48/EEC:OJ 1992 L 209/25.

feature of EC regulation of transport.[4] Our discussion of EC regulation of tourism in Chap. 7 indicates some concern for safety, for instance, the (admittedly non–binding) recommendation on fire safety in hotels and tour operator's liability for locally provided services, which should increase the incentives for them to demand higher standards. However, the EC lacks a coherent policy for promoting service safety and this is reflected in the lack of any horizontal legislation.

B.   The Proposal for a Service Liability Directive

In 1990 a proposal for a Council Directive on the liability of suppliers of services was submitted by the Commission,[5] This was seen as complementary to the Product Liability Directive, but instead of adopting a strict liability standard it simply reversed the burden of proving fault by requiring the supplier to prove absence of fault (art. 1(2)). The fault concept was shorn up by the requirement that the behaviour of the supplier was to be taken into account with the assumption that in normal and reasonably foreseeable conditions he should ensure the safety which may reasonably be expected (art. 1(3)). Ironically, due to the weak form of strict liability introduced by the Product Liability Directive, it might actually have been easier to have brought a claim for service liability (with the benefit of the reversal of the burden of proof) than under strict products liability. The benefits of the reversal of the burden of proof may, however, have been diminished by the requirement that the injured party provide proof of the causal relationship between the performance of the service and the damage (art. 5). This would have meant that the consumer would most likely have had to show (without the benefit of a reversal of the burden of proof) how the fault of the supplier caused the accident. In the event the proposal has been withdrawn.[6] From the outset the proposal had been controversial with the

---

4   The Maastricht Treaty inserted art. 75(1)(c) which requires the Council to lay down measures to improve transport safety when establishing a common transport policy.

5   OJ 1991 C 12/8, see Th. Bourgoignie, 'Liability of Suppliers of Services in the European Community: the Draft Council Directive' [1991] *E.Consum.L.J.* 3.

6   For a discussion of why the draft was not enacted see J. Shaw, 'A Proposal too Far? Lawyers and Legal Discourse in the Representation of Interests in the European Union', paper presented at the 1996 W.G. Hart Workshop, proceedings to be published in P. Craig and C. Harlow (eds), *Lawmaking in the European Union* (Sweet and Maxwell Ireland, forthcoming). She cites weaknesses in the original draft (lack of clarity as to why reversal of the burden of proof should be the basis of liability and failure to exclude certain key sectors) and the outmanoeuvring of the

Commission having been persuaded to remove the medical and construction sectors from the scope of the Directive on the condition that they be subject to specific directives. The final nails in the Directive's coffin were the review of existing and proposed legislation following the Sutherland report and the need to apply the subsidiarity principle following the Maastricht revisions to the Treaty.[7]

C. Explanations for the Lack of EC Activity with Regard to Service Safety

The hesitation of the EC to act in the service field with the same vigour as it has done in relation to products has at least two explanations. First, a traditional reluctance of law makers to subject services to the same standards as products. Second, a particular view that there is less of a Community dimension to the supply of services than goods.

(i) The Goods/Services Distinction[8]

Although a distinction is often drawn between the standards of liability for goods and services it is doubtful whether this is tenable either in terms of policy justifications or as a matter of practicality. In practice it can be hard to determine whether some things are goods or services. For instance, are software programmes goods or services? Equally, it is sometimes difficult to determine whether an accident was caused by the failure of a product, or the actions of someone who had repaired the product (perhaps ineffectively) or had operated it incorrectly.

One of the major justifications for differentiating between products is the claim that one can judge the final product objectively, without having to assess producer behaviour. This claim does not stand up, at least in relation to design defects, for, as we shall see, even under the Directive's strict product liability regime one is forced to consider the producer's behaviour. In truth all product defects are caused by human conduct, be it by the designer, quality assurance manager or production worker. The effect of subjecting service providers to a lower standard than product suppliers will be to channel liability to producers, when the fault may rest with an upstream link in the manufacturing chain, such as a designer.

Commission and consumer lobby in the lobbying process as reasons why the Directive never made the statute book.

7   See V. Kendall, *EC Consumer Law*, (Chancery Law, 1994) at 84.

8   See J. Stapleton, *Product Liability*, (Butterworths, 1994) at 323 *et seq*.

The differential standard applied to goods and services appears rather arbitrary, given that it can be a matter of chance or convenience whether a consumer uses goods or services. This is true across a range of activities, from choices made as to whether to purchase equipment to clean one's car or to take it to be valeted, through to whether some medical conditions should be treated by surgery or drug treatment. Regardless of whether goods or services are involved the consumer does not expect to be injured and it seems objectionable that different standards are applied.

It is sometimes argued that strict liability cannot be applied to services because services are more individualistic and depend upon a unique interaction between the supplier and the person (or thing) on whom the service is being provided. In other words whilst the producer can control the condition of the final product, the service provider cannot guarantee the outcome. However, strict liability should not be confused with absolute liability. Service providers would be able to protect themselves by informing of possible side–effects or risks of failure and consumers would be responsible for any damage caused by their own negligence. It is perhaps not fully appreciated that many services are to–day just as much mass–supplied as products are mass–produced and even if servicing and repairs are carried out by local mechanics, they will be performed in accordance with standardised work schedules. Certainly consumers expect many everyday services to produce guaranteed results.

Even if some services remain very small scale and personal this should not be a reason for excluding them from the liability or regulatory regime; a similar attempt to exclude craft industries from the Product Liability Directive was rightly rejected. It is sometimes suggested that there are too many different kinds of services to be brought within a common regime. However, this argument does not pass muster as there is also a wide range of products and yet common rules are applied to them all. The open–textured norms included in general horizontal directives are sufficiently flexible to take the particularities of different service sectors into account. There should be a heavy burden of proof on any sector which wished to be excluded from such general regulation. The medical sector would for instance have to establish that such rules would indeed impose an intolerable burden or lead to defensive practices.

The same arguments about loss distribution and channelling of liability which are used to justify strict products liability can be applied equally to service liability. There is also just as much need for regulatory controls of services as there is for product safety regulation. Indeed in some ways the need is greater for controls on services, for whilst a final product can always be inspected (admittedly dangers are sometimes hidden), a service supplier often has to start performing the service before one may be alerted to any danger.

The regulatory tools may possibly have to be different for services than products. For some services it may be impossible to require that a set outcome be achieved, if the service provider is not prepared to guarantee a particular result. For some services the most effective controls will not be on the final 'product', but rather on the inputs in terms of the quality of personnel and equipment used together with possibly some follow up monitoring of the outcomes of the service provision.

(ii) The Community Dimension

The traditional reluctance to equate services with goods and the powerful lobbying power of many service providers perhaps explain to a great extent the lack of progress made in EC consumer service safety law. The service providers opposition to a service liability directive[9] was made easier by the adoption of the subsidiarity principle. They were then able to build on the argument that there was less need for a Community involvement in services than goods. This argument suggests that whilst goods are easily transportable across boundaries, services tend to be more locally based.

There are several flaws in the argument that services lack a Community dimension. First, whilst most consumers would not cross borders for their regular services, car repairs, hair cuts, dry–cleaning etc., these services might, however, be operated by European wide organisations which would derive the same benefits from operating in a harmonised legal context as accrue to product manufacturers as a result of harmonisation.[10] One might also foresee consumers crossing borders for certain types of specialist services, particularly in the medical sector. This happens, currently, to some extent with abortion operations for instance, which for cultural and legal reasons are not encouraged or are illegal in some states. One can envisage the development of a cross–border market for certain services, especially those such as cosmetic surgery which are typically not covered by state or private health care insurance.

However, even if services are carried out locally their effects may occur in other Member States. Thus if Wilhelmsson has his car brakes incorrectly repaired in Helsinki before setting off to visit Howells in Sheffield, it is likely that the results will materialise on the German Autobahn. Thus all Europe's citizens have an interest in the regulation of the safety of services supplied

---

9   Work on a general service safety directive to impose similar controls to the General Product Safety Directive (see below) has never progressed beyond the ideas stage.

10   It will be noted in our discussion of the product sector that most of the benefits result from the harmonisation of standards and regulatory rules and controls rather than liability rules.

throughout the Community, both to attempt to ensure accidents do not arise and to provide compensation if they do.

Moreover as we circulate the Community with increasing frequency we will be bound to call upon service suppliers in other Member States and will want to be assured of their safety. Whilst using some services when abroad may be optional (e.g. hairdressers), others cannot be avoided in emergencies (e.g. doctors, dentists, car repairers) and some have to be utilised of necessity (e.g. hotels, restaurants, taxis and public transport). Thus for consumers ensuring all services provided within the Community are safe may in fact be a higher priority than product safety: for whilst one can select the countries from which goods are purchased, sometimes one has no option but to use the services of a country being visited. The lack of a Community consumer service safety policy is a major gap in the level of protection Europe offers its citizens.

(iii)   A Third Explanation?

It is has also been suggested that another reason why the EC has not given the same priority to service as product safety has been the lack of a highly public scandal.[11] It is true that the thalidomide tragedy provided much of the impetus for product liability reform. Many service failures do affect isolated individuals (the lady whose hair is damaged by a perm incorrectly applied, the driver whose car was improperly repaired) rather than large groups, but also many product related accidents are isolated incidents. It is, however, plainly not true that there have not been many widely publicised consumer service tragedies: the Hillsborough football stadium tragedy, the Herald of Free Enterprise ferry disaster and last summer's tragic flooding of a campsite in Northern Spain are just three of many examples which could be cited. The difference from the product sphere is perhaps that they are viewed as discrete events. Services are not so easily put together in one category as products are. There is no logical reason why this should be the case, but the physical existence of a product seems to give all products a common identity. Also consumer service disasters can often be explained as being in part the consequence of a freak accident, even if underlying causes can eventually be shown to have created the conditions which permitted the accident to happen or to inflict the damage it did. In short there have been no shortage of consumer service disasters, but there has been a failure to demand more coherent regulation of services, instead of *ad hoc* solutions to particular problems.

---

[11]   See Shaw, *op. cit.*

D. National Developments

On a more optimistic note, there is evidence that some Member States have used the occasion of implementing the product liability and safety directives to extend the scope of those laws to services or at least to modernise their law relating to services. Since 1983 France has applied the same principles to goods and services.[12] Belgium has now copied this approach, whilst the Finnish Product Safety Act has been extended to cover services. Greece has placed its fault liability on a statutory basis and requires the courts to take into account factors such as the subject matter and type of service and the time the service was rendered.[13]

3. PRODUCT LIABILITY

A. Introduction

Ever since the Thalidomide drug tragedy of the early 1970s there had been proposals for the development of strict product liability standards so those injured by dangerous products would be able to secure compensation. At the national level domestic industry was able to resist reforms by arguing that introducing strict liability would place it at a competitive disadvantage with its trading partners in Europe. The achievement of Europe was to provide a level playing field so that industry could no longer resist reforms by playing the protectionist card. This illustrates how common European action can promote civilised standards and act as a brake on the so–called 'race to the bottom' which is a growing threat as Europe moves towards increased free trade and open borders.

However, the Directive was not easily agreed upon by the Member States. The Product Liability Directive[14] was only adopted nine years after the original draft was published.[15] The main problem was the fear that introducing strict liability would lead to a US style product liability crisis. In

---

12 See J. Calais–Auloy and F. Steinmetz, *Droit de la Consommation*, (4 ed., Dalloz, 1996) at 236 *et seq.*

13 A. Vamvoukos, 'Consumer Law in Greece – the State of Play' [1996] *Consum.L.J.* 7.

14 Council Directive 85/374/EEC on the approximation of the laws, regulations and administrative provisions of the Member States concerning liability for defective products: OJ 1985 L210/29. For more detailed analysis of the Directive see G. Howells, *Comparative Product Liability*, (Dartmouth, 1993) Ch. 3 and G. Howells, 'Europe's Solution to the Product Liability Phenomenon' (1991) 20 *Anglo–Am. L.R.* 204.

15 OJ 1976 C 241/9.

fact this was unlikely to happen as European countries do not have the dangerous cocktail (of jury awards, high medical costs, contingency fees and the absence of a costs follow the award rule) which contributes to the burden products liability places on some sectors of the US industry, more than strict liability *per se*.

Nevertheless, it was only possible to have the Directive adopted by giving Member States options on whether (i) to provide a development risks defence (which excuses producers from liability for defects which were impossible to discover given the state of scientific and technical knowledge); (ii) to introduce a cap on personal injury damages; and (iii) to include primary agricultural produce. Most Member States have retained the development risks defence. Only Luxembourg and Finland have excluded it, whilst Spain has the defence but curiously not for food and drugs (the areas where it has most relevance). Luxembourg, Finland, Sweden and Greece have included primary agricultural produce.[16] Caps on personal injury damages are only to be found in Germany, Portugal and Spain.[17] These options obviously reduce, to some extent, the value of the Directive as a harmonising measure. The Directive provided for the options to be reviewed after ten year. A brief report concluded that it was too early for any revisions to be suggested, but did consider that the exclusion for primary agricultural produce could be reviewed.[18]

Furthermore the Directive leaves certain other questions to national laws. For example, it does not affect national rules regulating the suspension or interruption of limitation periods. Also the question of recovery for non–material damage as well as the measure of damages is left to the Member States. In Germany the implementing legislation simply does not allow non–material damages to be recovered under the strict liability regime. This emphasises the continued need to view the new strict liability regime alongside existing contractual and tortious sources of liability which are expressly preserved by art. 13.[19]

---

[16]   The French implementing legislation is likely to cover agricultural produce. France has yet to implement the Directive. Indeed implementation was slow with only the United Kingdom, Italy and Greece meeting the July 1988 deadline.

[17]   Greece did have such a cap in its first implementing law but removed it when it revised its law.

[18]   See COM(95) 617, this point was also mentioned in the Commission's latest three year plan: COM(95) 519 at 9. The EC review was preceded by a study carried out by McKenna's, *Report for the Commission of the European Communities on the application of Directive 85/374/EEC on liability for defective products*, Contract ETD/93/B5–3000/MI/06.

[19]   For a survey of existing laws in the Member States, see Howells (1993), *op. cit.*.

In the United Kingdom, for instance, it may often be easier to establish a breach of the implied condition that goods must be of satisfactory quality rather than to prove that they are defective. French legal tradition dislikes this overlapping of sources of liability. Thus in France it was initially proposed that the new regime of strict product liability should be the sole source of an injured person's remedies. This principle was part of an ambitious reform seeking to integrate sale and product liability law, but is unlikely to be found in any law which is eventually enacted to implement the Directive. As it is likely that any such law will contain the development risks defence, resort to the existing highly protective contractual and delictual principles will remain important means of redress for French consumers.

The justifications for the Directive are to be found in its preamble where both internal market and consumer protection objectives are cited. As the Directive was based on art. 100 it had to be shown that the measure directly affected the establishment and functioning of the common market. Accordingly it argued that 'existing divergences may distort competition and affect the movement of goods within the common market' (recital 1). We are in fact sceptical of the extent to which liability laws have this effect. Only when divergences in liability regimes are so great that they justify and require the development of new designs or labelling requirements will they seriously impede community trade. Product safety regulations which require certain construction, design or labelling requirements before access to a market is permitted are far more effective means of partitioning the market than downstream liability rules which generally only have a marginal impact on trading costs. The recital did, however, go on to express concern at the differing degrees of protection afforded the consumer in different legal systems. In this we can see the germ of the notion of a 'Community with a social face' which sees consumer protection as a worthy objective. Liability without fault was said to be the 'sole means of adequately solving the problem, peculiar to our age of increasing technicality, of a fair apportionment of the risks inherent in modern technological production' (recital 2).

B. Scope

Liability under the Directive is delimited by the concept of 'product' (art. 2). This covers all moveables even when incorporated into another moveable or an immoveable. Electricity is expressly included within the definition. The only exception provided for is in relation to primary agricultural products and game.

Primary agricultural produce means the products of the soil, of stock–farming and of fisheries which have not undergone initial[20] processing. There seems to be no explanation for this exclusion other than that it is a sop to the powerful farming lobby. We have already noted that the Commission seems to favour its removal. We agree that this would be the best approach and would therefore avoid the need to address difficult questions which the wording of the exclusion gives rise to, such as to what amounts to 'initial' or 'industrial' processing.

Other difficult questions surrounding the meaning of 'product' relate to whether it covers (a) blood products (to which the answer is, probably, yes),[21] and (b) software (as regards which a distinction might be drawn between off the peg programmes which are likely to be treated as products and individualised programmes, which are more likely to be treated as services).[22]

It should also be remembered that the Product Liability Directive, although undoubtedly inspired by consumer protection motives, is not restricted to assisting consumers. All products, not merely consumer products can be the cause of a claim under the Directive. As regards damages, we shall see that anyone can recover for personal injury and death caused by a defective product, although only property damage caused to consumer goods can be compensated.

C.   Channelling of Liability

The policy of the Product Liability Directive is to channel liability towards the producer, although as we shall see the term producer is broadly defined. Indeed the extended range of defendants provided by this expansive definition may prove to be one of the greatest practical improvements in the consumer's position brought about by the Directive. The channelling of liability to the producer reflects the reality that the producer has most control over the quality of the product and therefore is best placed to control its risks and should therefore be able to obtain the most favourable insurance terms.

---

20   Recital 3 of the preamble confuses matters by referring to processing of an *industrial* rather than an *initial* nature. This may exclude a wider range of product. This broader exclusion has been favoured in the United Kingdom implementing legislation: see, s.2(4) of the Consumer Protection Act 1987.

21   See A. Clark, *Product Liability*, (Sweet & Maxwell, 1989) at 61–65.

22   See J. Adams, *Atiyah's Sale of Goods*, (Pitman, 1995) at 46–7 (dealing with a similar issue in sale of goods law).

Under the Directive the supplier simply has a subsidiary liability which is triggered when the producer (or importer) cannot be identified and the supplier fails to inform the injured person of the identity of the producer (importer in the case of imported goods) or the person who supplied him (art. 3(3)). It is, perhaps, unfortunate that the supplier can fulfil his duties by simply providing the name of his supplier as this can cause the consumer to be left running from one link in the supply chain to another. If the chain is broken for any reason (perhaps insolvency) then the consumer is left high and dry. It would have been more protective to have made suppliers liable, but with a right of contribution against producers, or even with the requirement that any available producer be sued in the first instance.

The Directive's definition of 'producer' covers the manufacturer of a finished product, the producer of any raw material and the manufacturer of a component part (art. 3(1)). The policy of channelling liability to the producer is deviated from in two instances. First, it is extended to include anyone who by putting his name, trade mark or other distinguishing feature on the product presents himself as its producer (art. 3(1)). It might be thought that the policy behind this was to increase consumer protection by taking note of the economic power of the parties who might be caught by this provision – supermarket own–branders, franchisers, licensors etc. However, one might see the objective to be the more limited one of covering situations where it was not obvious that the goods had been produced by another party. If one adopts this starting–point it would seem that a person who had placed his name etc. prominently on a product could nevertheless escape liability if somewhere on the product or its packaging there was a statement that in fact the goods were produced by another party, as then the own–brander could not be said to be presenting himself as the producer. The name of the other party would not even have to be given, but if the brander was also the supplier this person would have to reveal the identity of the producer or their supplier. This policy seems to be wrong. The extension of liability to own–branders etc. should not be for purely practical reasons, but rather should be linked to consumer expectations. Consumers should be entitled to expect that anyone who puts their name on a product has sufficient confidence in it to accept liability should things go wrong.

The second extension of the definition of producer provides that anyone who, in the course of a business, imports a product into the Community for sale, hire, leasing or any form of distribution will be deemed to be the producer (art. 3(2)). This seeks to prevent the consumer being left with a worthless remedy against a distant overseas producer. The weakness in the provision is that liability attaches to the first importer into the Community, not the importer into the Member State where the harm occurred. The EC is keen to build the image of the fully functioning single market, but for a consumer injured in England it may be just as difficult (if not more so) to sue a Finnish importer than, say, an American manufacturer.

D.   Defectiveness

Under a strict liability regime the injured party still has to prove that his damage was caused by a defect in the product. The improvement over a negligence standard is said to be that there is no longer any need to prove that the defect was caused by the producer's fault. However, strict liability is not the same as absolute liability, for products must first be found to be defective and some specific defences are available. Supposedly attention should focus on the condition of the product rather than the conduct of the producer. The strictness of the liability regime can also be gauged by the extent to which it judges a product with the benefit of hindsight knowledge of dangers which only became available after it had been marketed.

Strict liability standards tend to involve either judging the product against consumer expectations or by subjecting the product to a risk:utility analysis. The Americans, who have had the greatest experience of products liability, have tended to reject the consumer expectation standard (as being too subjective and unable to deal adequately with patent defects) in favour of the more objective risk:utility standard or a dual standard comprising both tests.[23] The European reformers nevertheless ignored the US experience and adopted an essentially consumer expectation standard.[24] The basic objection to this approach is that it tends to reflect prevailing expectations of safety, rather than subject the product to a rigorous risk:utility analysis. It is perhaps significant that the subsequent General Product Safety Directive does adopt this more objective method of assessing safety (see section 4E). This gives rise to an intriguing possibility. If this safety standard is more

---

[23]   However, in fact determining which test applies in which state of the United States is both a complex and controversial question. The American Law Institute is looking to revise its Restatement on Torts, but it is proving hard to find agreement on a consensus position: see J. Vargo, 'The Emperor's New Clothes: The American Law Institute Adorns a "New Cloth" for Section 402A Products Liability Design Defects – A Survey of the States Reveals a Different Weave' (1996 26 *U. Memphis L. rev.* 493. Nevertheless the arguments against the consumer expectation test remain convincing.

[24]   Ironically this looks like becoming the common global definition of defect, see *Product Liability in the Asia–Pacific*, J. Kellam (ed.), (Legal Books, 1995). C.f. the moves in the United States to redraft the Restatement (Second) of Torts to provide for a negligence–style standard for design defects: see K. Ross and H. Bowbeer, 'American Product Liability Law Undergoing Revision' [1994] *Consum.L.J.* 96 and Vargo, *op. cit.*

rigorous than that apparently provided by the Product Liability Directive, it could be argued that it now forms part of a consumer's expectations that products comply with the General Product Safety Directive. The Product Liability Directive's defectiveness standard would then have to incorporate the conception of safety found in the General Product Safety Directive.

Art. 6 of the Directive provides that a product is defective 'when it does not provide the safety which a person is entitled to expect'. It then goes on to provide that this should be assessed taking all the circumstances into account, including some particular factors. These will be considered shortly, but for the moment we will reflect on this general standard. The most obvious point is that it is rather unhelpful in guiding one to know how much safety one should be entitled to. Is a person entitled to expect: that products never injure him, or simply that products are produced carefully, or does the answer lie somewhere in between? Evidently there is still much to be played for as this phrase is interpreted and applied in lawyers' offices and courts. The strictness of the new regime is still to be determined.

There is also scope for the application of the test to vary from one state to another (according to local customs and appreciations of risk) and even from one decision–maker to another. Attitudes to this may differ between the common and civil law worlds. In the civil law tradition the judge is considered to decide individual cases by reference to the written law and there is some latitude for applications to vary from one case to another. The common law tradition requires judges to be more detailed in their justifications for decisions and as the case has a precedent value there is more concern about inconsistent applications of standards.[25]

A difference can be appreciated in how the new defectiveness standard is applied to various categories of product defect. Where the complaint is of a manufacturing defect, then one can legitimately argue that a consumer is entitled to expect the product to be as safe as a correctly produced product would have been. Here the focus is clearly on the condition of the product. When, however, the complaint concerns a conscious design choice or the allegation that inadequate warnings or instructions were provided, then, the focus inevitably turns to the behaviour of the producer. Then, when asking whether the product was as safe as consumers were entitled to expect, the focus is on whether it was as safe as producers could have been expected to make it.[26] Thus we seem to have a true form of strict liability for

---

25 A similar concern is reflected in the hesitation common lawyers feel in applying the good faith test in the Unfair Contract Terms Directive (see Chap. 3 section 2C(i)). It is not so much the novelty of the concept as its vagueness which causes common lawyers consternation.

26 C.f. the comment in the US case of *Seattle–First Nat. Bank v Tabert* 542 P 2d 774 (1975) at 779 that 'In considering the reasonable expectations of the ordinary

manufacturing defects, but something which is perhaps best described as a stricter form of negligence for design and failure to warn defects. How much stricter this is than traditional negligence will turn on the time frame within which the producer's conduct is judged. This is considered below, but so far one could argue that few outcomes will be different under a strict liability than a fault based system.

However, much will depend upon how the defectiveness test is applied. The psychological impact of the shift from fault to strict liability may encourage judges to find liability where previously they would have been reluctant to do so, perhaps because it involved condemning the behaviour of the producer.

One of the factors to be taken into account when assessing defectiveness is the presentation of the product. This would cover the packaging or container which comes with the product, any accompanying literature as well as the manner in which it is displayed and arranged. It might also cover advertising and promotional material, but in any event such matters could be treated as one of the general circumstances to be taken into account. It is likely that producers will use the information they provide to limit the range of purposes for which they advise the use of the product and provide warnings against possible dangers. There is a real threat of information overload with important warnings being lost amongst a welter of others included simply to cover the producer against possible claims. A product supplied with too much information provided and with little differentiation between the most important messages and the rest could be found to be defective on the basis that the warnings had not been effectively brought to the consumer's attention. Whether judges will be prepared to hold such products to be defective is yet to be discovered, but we suspect that this is one area where there may be significant variations between Member States depending upon legal culture. However, warnings should never be adequate if products could be made safer relatively easily.

A producer ought not to be able to avoid liability by specifying a narrow range of uses and disclaiming liability if the consumer steps outside those parameters. This is because the Directive directs that account be taken of the 'use to which it could reasonably be expected that the product would be put'. This would seem to allow for a certain tolerance for foreseeable misuse. Producers should always be aware of the possibility that children may use certain products and this may mean that they may be more easily misused or that warnings suitable for adults may not be effective to get a message over to children.

---

consumer, a number of factors must be considered including the relative cost of the product, the gravity of the potential harm from the claimed defect *and the cost and feasibility of eliminating or minimising the risk* (emphasis added).

The other specific factor to which the Directive directs attention is the time when the product was put into circulation.[27] This means that the state of the art is to be taken into account when determining the question of defectiveness. Products should be judged by the safety standards current when they were marketed. Thus a fridge with a locking handle (which posed a danger of children being trapped inside) would have been acceptable in the 1950s, but would not be nowadays given that a foam seal has been developed which does not pose the same risk to children.

E.   Development Risks

Distinct from state of the art considerations, there are also development risks, that is risks which would have been unacceptable at the time of marketing if they could have been discovered. The classic example is of a drug side effect which has a long latency period and only materialises some years after being marketed. Whether such risks are included is one of the touchstones of how strict a product liability system is. Not unsurprisingly, this matter gave rise to a great deal of controversy when the Product Liability Directive was being proposed. The eventual solution was – contrary to the original proposal and against the better judgment of the Commission – to provide producers with a defence against development risks (art. 7(e)).[28] Member States were free to exclude the defence, but we have seen that few chose to do so.

The defence is available to a producer who proves that 'the scientific and technical knowledge at the time when he put the product into circulation was not such as to enable the existence of the defect to be discovered' (art. 7(e)). For some commentators, the inclusion of this defence means that there is little difference between the Directive's version of strict liability and a negligence standard, the only improvement being that the burden of establishing scientific knowledge is placed on the producer.[29] In fact that may only be a cosmetic improvement for it will be fairly easy for a producer to lead plausible evidence of what he understood the state of knowledge to be and the injured party would then be forced to refute this.

---

27   Art. 6(2) goes on to stress that a product shall not be considered defective for the sole reason that a better product is subsequently put into circulation. Subsequent improvements could, however, be used as evidence that those changes were practical at the time the product was put into circulation.

28   It was included at the instigation of the European Parliament: OJ 1979 C 127/61 at 62.

29   See generally on the relationship of strict liability to negligence J. Stapleton, 'Products Liability Reform – Real or Illusory' (1986) 6 *O.J.L.S.* 392 and *op. cit.*; C. Newdick, 'The Future of Negligence in Product Liability' (1987) 104 *L.Q.R.* 288.

In truth, everything depends upon the interpretation given to the defence. Just as with the defectiveness concept, one is left looking into a crystal ball and trying to predict how the courts will interpret the defence.[30] For instance, does knowledge have to be accepted by the majority of the scientific community before producers have to take note of it? What is the status of research which is disputed or only available in obscure publications? What if various pieces of knowledge had existed which could have revealed the risk, but the connection had not been made between them? What if there was knowledge of the risk, but no technical means of taking advantage of that knowledge?

The European Commission clearly favours a narrow test for the defence based on discoverability. This will be soon tested in the ECJ as the Commission is bringing proceedings against the United Kingdom whose implementing legislation provides a defence if 'the state of scientific and technical knowledge... was not such that a producer of products of the same description as the product in question might be expected to have discovered the defect if it had existed in his product while they were under his control'.[31] This introduces the concept of expectancy of discoverability and also judges producers according to the type of business they are in. It leaves open the possibility that a producer could defend a claim on the basis, not that the risk was unknown, but that someone with his resources could not have discovered it.[32]

Some commentators support the United Kingdom Government's interpretation of the defence arguing that if there is going to be a development risks defence it is only rational for it to be pitched at a level which individual producers can actually achieve. To make producers liable on the basis of knowledge which they could not be expected to have known

---

[30]   The German Federal Court of Justice ([1995] NJW 2162, Bundesgerichtshof) has held that the defence does not apply to manufacturing defects. Although it will rarely be the case that manufacturing defects cannot be discovered, there may be instances where quality control equipment is not sufficient to detect flaws. Thus the decision is difficult to justify especially if one remembers that the defence refers to technical as well as scientific knowledge. However, it fits into a pattern of courts being willing to find liability for manufacturing defects, presumably because the extent of liability tends to be fairly limited and the defect can be easily established by comparison with the perfect product.

[31]   S.4(1)(e) of the Consumer Protection Act 1987.

[32]   Just such a defence was being run by the manufacturers of hazelnut yoghurt in the United Kingdom: see M. Mildred, 'The Impact of the Directive in the United Kingdom', in *Directive 85/374/EEC on Product Liability: Ten Years After*, M. Goyens (ed.), (CDC, 1996). It is understood the case has now been settled out of court.

of is, so the argument runs, counter to the principle behind the defence.[33] This line of argument assumes legal rules should form a coherent and consistent pattern. This is an ideal, but one which cannot be achieved when the principles of liability without fault and exoneration for development risks are juxtaposed. The development risks defence is inconsistent with the rationales of risk spreading and loss distribution which motivated the introduction of strict liability. It should not be viewed as a principled exception, but rather as an expedient concession to ensure all Member States accepted the Directive. Therefore it will hopefully be confined within as narrow a boundary as possible by the ECJ. It is to be regretted that the recent ten year review of the Directive did not recommend the removal of this defence in the near future. Hopefully the experience of those states which have chosen to impose liability for development risks will in time encourage the Commission that this should be the norm throughout the Community.

F. Defences

In addition to the development risks defence, art. 7 provides producers with several other defences. In each case the burden is on the producer to establish the defence. These can be invoked if (a) the producer did not put the product into circulation; (b) the defect did not exist when he put the product into circulation; (c) he neither manufactured the product for sale or any other form of distribution for economic purposes nor distributed it in the course of his business;[34] (d) the defect was due to compliance with mandatory regulations issued by public authorities;[35] (e) a component manufacturer can show the defect was attributable to the design of the end product or to instructions given by the manufacturer of the product. Liability under the Directive cannot be excluded or limited (art. 12). Although the producer's liability cannot be reduced because the damage was also caused by the act or omission of a third party (art. 8(1)), it may be reduced or disallowed because of the fault of the injured party or someone for whom he is responsible (art. 8(2)).

---

[33] C. Newdick, 'The development risks defence of the Consumer Protection Act 1987' (1988) *Camb.L.J.* 455; C. Newdick, 'Risk, Uncertainty and "Knowledge" in the development risks defence' (1991) 20 *Anglo–Am.L.Rev.* 309.

[34] Both these limbs must be satisfied before the defence is available.

[35] This defence is narrower than is sometimes assumed. It does not provide a defence where there has simply been compliance with voluntary standards (e.g. CEN standards), moreover, the compliance with the mandatory regulations must have caused the defect (there must have been no way in which a safe product could have been manufactured in accordance with the standard).

Liability can only be incurred for products marketed after national implementing legislation came into force (art. 17).[36] There is also a limitation period of three years which begins to run once the plaintiff is aware, or should have reasonably been aware, of the damage, the defect and the identity of the producer (art. 10(1)). A ten year period of repose bars claims lodged more than ten years after the product was put into circulation by the producer (art. 11). This was in the original draft of the Directive as a trade off for producers carrying the development risks. Now that there is a development risks defence this arbitrary cut–off point is indefensible.[37] The harshness of this rule is not yet apparent as no cases have fallen foul of the rule because the new law has not been in force for ten years in any Member State. However, the problem has been appreciated in Australia, which adopted similar legislation to the Directive including the ten year period of repose. There the Government has proposed exempting 'toxic harm' from the ten year repose period.[38] However, it may be difficult to define 'toxic harm' and the sounder approach may be simply to remove the ten year period of repose.

G. Damages

Damages for personal injury and death are recoverable (art. 9(a)). As already noted, Member States have the option of placing a ceiling of not less than 70M ECU on damage resulting from a death or personal injury caused by identical items having the same defect. This option was included because in some states, notably Germany, there is a tradition of combining strict liability with a limit on damages. This approach does, however, give rise to a host of practical problems. For instance, having to convert a figure expressed in ECUs into national currency has caused problems; at one time Greece's ceiling was about half of the permitted level.[39] There is also uncertainty as to what amounts to an 'identical item' or the 'same defect' and as to whether the

---

36   For products marketed prior to national legislation coming into force, but after the Directive's implementation date (and in cases where claims would fail because of inadequate implementation of the Directive) there may be a possible claim against national governments under the *Francovich* principle.

37   It is sometimes suggested that a period of repose is needed so that producers are able to put a limit on the time they hold records. But this is not a very convincing reason, especially when one bears in mind that records may need to be kept longer to defend contractual or negligence actions.

38   See Kellam, *op. cit.*, at 29. Since then the Government has changed to a Liberal administration and it is uncertain whether these reforms will be carried through.

39   Greece subsequently removed the ceiling.

limit applies within each state or Community–wide. In those countries which have adopted a ceiling it is not clear whether claims should be paid on a first come first paid basis or apportioned between all claimants. If the latter rule applies, there is, however, no guidance on how long the parties should wait for potential claimants to come forward.

Non–material damages remain the province of national law. This is significant because Germany does not allow such damages to be recovered under its new strict product liability regime.

In fact, there is a wide range in the level of personal injury damages awarded throughout the Community.[40] Whilst differences in the level of damages is to be expected to reflect variations in levels of affluence and the availability of social security and public health care in the different states, some unease can be expressed at the differing, and sometimes unprincipled, methods of calculating damages between Members States.[41] This is a matter which needs attention, although was perhaps outside the ambit of the Product Liability Directive. Variations in levels of damages between Member States are bound to ensure that forum shopping remains a feature of European product liability litigation.

Although liability attaches to all products which cause damage, compensation is only payable for damaged or destroyed property if it was of a type ordinarily intended for private use or consumption and which was in fact also mainly used by the injured person for such purposes (art. 9(b)). In addition claims for property damage have a threshold of 500 ECU.[42] Although the English language version describes this as a threshold, so that claims above this figure are recoverable in full, other language versions treat it like an insurance excess deductible from all claims.[43] Although there was apparently an error in translation and the figure was meant to be a deduction, in fact the English approach seems the more sensible way of achieving the objective of 'avoiding litigation in an excessive number of cases' (recital 9),

---

[40] One study suggests that there is a three or four fold difference in tort damage levels between European countries: see P. Szöllösi, 'The Standard of Compensation for Personal Injury and Death in European Countries' (1983) 63 *Nordisk Försäkringstidskrift* 128. See also D. McIntosh and M. Holmes, *Personal Injury Awards in E.C. Countries*, (2 ed., Lloyds of London Press, 1994).

[41] McKenna's, *op. cit.*, at 12.

[42] Luxembourg, in its implementing legislation, adopts the sensible approach of stating the amount to be the Luxembourg franc equivalent of 500 ECUs at the relevant date, thereby avoiding the problem of national legislation breaching EC law because of currency fluctuations.

[43] The French version talks of a 'franchise' and the German version of a 'Selbstbeteiligung'. The Republic of Ireland has fallen into line with other European states and treats it as a deduction.

since a deduction allows people to continue to sue for small amounts and once litigation is undertaken there seems little rationale for not providing full compensation. Indeed the threshold seems to exclude many potential consumer claims. The suggestion that small consumer claims are unimportant is one which we would contest.

Property damage is recoverable for 'any item of property other than the defective product itself' (art. 9(b)). This tries to distinguish product liability from sales law which is concerned with the quality of the goods. However, there are borderline problems where part of a product damages the rest of it. As components are products in their own right one might have imagined that there could be recovery in such cases, but national implementing legislation seems to suggest otherwise. This could result in the irony that, for instance, if a battery catches fire and destroys a car there will only be compensation if the battery is a replacement!

H. Conclusions

The Product Liability Directive has been taken as a model for law reform in many countries around the world.[44] This could be considered to be rather depressing for, whilst strict liability has been a major demand of consumer groups, we have made trenchant criticisms of two of its central features – its choice of a defectiveness standard based on consumer expectations and inclusion of the development risks defence. Moreover, major problems continue to exist for consumers in establishing causation in toxic tort cases and securing access to justice.

More rationale solutions do exist, which separate out more clearly the law's compensation role from its deterrence function. Inspiration might be sought from, for instance, the pharmaceutical sector in Scandinavia where claims are met from an insurance fund[45] or from New Zealand where tort actions have been abolished for personal injuries and have been replaced by state accident compensation payments.[46] The Product Liability Directive, although possibly a short term advance in consumer rights, may make the development of a more consumer friendly and efficient accident compensation policy more difficult for two reasons.

First, it creates another set of potentially privileged plaintiffs, who may not be willing to forego the possibility of full tort compensation for the lower levels of compensation likely to be awarded under a universal scheme. Second, it may pose a legal obstacle to more favourable consumer reforms.

---

44 See Kellam, *op. cit.*

45 Howells (1993), *op. cit.*, at 164–170

46 Howells (1993), *op. cit.*, Ch. 16.

Many commentators and indeed the Commission consider the Product Liability Directive to be a maximalist Directive preventing further national initiatives: they point to the fact that the Directive lacks an express minimum directive clause and to art. 13 which preserves existing national laws, but does not mention the possibility of Member States going further. Also it is argued that the inclusion of some options on which Member States can choose to go further than the solutions adopted by the Directive would be superfluous if they had this right in any event. This view can however be questioned. The existence of options may be viewed as ways of defusing contentious debates rather than as setting firm principles for the future development of the law. Certainly the options on the development risks defence and primary agricultural products are best viewed as an attempt to encourage states to go further rather than as a limit on future reforms. Indeed art. 13 preserves existing laws, which can themselves evolve to be more protective, as has indeed been the case with the domestic laws of the Member States even prior to the Directive.[47] However, the possibility remains that the Directive will be used as a brake on further national initiatives.

Although it has been argued that the substantive rights of consumers have not necessarily been greatly improved by the Directive (although much still depends upon how the courts interpret some key provisions), the Directive has raised the profile of consumer safety. Defence lawyers have brought potential liability to the attention of firms and proactive plaintiff lawyers have made consumers more aware of their rights. This has in turn encouraged reforms in some states (such as the introduction of contingency fees and class actions) which make it easier for injured persons to bring claims.

However, liability rules are only one form of control on product safety. In practice the technical rules governing product standards and the controls by regulatory authorities may have an even greater impact on product safety. It is to these matters that we now turn our attention.

---

[47] See especially the development of French and German law, outlined in Howells (1993), *op. cit.*, Chaps 7 and 8.

4.   PRODUCT SAFETY[48]

A.   Introduction

Although we expressed doubts as to whether product liability laws needed to be harmonised for internal market considerations, it is clear that the technical standards governing product safety do need to be harmonised if Europe is to become a true single market. Furthermore, producers should be able to establish compliance with standards in one Member State and use this as a passport to trade throughout the whole Community. In addition consumer confidence needs to be assured by national authorities having the necessary powers to react to emergencies. EC law provides a fairly well developed framework to achieve these objectives, although we shall point out some problems which might still create dangers for consumers.

It is worth emphasising that the motivation for EC rules in this area is probably more related to internal market considerations than to consumer protection. Indeed consumer protection could be threatened if strict national laws, standards and certification procedures are replaced by harmonised rules pitched at a low common denominator.

EC intervention is needed because although national technical rules on product safety will fall foul of art. 30, as being measures having equivalent effects to quantative restrictions on imports, they will usually be saved either by art. 36 as they protect the health and life of humans or because they satisfy the mandatory requirements, of protecting public health and the defence of the consumer, as laid down in the Cassis de Dijon judgment.[49] The approach of the EC has been to monitor national activity so that the number of new national regulations is limited to those which are really necessary, whilst seeking to harmonise sectors at the European level and introducing a horizontal general safety requirement.

B.   Technical Standards Directive

The EC's General Programme for the Elimination of Technical Barriers to Trade Caused by Disparities Among National Legislation of May 1969 contained a 'gentleman's agreement' not to legislate at the national level where EC legislation was planned. This agreement was of little value and new national regulations could be passed in areas not covered by the

---

48   Much of the material for this section of the chapter is derived from G. Howells, *Comparative Product Safety*, (Dartmouth, forthcoming).

49   *Rewe–Zentral v Bundesmonopolverwaltung für Branntwein*, Case 120/78 [1979] ECR 649.

programme. Even in areas covered by the programme Member States were not very good at providing the Commission with information on new national measures. Thus, the Technical Standards Directive[50] introduced procedures to monitor national activity to ensure that so far as possible differences between national rules are reduced and new national initiatives do not create additional barriers to trade.

The Technical Standards Directive requires Member States immediately to communicate any draft technical regulation[51] to the Commission, unless the regulation is simply transposing the full text of an International or European standard (in which case information on the relevant standard suffices) (arts 8–10). This procedure, in effect, provides for at least a three month standstill during which regulations should not be adopted whilst Member States and the Commission are given the opportunity to comment on or object to the proposed regulation. If within this time a Member State or the Commission delivers a detailed opinion to the effect that the measure should be amended to eliminate or reduce any barriers it might create to the free movement of goods the measure should be postponed for six months

---

[50] Council Directive 83/189/EEC laying down a procedure for the provision of information in the field of technical standards and regulations: OJ 1983 L 109/8 (as amended by Directive 88/182/EEC: OJ 1988 L 81/75 and Directive 94/10/EEC: OJ 1994 L 100/30) (hereafter Technical Standards Directive).

[51] A technical regulation refers to technical specifications and other requirements, including relevant administrative provisions, which are compulsory, *de jure* or *de facto*, in the marketing or use of a product in a Member State or major part thereof, as well as laws, regulation and administrative provisions of Member States prohibiting the manufacture, importation, marketing or use of a product (art. 1(9)). *De facto* technical regulations are said to include situations where a law etc. refers to a technical specification or code of practice compliance with which provides a presumption of conformity, voluntary agreements (other than public procurement tender specifications) to which a public authority is a contracting party, and where compliance with technical specifications is encouraged by fiscal and financial measures (but not those linked to social security systems). Technical specification is in turn defined as a specification contained in a document which lays down the characteristics required of a product such as levels of quality, performance, safety or dimensions, including requirements regarding the name under which the product is sold, terminology, symbols, testing and test methods, packaging, marking or labelling and conformity assessment procedures. It also covers the production methods and procedures for agricultural products, products intended for human and animal consumption, medicinal products and other products where these have an effect on their characteristics (art. 1(2)).

from its notification.[52] This period is extended to 12 months if the Commission gives notice of its intention to propose or adopt a directive, regulation or decision on the subject or that such a proposal already exists. If the Council adopts a Common Position during this standstill period the period is extended to 18 months.

These rules on notification and standstill procedures do not apply where Member States are fulfilling Community obligations or obligations arising from international agreements which result in the adoption of common Community technical specifications or in certain other situations, such as when the regulations give effect to a judgment of the ECJ or make use of safeguard clauses. The standstill procedure does not apply where, for urgent reasons relating to the protection of public health or safety or the protection of the health and life of animals or plants, a Member State is obliged to prepare technical regulations in a very short space of time in order to enact and introduce them immediately without any consultations being possible. However, when the Member State notifies the draft regulation it must state the reasons for the urgency of the measures taken and the Commission is required to take appropriate action where improper use is made of this procedure.

In practice national technical standards may have the same effect on the free movement of goods as technical regulations. Accordingly procedures are put in place to require national standardisation bodies to inform equivalent bodies in other Member States, European standardisation bodies and the Commission of new standards work (arts 2–4).[53] Standardisation bodies have the right to be involved passively or actively (by sending an observer) in the work of standards bodies in other Member States. This right has not been greatly utilised, partly because the European standards bodies have their own co–operation procedures.

A Standing Committee meets with representatives of the standards institutions at least twice a year to consider a Commission report on the above stated procedures (arts 5–7). In expressing its opinion the Committee may propose that the Commission request the European standards institutions draw up a European standard within a given time. Member States must then take all appropriate measures to ensure that their standards institutions do not draw up or introduce standards in that field whilst the European standard is being drawn up. The obligation to postpone

---

[52]   The period is four months for *de facto* technical regulations in the form of voluntary agreements to which a public body is a contracting party.

[53]   Standards means a technical specification approved by a recognised standardisation body for repeated or continuous application, with which compliance is not compulsory and which can be either an international, European or national standard (art. 1(4)).

development of standards does not apply if the work of the standards institution is being undertaken at the request of the public authorities in order to draw up technical specifications or a standard for the purpose of enacting a technical regulation for such products. Such measures should be referred to the Commission as draft technical regulations, under the procedures outlined above.

Instead of seeking to have a matter referred to a European standardisation body, the Standing Committee may prefer to ask the Commission (i) to ensure that initially, Member States be asked to decide amongst themselves on appropriate measures to avoid the risk of barriers to trade; or (ii) to take all appropriate measures; or (iii) to identify areas where harmonisation appears necessary and, should the case arise, undertake appropriate harmonisation in a given sector.

C. Positive Harmonisation

In 1985 the EC started the process of establishing a new approach to technical harmonisation in its Council Resolution on the New Approach to Technical Harmonisation and Standardisation.[54] This marked a move away from detailed technical rules to broad sectoral directives which lay down essential safety requirements which are fleshed out by European standards.

A further stage in this development was the Council Resolution on a Global Approach to Conformity Assessment.[55] This sought to create a harmonised approach to conformity assessment so that Member States could have confidence that all products stated to conform to the European standard actually did so conform. We shall see that assuring conformity is one of the biggest practical problems created by the new approach to technical harmonisation.

Standardisation is central to the new and global approaches. This was recognised in 1990 by the adoption of a Commission *Green Paper on the Development of European Standardisation: Action for Faster Technological Convergence in Europe*[56] and the follow up document in 1991, *Standardisation in the European Economy*.[57]

---

54 OJ 1985 C 136/1.
55 OJ 1990 C 10/1. For a critique of this document see H. Micklitz, *Inquiry on EC and Current National Certification Schemes for Particular Consumer Goods*, (SECO, 1990).
56 OJ 1991 C 20/1.
57 COM(91) 521.

Thus the new approach has three limbs (i) more flexible legislation, (ii) a prominent role for standardisation, and (iii) reliance on conformity assessment procedures (leading to the award of the CE mark which allows access to the European market). These three elements will be considered in turn.

(i)   Technical Harmonisation

The old approach to technical harmonisation had been over ambitious.[58] It sought to set out in detail all the performance objectives and design specifications for the products covered. The resulting legislation was too inflexible; failed to allow regional considerations to be adequately taken into account; did not encourage product innovations; failed to integrate EC standardisation work; did not take the interests of third country producers into account and although the directives might encourage mutual recognition of testing and certification procedures carried out in other Member States, this was not required and did not occur in practice. In addition, adoption had been slow because of the unanimity requirement in art. 100 and because a lot of preparatory work by experts was needed.

In 1985 the EC adopted a new approach to technical harmonisation which places an emphasis on reference to standardisation work. This is clearly influenced by the German tradition where standards have traditionally played a significant role.[59] Traces of this new approach can be perceived as early as the 1973 Low Voltage Directive.[60]

New approach directives which affect product safety cover:

- simple pressure vessels,[61]
- toy safety,[62]

---

58   See, S. Farr, *Harmonisation of Technical Standards in the EC*, (Chancery Law, 1992) at 4–6.

59   See, C. Joerges, J. Falke, H–W. Micklitz and G. Brüggemeier, *Die Sicherheit von Konsumgütern und die Entwicklung der Europäischen Gemeinschaft*, (Nomos, 1988) at 132 *et seq.*

60   Council Directive 73/23 on the harmonisation of the laws of the Member States relating to electrical equipment designed for use within certain voltage limits: OJ 1973 L 77/29.

61   Council Directive 87/404/EEC on the harmonisation of the laws of the Member States relating to simple pressure vessels: OJ 1987 L 220/48.

62   Council Directive 88/378/EEC on the approximation of the laws of the Member States concerning the safety of toys: OJ 1988 L 187/1.

- construction products,[63]
- machinery,[64]
- personal protective equipment,[65]
- implantable medical equipment,[66]
- medical devices,[67]
- gas burning appliances,[68]
- telecommunications terminal equipment.[69]

New approach directives are considered to be 'total harmonisation' directives. The ECJ has consistently held that national regulation is incompatible with the presence of Directives which have established harmonised regimes.[70] Indeed new approach directives are most unlikely to be construed as being minimal in character since their purpose is to provide a level playing field. However, it is always possible that a new approach directive will not be construed as covering all risks and art. 100a(4) of the Treaty now expressly foresees continued reliance on art. 36 to justify national provision even in harmonised areas.

The basic principles of the new approach to technical harmonisation are set out in the 1985 Resolution as being:

- harmonising legislation should be limited to adopting 'essential safety requirements' to which products should conform; if they do so conform

63 Council Directive 89/106/EEC on the approximation of laws, regulations and administrative provisions of the Member States relating to construction products: OJ 1989 L 40/12.
64 Council Directive 89/392/EEC on the approximation of the laws of the Member States relating to machinery: OJ 1989 L 198/16; amended by Directive 91/368/EEC to cover mobile machinery and light equipment: OJ 1991 L 198/16.
65 Council Directive 89/686/EEC on the approximation of the laws of the Member States relating to personal protective equipment: OJ 1989 L 399/18.
66 Council Directive 90/385/EEC on the approximation of the laws of the Member States relating to active implantable medical devices: OJ 1990 L 189/17.
67 Council Directive 93/42/EEC concerning medical devices: OJ 1993 L 169/1.
68 Council Directive 90/396/EEC on the approximation of the laws of the Member States relating to appliances burning gaseous fuels: OJ 1990 L 196/15.
69 Council Directive 91/263/EEC on the approximation of the laws of the Member States concerning telecommunications terminal equipment, including the mutual recognition of their conformity: OJ 1991 L 128/1.
70 *Oberkreisdirektor des Kreises Borken v Handelsonderneming Moormann*, Case 190/87 [1988] ECR 4689; *Firma Eau de Cologne & Parfumerie–Fabrik Glockengasse v Provide*, C–150/88 [1989] ECR 3891 and *Commission v United Kingdom*, Case 60/86 [1988] ECR 3921.

this should be their passport to free movement throughout the Community;

- standardisation organisations should be entrusted with the task of drawing up the technical specifications needed for the production and placing on the market of products conforming to the essential requirements;
- these specification should be voluntary;
- national authorities are obliged to recognise that products conforming to the harmonised standards are presumed to conform to the essential requirements, but manufacturers should have the choice of not manufacturing in conformity with the standard. If the latter option is adopted manufacturers should be obliged to prove that their products conform to the essential requirements.

The presumption of conformity is, of course, just that – merely a presumption. Its purpose is to prevent the routine testing of products or requirements that documentation be produced once the product has been found to conform to the Directive. We shall see that this is typically signified by the CE mark, which is the effective passport for products to circulate within Europe. However, the new approach directives also have safeguard clauses and the 1985 Resolution makes it clear that where all the essential requirements are not covered then action under art. 36 (and presumably also under the mandatory requirements proviso) remains possible.

The 1985 Resolution justifies the new approach to technical harmonisation because of the need to harmonise safety legislation without lowering existing and justified levels of protection. Directives should specify their sphere of application according to the type of hazard involved (safety, health, environmental, consumer protection) and if need be the relevant circumstances (at home, at work, under road traffic conditions, during leisure activities etc.).

New approach directives include clauses dealing with:

(a) The scope of the Directive; they normally cover a broad category so as to avoid the proliferation of directives on specific products.
(b) A general clause providing that products covered by the Directive may only be placed on the market if they do not endanger the safety of persons, domestic animals or goods when properly installed and maintained and used for the purposes for which they are intended. However, particularly in the case of worker or consumer protection this can be strengthened to include foreseeable as well as intended uses.
(c) Essential safety requirements which will be used to assess whether the general safety requirement is satisfied. These essential requirements should be worded precisely enough so that when implemented in

national legislation they create legally binding obligations which can be enforced.

(d) The means of attestation of conformity which may be used. These include:

    (i) certificates and marks of conformity issued by a third party;

    (ii) results of tests carried out by a third party;

    (iii) declaration of conformity issued by the manufacturer or his agent based in the Community, possibly coupled with the requirement for a surveillance system; or

    (iv) such other means as specified in the Directives.

Specific directives establish the appropriate means of attestation and in so doing may limit or restrict the above range of options. Third party certification will be needed where there are no standards or the manufacturer chooses not to observe the standards. Where a manufacturer's declaration is relied upon national authorities, if they have good grounds for believing that a product does not offer the safety required in all respects, have the right to ask the manufacturer or importer for the data from the safety tests on which they rely. If this is not forthcoming then there is sufficient reason to doubt the presumption of conformity. Only through the use of one of the specified means of attestation can the product benefit from the presumption of conformity. However, the trader remains free to use any means he sees fit to establish that his product complies with the general safety obligation and the essential requirements.

(e) A free movement clause which obliges Member States to accept goods which conform to the general safety obligation and the essential requirements. Proof of conformity can be assured by one of the means of attestation referred to above declaring that the product is in conformity with a European harmonised standard, or (as a transitional measure) national standards.

(f) A safeguard clause so that even if a product is accompanied by a means of attestation, a Member State must take all appropriate measures to withdraw or prohibit the placing on the market of the product in question or to restrict its free movement, where it finds that it might compromise the safety of individuals, domestic animals or property. If the product was accompanied by a means of attestation of conformity with the relevant directive, the Member State must inform the Commission of such measures stating the reason for its decision and indicating whether the non–conformity resulted from, in the case where the product did not claim to conform to a standard, non–compliance with the general safety or the essential safety requirement, or in other cases an incorrect application of the relevant standard or a shortcoming in the actual standard.

If a Member State intends to keep such a measure in place the Commission will refer the matter to the Standing Committee. If the measure is found to be justified the Commission will inform the Member State in question and point out to the other states that (all else being equal) they should also prevent the product in question being marketed. If the failure of the product results from shortcomings in a harmonised or national standard then the Standing Committee should give its opinion as a matter of urgency. In the light of the Committee's opinion the Commission will notify the Member States as to whether or not the standard needs to be withdrawn. Where the non–conforming product was accompanied by a means of attestation the competent Member State should take appropriate action against the author of the attestation.

The relationship between the essential safety requirements and standards is central to the new approach. In theory it provides the means to ensure safety in a manner which is compatible with economic development. The safety objectives are set down by the politicians in the Directives, whilst the technocrats from industry take part in the standardisation process to ensure the means to achieve those goals are acceptable to industry.

However, inevitably, the distinction between standard setting and technical implementation is not always clear cut. A perusal of the essential safety requirements in the annexes to the new approach directives shows that the rules they contain vary in character. Some rules are very clear and precise, but many of the essential safety requirements set down vague objectives and refer, for instance to the need to minimise risks or reduce them as far as possible or to ensure temperatures do not cause burning (leaving it for experts to decide what temperatures are appropriate). Requirements phrased in this way leave a great deal of room for debate as to how far risks can be minimised or reduced or what the maximum temperature should be. The clear danger is that the Directives can produce the symbolism of safety, but the standards fail to back this up by providing concrete safety. As a general rule even the standards do not themselves prescribe the means by which safety should be assured. They are generally framed in terms of performance rather than means, with the belief being that:

> 'only people of the trade can be responsible for choosing the necessary and sufficient technical solutions to obtain the performances defined by the standards so as to meet the essential requirements specified by the directive and intended to guarantee user safety.'[71]

Thus new approach directives provide four layers of controls – the general safety clause in the body of the Directive, the essential requirements to be

---

71   See comment by Jeanne Milhaïlov in *The New Approach*, (CEN, 1994) at 198.

found in the annex, harmonised standards and the means chosen by manufacturers to achieve those standards. Clearly the content of the standards is pivotal as these will be the basis for manufacturers' design and production decision–making and also the measure against which products will be judged in order to obtain the CE marking and thereby access to free movement within the EC. It is also clear that this process is more than just a technical process. Standards do not just provide the technical details to supplement the safety standards laid down in the essential requirements. More precisely the essential requirements tend to set down the need for various safety concerns to be addressed, whilst the standards give meaning to those exhortations. To put it more bluntly, the directives say that products should be safe, the standards tell us what safe means.

(ii) Standardisation

There are three European standards organisations CEN (European Committee for Standardisation), CENELEC (European Committee for Electrotechnical Standardisation) and ETSI (European Telecommunications Standards Institute). We shall concentrate on CEN as it is the largest organisation.

One of the criticisms of CEN and European standardisation in general is that it lacks a rigorous structure. The Commission had suggested that European standardisation be re–organised.[72] It proposed the establishment of a European Standardisation Council responsible for the strategic direction of European standardisation. This would have had an executive body, the European Standardisation Board, responsible for co–ordinating the work of the European standardisation bodies. It was envisaged that in the future other sectors (than just the telecommunications sector, which has ETSI) may wish to develop their own European standardisation bodies. The Commission wished to encourage this in the hope that industry would then become more involved in and committed to standardisation, but saw its European Standardisation System as a means of retaining coherency in the system.

There was opposition to the Commission's proposals which were seen as adding a needless bureaucratic layer,[73] but they did cause the three European Standardisation Bodies to appreciate the need to work more closely together. There is now a Joint Presidents Groups to reach understandings on strategic issues; a Joint Co–ordination Group to monitor co–operation between technical bodies of the three organisations in areas of common interest and which also acts as a court of last resort in the event of conflicts not resolved

---

[72]   See OJ 1991 C 20/1, *op. cit.*
[73]   See COM(91) 521 at 4.

through normal processes, as well as an Information Technology Steering Committee (now the ICT Standards Board).[74]

CEN has been criticised for its slow procedures, failing to promote the European dimension of standardisation and not fully integrating social partners, such as consumers into its structures and working methods.[75] Although many of these criticisms are valid, it is worthwhile setting them in the context of both the origins of CEN and the changed role it has been called upon to play.

When CEN was established in 1961 its primary role was not to harmonise standards, but rather to ensure the more effective implementation of international standards by national standardisation bodies in Europe. Between 1961 and 1982 CEN only adopted 96 standards. By 1995 1,700 European standards were in existence with a further 8,300 projected.[76] Not only the new approach directives, but other moves towards European integration, for instance in the public procurement sphere, have placed increased workloads on CEN. Thus CEN is trying to perform a task – harmonisation – which it was not originally established to achieve and the size of the harmonisation task has grown exponentially in recent years.

CENs constitution as a body representing and comprising national standardisation bodies causes some problems.[77] Industry does not feel it 'owns' the European standardisation process and therefore does not see why it should fund it.[78] The national bodies are themselves industry oriented and so other social partners feel excluded. The need to reach consensus between national interests and traditions may both water down proposals and cause them to be delayed. Also the end result continues to be national standards giving effect to European standards. This can help maintain the idea of

---

74   These arrangements are explained in the pamphlet, *European Standardisation,* published by CEN, CENELEC and ETSI.

75   For a useful discussion of the attempts to improve consumer representation in the standardisation process: see B. Farquhar, 'Consumer Representation in Standardisation' [1995] *Consum.L.J.* 56. Consumers are represented both on national delegations and directly at the European level by ANEC, a Commission sponsored co–ordinating body for consumer representation in standardisation. In truth consumers are always going to lack the expertise and resources to challenge business on an even footing. The need to co–ordinate at a European level creates additional costs of co–ordinating national consumer bodies, but equally could permit savings to be made if consumer research in the Member States was properly focused and co-ordinated.

76   CEN, *Standards for Access to the European Market,* (2 ed., CEN, 1995) at 13.

77   C.f. ETSI where individual companies are members.

78   70% of CENs funding used to come from EC mandates and subsidies: see OJ 1991 C 20/1, *op. cit.,* at 20. The percentage has reduced in recent years.

market segmentation, especially as national marks continue to be permitted (see below).

(iii) Conformity Assessment

Setting harmonised standards under the new approach is only half the battle to freeing up barriers to trade, because even if products are made to common standards they still need to provide proof of this. If states differ in the forms of proof they require, or do not recognise test results or certification carried out in other states then these can be major practical hurdles to the creation of an internal market. Furthermore problems can arise if different marks are either required to be used, or permitted, in Member States. A Community solution to these problems is necessary. This problem does not only affect products governed by new approach directives, but also products subject to national regulations or even those with no regulatory requirements, because increasingly firms are seeking assurances of compliance with standards from contractors as part of their attempts to limit their liability exposure.

Conformity assessment is, however, a difficult matter to control on a European wide level. Given the policy of restricting public authority controls to a limited number of products where it is absolutely necessary, it requires states (and consumers) to have confidence that manufacturers, testing and certification bodies in other Member States will competently and diligently carry out the necessary procedures to ensure compliance with standards.

The Resolution of 7 May 1985 on technical harmonisation recognised 'that the new approach will have to be accompanied by a policy on the assessment of conformity'. The Commission's response was to develop the *Global Approach to Certification and Testing*[79] which was encouraged by the adoption of a council resolution on a Global Approach to Conformity Assessment on 21 December 1989.[80] The concrete outcomes of this global approach have included Council Decision 93/465/EEC concerning the modules for the various phases of the conformity assessment procedures and the rules for the affixing and use of the CE conformity marking, which are intended to be used in the technical harmonisation directives[81] and the establishment of the European Organisation for Testing and Certification (EOTC).

---

[79]   OJ 1989 C 231/3.

[80]   OJ 1990 C 10/1.

[81]   OJ 1993 L 220/23 (hereafter Conformity Assessment and CE Marking Decision). At the same time Council Directive 93/68/EEC was passed amending various new approach technical harmonisation directives to bring them into line with the Council decision: see OJ 1993 L 220/1.

Resolving the conformity assessment problem requires (a) that the means of assuring conformity are harmonised, (b) that testing procedures are also harmonised and competency of those involved in the process is assured, and (c) that conforming products are awarded a mark which assures them access to the whole of the internal market. The dangers to consumers are that the European rules and practices may be less demanding than those which existed under national laws and as conformity can be established in any Member State there may be a drift towards undertaking compliance procedures where they are, at least perceived to be, less demanding. Further problems about the relationship between European certification marks and national marks also arise.

(a)   Conformity assessment procedures

The Conformity Assessment and CE Marking Decision[82] states that the essential objective of conformity assurance is to enable public authorities to ensure that products placed on the market conform to Directives, particularly with regard to the health and safety of users and consumers (annex 1A(a)). It explains that conformity assessment can be divided into modules relating to both the design and production phases and produces eight modules which in various combinations produce 17 possible permutations. However, there are three broad categories of conformity assessment: self–declaration by the manufacturer, third party certification and quality assessment procedures supervised and controlled by a third party.[83]

Normally products must be subject to assessment at both their design and production stages. For each particular product sector the directive will select the appropriate modules taking into account the type of products, the nature of the risks involved, whether third party testing facilities exist, the types and importance of production etc. However, the emphasis is clearly on reducing the burden on manufacturers. Thus the Decision provides that the directives should leave the manufacturer with as wide a choice of modules as is consistent with meeting the requirements and avoid imposing unnecessarily modules which are too onerous relative to the directive's objectives. Notified bodies are also to be encouraged to apply the modules without placing unnecessary burdens on economic operators and the technical documentation required has to be limited to that which is required solely for conformity assessment purposes, with protection being afforded to confidential information.

---

[82]   The principal guidelines for the use of conformity assessment procedures are found in Annex IA.

[83]   See Micklitz, *op. cit.*, at 8.

One problem is that the Decision only provides modules for the future. In contrast to the position with regard to the CE marking, there is no complementary measure revising existing new approach directives, although many of the existing directives followed patterns of conformity assessment which resemble those laid down in the Decision.

The Commission, in co–operation with Member States, is to ensure close co–operation between the Member States to ensure consistent technical application of the modules. This, combined with competition between notified bodies (since approval by any one body affords access to the single market), will have a tendency to restrict the freedom of testing bodies to be more demanding than the basic requirements of the directives. Unless the requirements of a particular directive require the application of a certain procedure then the manufacturer should be given the choice whether or not he uses modules based on quality assurance techniques. To the extent that this reduces third party certification, it requires consumers to have a degree of confidence in quality assurance systems and third party surveillance of them, which perhaps does not yet exist and is perhaps not yet justified.

(b) Testing and certification bodies

Wherever possible the approach is therefore to permit manufacturers to undertake as much of the conformity assurance as possible themselves. Although not referred to in the Conformity Assessment and CE Marking Decision the Community has a policy of promoting quality assurance systems which comply with the European standard series EN 29 000.[84]

The Decision does require Member States to notify bodies within their jurisdiction which they have approved as being technically competent and complying with the requirements of the directives.[85] Member States must then ensure that these 'notified bodies' retain the requisite qualifications and also keep the competent national authorities informed of their performance. In keeping with the new approach to technical harmonisation, notified bodies which can prove their conformity with harmonised standards (the EN 45 000 series European standards) will be presumed to conform to the requirements of the directives by submitting an accreditation certificate or other documentary evidence. Member States can notify bodies not able to provide this evidence, but then the Commission can ask the Member State to provide documentary evidence of the basis on which notification was carried out. Notified bodies are listed in the Official Journal. Confidence can be built by testing laboratories and certification and inspection bodies being accredited

---

84 See Council Resolution of 21 December 1989, *op. cit.*
85 Annex IA(k).

by third parties in accordance with EN 45 000 series standards.[86] This is particularly important in areas not covered by directives if free trade is to be realised. One of the roles of the European Organisation for Testing and Certification (EOTC) is to develop mutual recognition agreements between national networks. Absent harmonisation or mutual recognition, the next best thing is knowledge of the relevant procedures and bodies: These have been collated by the Commission in the PROMOLOG– CERTIFICAT data base.

Council Directives 87/18/EEC[87] and 87/19/EEC[88] adopt a different approach and make mandatory the use of the Good Laboratory Practice guidelines, which originated from the OECD. These directives are, however, exceptional in this respect and indeed are likely to be revised to see which aspects can be covered by EN 45 000 standards. Whilst one can accept the principle of self regulation, there are certain reasons for being cautious about the way it is being applied in relation to conformity assessment. First, standards under the new approach are attempting to flesh out essential safety requirements. The EN 45 000 standards, on the other hand, set standards within no legislative framework. Furthermore, product standards are subject to safeguard clauses and post–marketing controls, yet outside their rather imprecise responsibility for notified bodies there is no obligation on Member States to ensure the proper functioning of testing, certification and inspection bodies.

(c)   CE marking

The CE marking is the linchpin of the system. Goods bearing this marking are in principle assured access to European markets, subject to safeguard controls. Prior to 1993 Community directives had provided for several different Community marks of varying significance.[89] Annex 1B of the Conformity Assessment and CE Marking Decision provides the principal guidelines for affixing and use of the CE marking.

---

86   In 1989 eight Member States had accreditation networks for testing laboratories, but only three had similar networks for certification and inspection bodies: COM(89) 20, Annex at 22.

87   Council Directive 87/18/EEC on the harmonisation of laws, regulations and administrative provisions relating to the application of the principles of good laboratory practice and the verification of their applications for tests on chemical substances: OJ 1987 L 15/29.

88   Council Directive 87/18/EEC amending Directive 75/318/EEC on the approximation of the laws of the Member States relating to analytical, pharmaco–toxicological and clinical standards and protocols in respect of the testing of proprietary medicinal products: OJ 1987 L 15/31.

89   COM(89) 209 Annex 1 at 37.

The CE marking symbolises conformity to all obligations imposed on manufacturers by virtue of directives which provide for its affixation. This need not be limited to the essential requirements, since some directives may impose specific obligations not necessarily forming part of the essential requirements. The person affixing the CE marking verifies that the product conforms to all Community total harmonisation provisions and has been subject to the appropriate conformity evaluation procedures. Where several directives apply to the product each requiring a CE marking then the marking must indicate conformity to all the directives.

The Decision specifies the design of the CE marking. The identification number of any notified body involved in the production control phase must follow the CE marking. This can be followed by a pictogram or other mark, where it is necessary to lay down conditions for the use of certain products. The marking must be visible, legible and indelible. In principle it should be affixed to the product or its data plate, although if more appropriate it can be affixed to packaging or any accompanying documents. The CE marking must be affixed at the end of the production control stage by the manufacturer or his agent established within the Community, or if exceptionally provided for in directives, the person responsible for placing the product on the Community market. The notified body's identification number should be affixed under its responsibility either by itself or the manufacturer or agent established within the Community.

The CE marking establishes no more and no less than that the product conforms to the directives based on the global approach. One danger is that consumers believe that the CE marking warrants all aspects of the product or that it is an express indication of safety.

Member States must refrain from introducing other marks to demonstrate compliance with these directives. Member States must also take all possible steps to exclude the possibility of confusion and to prevent abuse of the CE marking. But products can also carry other marks besides the CE marking, for instance marks which indicate conformity to national or European standards or to traditional–style optional directives, provided that such marks are not liable to cause confusion with the CE marking. The legibility or visibility of the CE marking must not be reduced by these other marks being affixed to the product, its packaging or the accompanying documentation. In practice other marks, especially national marks, remain important.

Without prejudice to safeguard clauses in directives, where a Member State establishes that the CE marking has been improperly affixed then the person responsible for affixing the CE marking can be obliged to make the product comply and to end the infringement under conditions imposed by the Member States. If non–compliance continues the Member State must take all appropriate measures to restrict or prohibit the placing of the product on the market or to ensure that it is withdrawn from the market in accordance with the safeguard clauses.

Accurate information on which products pose the greatest threats to consumer safety is important if resources are to be effectively targeted. It allows regulators and standardisers to prioritise their work and can result in better standards and more successful consumer education campaigns.

Within Europe only the United Kingdom, the Netherlands and Denmark already had national systems for collecting data on home and leisure accidents. The need for such systems in all Member States became apparent. Therefore the Community has moved tentatively towards a European system EHLASS (European Home and Leisure Accident Surveillance System). This development has been marked with caution. In 1981 a 30 month pilot experiment was established.[90] In 1986 a demonstration project was set up,[91] which was amended and extended in 1990.[92] Finally a system was introduced in 1993, but for only one year.[93] The current system was established in 1994.[94]

The system is primarily based upon collecting data from 65 hospital casualty departments across the Community concerning persons injured in product related accidents. Germany has opposed this method of collecting data, so it (and now also Spain and Luxembourg) are allowed to provide equivalent data based on household questionnaires. The Commission meets 80% of the cost of both methods of data collection as well as providing funds for supporting those Member States with less developed national infra-structures.

Member States must submit annual reports to the Commission. The Commission role is to make the material available and also to undertake information campaigns if these appear necessary at the European level.

The EHLASS system has certainly been successful in encouraging the development of national systems of accident data collection in some countries where these did not previously exist. It is less obvious that much use is made of the reports from other Member States and currently no attempt is made to compile centralised European statistics. One reason for this is the need to take further steps to ensure that data is collected in a consistent manner in the different states. The EHLASS system is still embryonic and the jury must be out on its effectiveness. It is understood that the Commission is considering

---

90   Council Decision 81/623/EEC: OJ 1981 L 229/1.
91   Council Decision 86/138/EEC: OJ 1986 L 109/23.
92   Council Decision 90/534/EEC: OJ 1990 L 296/64.
93   Council Decision 93/683/EEC: OJ 1993 L 319/40.
94   Council Decision 3092/94/EC: OJ 1994 L 331/1 as amended by Council Decision 95/184/EEC: OJ 1995 L 120/37.

ways in which the information can be brought together to produce European wide data.

D.   General Product Safety Directive

(i)   Introduction

A General Product Safety Directive was first proposed in 1989,[95] an amended proposal was submitted in 1990[96] with the Directive being adopted in 1992.[97] This Directive is seen as the final piece in the jigsaw fitting alongside the technical harmonisation directives.

The Directive's preamble cites disparities between, or the absence of, national horizontal product safety regulation as justifying the Directive in order to prevent the creation of barriers to trade and distortions to competition (recital 2). This type of argumentation is stronger in this context than when it is applied to product liability. The actions of national authorities can actually prohibit the marketing of products, whereas different product liability laws simply affect the risk should something go wrong. However, the general obligations are less crucial than technical specifications discussed in section 4B, for they do not dictate a particular form of manufacture or design.

The General Product Safety Directive also seems to be motivated by the desire to ensure consumer protection in the new internal market. This is reflected in recital 3 of the preamble which talks of the need to include products not subject to Community legislation and to cover lacunae in specific legislation. It particularly refers to the requirement of art. 100a(3) to ensure a high level of protection of safety and health of persons.

The General Product Safety Directive imposes a general safety requirement on producers and distributors (arts 3–4); requires Member States to have authorities to monitor product safety (arts 5–6); provides for notification procedures and exchanges of information (arts 7–8 and Annex) and provides for an emergency Community procedure (arts 9–11).

(ii)   Scope

The Directive applies to 'products' which are both:
(a)   intended for consumers or likely to be used by consumers; and

---

95   OJ 1989 C 193/1.

96   OJ 1990 C 156/8.

97   Council Directive 92/59/EEC on general product safety: OJ 1992 L 228/24.

(b) supplied, whether for consideration or not in the course of a commercial activity (art. 2(a)).

Here of course the definition is applied directly to the product rather than the characteristics of a potential consumer or user of them. The Directive would therefore apply even if there had been no use by consumers so long as such use was likely. Consumer would seem to be intended to be given its narrow meaning referring to private individuals who use products outside their trade or profession.

Recital 5 of the Directive's preamble states that production equipment, capital goods and other products used exclusively in the context of a trade or business are not covered. Whilst the Directive is clearly restricted to consumer goods it, surprisingly, gives little help in determining the meaning of the word 'product' itself. It is, however, stated to cover new, used and reconditioned products. The only exceptions to this are for (a) second–hand goods supplied as antiques and (b) products which need to be repaired or reconditioned prior to use where the supplier clearly informs the buyer of that fact (art. 2(a)).

(iii) Relationship with Vertical Regulation

Although it might have been attractive to consumers for the General Product Safety Directive to be viewed as a safety net which applied concurrently with specific vertical rules, this is not the solution adopted by the Directive. Art. 1(2) first indent states that its provisions shall only apply 'in so far as there are no specific provisions in rules of Community law governing the safety of the product concerned'. This would seem to point in favour of a vertical directive pre–empting the horizontal directive. Recital 7 of the preamble is even more explicit, stating

> 'when there are specific rules of Community law, of the total harmonisation type, and in particular rules adopted on the basis of the new approach, which lay down obligations regarding product safety, further obligations should not be imposed on economic operators as regards the placing on the market of products covered by such rules'.

However, whilst the goal of new approach directives may be to cover all safety aspects, this is not achieved in practice. It is therefore possible to read the General Product Safety Directive as having some relevance even for products covered by new approach directives. The second indent of art. 1(2) seems to qualify the general exclusion in the first indent by stating that when specific rules impose safety requirements then the provisions in arts 2–4 shall not in any event apply, implying that the other provisions may. Thus the General Product Safety Directive could be seen as having a role in relation to new approach directives by supplementing them with notification, information exchange and emergency procedures where these features are absent from product specific directives, as well as ensuring the enforcement authorities have adequate powers. This view is supported by recital 7 which only seeks to prevent further controls concerning the placing on the market of products and so would not affect post–marketing controls.

The second indent of art. 1(2) suggests that a provision in a specific directive ousts the general safety requirement even if it offers less protection. However, the third indent clarifies the second indent, by stating that where only certain safety aspects are covered by the specific regulations, then those provisions apply to the product for the relevant safety aspect or risk. This implies that other aspects or risks could be dealt with under the general safety requirement.

(iv) Safe product

The Directive's central organising concept is that of the 'safe product' (art. 2(b)).[98] It is defined as meaning:

> 'any product which, under normal or reasonably foreseeable conditions of use, including duration, does not present any risk or only the minimum risks compatible with the product's use, considered as acceptable and consistent with a high level of protection for the safety and health of persons, taking into account the following points in particular:
> – the characteristics of the product, including its composition, packaging, instructions for assembly and maintenance,
> – the effect on other products, where it is reasonably foreseeable that it will be used with other products,
> – the presentation of the product, the labelling, any instructions for its use and disposal and any other indication or information provided by the producer,
> – the categories of consumers at serious risk when using the product, in particular children.
>
> The feasibility of obtaining higher levels of safety or the availability of other products presenting a lesser degree of risk shall not constitute grounds for considering a product to be "unsafe" or "dangerous".'

---

98   Sometimes reference is made in the Directive to a *dangerous product*, but this is simply a product which does not meet the definition of a *safe product*: art. 2(c).

From a consumer perspective there are several positive aspects of this definition. It is rather objective, assessing the actual risks. In this respect it compares favourably with the defectiveness standard in the Product Liability Directive which depends upon the expectations of consumers.[99]

The General Product Safety Directive only accepts as safe products which either (a) do not present any risk, or (b) only the minimum risks compatible with the product's use. Even these minimum risks must be acceptable. Thus it is not necessarily sufficient that a product has the safest design to perform its intended function. The utility of the purpose must be balanced against the minimum inherent risks to judge whether these are acceptable. Although there is room for debate about what is considered acceptable, the Directive indicates that it should be pitched at a high level by stressing that the risks must be compatible with a high level of protection for the safety and health of persons.

The function of a safety standard in a regulatory regime is not to remove all risks from the market, but only those not justified by the benefits derived from the product or because safer alternatives exist. Thus the basic definition seems to strike the right balance. However, to some extent this rather stringent definition is undermined by the situations in which art. 4 treats products as being safe (see below).

In determining whether a product is safe, the Directive lists factors which should be particularly taken into account. These include the product's durability, characteristics, presentation, labelling, instructions and the information which is provided, as well as its effect on other products.

The product must be judged according to its normal or reasonably foreseeable conditions of use. This is a compromise standard. It does not let the manufacturer arbitrarily restrict the uses to which the product can be put. Equally, the consumer is not to be protected against all misuses, only those which are reasonably foreseeable.

It is pleasing that the definition refers to the need to consider the categories of consumers at serious risk when using the product. It states that, in particular, the needs of children should be taken into account; but this should not prevent the interests of other groups, such as the elderly, blind, deaf and disabled etc., being considered.

The definition of safe product forms the foundation of the general safety requirement in art. 3. This places on producers the obligation to place only safe products on the market and on distributors the duty to take due care to help ensure compliance with that requirement. However, for these purposes the definition of a safe product has to be read in the light of art. 4. This provision lays down a hierarchy of rules and standards against which a product should be judged to determine whether the general safety

---

[99]   But note the introduction of consumer expectations in art. 4(2): see below.

requirement is satisfied. However, this is expressly said not to bar the competent authorities from taking appropriate measures to impose restrictions on the placing of the product on the market or to require its withdrawal, where there is evidence that despite conformity with the requirement the product is dangerous to the health and safety of consumers.

Art. 4(1) provides that a product shall be deemed safe when it conforms to (a) specific Community provisions governing the safety of the products in question, or (b) failing such provisions specific rules of national law of the Member State in whose territory it is circulating which lay down health and safety requirements which the product must satisfy.

Art. 4(2) states that conformity to the general safety requirement shall be assessed having regard to a list of criteria. It does not provide that products fulfilling these criteria are to be deemed safe. Although art. 4(3) seems to imply that conformity with one of these criteria would satisfy the general safety requirement, it is possible to argue that this need not be an automatic consequence. The criteria although not expressly stated to be hierarchical are listed in such a way that implies the drafters conceived of a hierarchy along the following lines:

- voluntary national standards giving effect to a European standard,
- Community technical specifications,[100]
- standards drawn up in the Member States in which the product is in circulation,
- codes of good practice in respect of health and safety in the sector concerned,
- the state of the art,
- safety which consumers may reasonably expect.

The inclusion of the last two criteria exposes the dangers created if products which conform to these standards are deemed to satisfy the general safety requirement. An enforcement authority could take a perfectly proper prosecution against an unsafe product only to be met with defences that it complied with the state of the art or that it offered the safety which consumers might reasonably expect. Determining the merits of such defences involves complex technical questions requiring a great deal of expert evidence and resources which enforcement authorities would often not feel they could devote to the prosecution of the case.

---

[100] There is some uncertainty as to what this phrase means. It might simply refer to CEN standards which have not, yet, been adopted at the national level or it could also refer to other European specifications such as harmonisation documents and European pre-norms: c.f. the very broad definition of the term in the Technical Standards Directive, see section 4B.

(v)   General Safety Requirement

(a)   Definition of producer and distributor

The general safety requirement places different obligations on producers and distributors.[101] In theory the principle obligation to assure safety is placed on producers with distributors having a supportive role. The Directive gives a broad definition of producer (art. 2(d)). This includes the manufacturer, if established within the Community, otherwise his representative will be treated as the producer. If neither are established in the Community the importer[102] will be treated as the producer. Any person who presents himself as the manufacturer by affixing to the product his name, trademark or other distinctive mark[103] and any person who reconditions a product is also treated as producers.

Also included within the definition of producer are other professionals in the supply chain, insofar as their activities may affect the safety properties of a product placed on the market. The definition of distributor is the mirror image of this, namely those professionals in the supply chain whose activity does not affect the safety properties of the product (art. 2(e)).

Thus it is crucial to consider whether a party has affected the safety properties of the product. Certainly this would cover anyone who affected the design or construction of the product. Thus a party who modified the product or helped assemble it or install it might fall within the definition of producer. Those who simply stored, transported or displayed the product may be treated as producers but only if their activities affected the safety properties of the product. This will not be the case with most products, but the safety of many food products, for instance, might easily be affected by such activities. Thus many parties whom one would colloquially speak of as distributors or retailers, will in fact fall within the definition of producer.

(b)   Obligations of the producer

Art. 3(1) obliges producers to place only safe products on the market. This obligation is strict in the sense that it is breached by the mere fact of marketing an unsafe product without regard to any question of the degree

---

101   In the first draft directive these obligations had not been placed directly on the producers and distributors, but rather on the Member States to ensure these objective were achieved: see OJ 1989 C 193/1, arts 4 and 6. The Directive's reference to these obligations being those of the producer or distributor may only be symbolic given that Member States still have to implement the Directive, but is to be welcomed.

102   Unlike the Product Liability Directive it does not expressly state it is the importer into the Community, but such an interpretation is likely to be given.

103   C.f. discussion in the context of the Product Liability Directive in section 3C.

of care taken by the producer. Art. 3(2) outlines two types of supporting 'information obligations' placed on producers.

One set of obligations involves providing consumers with the relevant information to enable them to assess the risks inherent in a product throughout the normal or reasonably foreseeable period of its use, where such risks are not immediately obvious without adequate warnings. The information must be such as to enable the consumer to take precautions against those risks. Here we have an illustration of the faith EC law places in information as a consumer protection strategy. The relationship between this approach and the expressed concern for vulnerable consumers, such as children, clearly needs to be carefully worked out.

Producers should also take measures commensurate with the products they supply (i) to enable them to be informed of risks which these products might present, and (ii) to take appropriate action to avoid those risks, including, if necessary, withdrawing the product from the market. The list of examples of measures which should be included, whenever appropriate, involve the marking of products or product batches, sample testing, the investigation of complaints and keeping distributors informed of such monitoring.

However, producers need only undertake such of the above obligations as could be expected of them within the limits of their activities. This proviso is needed, because of the broad definition of producer, so as not to impose too onerous obligations on parties who have affected the safety of the product in only a marginal way. A retailer who affected the safety properties by storing, assembling or installing a product would not, for instance, usually be expected to warn of the product's inherent risks.

(c) Obligations of the distributor

The role of the distributor is, at least at first glance, subsidiary to that of the producer. He is required to act with due care to help ensure compliance with the general safety requirement. Due care suggests that the distributor will only breach the general safety requirement if he has unreasonably failed to help assist in satisfying the general safety requirement. The assessment of the distributor's action seems to be premised on fault. However, due care involves an objective standard against which the distributor is judged. This is underpinned by the Directive, which states that in particular distributors should not supply products which they know, or should have assumed, do not comply with the general safety requirement. Their constructive knowledge is to be assessed having regard both to information in their possession and as professionals. The due care standard ought to be sufficiently flexible to expect different standards from different kinds of distributors. Thus large and/or specialist retailers should be judged by higher standards than local small shopkeepers.

A particular duty placed on distributors requires them to participate in monitoring the safety of products placed on the market. The extent of this obligation is related to what could be expected of them within the limits of their respective activities. This should require them to pass on information on product risks and to co–operate in the action taken to avoid these risks (by, for example, displaying posters or contacting customers affected by product recalls).

The distinction between the primary strict obligation of producers only to market safe products and the secondary obligation of distributors to assist in ensuring that the obligation is satisfied is not clear cut. Although the primary obligation of producers to market only safe products is strict, the additional obligations placed on producers depend upon the limits of their activities. By contrast, the practical requirements resulting from the distributor's duty to act with due care will vary according to the nature of his professional involvement and can be quite onerous for large and/or specialist organisations. Thus it is better to see the obligations of producers and distributors in terms of a continuum, with indeed some overlap, for some distributors may be expected to do more than some producers (compare the obligations of a large specialist distributor with those of a small retailer who is only a producer because he assembles the final product).

(vi) Enforcement of Duties

Art. 5 requires Member States to introduce the necessary laws, regulations and administrative provisions to make producers and distributors comply with their obligations under the Directive so that only safe products are placed on the market. However, laws are only as good as their enforcement, so it goes on to provide that in particular states should establish or nominate authorities to monitor compliance with the obligation only to place safe products on the market. The Commission shall be notified of these authorities and this information shall be passed on to the other Member States. The requirement to ensure there are specific authorities to regulate consumer product safety is a major structural improvement brought about by the Directive. Although many states already had such agencies, others, particularly in the South of Europe, had no consumer safety authorities, or at least none that were properly organised. The existence of such agencies is an essential pre–condition to the effectiveness of the controls put in place by the Directive. This spur to administrative reform is therefore most welcome, but of course these agencies need to be well equipped, trained and financed if they are to make a real impact.

The national authorities must be given the necessary powers to fulfil their obligations under the Directive. Art. 6(1) lists a series of objectives which these powers should ensure are achieved. The first three of these powers are concerned with ensuring the authorities have the powers to undertake adequate surveillance of products, whilst the remaining five relate to controls which they should be able to impose on the marketing of products.

Enforcement authorities must be able to:

(a) Organise appropriate checks on the safety properties of products.

(b) Require all necessary information from the parties concerned.

(c) Take samples of a product or product line and subject them to safety checks.

(d) Subject product marketing to prior conditions designed to ensure product safety and require suitable warnings to be affixed regarding the risks which the product may present.

(e) Make arrangements to ensure that persons who might be exposed to a risk from a product are informed of it within good time and in a suitable manner. This is said to include the publication of special warnings.

(f) Prohibit temporarily (whilst checks are being carried out) anyone from supplying, offering to supply or exhibiting a product or product batch, whenever there are precise and consistent indications that they are dangerous.

(g) Prohibit the placing on the market of a product or product batch which has proved to be dangerous. Accompanying measures to ensure the ban is complied with should also be available.

(h) Organise the effective and immediate withdrawal of a product or product batch already on the market. If necessary this should involve destruction of the product under appropriate conditions. Nothing is said about the issue of compensation for the consumer who has paid for a dangerous product which has been recalled, although of course this would usually be covered by the civil law. There is an ambiguity as to what is meant by goods 'on the market'. Does it simply refer to goods 'on the market' waiting to be sold or does it extend to goods which have already been sold and are now in the possession of consumers. Consumer protection would seem to demand that measures be taken to require recall procedures to extend to dangerous products which are actually in the possession of consumers;[104] but the United Kingdom

---

104 Many states which did not have such a power are introducing one to comply with the Directive, see for example s.13a of the Finnish Products Safety Act, Act 18.6.1993/539.

Government clearly takes a more restricted view of this provision as it has no powers to require recall campaigns of this nature.

Enforcement authorities must exercise their powers in accordance with the degree of risk[105] and with the Treaty, particularly arts 30–36. The powers shall be addressed as appropriate to both producers and distributors; but regarding distributors, measures should only be addressed to them within the limits of their activities. In particular the distributor responsible for the first stage of distribution on the national market is targeted for enforcement action. This is a welcome recognition of the continued need for controls at the national as well as European level. In addition measures can be addressed to any other person where this is necessary to ensure co–operation in action taken to avoid risks arising from a product.

Art. 5 makes it clear that the powers of the enforcement authorities should include the possibility of imposing suitable penalties. Reference to the word penalties would seem to indicate that there should be some form of regulatory sanction besides civil law sanctions. According to national traditions this might take the form of criminal sanctions, administrative fines etc. and of course under general EC law principles the size of any fine must be adequate and effective.[106] This direction that the sanctions should be more than those of the civil law is a welcome contrast with the absence of such a provision in many other EC consumer law directives.

(vii) Notification and Exchange of Information

The Sutherland Report, *The internal market after 1992: meeting the challenge*, drew attention both to the need to review existing mechanisms for handling urgent and serious consumer problems[107] and for the Commission to have a partnership with Member States to ensure the implementation of Community rules and more specifically to ensure the effective handling of urgent problems.[108] In fact the General Product Safety Directive has two procedures under which information must be notified to the Commission by Member States. Such procedures have three possible objectives: supervising the appropriateness of the actions of Member States, informing other Member States of possible dangers and alerting authorities to the need to take action at the Community level, where appropriate.

---

105   There seems to be a typing error in the text of the English language version of the OJ which says 'degree or risk'.

106   *Marshall v Southampton A.H.A. (No. 2)*, Case 271/91[1993] 3 CMLR 293.

107   Recommendation 24.

108   Recommendation 33.

(a) Art. 7 notification

Art. 7 is the procedure intended for non–emergency situations. The duty of the Member States to notify the Commission arises when they have taken measures restricting the marketing of a product or requiring its withdrawal (as provided for in art. 6(1)(d–h)).

The obligation to notify does not apply if such notification is required under another specific Community legislation or 'if the measures relate to an event which is local in effect and in any case limited to the territory of the Member State concerned'. One might question the wisdom of the second limitation. Products can easily cross borders and indeed sales might be diverted to other Member States once restrictive measures are applied. Equally similar, but not identical products, may be in circulation in other Member States.

Once the Commission receives information under art. 7 it enters into consultations with the parties. If it concludes that the measure was justified it immediately informs all Member States. If it considers the measure was not justified it immediately informs the Member State which initiated the action.

(b) RAPEX

Established in 1984 the system for the rapid exchange of information arising from the use of consumer products (RAPEX) now has its legal base in art. 8 of the General Product Safety Directive together with an annex setting out detailed procedures for the operation of the scheme. The notification obligation arises in relation to all products which fall within the scope of the Directive, unless they are covered by similar procedures in other Community legislation. The RAPEX system is in fact two systems – one for food products organised by D–G III[109] and the other for non–food products run by D–G XXIV (formerly the Consumer Policy Service). Both food and non–food systems operate similarly, but with some minor differences. We will concentrate on the non–food sector RAPEX system.

Once a serious and immediate risk is detected the national authorities should obtain the maximum amount of information about the product and the nature of the danger, by in particular consulting the producer or distributor of the product. This should not compromise the need for quick action. Where because of a serious and immediate risk a Member State decides on or adopts measures to prevent, restrict or impose specific conditions on the possible marketing or use of the product within its own territory it must

---

[109] Prior to the establishment of the RAPEX system there had been an informal system for food safety which worked well and it was decided not to disturb it.

inform the Commission forthwith.[110] Member States may pass on information about serious and immediate risks even before they decide to adopt a measure.

The communication should be in writing, usually by fax and accompanied by a photo of the product, although this can be preceded by a telephone call. It is hoped in the near future that trials will enable information to be sent, processed and received by computer. The notification will be in the language of the Member State making the notification.

Member States can specify that certain information be treated as confidential. However, such a request must be justified bearing in mind that the need to take effective measures to protect consumers normally outweighs confidentiality, especially as the Commission and all members of the network take precautions to avoid any unnecessary disclosure of information likely to harm the reputation of the product. Although criticised by consumer groups the confidentiality provision is said to be almost never invoked.[111]

On receiving a notification the Commission will check that it conforms to the requirements of art. 8. These conditions are very restrictive and the Commission has aggravated the problem by its strict interpretation of these requirements, particularly the 'serious and immediate' condition. The Commission seeks to make a neat distinction between emergency situations

---

110   The duty to notify only arises when measures are taken by the state, there is no duty to notify when measures are taken by a firm voluntarily. Zahlen suggests the duty covers voluntary measures taken following an intervention of the public authorities: G. Zahlen, 'The Community System of Exchange of Information on Dangerous Consumer Products (RAPEX)' in A–C Lacoste (ed.), *Rapid Exchange of Information Systems on Dangers Arising from Consumer Products*, (Centre de Droit de la Consommation, 1996) at 34–5. However, the Directive's requirement that there be a 'measure' seems strictly to make the duty dependant on there being a formal measure causing the firm to act rather than simply informal negotiations. This can be seen as a lacuna as it would be desirable that where voluntary measures are taken other Member States should be alerted to take similar safeguards, possibly also on a voluntary basis. Member States could notify on the basis of their discretionary power to notify cases involving serious and immediate risks, although strictly (as this discretion is only available prior to adopting a measure) it could be argued it did not apply where authorities had decided not to adopt a measure because voluntary measures had been put in place. J. Falke comments that a large number of notifications do in fact relate to measures taken by producers or importers on their own account: see J. Falke, 'The Community system for the rapid exchange of information on dangers arising from the use of consumer products' in H. Micklitz, T. Roethe, S. Weatherill (eds), *Federalism and Responsibility*, (Graham & Trotman, 1994) at 220.

111   Zahlen, *op. cit.*, at 36.

when the art. 8 RAPEX system is to be invoked and more long term problems to which art. 7 applies. However, as the annex to the Directive itself notes it is impossible to lay down specific criteria as to what amounts to a serious and immediate risk and the national authorities have to judge each individual case on its merits.[112] It is therefore possible to give a broad or narrow interpretation to the condition.

One would have imagined that the Commission would have wanted Member States to err on the side of sending too many rather than too few RAPEX notifications: after all the system is rather innocuous, simply alerting national authorities to potential risks their consumers may be exposed to. Although they should investigate such risks, it leaves the Member States free to make their own assessment of the dangers and decide what measures, if any, are appropriate for them to adopt. Thus it seems absurd to be strict about the conditions for entry to the RAPEX system. Other notifications systems may be equally efficient, but the RAPEX system is not overloaded. In 1994 only nine notifications were accepted under the RAPEX system (with 12 being refused). Between 1984–90 there had only been 90 notifications. The Commission became more restrictive when the number of notifications jumped to 96 in 1991.[113] That increase was due to more countries making use of the system (something which should be applauded) and in particular by Belgium leaping from zero notifications in 1990 to 49 in 1991! Whilst it might have been worthwhile having a quiet word with the Belgium authorities, a blanket policy of strictly interpreting the notification conditions is potentially harmful.

A major weakness of the system lies in the lack of commitment by national authorities to participate in it. The former Head of the Unit administering the RAPEX system had concluded 'that all national controlling authorities have not yet fully integrated the Internal Market dimension and their corresponding responsibility into their work.'[114] Given that conclusion it seems contradictory to send out signals discouraging RAPEX notifications except in very exceptional circumstances.

The notification will be received in DG XXIV by a fax dedicated to the RAPEX system, translated within 48 hours into four or five official languages of the EC (English, French, German, Spanish and Italian) and forwarded to a network of national contacts. These national contacts may be in Economic Affairs, Trade and Industry and Health Ministries or consumer bodies attached to a Ministry.

---

[112] The Commission has attempted to commence a dialogue about the content of this phrase through the auspices of the Committee on Product Safety Emergencies.

[113] SEC (92) 618 final, at 5–6.

[114] Zahlen, *op. cit.*, at 39.

The circle of contacts can be criticised for being rather limited. Although to some extent one can expect the national authority to disseminate the information within its borders, there seems little justification for the Commission sending information to the French enforcement authority (the DGGCRF) but refusing to send notifications direct to the Consumer Safety Commission, which is actually the body responsible in France for consumer information on product safety. A consequence of the RAPEX system of national contacts may well be a centralisation of power, whereas in many countries decentralised regional or local enforcement has been found to be effective. Germany, for instance, is having internal difficulties because the Länder resent the need to develop central Government institutions to satisfy the RAPEX system in an area where law enforcement has for constitutional reasons been their responsibility.

At an early stage in the development of the RAPEX system the suggestion had been made that information should be conveyed to European consumer organisations. The Commission opposed this on the ground that it threatened confidentiality. Whilst the risk of leaks would be serious were the information given to every consumer organisation it should be possible to trust a co-ordinating body like BEUC with the information so that it could assess the risk from the consumers' perspective, make representations and monitor the response of national authorities.

On receiving a notification the Member States should, wherever possible, inform the Commission without delay of whether the product has been marketed in its territory and any supplementary information it has obtained, including test/analyses results. In any case the Commission must be informed as soon as possible of any measures taken in respect of the product,[115] or the reason why no measures were taken if the product had been found within their territory. The reaction of the Member States is crucial. The purpose of RAPEX is to prevent accidents by alerting enforcement authorities in other Member States to potentially dangerous products. In turn it is hoped that when surveying the market they may uncover similar dangerous products which could be subject to separate notification procedures. The feedback to the Commission can inform the debate as to whether there needs to be Community action because different responses are threatening the internal market.

The Commission takes the view that Member States must systematically react to all notifications, even if only to say that no measures have been taken. However, prior to 1994 the average number of Member States reacting to notifications was four. This paltry figure had risen to nine by October 1995.[116] It may be that national authorities do consider the

---

[115] This information is then passed on to the network.

[116] Zahlen, *op. cit.*, at 40.

notifications, but simply do not have the time or systems in place to ensure a response is sent to Brussels. This, however, only serves to underline the reluctance of national authorities to see their function as having an internal market dimension. This is not true of all authorities. Again, as with the practice of making notifications, there is a great deal of variation between the response rate of national authorities. Nevertheless, there remains a rump of national authorities failing to meet their obligations under the Directive. In many cases this is likely to be because of a lack of infrastructure. This places citizens in those countries at risk from dangerous products which go undetected or uncontrolled. In the internal market this places at risk not only citizens of those states, but also all citizens of the Union. In a minority of cases there is suspicion that even some well organised national authorities view the EC dimension as an irritating irrelevance to their work and give it low priority. This attitude is dangerous and shows ignorance of the interdependency of Member States.

The Commission, in the light of the evolution of the case and the information received from Member States or a representative of a Member State, can request the Committee on Emergencies be convened in order to exchange views on results obtained and to evaluate the measures taken. The Committee on Emergencies will also be periodically informed of all notifications received and the follow up in order to allow it to have an overview of the situation.

(viii) Emergency Procedures

So far the thrust of the Directive has been to ensure that Member States have procedures in place to deal with dangerous products. The role of the Commission has been restricted to that of a distributor of messages between Member States. However, arts 9–11 provide the Commission with more interventionist powers in relation to emergency situations. Nevertheless, because of the conditions imposed on the use of these powers, the Commission's freedom of action remains rather limited. Although some commentators think it would be relatively easy to by–pass these restraints,[117] DG XXIV does not evidence a willingness to push its powers to their limits.

The Community emergency powers can only be activated once the Commission has become aware of the existence of a serious and immediate risk from a product to the health and safety of consumers in various Member States. As under RAPEX, the conditions 'serious and immediate' are

---

[117] H. Micklitz and T. Roethe, 'Federalism in Process' in Micklitz, Roethe, Weatherill (eds), *op. cit.*, at 58.

cumulative conditions and one can expect them to be interpreted in the same way. Member States may make the Commission aware of a risk by notifying it of a situation to which the emergency procedures apply or else the information provided under arts 7–8 may indicate that such a situation exists.

The influence of the Member States is evidenced not only by the fact that the Commission must become aware of the emergency through them, but also because the Commission's powers are only activated once one or more Member States have adopted measures entailing restrictions on the marketing of the products or requiring its withdrawal from the market.[118] Furthermore the Commission's powers depend upon Member States adopting different measures to deal with the risk in question. This would seem to cover situations where Member States adopted different measures and where some adopted a measure and others failed to adopt any measures.

It is absurd that an emergency procedure should require a Member State to have adopted a measure before it can be invoked. As it stands the Directive reviews measures taken to protect consumers, but it is impotent to review decisions to leave consumers unprotected. Similarly, why should the power of review only arise when states differ in their reactions? The broader perspective of the European regulator may throw a new light on the problem and suggest different solutions than those thought appropriate by national authorities. Certainly where there is a risk of the danger spreading the Commission should be able to protect the interests of citizens in those states whose authorities have not yet had occasion to consider the problem. The need for the Commission to have this broader role need not threaten the Member States unduly as in most instances it should simply involve informing states of the situation and co–ordinating information and responses.

There are two further pre–conditions for Community emergency action. The safety issue posed by the product must be such that the risk cannot be dealt with in a manner compatible with the urgency of the case, under other procedures laid down by the specific Community legislation applicable to the product or category of products concerned. The risk must also be one which can only be eliminated effectively by adopting appropriate measures at the Community level. The Community dimension must be needed to ensure the protection of the health and safety of consumers and the proper functioning of the common market.

Whilst one can see that different solutions could potentially affect the functioning of the common market, it is hard to see how a Community

---

118   Art. 9(1)(a) goes on to refer to measures 'such as those provided for in art. 6(1)(d)–(h)' but the phrase 'such as' would indicate that the measures are not limited to those cited.

dimension is especially needed to protect consumers. National authorities ought to be able to protect their citizens with the other powers provided by the Directives. This does not mean that the Commission should not have a role in ensuring national authorities take appropriate action, simply that the right of action ought to be premised on a conceptualisation of a European dimension to the risk. Involvement of the Commission should not be that of a broker negotiating between different responses, but rather that of an advisor or co–ordinator seeking out the best response to emergency situations and ensuring these are adhered to wherever necessary throughout the Community.

Although the need for Community action is a pre–condition to the Commission becoming involved this, surprisingly, does not guarantee that the emergency process will result in a decision. It only gives the Commission the power to consult Member States – a process which may lead to a decision but only if at least one Member State so requests. This not only underscores the subsidiary role of the Commission, but further emphasises that internal market philosophy dominates. States will have little incentive to seek a Community decision for consumer protection reasons, since they can use domestic law to protect their own citizens. States will, however, be concerned that measures taken by other states do not affect their exports. Thus the most likely use of the emergency procedure is as a means for Member States to negotiate down to a lowest common denominator the various responses to emergencies made by national authorities throughout the Community.

Earlier drafts of the Directive had given the Commission a clearer investigative role. Whilst point 8 of the technical annex dealing with RAPEX does give the Commission the option in 'exceptional circumstances' of instituting its own investigation, the general failure to spell out the Commission's investigative powers underlines the view of the Commission's emergency powers as 'an instrument of last resort'[119] and of the Commission as predominantly a broker between Member States rather than as a protector of the consumer interest. Of course there is scope for the Commission to give a broad interpretation to 'exceptional circumstances', as all serious and immediate risks to consumer health and safety could be so defined.[120] However, there seems no sign that the Commission is actively looking for occasions to flex its muscle.

If requested by a Member State, the Commission may after consultation with the Member States adopt a decision requiring Member States to take temporary measures from those listed in arts 6(1)(d)–(h). It has been said

---

[119] B. Lorz, 'The Draft General Product Safety Directive: the Core Element of an Integrated Approach to Product Safety' [1991] *E.Consum.L.J.* 129 at 135.

[120] Micklitz and Roethe, *op. cit.*, at 57.

that the 'principles of appropriateness and proportionality' apply so that 'a Community–wide recall or withdrawal of a product is not necessarily the result of such procedure'.[121]

Measures adopted under this procedure are valid for no more than three months,[122] but the same procedure can be used to prolong the period. Obviously the temporary measure is intended to provide a breathing space during which more permanent solutions can be adopted, if necessary.

The procedure for adopting a decision is fairly cumbersome considering one is responding to serious and immediate risks. It involves the Commission submitting a draft decision to the Committee on Product Safety Emergencies. If the Committee does not agree with it the matter has to be referred to the Council. It would be preferable if in very urgent cases the Commission be given exceptional powers to issue a decision of immediate effect which could then be subject to review.

The eventual decision is addressed to Member States. Thus the Commission cannot impose any obligations on economic actors. This is the duty of the Member States. Although the Commission could invoke art. 169 procedures against a Member State which has failed to fulfil its obligations under the decision, any victory would be rather pyrrhic and of only symbolic value in the context of emergency measures.

As the Member State is the party taking the measure against economic actors in its territory, this has the consequence that the Member State and not the Commission would be liable in damages if the measure turned out to be unjustified. Leaving aside any general objections to the liability of enforcement authorities, it seems unfair that national authorities should be responsible for the consequences of a measure they were required to take by the EC. If any damages are to flow from a measure adopted by the collective decision of the Community then the cost of any errors should be borne communally. This might also weaken resistance by national authorities to a more active involvement by the Commission in emergencies. The arguments against such liability are purely pragmatic: namely that the Commission may be reluctant to propose measures if it exposes itself to Community wide liability and that as new resources are unlikely to be forthcoming any claim can only deplete the limited funds dedicated to consumer protection at the EC level. One answer would, of course, be to limit the circumstances and amounts of damages which can be recovered.

Despite the limited nature of the Commission's powers to act in emergencies, the sensitivity of the principle that the Community can require

---

121 D. Hoffmann, 'Product Safety in the Internal Market: the Proposed Community Emergency Procedure' in *Product Safety and Control Processes in the European Community*, M. Fallon and F. Maniet (eds), (Story Scientia, 1990) at 75.

122 Earlier drafts of the Directive allowed the temporary measures to last for six months.

Member States to take action against dangerous products is seen in the German challenge to art. 9 of the Directive.[123] Essentially the German Government objected to the Commission having more power than itself to tell its Länder what to do with respect to product safety matters! The ECJ upheld the validity of the Community emergency measures imposing specific measures against individual products as being justified in terms of the establishment and functioning of the internal market and as not being disproportionate to the achievement of that goal. The positive decision of the ECJ is to be welcomed, but the reluctance of some states to see consumer product safety as requiring genuine collaboration and co–ordination between national and European authorities is disheartening.

5. CONCLUSIONS

The length of this chapter reflects the extent of EC regulations affecting consumer safety. The bulk of activity has concentrated on products, with service safety being given a lower priority. Indeed, the Commission failed to have the draft directive on service liability adopted. The lack of positive regulation, particularly of a horizontal nature, concerning service safety is to be regretted. However, there are signs that national laws are beginning to improve the regulation of service safety. Partly this has resulted from a general review of their legislation because of the need to implement EC laws on product liability and safety. This may in turn cause the Commission to be more confident about the need for EC regulation of service safety if it considers the matter again in the future. We have tried to show that this is justified by internal market considerations, but it is certainly required if the Community wishes to develop an autonomous consumer policy.

Some regulation of product safety would have been required by purely internal market considerations. However, this could have been restricted to matters of technical harmonisation. The Product Liability Directive and General Product Safety Directive claim to be partly based on internal market considerations. However, we doubt whether liability rules and general safety requirements have a serious affect on trade. Instead we see in them some genuine concern to protect the consumer. However, we question whether the Product Liability Directive adopts the correct approach by preferring private law remedies for accident victims rather than more 'social' forms of accident compensation schemes. We also wonder whether it has adopted the most appropriate defectiveness standard: one based on a risk:utility analysis might have been more demanding than one based on consumer expectations.

---

[123] *Germany v Council*, Case 359/92 [1994] ECR I–3681.

The practical impact of the General Product Safety Directive is yet to be demonstrated. The lack of resources available to enforcement agencies in many countries is a matter of concern. The presence of a general safety requirement may ease their enforcement work. As a matter of practice it seems likely, however, that producers will pay more attention to the detailed rules set out in the new approach directives and standards than to the general exhortation to market only safe goods. Although it is hoped that the practical obligations the Directive imposes on producers and distributors will improve industry practice.

The new approach to technical harmonisation and global approach to conformity assessment have great potential to provide a framework, combining generally framed statutory norms with 'soft law' standards, in a way which permits legislators, industry and consumers to work together to reduce barriers to trade whilst ensuring the safety of goods circulating in the internal market. However, weaknesses in the present arrangements do exist. These include the lack of adequate consumer representation in the standardisation process; inadequate controls over testing and certification as well as a lack of harmonisation of testing methods and confusion over the meaning of the CE marking and its relationship to national marks. These problems need to be addressed if consumers are to have confidence in the internal market and are not to retreat to the security of national standards.

Information plays an important role even in EC policy on safety, where one might expect more mandatory design standards. Thus product liability can in some circumstances be avoided by warnings. The General Product Safety Directive accepts some risks so long as consumers are informed of them and can therefore make their own assessment or take precautions where the risk is not obvious. Standards often use information as a means of assuring safety. Clearly there is a role for information and warnings. One would have to turn the clock back two centuries or more if one wanted dramatically to reduce the risks created by modern consumer products. For instance, all electrical goods would have to be removed. However, information should not be used as an alternative to design improvement. For instance, rather than warning about a dangerous blade it would be better to enclose it, if possible. Also the General Product Safety Directive claims to have concern for vulnerable consumers, particularly children. If this policy is to be taken seriously then information strategies should be closely scrutinised to see whether they adequately take the interests of these groups into account. However, in the safety field there is an appreciation that the consequences of ineffective regulation can be very severe. Therefore, there is not the same uncritical acceptance that the well informed consumer is able to protect himself, which we shall find in some of the other areas of consumer protection which we identify in subsequent chapters.

3 Consumer Contracts – General Principles

1. INTRODUCTION

The consumer rules of the EC are not only concerned with the protection of the physical safety of the consumer. The preponderant part of the directives and other rules issued in the consumer law area relate to the protection of the economic interests of consumers. There are a variety of enactments covering general issues concerning consumer contracts and advertising as well as specific contractual relations in areas like credit and tourism. This chapter will deal with some general issues in the field of consumer contract law.

In general, the EC has refrained from making thorough harmonisation projects in the private law sphere. The principles of the common law, Bürgerliches Gesetzbuch and Code Civile are almost as far apart from each other as when the EC was founded. The Community law measures affecting contract law are mainly to be found in the consumer law area; EC contract legislation in other fields, like the Commercial Agents Directive[1] and the labour law directives, is much more specifically focused.[2]

The growing recognition that the EC influences private law is therefore mainly due to the development of consumer legislation. Community contract law is to a large extent consumer law. Thus, what is said in this chapter does not necessarily have an impact on consumer law alone. It can also have wider implications for the harmonisation of contract law, which, however, cannot be dealt with in this context.[3] It should, however, be mentioned that the Commission on European Contract Law, which aims at developing uniform principles for contract law in the European Community,[4] has

---

[1] Council Directive 86/653/EEC on the co–ordination of the laws of the Member States relating to self–employed commercial agents: OJ 1986 L 382/17.

[2] See, on EC contract law in general, T. Wilhelmsson, *Social Contract Law and European Integration*, (Dartmouth, 1995). Many of the standpoints taken in this chapter are based on this book.

[3] The discussion among scholars interested in comparative law on the unification of European private law has been intense during the last years, see on the rapidly growing literature Wilhelmsson, *op. cit.*, 89 *et seq*.

[4] The Commission is a group of lawyers, mostly law professors, established in 1980 with the aim of drafting a collection of General Principles of Contract Law for the EC countries. The group is unofficial and has not been appointed by any government or

decided to include the main rules of the Unfair Contract Terms Directive in its final proposal.[5] Below, we discuss how this Directive might function as one of the means through which the Principles adopted by the Commission on European Contract Law can receive legal effect.

As noted earlier (Chapter 1, section 1A) harmonisation of consumer law in the EC may take place by negative as well as positive harmonisation. In the contract law area, however, there are very few signs of negative harmonisation aiming at the removal of so called barriers of trade. In fact, the ECJ has in a couple of recent cases refrained from outlawing national provisions of contract law, alleged to function as barriers to trade. One should especially mention the *Alsthom* case.[6] This is not a consumer case, but nevertheless gave the EC Commission, in its Green Paper on guarantees for consumer goods and after–sales services, reason to claim that national guarantee rules favourable to consumers are not contrary to EC law.[7] Although this is perhaps a too far–reaching interpretation of that case by itself,[8] other cases show the same inclination of the Court to leave national contract rules untouched. Directly concerned with consumers is the case *CMC Motorradcenter GmbH v. Pelin Baskiciogullari*[9] which involved the German case law on the pre–contractual duty to provide information. It was alleged that a rule which required German parallel importers of motorcycles to inform the buyers that German dealers frequently refused to effect repairs under the guarantee for such parallel imported motorcycles was to be

---

interest group. The Principles are intended to function as a guideline for arbitrators developing a European *lex mercatoria*, and also for the ECJ when it deals with contract law cases. The first results of the work are published in O. Lando & H. Beale (eds), *Principles of European Contract Law, Part I: Performance, Non–performance and Remedies*, (Martinus Nijhoff, 1995). The complete collection, in the preparation of which one of the authors of this book (Wilhelmsson) has participated, is due to be published in 1997.

5   These will not be limited to consumer contracts, but will cover all contract terms which have not been individually negotiated.

6   See *Alsthom Atlantique SA v Compagnie de construction mécanique Sulzer SA*, Case C–339/89 [1991] ECR 107.

7   COM(93) 509 at 57.

8   As the Court in its reasoning expressly referred to the fact that the parties could have avoided the contract law rule alleged to form a barrier of trade with the help of a choice of law clause, the decision cannot be interpreted as a general denial of the possibility to intervene against private law norms, see O. Remien, 'Möglichkeiten und Grenzen eines europäischen Privatrechts' in *Jahrbuch Junger Zivilrechtswissenschaftler 1991*, (Richard Boorberg Verlag, 1991) at 21.

9   Case C–93/92 [1993] ECR I–5009. See also the insurance case *Commission v. Germany*, Case 205/84 [1986] ECR 3755.

considered a barrier to trade infringing art. 30 of the Treaty of Rome. However, the ECJ held the German national rule was permissible.

The general picture, that the ECJ does not want to intervene in consumer contract law matters on the basis of the Treaty of Rome, is not changed by the fact that the Court in some cases has contested price regulation measures with reference to art. 30 of the Treaty.[10] These cases do not contain any general prohibitions or restrictions on national price regulation measures. Only if the measures are practised in a discriminatory way or lead to discriminatory effects are they considered to violate the Treaty: for example, if the prices are fixed at such a level that it becomes impossible or more difficult to sell imported products, the measure will be considered to have an equivalent effect to a quantitative restriction of trade.[11] The reluctance of the Court to intervene against these kinds of national measures is reinforced by the famous *Keck* decision in which national rules which forbade retailers to sell goods cheaper than they were bought for were not considered to violate the Treaty of Rome.[12]

As the application of the Treaty of Rome has to–date left national consumer contract law more or less untouched, the harmonisation pressure in this area stems almost exclusively from positive legislative measures of the EC. Community consumer contract law consists mainly of directives, although regulations and recommendations are not completely unknown in this area either.[13]

The most important of the consumer contract law directives is certainly the Unfair Contract Terms Directive.[14] Many rules in this Directive directly mirror the prevailing consumer contract ideology in the Community. The Directive will therefore be analysed extensively.

Usually the sales contract is thought of as the most important contract type. The rules on sale of goods are often used as models for developing rules on other contract types as well. The regulation of consumer sales is therefore of central importance for the development of general EC consumer contract law. The proposals in this field are therefore also scrutinised, although as they are still only proposals only their general features are

---

10 See in more detail, N. Reich, *Europäisches Verbraucherrecht*, (3rd ed., Nomos, 1996) 94 *et seq.*

11 See *Roussel Laboratoria BV and Others v The Netherlands*, Case 181/82 [1983] ECR 3849 and *Re Pharmaceutical Prices: E.C. Commission v Belgium*, Case C–249/88 [1991] ECR I–1275.

12 *Criminal proceedings against Bernard Keck and Daniel Mithouard*, Joined Cases C–267/91 and C–268/91 [1993] ECR I–6097.

13 See especially Chap. 6 on financial services and Chap. 7 on tourism.

14 Council Directive 93/13/EEC on unfair terms in consumer contracts: OJ 1993 L 95/29.

presented. Other more specific contract law rules are analysed in the chapters on trade practices, financial services and tourism.

2.   THE UNFAIR CONTRACT TERMS DIRECTIVE

A.   Introduction

The work on the approximation of rules on unfair terms in consumer contracts started in the 1970s.[15] During the lengthy preparation of the Directive its ambitions were lowered as has so often happened during the preparation of EC legislation. A good example of this is offered by the development of the scope of application of the Directive. The starting point of the Commission Proposals of 1990[16] and 1992[17] was that the Directive would cover both individually negotiated contracts and standard form contracts, but the common position adopted in the EC Council in September 1992 delimited the scope of the Directive to a term 'which has not been individually negotiated'.[18] This delimitation is also included in the final Directive (art. 3).

In another respect, however, the Directive has retained its general character. It is not limited to certain contract types, rather it covers all kinds of consumer contracts.[19] It applies to contracts for the sale of goods as well as for the supply of services, including banking and insurance services. In this sense it can be said to institute a general fairness standard for European consumer contract law.

The material provisions of the Directive can be divided into three groups. First and foremost, there is of course the attempt to formulate a European concept of unfairness. The basic provision of the Directive is a general clause, under which a term which has not been individually negotiated shall be considered unfair if, contrary to the requirement of good faith, it causes a significant imbalance in the parties' rights and obligations, to the detriment of

---

15   See e.g. Preliminary programme for consumer protection and information policy, OJ 1975 C 92/1, at 18, 19, 24, 25. In the 1970s also the Council of Europe was engaged in the work, see Resolution (76)47 on unfair terms in consumer contracts and on appropriate method of control, adopted by the Committee of Ministers 16.11.1976.

16   OJ 1990 C 243/2.

17   OJ 1992 C 73/7.

18   Common position adopted by the Council on 22 September 1992 with a view to the adoption of Council Directive 92/ /EEC on unfair terms in consumer contracts, art. 3. The Document was later published in the Journal of Consumer Policy at (1992) 15 *J.C.P.* 473.

19   As to the definition of 'consumer' in the Directive, see above Chap. 1 section 1B.

the consumer (art. 3). The general clause is supplemented by a fairly extensive indicative list of examples on unfair contract terms (Annex). The Directive also contains general guidelines on the assessment of unfairness, referring, among other things, to the nature of the goods or services for which the contract was concluded, the other terms of the contract and the circumstances attending the conclusion of the contract (art. 4(1)). A significant delimitation of the scope is contained in the provision under which the assessment of the unfair nature shall relate neither to the definition of the main subject matter of the contract nor to the adequacy of the price and remuneration in so far as these terms are in plain, intelligible language (art. 4(2)).

Second, the Directive addresses the question of interpretation. In art. 5 the Directive emphasises the significance of plain, intelligible language in the drafting of the contract terms and confirms the principle of *in dubio contra stipulatorem* in the interpretation of the terms.

Third, the legal consequences of unfairness are spelled out. The consequences of the use of an unfair term relate both to contract law and public law. An unfair term is not binding on the consumer (art. 6) and the Member States shall, furthermore, ensure that adequate and effective means exist to prevent the use of unfair terms (art. 7).

The reasons given to justify the Directive show the same kind of Janus–faced ideology as one finds behind most of the EC consumer law. On the one hand the aim to improve consumer protection is clearly spelled out. The preamble of the Directive directly refers to the consumer protection programmes when stating that 'acquirers of goods and services should be protected against the abuse of power by the seller or supplier, in particular against one–sided standard contracts and the unfair exclusion of essential rights in contracts' (recital 9). On the other hand the internal market aspect is underlined as well. According to the preamble varying rules on unfair contracts may lead to distortions of competition and also deter active internal market consumers from making purchases in other Member States (recitals 2 and 5). Against this background (and as the Directive is primarily concerned with standard form contracts) one could even claim that the Directive aims at promoting a reasonable standardisation of consumer contract forms in order to improve the operation of the single market. However, as the requirement in the Directive concerning intelligibility of standard terms is thought to imply some, albeit unclear restrictions concerning choice of language of the terms,[20] this latter goal cannot be said to have been pursued very efficiently. One cannot therefore speak about a measure primarily safeguarding the free movement of standard form contracts.

---

[20] See below at section 2D(i).

It should also be noted that the Directive does not aim at any complete harmonisation of the unfairness rules, which a really free movement of standard form contracts would require. Considerable freedom is given to the Member States in editing the practically important Annex and, even more importantly, the Directive is clearly stated to be a minimum Directive. As art. 8 allows Member States to adopt or retain the most stringent provisions compatible with the Treaty in the area covered by the Directive, to ensure a maximum degree of protection for the consumer, the fairness standards and practices in the various Member States will also in the future differ, at least to some extent. The Directive only fixes the minimum level of protection.

The content of the Directive naturally has been influenced by many of the laws in force in the various Member States.[21] However, this Directive seems to have gained most inspiration from German law and its Act on General Conditions of Contract.[22] It has been claimed, as will be elaborated later, that some of its provisions, like the good faith requirement and the rules on organisational action, seem rather unfamiliar to an English lawyer.

The various Member States have also chosen very different ways for implementing the Directive. In the United Kingdom the Directive is implemented through special regulations, the Unfair Terms in Consumer Contracts Regulations 1994,[23] closely following the wording of the Directive. In Germany the proposed implementation mechanism is the amendment of the existing Act on General Conditions of Contract.[24] Even in Nordic law various models have been resorted to: in Sweden a new Act on Contract Terms in Consumer Relations has been enacted,[25] in Denmark some amendments have been made in the general Contracts Act[26] and in Finland implementation has been effected through amendments of the Consumer Protection Act.[27] The differences do not, however, concern only the form of implementation. A comparison of the contents of the rules on

---

[21] The work was based on an analysis of the laws of the Member States as well as of some other states by E. Hondius, *Unfair Terms in Consumer Contracts*, (Molengraaff Instituut voor Privaatrecht, 1987).

[22] Gesetz zur Regelung des Rechts der Allgemeinen Geschäftsbedingungen 1976, *BGBl* 76 I 3317.

[23] S.I. 1994/3159. See, R. Brownsword & G. Howells, 'The Implementation of the EC Directive on Unfair Terms in Consumer Contracts – Some Unresolved Questions' (1995) *J.B.L.* 243.

[24] See the Government proposal, *Regierungsentwurf* BR–Dr 528/95 and H.–W. Micklitz, 'Richtlinie 93/13/EWG – Stand der Umsetzung' (1996) 11 *Verbraucher und Recht* 75.

[25] Act 1994:1512.

[26] Act 1098/1994.

[27] Act 1259/1994.

unfair contract terms shows very clearly that these rules are far from harmonised in the EC area. As will be noted below, the limitations of the scope of the Directive, not to cover individually negotiated contracts and the price/performance–relationship, are not considered necessary in all Member States (which because of the minimum character of the Directive is perfectly acceptable). The important Annex is implemented in various ways in the different Member States and other differences could be cited.

The Directive is relatively detailed. It has already in the implementation stage given rise to several questions of interpretation. All of them cannot be dealt with here. The focus is on those rules of the Directive which reflect more general ideas concerning fairness controls of consumer contracts. Through the analysis of these rules one may detect the contractual thinking, the contract paradigm, which lies behind the Directive.

B. Respect for Individual Contracting

(i) Individually Negotiated Contracts Excluded

The Directive contains some limitations of its scope of application which clearly reflect the contract paradigm prevailing behind the Directive. The most important of these is probably the already above–mentioned limitation of the scope to contract terms which have not been individually negotiated (art. 3).

The grounds for the drafting of the Unfair Contract Terms Directive were of course largely related to problems appearing in connection with standard form contracts. Still, the starting point of the 1990 proposal for the Directive was that it would be applied to all types of consumer contracts, both to standard form contracts and to individually negotiated contracts. This was criticised in German legal literature, especially, because the fairness control of individually negotiated contracts was said to be in conflict with private autonomy and the functioning of the market economy.[28] This criticism eventually had results. The 1992 proposal had already adopted a special category of individually negotiated contracts, with a higher adjustment threshold than would be the case with standard form contracts. In the final Directive, this respect for private autonomy was taken to its logical end–point. The Directive only applies to a term 'which has not been individually negotiated' (art. 3). Individually negotiated contracts are not within the scope of the Directive: because since it has been possible for a

---

28 H.E. Brandner & P. Ulmer, 'The Community Directive on Unfair Terms in Consumer Contracts: Some Critical Remarks on the Proposal Submitted by the EC Commission' (1991) 28 *C.M.L.R.* 647 at 652 *et seq.*

rational consumer to affect the contents of an individually negotiated contract, he does not need the substantive protection afforded by the Directive. The limitation of the scope of the Directive 'represents a victory for the consumer choice perspective'.[29] The basic idea of the EC consumer contract model is still freedom of contract and private autonomy.

The solution may be seen as a compromise to make the adoption of the Directive possible. Indeed, the preamble of the Directive notes, in an almost lamentable tone, that national laws, as they now stand, allow only partial harmonisation to be envisaged, and that it has therefore been necessary to restrict the Directive only to contractual terms which have not been individually negotiated (recital 12). For this reason, and as the Directive is a minimum Directive, nothing in the Directive prevents Member States also imposing a fairness test on individually negotiated contract terms. Such rules are to be found in the Nordic countries.

One should also note that the concept 'not individually negotiated contracts' has been given a very broad definition in the Directive, so as not excessively to limit the scope of application of the Directive. The Directive covers not only standard form contracts proper, but also individual terms put forward by the seller or supplier concerning which there has been no negotiation. One could speak about 'pre–formulated individual terms'.[30] This could be said to reflect a commitment to a relatively strong version of the consumer choice model. The possibility of choice should not be purely symbolic.

The precise meaning of 'negotiation' in this rule is of course unclear. What kind of negotiation activity is required for the term to be individually negotiated? Taking into account the wording of art. 3(2) of the Directive ('and the consumer has therefore not been able to influence the substance of the term'), the most reasonable interpretation seems to be that it is a question of whether the consumer had a real possibility of influencing the content of the term or not.[31] If no such possibility was at hand the situation would be within the scope of the Directive. If a term which looks like an individual term in fact was formulated in advance and the consumer thus did not have the possibility to influence the substance of the term, the Unfair Contract Terms Directive should apply to the term. If the consumer was presented with two or more pre–formulated alternatives to choose from, one cannot

[29]   H. Collins, 'Good Faith in European Contract Law' (1994) 14 *O.J.L.S.* 229 at 239.

[30]   'Vorformulierte Individualklauseln', see H.–W. Micklitz, 'AGB–Gesetz und die EG–Richtlinie über missbräuchliche Vertragsklauseln in Verbraucherverträgen' (1993) *Zeitschrift für Europäisches Privatrecht* 522 at 526.

[31]   See H.–W. Eckert, 'Die EG–Richtlinie über missbräuchliche Klauseln in Verbraucherverträgen und ihre Auswirkungen auf das deutsche Recht' (1993) 47 *Zeitschrift für Wirtschafts– und Bankrecht* 1070 at 1073.

speak of any individual negotiation either.[32] Even oral agreements made in this way are covered by the Directive: according to the preamble 'the consumer must receive equal protection under contracts concluded by word of mouth and written contracts' (recital 11).

The effect of this broad definition is strengthened further by a provision on burden of proof, in art. 3(2) of the Directive, according to which a seller, who claims that a standard term has been individually negotiated, has the burden of proving his claim. The seller should not be able to satisfy this burden of proof only by showing that some negotiations have been conducted concerning the term. If the seller has confronted the buyer with a standard term which after negotiations has been taken into the contract without any changes the Directive should normally still apply,[33] if the seller cannot prove that the acceptance of the term was based on effective and balanced negotiations.

Finally, one should mention the very obscure second passage of art. 3(2) of the Directive, according to which the fact that certain aspects of a term or one specific term have been individually negotiated shall not exclude the application of the Article to the rest of a contract if an overall assessment of the contract indicates that it is nevertheless a pre–formulated standard contract. This rule is absurd in the light of the fact that all other parts of art. 3 focus on the nature of 'a term', not on the contract as a whole.[34] There does not therefore seem to exist any real need to define the term 'pre–formulated standard contract'; it may only refer to the very vague and only guiding (in fact superfluous) expression in the preceding sentence 'particularly in the context of a pre–formulated standard contract'. At least one should not draw the conclusion that terms, which have not been individually negotiated, fall outside the scope of the Directive simple because they are in a contract that contains one or more individually negotiated terms.

---

32 See, on English law, A. Padfield, 'The Impact on English Contract Law of the EC Directive on Unfair Terms in Consumer Contracts', (1995) 10 *Journal of International Banking Law* 175 at 176. The rule is the same in German law on standard form contracts, see F.A. Bultmann, 'Änderungen des AGBG aufgrund der Richtlinie über missbräuchliche Klauseln?' (1994) *Verbraucher und Recht* 137 at 140.

33 See, on German law, Bultmann, *op. cit.*, at 140 *et seq.*

34 See also M. Tenreiro, 'Protection des intérêts economiques des consommateurs' (1993) *Le droit des contrats, Juris–classeurs, Europe, Editions Techniques,* Fascicule 2011 at 16 and R. Bragg, 'Implementation of the E.C. Directive on Unfair Terms in Consumer Contracts' [1994] *Consum.L.J.* 29 at 31, 34.

(ii) Core Provisions of Contract Excluded

In the same liberalist line of reasoning is the rule concerning 'the so called core provisions of contract'[35] in art. 4(2) of the Directive. It expressly states that the assessment of the unfair nature of the terms shall relate neither to the definition of the main subject matter of the contract nor to the adequacy of the price or remuneration. These central terms of the contract may be intervened against only if they are not in plain, intelligible language. This delineation, which was not included in the Directive until the final preparatory stages, is based on the thought that the relationship between the price and the performance of the contract has to be determined by the market mechanism and not through regulation.[36] The EC Council actually justified the inclusion of this delineation in the Directive by the wish to exclude from the scope of the Directive 'anything resulting directly from the contractual freedom of the parties'.[37] Again one encounters a rather traditional view on contract law, based on the thought of freedom of contract functioning in an efficient market.

In other words, the Directive does not purport to regulate the most important point of the contractual relation, that is the balance between performance and price, as long as this relation is agreed upon in plain intelligible language. There is no hint in the preamble that this solution has been adopted only because there had been a need to limit the sphere of the Directive to questions on which the Member States could reach an agreement. The solution rather seems to reflect a relatively common starting point. With regard to insurance contracts the preamble even expressly states that 'the terms which clearly define or circumscribe the insured risk and the insurer's liability shall not be subject to such assessment since these restrictions are taken into account in calculating the premium paid by the consumer' (recital 19). In spite of this, as the Directive is a minimum Directive, nothing prevents the Member States from including in their national laws rules on adjustment of the price and other core provisions of the contract. Again such rules are to be found in Nordic law, where the

---

35   Department of Trade and Industry, *Implementation of the EC Directive on unfair terms in consumer contracts (93/13/EEC), A Consultation Document*, (London, 1993), at comment to art. 4(2) and *Further Consultation Document*, (London, 1994) at 17.

36   See the criticism of the earlier proposals in Brandner & Ulmer, *op. cit.*, at 656.

37   Common Position adopted by the Council on 22 September 1992 with a view to the adoption of Council Directive 92/ /EEC on unfair terms in consumer contracts, the Council's reasons at p. 5. The Council's reasons document has later been published at (1992) 15 *J.C.P.* 483.

general fairness rule is applicable also to the price and the main subject matter of the contract.

The relationship between price and performance is, however, not completely irrelevant in the application of the Directive. According to the preamble 'the main subject matter of the contract and the price/quality ratio may nevertheless be taken into account in assessing the fairness of other terms' (recital 19). This gives some possibilities for at least an indirect fairness control of the contractual balance in certain situations. One might imagine that a high price would lead to expectations of better warranties. However, one should be rather cautious in employing these kind of price arguments. Especially the inverse situation, that a low price could legitimise otherwise voidable terms, does not seem acceptable: not only would such a solution in many cases hit poor consumers, buying cheap products, especially hard, it would also be in conflict with transparency requirements, as the consumer usually is not able to see and calculate the possible connection between price and contract terms.[38]

The limitation of the sphere of application of the Directive by art. 4(2) is not very clear and precise. The expression 'main subject matter of the contract' may be interpreted in various ways. In a sales contract it certainly covers the definition of the type of goods to be delivered as well as the quantity of the goods. On the other hand it seems equally clear that all minor details in the description of the qualities of the goods, exclusion clauses relating to such details etc. do not relate to the main subject matter of the contract. Where precisely one should draw the line seems at this stage impossible to say.[39]

One point should, however, be made in this context: whether or not a certain term in a contract is taken into account in calculating the price paid by the consumer cannot be decisive (even though the statement in the preamble concerning insurance, cited above, would seem to indicate otherwise). As most terms – and most certainly exclusion clauses – can have an effect on the price, such an interpretation would make the scope of the Directive far too narrow.

A similar interpretation problem is connected also with the words 'the adequacy of the price and remuneration'. This limitation should not cover all terms which have an effect on the price. Although the price level as such is outside the scope of the Directive, various indexation clauses and other terms

---

[38] The transparency objection is emphasised by B. Stauder, 'Schwerpunkte der Richtlinie vom 5 April 1993 über Missbräuchliche Klauseln in Verbraucherverträgen' in *Die Bedeutung der AGB–Richtlinie der Europäischen Union für Schweizer Unternehmen, Studien zum Verbraucherrecht, Band 3* (Schulthess, 1996) at 37 *et seq.*

[39] For a discussion of the subject from the point of view of English law, see Brownsword & Howells, *op. cit.*, at 247 *et seq.*

affecting the calculation of the price may very well be within the ambit of the Directive.

C.   The Fairness Test

(i)   *Imbalance and Good Faith*

According to art. 3 of the Directive a term shall be regarded as unfair if, contrary to the requirement of good faith, it causes a significant imbalance in the parties' rights and obligations arising under the contract, to the detriment of the consumer. In this general clause there are mentioned two cumulative criteria[40] for unfairness:

a)   significant imbalance, and
b)   contrary to good faith.

The question arises concerning the content of and relationship between these criteria.

As a starting point the meaning of 'significant imbalance' seems relatively clear, although it is of course also very vague. It seeks merely to express the idea that not every imbalance in the contract to the detriment of the consumer should be interpreted as violating the fairness test. There is a certain threshold above which the imbalance has to reach before the term can be called unfair. The exact height of this threshold is of course not determined by just one word. One cannot steer the application of a general clause only by a choice of words. The attitudes of the courts and other juridical actors with regard to the general clause are important as well. There might, however, be some difference in the approaches of an English and a continental court in this respect. Certainly an English court would look more closely to the dictionary meaning of the words when applying even a general clause than a Nordic one would do. Anyway, to some extent it is always up to the courts to decide what imbalance will be considered relevant.

---

[40]   The expression 'to the detriment of the consumer' could perhaps be seen as a third criterion. However, its task seems mainly to be to indicate that the Directive is not concerned with situations where the seller or supplier claims unfairness. In special situations, however, it might be relevant to ask whether a certain clause – e.g. a clause permitting the provider of credit to have access to protected data concerning the consumer – *de facto* has a detrimental effect on the consumer, see G. Howells, 'Data Protection, Confidentiality, Unfair Contract Terms, Consumer Protection and Credit Reference Agencies' (1995) *J.B.L.* 343 at 354 *et seq.*

Even though from a consumer perspective one may criticise the inclusion of the word 'significant' in the text,[41] its practical impact is not likely to be great. In theory it of course underlines the strong attachment to traditional contract thinking which lies behind the Directive: the fairness test should apply only in more obvious cases. However, the wording is so vague that it certainly does not prevent practice from developing in a more consumer–friendly direction.

Of course the drafters of the Directive have been well aware of the problems connected with the vagueness of the central expressions. This is the main reason for the attempts to steer the application of the Directive with the help of a list of examples in the Annex. This matter will be dealt with later.

The second requirement in art. 3, 'good faith', seems to pose more problems of an interpretative nature. In particular the relationship between this criterion and the 'significant imbalance' is rather unclear.[42] One possible interpretation is to see these requirements as overlapping. If there is significant imbalance, one must assume that there also is a breach of good faith. The good faith requirement would then add nothing to the requirement that there should not be a significant imbalance in the contract. One could pay little attention to the expression 'contrary to the requirement of good faith' when applying art. 3 of the Directive. On the other hand one could argue that the fulfilment of the requirement of substantive unfairness, that is 'a significant imbalance', is not sufficient for a term to be deemed unfair according to the Directive. In addition to this one would have to show the absence of good faith, which might, according to one possible interpretation, imply the existence of some procedural unfairness.

Such a procedural interpretation of the good faith requirement seems to be indicated by the preamble to the Directive:

> 'whereas, in making an assessment of good faith, particular regard shall be had to the strength of the bargaining positions of the parties, whether the consumer had an inducement to agree to the term and whether the goods or services were sold or supplied to the special order of the consumer; whereas the requirement of good faith may be satisfied by the

---

41   See, European Consumer Law Group, 'Opinion on the Proposal for a Council Directive on Unfair Terms in Consumer Contracts' (1991) 14 *J.C.P.* 107 at 112 and T. Wilhelmsson, 'The Proposal for an Unfair Contracts Directive – a Nordic Perspective' [1992] *E.Consum.L.J.* 77 at 85.

42   See, R. Brownsword, G. Howells & T. Wilhelmsson, 'Between Market and Welfare: Some Reflections on Article 3 of the E.C. Directive on Unfair Terms in Consumer Contracts' in C. Willett (ed.), *Fairness in Contract*, (Blackstone Press, 1996).

seller or supplier where he deals fairly and equitably with the other party whose legitimate interests he has to take into account;' (recital 16)

This procedural view on the good faith requirement is adopted also in the English implementation of the Directive. Schedule 2 of the Unfair Terms in Consumer Contracts Regulations 1994 repeats the description of good faith given in the above-mentioned recital. Such a clarification seems to be needed as the concept of good faith in this context is rather unfamiliar for an English lawyer.[43]

However, these definitions in the preamble and the English Regulations do not make it very clear what kind of procedural requirement one is speaking about. There are several possibilities. Some may read it as a subjective requirement, others as being more objective. A subjective reading may refer to the state of mind of different persons: one might refer to a moral condemnation of the behaviour of the seller or to the good faith (understanding) of the other party. If one focuses more objectively on what happened when the contract was made, the good faith requirement may point at information (transparency) requirements, but it can also lead one to take into account situations where there has been a lack of choice of the consumer. In short: the good faith requirement does certainly not contribute to a harmonised application of the fairness principle. A strongly procedural emphasis on the good faith requirement does therefore not appear as unavoidable, at least in the light of the sources available at the moment.[44] One could argue that the existence of a significant imbalance as such should be sufficient proof for the breach of the good faith requirement. The concept of good faith could – and from a consumer protection point of view should – at least partly be given a substantive content.[45] Some imbalances would automatically be considered contrary to the good faith requirement; in other cases – the borderline cases – one might, however, require some procedural support for a claim concerning unfairness.

---

[43] As M. Dean, 'Unfair Contract Terms: The European Approach' (1993) 56 *M.L.R.* 581 at 584 points out, the concept may cause problems for English lawyers, as 'under English law "good faith" is not an established, well-defined and coherent concept in general use.' The concept 'is mysterious and exciting to an English lawyer', Collins, *op. cit.*, at 249.

[44] Certainly the Commission official responsible for the passage of the Directive describes the efforts to retain a reference to 'good faith' as being inspired by a desire to enhance consumer protection and to make connections with existing jurisprudence, rather than by a desire to place extra hurdles in the way of consumers, see M. Tenreiro, 'The Community Directive on Unfair Terms and National Legal Systems' (1995) 3 *Eur. Rev. Private Law* 273 at 276.

[45] See also Collins, *op. cit.*, at 250.

Such an interpretation would not be very strange, if one looks at the genesis of the Directive. As the Directive is strongly influenced by German law, it is natural to find a concept like good faith in the Directive. It is obviously intended to refer to the German concept 'Treu und Glaube' and similar concepts in some other countries. One therefore does not have to treat the good faith requirement as an additional requirement, cumulated with 'significant imbalance'. It can merely be seen as a signal tying the assessment of unfairness to ideas prevailing in those continental countries. Those ideas are of course relatively vague and dispersed. One might perhaps speak about connecting the assessment of contractual behaviour to some ethical standard, condemning an absolute egoism of the parties and implying some obligation to take into account the interests of the other party and his reliance.[46] This reading of the good faith requirement, as stating a kind of duty of co-operation, is in fact expressed at the end of the above citation from the preamble: 'deals fairly and equitably with the other party whose legitimate interests he has to take into account.' Through the good faith requirement one again encounters one of the basic principles of EC consumer law: the duty of the enterprise to take into account the legitimate expectations of the consumer.[47]

The breach of this duty can in many cases be inferred directly from the content of the contract. This does not mean, however, that there should be no procedural arguments used in the assessment of unfairness. Already art. 4 of the Directive clearly shows the relevance of such arguments. One should only refrain from making procedural reasoning a necessary precondition for unfairness. In many cases it should be sufficient to prove significant imbalance for the fairness rule to be applicable.

(ii) Concrete or Abstract Assessment?

If one accepts the idea that procedural requirements need not necessarily be fulfilled in order to make it possible to declare a term unfair the assessment of unfairness may take place in two ways. On the one hand one may focus only on the substantive content of the contract term at hand. This could be called a purely abstract assessment. On the other hand one may look at the

---

46   M. Mononen, *Kohtuuttomat sopimusehdot EY:n ja Suomen kuluttajaoikeudessa,* (Helsingin yliopiston yksityisoikeuden laitos, 1993) at 87 *et seq.*

47   This reading of the good faith principle is advocated by H.–W. Micklitz, 'Principles of Justice in Private Law within the European Union' in E. Paasivirta & K. Rissanen (eds), *Principles of Justice and the Law of the European Union*, (Institute of International Economic Law, University of Helsinki, 1995) at 289 *et seq.*: see discussion in Chap. 9 section 4.

concrete term in the particular contract, taking into account also the way in which the contract was made. The contract term is declared unfair on the basis of a concrete assessment. What type of assessment is provided for in the Directive?

In answering this question one should remember that the Directive regulates both for private law voidness of an unfair term in a particular contract and prevention of the use of unfair terms on a more collective level (art. 7). Obviously the assessment of unfairness in cases of the latter kind must by necessity be relatively abstract. There is no concrete case to relate the assessment to. This explains why the guidance for the assessment of unfairness in art. 4 is stated to be without prejudice to the preventative, collective application of the fairness rule. Although where appropriate some of those factors could be relevant in a collective challenge to an unfair term and there would be nothing to prevent them being taken into account.

The question concerning concrete and abstract assessment is, in other words, practical only when speaking about cases concerning voidance of concrete terms in particular contracts. For these situations an attempt to prescribe the relevant types of arguments in the assessment of unfairness is contained in art. 4(1) of the Directive. According to this Article the unfairness of a contractual term shall be assessed, taking into account the nature of the goods or services for which the contract was concluded and by referring, at the time of conclusion of the contract, to all the circumstances attending the conclusion of the contract and to all the other terms of the contract or of another contract on which it is dependent.

The need to take into account all the circumstances surrounding the making of a contract is emphasised. This points at a very situation–specific and concrete assessment of unfairness. This has caused many German legal writers to see the fairness control of the Unfair Contract Terms Directive as 'concrete–individual' in comparison with the 'supraindividual–generalising' control in German law.[48] This obviously means that a normally perfectly fair clause can be considered unfair *in casu*, if this is warranted by the specific situation in which the contract was made.[49]

However, one should not over emphasise the concrete character of the assessment based on the Directive. The circumstances mentioned in art. 4

---

[48]   See R. Damm, 'Europäisches Verbrauchervertragsrecht und AGB–Recht' (1994) 49 *Juristenzeitung* 161 at 172 *et seq.*, Eckert, *op. cit.*, at 1075 and P. Hommelhoff and K.–U. Wiedenmann, 'Allgemeine Geschäftsbedingungen gegenüber Kaufleuten und unausgehandelte Klauseln in Verbraucherverträgen' (1993) 14 *ZIP, Zeitschrift für Wirtschaftsrecht* 562 at 568. Criticism by O. Remien, 'AGB–Gesetz und Richtlinie über missbräuchliche Verbrauchervertragsklauseln in ihrem europäischen Umfeld' (1994) 2 *Zeitschrift für Europäisches Privatrecht* 34 at 52 *et seq.*

[49]   Bultmann, *op. cit.*, at 142.

only refer to facts attending the conclusion of the contract. One might therefore not, according to the Directive, be allowed to pay very extensive attention, for example, to the consequences of application of the contract to the facts prevailing subsequently. This is possible in Nordic law. The evaluation according to the Directive is therefore static and fails to take into account the fact that the contractual setting may change over time in ways which legitimately should be considered relevant; such changes should according to the philosophy of the Directive be taken into account primarily through specific legal doctrines like the English doctrine of frustration or the German doctrine of the basis of contract (*Geschäftsgrundlage*). In this sense the approach of the Directive again has been based on very cautious thinking.[50] Traditional models of contract, focusing on the will or reliance of the parties as the basis of contractual obligation, usually lock the normative situation to the time when the contract was made.

Perhaps of even more significance is the fact that the remaining structure of the Directive strongly suggests that the purpose has been to give *in casu* consideration as such a relatively insignificant role. The limitation of the scope of the Directive to cover only terms which have not been individually negotiated, results in predominantly abstract consideration of terms. Also the fact that the Directive, at least partly, makes use of the same material rules for both individual adjustment and collective regulation – although art. 4 states that it does not affect the collective regulation based on art. 7 – supports an assessment that is removed from the circumstances prevailing in an individual case. Collective regulation does not allow very extensive consideration of facts other than those related to the contents of the contract. Finally, the grey list of the Annex of the Directive leads one's thoughts to a method which mainly looks for concrete rules concerning the contents of unfair contract terms instead of a solution taking into account the needs of

---

50 There were some attempts during the preparation of the Directive to give it a more dynamic flavour. When the static approach adopted in the Directive was criticised during its preparation, the second criterion of unfairness, which had been contained in the original proposal, but had been removed from the Commission Proposal of 1992, was returned to the 1993 Commission Proposal; under this criterion, a term was to be considered unfair if it 'causes the performance of the contract to be significantly different from what the consumer could legitimately expect'. The solution was justified by the fact that it had 'the advantage of showing clearly that the requirement of good faith is not restricted to the circumstances prevailing at the time the contract is drawn up but extends to the probable consequences of its performance for the consumer', COM(93) 11 at 2. The cited point was, however, again removed from the final version of the Directive. The wording of art. 4, emphasising the static approach, was thus not even counterbalanced by a dynamic interpretation possibility based on art. 3.

the parties in an individual case. This emphasis is hardly changed by the fact that the list of unfair terms in the Annex is noted to be only indicative (art. 3(3)). If the ECJ will take on a prominent role in developing the fairness test it is also to be expected that many of its decisions probably will concern the fairness of certain types of contract clauses.

With regard to the harmonisation aims of the Unfair Contract Terms Directive, this type of attempt to reach a fairly formal assessment of unfairness is understandable. A black list or some other form of typification will certainly be needed if the aim is to harmonise, also on the practical level, the provisions on unfairness that are in force in Europe. The guiding effect of a general clause may also increase if one adopts a more typified approach in the solution of fairness cases.

The typifying approach is in line with the market–oriented contract regulation which can be seen to lie behind the Directive. In such an approach the rules on fairness just draw the boundaries around the field where private autonomy may play freely. A more concrete evaluation (also taking into account the effects of the clause on the situation at hand, including changes of circumstances) would point at a changed conception of contract. In such a conception contract would be seen primarily as an instrument for distribution of wealth in society which should be protected by the courts only in so far as it produces reasonably fair outcomes.

The relatively abstract approach of the Directive also makes it hard to take into account personal factors – the situation of the 'poor and ignorant man' – in the assessment of fairness. Admittedly the preamble to the Directive expressly states that, 'in making an assessment of good faith, particular regard shall be had to the strength of the bargaining positions of the parties' (recital 16), but the structures analysed above are not very favourable to such a line of argument. Even though some ability–oriented factors may be taken into account when assessing the procedure for concluding the contract, there seems to be little room for the type of need–oriented reasoning – focusing on the special needs of consumers arising from poverty, illness, unemployment etc. – which has emerged in the Nordic setting.[51] In this way the Directive reflects the relative insensitivity of EC law towards the special needs of weak and vulnerable consumers.

(iii) Substantive Models

Above the view was defended that the fairness test should focus strongly on the content of the term in question (and, of course, also on the content and nature of the whole contractual relation). However, this does not tell us very

---

51   See T. Wilhelmsson, *Critical Studies in Private Law*, (Kluwer, 1992).

much about the outcome of the fairness test. One has to ask what substantive requirements the fairness test puts on the content of consumer contracts. Where do we find the models for what could be considered fair contracts?

Two approaches are possible. On the one hand it is possible that the Unfair Contract Terms Directive to some extent may form the basis for the development of a truly European fairness doctrine. The ECJ may try to treat the concepts of the Directive as autonomous Community law concepts rather than just as mere reflections of the corresponding national concepts.[52] On the other hand the Court may draw heavily on national fairness doctrines and thereby give comparative law central importance. These perspectives are of course not mutually exclusive. Indeed they are closely interrelated; any autonomous fairness doctrine must obviously have a strong input from national conceptions of fairness. The models of fairness therefore can and should be taken from both Community law materials and national materials.

The main substantive model for an autonomous fairness doctrine is contained in the Annex to the Directive. The status and content of this Annex is analysed more closely in the next section. However, there are also some other European materials which should be mentioned in this context. On the EC level one should especially note the relevance of EC recommendations in deciding on the fairness of contract clauses. There are a few such recommendations in the consumer law field, of which at least one contains more extensive contract provisions: the Payment Systems Recommendation, which is dealt with in detail in Chapter 6. Obviously such a recommendation should be taken as one starting point when discussing the fairness of clauses in contracts within its sphere of application.[53] It should be noted in this context that the ECJ has expressly stated that certain EC recommendations should not be considered lacking legal effect altogether. On the contrary, national courts should take these 'recommendations into consideration in order to decide disputes submitted to them, in particular where they are capable of casting light on the interpretation of other provisions of national or Community law.'[54]

Other European materials may also be taken into account by the ECJ, if it seeks to shape an autonomous European fairness doctrine. A possible source is the Resolution of the Council of Europe on unfair terms in

---

52   N. Reich, 'Verbraucherschutzaspekte der AGB–Banken' in N. Horn (ed.), *Die AGB–Banken 1993*, (Walter de Gruyter, 1994) at 49.

53   P.–J.B. Guillen, 'Die Kriterien der Missbräuchlichkeit in der EG–Richtlinie über missbräuchliche Klauseln in Verbraucherverträgen' (1994) 9 *Verbraucher und Recht* 309 at 321.

54   *Salvatore Grimaldi v. Fonds des maladies professionelles*, Case C–322/88 [1989] ECR 4407 at 4422.

consumer contracts and on appropriate method of control[55] which contains a fairly extensive list of examples on unfair clauses. If the work of the Commission on European Contract Law, mentioned in the introduction, receives more widespread acceptance, it may also be used in this context. Although the developed principles are mainly non–mandatory and focus primarily on commercial contracts they can be seen as containing an average European standard for fair contracting with some relevance for consumer contracts as well.

Any control of unfair terms must obviously also to some extent be related to the substantive background rules and principles of the country of application. For instance, a term that denies the consumer a right – for example the right to demand the repair of a defective product – can usually be considered unfair only if the consumer would otherwise have this right.[56] This means that to some extent various background rules must by necessity lead to differing results in different countries.[57] This is also partly recognised in the Directive which expressly excludes the possibility of a fairness control of clauses in accordance with national legislation. According to art. 1(2) of the Directive contractual terms which reflect mandatory statutory or regulatory provisions – and this expression is, according to the preamble, also intended to cover non–mandatory rules which are applicable because no other arrangements have been established between the contracting parties (recital 13) – and the provisions or principles of international conventions to which the Member States of the Community are party, particularly in the transport area, shall not be subject to the provisions of the Directive. The reason for this exclusion is, again according to the preamble, that such provisions are presumed not to contain unfair terms. However, as this limitation of the scope of the Directive, as far as it concerns non–mandatory rules, is stated only in the preamble, it has been argued that this does not necessarily prevent a fairness control of terms which are in accordance with such rules.[58] This would be a bold step for a court to take, but if the ECJ wishes to develop an autonomous European fairness doctrine it might have to transgress the said limitation.

---

[55]   *Op. cit.*

[56]   It is against this background that Brandner & Ulmer, *op. cit.*, at 660 have criticised some of the examples of unfair terms in the proposed directive (as it then was).

[57]   Therefore Hondius, *op. cit.*, at 246 has called the varying national contract laws a 'time bomb' when looked at from the perspective of the control of unfair contract terms.

[58]   Reich (1996), *op. cit.*, at 343.

(iv) The Annex

During the preparation of the Unfair Contract Terms Directive the drafters clearly realised that a Directive based only on a general fairness clause would most likely be understood and interpreted very differently in different countries, depending on their contract law traditions. Any real approximation of the fairness doctrines of different countries would require a more detailed approach. Therefore an Annex is attached to the Directive which contains an extensive list of examples on unfair clauses. According to art. 3(3) of the Directive the Annex contains 'an indicative and non–exhaustive list of the terms which may be regarded as unfair'.

As the list is only 'indicative' it is usually called a grey–list, rather than a black–list. German law contains a black–list of terms which are always considered unfair. The exact meaning of 'indicative' is, however, unclear. All aspects of the interpretation of this word cannot be dealt with in this context;[59] some of them will undoubtedly sooner or later reach the ECJ. Some short remarks may suffice at this stage.

First, the indicative nature of the list refers to the obligations of both the Member States and their courts. The Member States can, according to the preamble of the Directive, let the scope of the terms 'be the subject of amplification or more restrictive editing... in their national laws';[60] (recital 17). The courts may, because of the indicative nature of the list, *in casu* accept a clause as fair even though it falls within one of the examples in the grey–list. In both situations, however, one may assume that the applicability of an example from the list reverses the burden of proof (or rather the burden of arguing that a term has to be considered unfair); both Member States and users of contract terms who want to claim that a term contained in the list is

---

[59] See in more detail, Wilhelmsson (1995), *op. cit.*, at 66 *et seq.*

[60] This could be understood to mean that at least some list is required in national law; the Nordic way of implementing the list only through *travaux préparatoires* would in that case not fulfil the demands of the Directive, see T. Wilhelmsson, 'The Implementation of the EC Directive on Unfair Contract Terms – an Assessment from a Nordic Point of View', in F. Maniet & B. Dunaj (eds), *The Implementation Process of E.U. Directives on Product Safety, Product Liability and Unfair Contract Terms*, (Centre de Droit de la Consommation, 1995) at 38 *et seq.* It also seems to be in conflict with the Community law principle of effective judicial protection, see especially the case *Commission v. Denmark*, Case 143/83 [1985] ECR 427, where a Danish implementation of a provision in a labour law directive through *travaux préparatoires* was found to be insufficient.

not unfair in a certain situation must produce the arguments to support such a claim.[61]

Regardless of how the Annex is implemented in national law it may of course gain legal effects directly as part of Community law. The obligation of national courts to interpret national law in accordance with Community law offers good grounds for arguing that the Annex of the Directive should be taken into account when applying national general clauses, even when the Member State in question has not implemented the Directive or the Annex.

Although the legal status of the Annex is somewhat unclear, it may have effects in practice as a kind of checklist for businesses when drafting standard form conditions. At least in countries like the United Kingdom where a general fairness principle is a novelty some businesses seem to use the Annex in this way. In countries with longer traditions of general fairness standards national practice might be more important.

The contents of the Annex cannot be analysed in detail in this book. The structure of the Annex does not seem to be built on any systematic principle and so there are various ways in which the examples could be systematised. They could, for instance, be grouped under the following four headings:[62]

I. Terms giving one party control over the contract terms or the performance of the contract:
    This covers terms which have the object or effect of:

'(i) irrevocably binding the consumer to terms with which he had no real opportunity of becoming acquainted before the conclusion of the contract;

(j) enabling the seller or supplier to alter the terms of the contract unilaterally without a valid reason which is specified in the contract;

(k) enabling the seller or supplier to alter unilaterally without a valid reason any characteristics of the product or service to be provided;

(l) providing for the price of goods to be determined at the time of delivery or allowing a seller of goods or supplier of services to increase their price without in both cases giving the consumer the corresponding right to cancel the contract if the final price is too high in relation to the price agreed when the contract was concluded;

---

61   Reich (1994), *op. cit.*, at 51. Compare, however, the implementation of the list in French law, according to which the plaintiff has to prove the unfairness of the term even if it is on the grey–list, see J. Franck [1995] *Consum.L.J.* CS 37.

62   This systematisation is taken from R. Brownsword, G. Howells & T. Wilhelmsson, 'The EC Unfair Contract Terms Directive and Welfarism' in R. Brownsword, G. Howells & T. Wilhelmsson (eds), *Welfarism in Contract Law*, (Dartmouth, 1994) at 284 *et seq.*

(m) giving the seller or supplier the right to determine whether the goods or services supplied are in conformity with the contract, or giving him the exclusive right to interpret any term of the contract;

(p) giving the seller or supplier the possibility of transferring his rights and obligations under the contract, where this may serve to reduce the guarantees for the consumer, without the latter's agreement.'

II. Terms which govern the duration of the contract:
This covers terms which have the object or effect of:

'(g) enabling the seller or supplier to terminate a contract of indeterminate duration without reasonable notice except where there are serious grounds for doing so;

(h) automatically extending a contract of fixed duration where the consumer does not indicate otherwise, when the deadline fixed for the consumer to express this desire not to extend the contract is unreasonably early.'

III. Terms which prevent the parties having equal rights:
This covers terms which have the object or effect of:

'(c) making an agreement binding on the consumer whereas provision of services by the seller or supplier is subject to a condition whose realisation depends on his own will alone;

(d) permitting the seller or supplier to retain sums paid by the consumer where the latter decides not to conclude or perform the contract, without providing for the consumer to receive compensation of an equivalent amount from the seller or supplier where the latter is the party cancelling the contract;

(f) authorising the seller or supplier to dissolve the contract on a discretionary basis where the same facility is not granted to the consumer, or permitting the seller or supplier to retain the sums paid for services not yet supplied by him where it is the seller or supplier himself who dissolves the contract;

(o) obliging the consumer to fulfil all his obligations where the seller or supplier does not perform his.'

IV. Exclusion, limitation and penalty clauses:
This covers terms which have the object or effect of:

'(a) excluding or limiting the legal liability of a seller or supplier in the event of the death of a consumer or personal injury to the latter resulting from an act or omission of that seller or supplier;

(b) inappropriately excluding or limiting the legal rights of the consumer *vis-à-vis* the seller or supplier or another party in the event of total or partial non–performance or inadequate performance by the seller or supplier of any of the contractual obligations, including the option of offsetting a debt owed to the seller or supplier against any claim which the consumer may have against him;

(e) requiring any consumer who fails to fulfil his obligation to pay a disproportionately high sum in compensation;

(n) limiting the seller's or supplier's obligations to respect commitments undertaken by his agents or making his commitments subject to compliance with a particular formality;

(q) excluding or hindering the consumer's right to take legal action or exercise any other legal remedy, particularly by requiring the consumer to take disputes exclusively to arbitration not covered by legal provisions, unduly restricting the evidence available to him or imposing on him a burden of proof which, according to the applicable law, should lie with another party to the contract.'

D.   Transparency

(i)   Interpretation and Language

The Unfair Contract Terms Directive is not a pure substantive piece of legislation. The strong emphasis in EC consumer law on information and transparency can clearly be seen in the Directive as well. Art. 5 of the Directive states the general rule that contract terms which are offered to the consumer in writing must always be drafted in plain, intelligible language. This requirement on clarity is even extended to terms which define the main subject matter of the contract and the adequacy of the price (art. 4(2)).

The private law consequence connected with this rule is a rule of interpretation, the very well known rule on interpretation *in dubio contra stipulatorem*. In the Directive this has been formulated as a positive rule of interpretation: in case of doubt, the interpretation most favourable to the consumer shall prevail (art. 5).

This sanction, however, does not necessarily have to be read as covering all cases of breach of the obligation to draft the terms in plain, intelligible language. One might claim that as the sanction requires there to be 'doubt about the meaning of a term', this does not cover all situations where a term appears unintelligible for certain groups of consumers. The argument would be that although the term cannot be considered plain and intelligible it might still be thought of as clear, particularly if read by a technical expert. However, such a reading is not in line with the protective spirit of the provision and certainly would undermine the idea, mentioned below, of protecting 'naive and inexperienced consumers' through a more subjective reading of the intelligibility requirement. Art. 5 of the Directive would certainly be more efficient, if all cases of breach of the intelligibility requirement would be considered to be situations of doubt when applying the interpretation rule.

Although art. 5 provides that the *in dubio contra stipulatorem* rule does not apply to the art. 7 collective injunction procedure, nevertheless the fact that terms are not drafted in a plain, intelligible language may still be relevant under this procedure.[63] Their unintelligibility could be considered as a relevant factor and possibly evidence of bad faith. This would at least be a possible way of understanding art. 7 and in line with Nordic practice.

The requirement concerning plain, intelligible language is open to interpretation. Should one focus more objectively on what is understandable for a reasonable consumer or is it possible also to take into account the special difficulties of the individual consumer? The importance of this interpretation rule obviously is greater, if, like Hugh Collins, one prefers a test referring to 'the naive and inexperienced consumer'.[64] The general attitude of the ECJ concerning the consumer image in the Community[65] does not, however, give reason to anticipate that the Court would endorse the use of such a test.

The question concerning subjective or objective assessment may be of greater theoretical than practical value. However, there is a more practical impreciseness in the requirement of transparency in the Unfair Contract Terms Directive. The Directive fails to address a problem that is quite significant in the internal market; that of the language in which the terms should be given to the consumer.[66] This problem has been addressed in various ways in several directives concerning labelling[67] as well as in the Timeshare Directive[68] and the Payment Systems Recommendation.[69] These rules are, however, heterogeneous and cannot be used to construct any general principle, although consumers often may prefer the consumer-friendly solution of the Timeshare Directive, requiring the contract to be

---

[63] See also Bragg, *op. cit.*, at 36 and Wilhelmsson (1995), *op. cit.*, at 133. See on the injunction procedures more closely below, at section 2E(ii).

[64] Collins, *op. cit.*, at 248.

[65] See below Chap. 9 section 3.

[66] See in more detail Wilhelmsson (1995), *op. cit.*, at 131 *et seq.*

[67] See *Communication from the Commission to the Council and the European Parliament concerning language use in the information of consumers in the Community*, COM(93) 456 at 3.

[68] See below Chap. 7 section 4C(iii).

[69] See below Chap. 6 section 3B(ii).

drawn up in at least the official Community language of the Member State in which the purchaser resides, or, if he so wishes, in the language of the Member State in which he is a national. At this stage, when we are waiting for cases to reach the ECJ, one can only surmise rather vaguely that the requirement of intelligibility ought to pose some restrictions on the choice of language in various parts of the Community. In this sense there should be a limitation on the automatic free movement of standard form conditions. At least they should be translated so that they are in an appropriate language for the market in which they are used.

(ii)   Access to Terms

Not only should the contract terms be plain and intelligible, they should also be accessible for the consumer. This principle can be inferred from example (i) of the Annex, according to which a term which has the object or effect of irrevocably binding the consumer to terms with which he had no real opportunity of becoming acquainted before the conclusion of the contract is to be regarded unfair. This may imply that even such a standard form contract which is signed by the consumer can be regarded as unenforceable, if the contract form was presented to the consumer at such a late stage in the contracting process that he had no opportunity of becoming acquainted with its content.[70]

Other parts of the Directive may also indirectly support the idea of giving consumers access to the contract terms. One might claim that the Directive indirectly demands that the standard terms be handed over to the consumer. Norbert Reich has proposed the deduction of a private law rule of this kind from the general requirement of adequate and effective means to prevent the use of unfair terms in art. 7 of the Directive.[71] Although the connection of such a rule with the Directive must be regarded as rather tenuous, it certainly can be defended from a consumer point of view. It is at least in line with the transparency principle emphasised elsewhere in Community consumer law. A rule demanding at least the availability of the terms also receives some support from Community competition law. The exemption granted by the Insurance Practices Regulation to insurance companies for co-operation for the establishment of standard policy

---

[70]   Padfield, *op. cit.*, at 178.

[71]   N. Reich, 'EG–Rechtliche Anforderungen an die Reform des deutschen Versicherungsvertragsrechts', in H.–P. Schwintowski (ed.), *Deregulierung, Private Krankenversicherung, Kfz–Haftpflichtversicherung*, (Nomos, 1994) at 38.

conditions applies only if the conditions are accessible to any interested person and are provided upon request.[72]

E. Sanctions

(i) Voidness

In individual disputes between a seller or supplier and a consumer the proper sanction for unfairness is voidance of the term. According to art. 6(1) of the Directive, Member States shall lay down that unfair terms in consumer contracts shall not be binding on the consumer and that the contract shall continue to bind the parties if it is capable of continuing in existence without the unfair terms. The exact meaning of 'not binding' is to be deemed on the basis of national law.

The Directive therefore prescribes complete voidness of the unfair term. The term should not only be adjusted by the court,[73] it should be completely disregarded. If this leads to a lacuna in the contract the general rules of contract law will apply so far as possible.

The complete elimination of the unfair term from the contract sometimes may lead to unfairness against the seller or supplier. In the Nordic countries, the courts in this case have had the possibility to adjust the whole contract in order to reach a fair solution. According to the Directive this does not seem possible.[74] The Directive therefore clearly contains a punitive element. At least in theory a seller or supplier who uses unfair terms has to face the risk of ending up in a situation where the contract is unfair against him but is still binding. Concrete examples of this possibility are, however, not very easy to invent.

(ii) Effective Means of Prevention

The private law sanction of voidness is not considered sufficient to counteract the use of unfair terms in consumer contracts. Thus, art. 7 requires Member States to ensure that adequate and effective means exist to prevent the continued use of unfair terms in consumer contracts. The means

---

[72] Commission Regulation (EEC) No 3932/92 of 21 December 1992 on the application of art. 85(3) of the Treaty to certain categories of agreements, decisions and concerted practices in the insurance sector: OJ 1992 L398/7, art. 6(1)(c).

[73] For courts in the Nordic countries this is possible.

[74] The Nordic laws have been changed accordingly. See, for Finland, Act 1259/1994, amending Chap. 4 of the Consumer Protection Act (this rule being found in 4:2.3).

for achieving this are not specified, except to the extent mentioned below. The required efficient protection can therefore be obtained in various ways. Criminal sanctions, injunction procedures by public officials (like the UK's Director General of Fair Trading and the Nordic Consumer Ombudsmen), or collective preventive action by consumer associations (like in Germany and France) can be mentioned as examples.

A certain specification of the obligation is given in art. 7(2), according to which the adequate and effective means shall include provisions whereby persons or organisations, having a legitimate interest under national law in protecting consumers, may take preventative action according to the national law concerned before the courts or before competent administrative bodies. This rule might seem to make it obligatory to allow for some sort of organisational action by consumer associations. The UK's solution of allowing only the Director General of Fair Trading to take action could therefore be problematic in this respect.[75] It might, however, be defended on the basis of the reference to the national law in the article.[76] On the other hand the reference to national law may have been included in the rule only to give the Member States the right to define the requirements for which organisations should have *locus standi*, not to make it possible to eliminate the right of organisations to take action altogether.[77] The problem is now brought to the ECJ in the form of a reference for a preliminary ruling;[78] the authors of this book are obviously very interested to see which of the two alternative interpretations the Court will choose.

Finally art. 7(3) contains an interesting rule on a kind of defendant class action. It permits the preventative legal remedies to be directed separately or jointly against a number of sellers or suppliers from the same economic sector or their associations which use or recommend the use of the same general contractual terms or similar terms. On account of this rule

---

[75] Consumer organisations do have the possibility to make a complaint to the Director General of Fair Trading who has to consider it; he does not, however, have any obligation to initiate proceedings in such a case.

[76] See Brownsword & Howells, *op. cit.*, at 260. A different (negative) view on the correctness of the implementation of the Directive in the UK in this respect is expressed by M. Clarke, 'The EC Directive on Unfair Terms as it affects Insurance Contracts – an English View' (1996) 81 *Svensk Juristtidning* 149 at 165.

[77] This standpoint is defended in T. Wilhelmsson, 'Public Interest Litigation on Unfair Terms', in H.-W. Micklitz and N. Reich (eds), *Public Interest Litigation Before European Courts*, (Noms, 1996). Although it is apparent that the authors take different views on what type of collective actions are required by the Directive, both agree upon the desirability of consumer organisations having standing in this type of case, even if the power is likely to be exercised infrequently in practice.

[78] Case C–82/96.

amendments have been made in Nordic law making it possible for the Consumer Ombudsman to institute injunction procedures directly against a trade association which draws up or recommends the use of certain contract terms.[79] This option is also included in the UK and German laws.

F. Protection Against Choice of Law

There is one special rule in which the Directive especially addresses the problems of cross–border consumer contracts. Art. 6(2) deals with choice of law clauses referring to the law of non–Member countries.

This rule is, according to the preamble, directed against the risk that a consumer may be deprived of the protection under the Directive by a contract term which designates the law of a non–Member country as the applicable law (recital 22). Therefore, according to the Directive, 'Member States shall take the necessary measures to ensure that the consumer does not lose the protection granted by this Directive by virtue of the choice of the law of a non–Member country as the law applicable to the contract if the latter has a close connection with the territory of the Member States.'

This rule limits the effects of choice of law clauses in relation to the Directive. However, it affects only clauses which refer to the law in a non–Member state. It has no bearing on clauses according to which the law of one Member state is chosen instead of the law of another. The rationale of art. 6(2) is only to secure the application of the minimum level of protection prescribed in the Directive, whenever there is a close connection to the territory of the EC. It does not seek to secure for consumers the availability of more consumer–friendly rules which may be in force in certain Member States.

One may of course question the need for art. 6(2) as there is a relatively wide restriction on the binding effect of choice of law clauses in consumer contracts imposed by art. 5 of the Rome Convention on the Law Applicable to Contractual Obligations.[80] However, as that article covers only goods, services and (certain forms of) credit, and as it deals only with certain specific situations, one can think of cases where the protection afforded by that Article does not apply. More significant, however, is the fact that the special rules on consumer contracts in the Rome Convention protect only the so called passive consumer, who usually enters into the contract in his own country. The special protection against choice of law clauses offered by the Unfair Contract Terms Directive might be particularly important for active consumers making purchases while travelling abroad on their own initiative.

---

[79] See e.g. in Finnish law Act 1259/1994, 3:1.1.
[80] See Chap. 8 section 2C(i)(a).

There is an interesting difference in the wording between the Directive and the Rome Convention. The protection afforded by the Directive applies when the contract has 'a close connection with the territory of the Member States', while the Rome Convention in art. 4 uses the expression 'most closely connected'. This could imply that the Directive should be applicable even in some situations where applicable law is not one of the laws of the Member States. On the other hand the difference in wording might just be the result of poor drafting. At least some reasons – such as the wording of the preamble according to which the rule is directed against the use of choice of law clauses to 'deprive' the consumer of protection – seem to indicate that the rule of the Directive is only concerned with situations where the law of a Member State is applicable according to the general rules.[81] A wider application of the requirement of 'close connection' is, however, also defendable.[82]

G.   Conclusions and Outlook

The Unfair Contract Terms Directive seems to be a rather important directive from both a theoretical and a practical perspective. It clearly acknowledges the principle of fairness as one of the leading principles of European consumer contract law. Thereby it forces those Member States in which this principle has not been recognised to introduce it in their legislation.[83]

On the other hand one should not overemphasise the radicalness of the Directive. We have seen that the contract thinking on which the Directive is based is still fairly traditional. The values of freedom of contract and private autonomy are reinforced by excluding individually negotiated contracts as well as the core provisions of the contract from the scope of the Directive. The fairness of the price and performance relationship is left to be determined by the market. The obsession with the events occurring when the contract was made – a typical characteristic of traditional contract law – is also repeated in the Directive.

The Directive can be considered important from another perspective.[84] It may play an important role in the development of a harmonised European

---

[81]   M. Bogdan, 'Avtalsvillkor i gränsöverskridande konsumentavtal' (1995) 80 *Svensk Juristtidning* 189 at 198.

[82]   See Reich (1996), *op. cit.*, at 353.

[83]   See, on the English law, Department of Trade and Industry, Implementation of the EC Directive on unfair terms in consumer contracts (93/13/EEC), *op. cit.*, at 1 where it states 'The main effect of the Directive will be to introduce for the first time a general concept of fairness into the UK law of contract'.

[84]   See, in more detail, Wilhelmsson (1995), *op. cit.*, at 93 *et seq.*

private law. It certainly adds to the pressure for the harmonisation of contract law in the European Community. As noted above, any control of unfair terms is always to some extent related to national substantive contract law. The adoption of the Directive will therefore necessarily lead to increased pressure towards the harmonisation of the material provisions of contract law.[85] The Directive also brings in the ECJ as a new actor in the field of the harmonisation game, as it gives the Court jurisdiction to give preliminary rulings in matters concerning the unfairness of the terms of consumer contracts.[86] By this means the Court may gain influence over the general development of European contract law.

3.   SALE OF CONSUMER GOODS

A.   Introduction

We have seen that, the Unfair Contract Terms Directive brings pressure for the harmonisation of other parts of contract law. Harmonised fairness principles cannot lead to similar results in practice, if the national background rules of contract law are very different. This was appreciated even during the first stages of preparation of the Unfair Contract Terms Directive. In the 1992 proposal[87] there was a specific provision (art. 6) according to which consumers who have been sold defective goods should have a choice of the remedies of reimbursement or reduction of price, or replacement or repair of the goods, as well as compensation for damage caused by the defect. This provision, which would have required some harmonisation of consumer sales law, was, however, removed from the adopted version of the Directive. The Council agreed to refer the question of harmonisation of guarantees to a specific directive.

The preparation of such a directive began immediately. In 1993 the Commission published a Green Paper on *Guarantees for Consumer Goods and After-sales Services*.[88] In the Green Paper the present situation in the Member States was described and assessed. The Green Paper also contained a discussion of possible solutions concerning three sets of questions. First, it analysed the possibility of harmonising the national provisions concerning

---

85   Micklitz (1993), *op. cit.*, at 535 claims that the Directive will start an avalanche towards the Europeanisation of private law.

86   The extent of this jurisdiction is of course somewhat unclear, as the application of law and the assessment of facts (which is not for the ECJ to perform) are often inseparably intertwined in a decision on contractual fairness.

87   OJ 1992 C 73/7.

88   COM(93) 509.

the legal guarantee, especially in relation to new, durable, movable consumer goods. This part concerned the rights of consumers flowing directly from the law on consumer sales. Second, it focused on commercial guarantees, that is contractual guarantees expressly given by the seller or manufacturer. Here the problems are connected with the commercial practices which relate to the guarantees as well as with the functioning of such guarantees in the context of the Single Market. Finally, some questions concerning after–sales services and the liability to stock spare parts were taken up.

Already the terminology of the Green Paper gives an indication of problems arising in the context of harmonising consumer sales law. The concept of the 'legal guarantee' which is used as a heading for the main part of the proposals is familiar to only some Member States. In English law one more commonly speak about implied terms and in German law about warranty rights (*Gewährleistungsrechte*). In Nordic law, the term guarantee is normally reserved only for phenomena which in the Green Paper are dealt with under the heading of commercial guarantees. In the proposal which has been published subsequently, the heading 'legal guarantee' is therefore removed. This is just one example of the conceptual difficulties attached to this project.

The Green Paper led to much debate. Opinions were divided on the issue of whether the Community should engage in legislation in this area which was in the heartland of private law. Some found that the suggestions in the Green Paper would not be very beneficial for consumers,[89] while others considered EC legislation along the lines proposed to be an advancement from a consumer point of view.[90] Anyway the preparation went on and in the spring 1995 an Expert Group participated in the drafting of a proposal for a directive.[91] After much delay caused by very different views in the Commission a proposal was published in summer 1996.[92]

The published proposal contains the text of a minimum directive which would ensure the consumer[93] some basic mandatory rights in case of non–

---

89   See R. Bradgate, 'Harmonisation of Legal Guarantees: A Common Law Perspective' [1995] *Consum.L.J.* 94. Such assessments depend upon both how protective one considers existing national remedies and also how effective one views the solutions proposed by the Commission.

90   See H.–W. Micklitz and F. Amtenbrink, 'Legal Guarantees – German Civil Law in the Light of the Green Paper' [1995] *Consum.L.J.* 117.

91   Both authors were members of this expert panel.

92   COM(95) 520.

93   The definition of 'consumer' in the proposal is a little different than those in most other consumer protection directives (see above Chap. 1 section 1B): 'any natural person who... is acting for purposes which are not *directly* related to his trade, business or profession'. (emphasis added). The drafters have orally stated that the

conformity of the goods. There is also a short provision on (commercial) guarantees offered by sellers and producers. If one compares the proposal with the discussion in the Green Paper and with the text drafted in co–operation with the Expert Group the proposal is very modest. The watering down process typical for EC consumer legislation has taken place already at this early stage. The most interesting parts, which really could have contributed to the development of consumer sales law in many Member States, have been left out. In the published proposal nothing is said about after–sales services and there are no rules about the consumer's right to take direct action against the producer of the goods. The coverage of commercial guarantees throughout the whole Community is not touched upon. The liability of the seller for delay is not included in the proposal.

B.   Main Contents of the Proposal

As the preparation of the directive has been surrounded with much controversy and it is not certain whether it will be adopted and with what precise content, only the main lines of the proposal will be presented here. The name of the proposal gives the impression of a relatively comprehensive enactment: Proposal for a European Parliament and Council Directive on the sale of consumer goods and associated guarantees.[94] However, in reality it only covers some aspects of consumer sales. The main provisions of the proposed directive concern the conformity of the goods and the consequences of non–conformity.

The definition of conformity in art. 2 of the proposal is very much inspired by the 1980 United Nations Convention on Contracts for the International Sale of Goods, art. 35.[95] The goods should be fit for the normal purposes of the goods in question as well as, under certain circumstances, for the particular purposes required by the buyer. In addition it is proposed that the quality and performance of the goods should be satisfactory given the nature of the goods and the price paid and taking into account the public statements made about them by the seller, the producer or his representative.

---

word 'directly' is intended to extend the scope of the directive to situations such as where a lawyer buys a coffee machine for his office. However, as this is not explained in the proposal, which on the contrary gives the impression that the definition is in line with previous definitions ('The definition of the consumer is inspired by the classical definitions already contained in other Directives', COM(95) 520 at 10), it is questionable whether this result can be achieved. Anyway it does not seem acceptable to try to 'sneak in' important changes of principle through one unexplained word.

[94]   COM(95) 520.
[95]   COM(95) 520 at 11.

The proposal does not expressly contain the notion of 'failure to meet the consumer's legitimate expectations' advocated in the Green Paper,[96] but it can probably be read as an attempt to describe somewhat more precisely what must be considered to be within the normal expectations of consumers.[97]

The provision that allows public statements to be taken into account when assessing whether the goods are satisfactory is an example of advertising being given contractual effect; we shall see another example of this, below, when we see the proposal that the content of the guarantee should be derived in part from associated advertising. The term 'public statements' would seem at least to include advertisements. However, it is presumably wider than this for in relation to guarantees the term advertising is expressly used. The width of the term is unclear and could usefully be clarified. Art. 3(2) seeks to prevent the seller having responsibility for public statements made by the producer or his representative where this would be unfair. Thus there is no liability if he corrected the statement at the time of sale. Equally he is not liable for statements of which he did not know and could not reasonably have known about; a qualification might be added to the effect that the consumer should have realised that the seller was unlikely to have known of the statement. The seller will also not be liable if he shows that the decision to buy the goods could not have been influenced by the statement.

The proposed rules on the relevant time for assessing conformity are consumer–friendly. The seller shall, according to art. 3(1) be liable for any lack of conformity existing at the time when the goods are delivered to the consumer. By means of a rule on the burden of proof concerning lack of conformity, any lack of conformity which becomes manifest within six months after delivery shall normally be presumed to have existed when the goods were delivered, unless the opposite is proved (art. 3(3)). This proposal would certainly improve the position of consumers in many Member States. It remains to be seen whether it will be found in the text of the directive at later stages of its preparation.

The remedies for non–conformity are listed in art. 3(4). The consumer shall be entitled to demand repair of the goods; replacement of the goods, when this is possible, price reduction or rescission (avoidance) of the contract. Obviously the choice of remedy is in principle left to the consumer. However, Member States are allowed to provide that the scope of the rights of the consumer are limited when the lack of conformity is a minor one. In

---

[96]   COM(93) 509 at 85.

[97]   See also COM(95) 520 at 11, where the solution based on a 'legitimate expectations' test is said to have been warmly welcomed by consumer advocates, but criticised by professional circles.

many legal systems as well as under the Vienna Convention on Contracts for the Sale of Goods it is not, as a main rule, permitted to avoid the contract, if the breach of contract is not fundamental. The proposed directive allows such a rule to be kept in force.

No rule about the fundamental remedy of damages is to be found in the proposal. This does not mean that this remedy is to be thought of as inappropriate. The problem is just left to national law. As the rules on contractual damages are very different in the Member States and as they are situated in the very heartland of contract law it has been considered wiser to refrain from dealing with this question in the proposed directive. Of course, the remedy of price reduction may fulfil the same function as parts of the rules of damages; the main point is that consequential damages are left to national law.

In order to be able to use the remedies the consumer has to notify the seller of the lack of conformity. The proposed period of notification is one month from the date when he detected the lack of conformity or ought to have detected it (art. 4). This notification duty is a traditional feature in some legal systems, such as the Nordic countries. For others, like the United Kingdom, it will be a novelty and there may be fears that consumers who are ignorant of the their legal rights and how to enforce them may be denied justice by this provision. Of course Member States are free not to include the obligation as the directive is a minimum harmonisation measure, but it may be better to leave Member States the option to require notification, rather than to have it as the main rule.

The ultimate limitation period according to the proposal would be two years. The seller would be liable for a lack of conformity becoming manifest within two years from delivery (art. 3(1)); however, the remedies of avoidance and replacement would be available only for a period of one year (art. 3(3)). The two year rule would prolong the limitation period in some countries such as Germany and would in those states be seen as an advancement from the consumer point of view. In others, such as the UK and Finland, the period seems short; however, as the directive would be a minimum directive it would not legally[98] prevent such countries from sticking to their present rules.

Finally there is a short provision on contractual (commercial) guarantees in art. 5. First, it states that a guarantee shall be binding on the seller or producer who offered the guarantee. In this context it notes that references in advertising to the content of the guarantee shall count as binding guarantee conditions. This is an expression of the principle that information given in

---

[98] The directive could certainly, in spite of this, be used as an argument by those who might want to change domestic law in a more consumer–unfriendly direction.

advertising usually is to be treated as part of the contract.[99] The provision then goes on to express a general principle of guarantees law in many countries, namely that the guarantee must put the beneficiary in a more advantageous position than he would have been in according to the applicable rules on consumer sales. Finally the article contains a transparency requirement. When a guarantee is given it should feature in a written document which contains certain particulars and is freely available for consultation. However, a breach of this rule would of course not affect the validity of the guarantee, but other measures taken by the Member States against breaches of the transparency rule are expected.[100]

C.   Conclusions

The work on a directive on consumer sales has been controversial and it is not certain that it will lead to the adoption of a Directive. From a consumer point of view the project in its present form does not seem very important. The proposal has been strongly watered down from the possibilities raised by the Green Paper, which had highlighted some areas of serious consumer concern. Most of the ideas which would have led to real improvements of the rights of the consumers in many countries have been dropped from the published proposal. Certainly some details of the proposal can be applauded from the consumer point of view in some countries – the obligatory extension of the limitation period to at least two years, the presumption of non–conformity having existed at the time of delivery, perhaps the introduction of the right of repair as a remedy in British law etc. – but by and large the proposal does not seem to bring very much new protection in this area in most Member States.

A directive in the area may, however, be assessed also from the more general point of view of harmonisation of European private law. A consumer sales directive could be seen as a first step towards a European sales law.[101] From this perspective a possible directive can be expected to be criticised by persons who feel sceptical about allowing the Community to play in a field which is central to private law, while those who are committed to building a European private law might show a more positive attitude. Even from the latter's point of view, however, the proposed directive, in its stripped version with only a few provisions, does not seem to offer very much.

---

99   COM(95) 520 at 15.

100   *Ibid.*

101   See A.K. Schnyder and R.M. Straub, 'Das EG–Grünbuch über Verbrauchsgütergarantien und Kundendienst – Erster Schritt zu einem einheitlichen EG–Kaufrecht?' (1996) *Zeitschrift für Europäisches Privatrecht* 8.

4 Advertising

1. INTRODUCTION

A. Starting Points

Advertising and other forms of marketing are key elements in a market economy, the importance of which is continuously growing in the post–industrialised society. One cannot therefore overlook the regulation of advertising when creating the framework for a functioning internal market. It is not surprising that European Community law contains some rules on advertising. One could rather express some surprise about the relatively few EC rules in this area; as will be noted below, advertising regulation at Community level is still rather fragmented and incomplete.

From an internal market point of view there is a strong case for Community legislative efforts in the area of advertising. As the marketing strategies of enterprises increasingly focus on multinational rather than national markets, the need for a harmonisation of the marketing rules becomes ever more obvious from the point of view of business. If the rules on advertising and other marketing practices are very different in the various Member States of the European Union, a multinational corporation or a multinational chain of enterprises marketing the same product in several Member States might have to create different marketing strategies for different parts of the internal market for purely legal reasons,[1] multiplying the cost of advertising.[2] This would not seem to be a good state of affairs from an internal market point of view.

Indeed the basic starting points for the regulation of advertising were very different in the Member States, at the time when the EC rules on marketing were being prepared. On the one extreme there was the English system mainly based on common law, containing only specialised legislation concerned just with false and misleading advertising, and depending much on soft law methods of control to regulate the fairness of advertising. In the middle there was German law – with similar solutions in some other

---

[1] Such a differentiated approach may, of course, obviously often be warranted by cultural reasons.

[2] If the Coca–Cola company could use its US advertising throughout the European Union it has been suggested that it would expect perhaps a 50 million dollar reduction in expenses, see U. Reese, *Grenzüberschreitende Werbung in der Europäischen Gemeinschaft*, (C.H. Beck, 1994) at 5.

continental countries – which in this area started from the legislation on unfair competition to which consumer protection thinking has later added. Finally, on the other extreme there was the Nordic (then represented by Denmark) model. This model placed a stronger emphasis on consumer protection as the basic starting point, giving the Consumer Ombudsmen relatively wide powers to intervene against unfair advertising. In contrast to the common law system, both the German and the Nordic legislation offered broad general clauses on unfairness on which the courts could base their decisions.[3]

From the point of view of the business world, which needs harmonisation of advertising rules, the EC measures so far adopted are certainly a disappointment. The Community legislation only addresses certain questions, like misleading advertising, or advertising through certain media, like TV advertising. There is no general principle forbidding unfair marketing codified in EC law. For example suggestive advertising, discriminatory advertising, advertising interfering with privacy, denigratory advertising and giving of inadequate information in advertising[4] are not subject to any general Community legislation. This largely seems due to the fact that no general clause on unfair advertising exists in the United Kingdom which led this country to resist such rules on the EC level.[5] The state of affairs which created the need for harmonisation – the large differences between the rules in the various Member States – has also paradoxically functioned as an obstacle to such harmonisation.

The content of the harmonised rules also to some extent reflects the conflicting starting points of various countries. The preparation of the Misleading Advertising Directive clearly began as a project which primarily concerned unfair competition. Later on the emphasis shifted more towards the consumer protection approach.[6] As will be seen later, both these aspects

---

3   For a more detailed comparison, see F.-K. Beier, 'Entwicklung und gegenwärtiger Stand des Wettbewerbsrechts in der Europäischen Wirtschaftsgemeinschaft' (1984) *Gewerblicher Rechtsschutz und Urheberrecht Internationaler Teil (GRUR Int.)* 61.

4   These types of advertising are enumerated by U. Bernitz as the major types of unfair advertising in 'The Legal Concept of Unfairness and the Economic and Social Environment: Fair Trade, Market Law and the Consumer Interest' in E. Balate (ed.), *Unfair Advertising and Comparative Advertising* (Story Scientia, 1988) at 61 *et seq.* It is easy to accept such an enumeration, if one understands 'suggestive marketing' to be a very broad category including various methods of commercial pressure, exploitation of feelings of various kinds, exploitation of the weaknesses of children and other vulnerable groups etc.

5   See L. Krämer, *EEC Consumer Law*, (Story Scientia, 1986) at 158–159.

6   See, on the history of the directive, N. Reich, *Europäisches Verbraucherrecht*, (3rd ed., Nomos, 1996) at 311.

are still present in the EC rules; for example the effort to harmonise the rules on comparative advertising seems to have more to do with unfair competition than with consumer protection, although the latter element certainly is present as well. Anyway, when analysing the content of the adopted measures it is important to bear in mind that many of these measures are not pure consumer protection rules, but they are expressly[7] designated to protect fair competition as well.

From a consumer point of view the need for Community legislation seems twofold. First, obviously, a harmonisation on a relatively high level, if that could be achieved, would here as elsewhere assist consumers in countries with less developed systems. Second, and this is a problem which affects consumers in all Member States, there is the rapidly growing phenomenon of cross–border malpractices. The present system where authorities or consumer organisations supervise marketing in their own country, having no means to attack advertisers based in another country, leaves large loopholes for those who wish to escape national regulations. This brings to the fore, among other questions, the issue of cross–border standing which is discussed later under the heading of access to justice (see Chap. 8 section 3).

Business also has an interest in the cross–border context in having to comply with just one rather than several control mechanisms. The discussion then focuses on the question of 'home country' control versus 'host country' control, that is whether the supervision and control should be effected by the authorities and the rules of the Member State from which the advertisement is sent (home county control) or whether the system of the receiving (host) country should be decisive.[8] This problem again is not dealt with very extensively or clearly in Community law on advertising. The fact that the TV Directive, as will be explained below, expresses the principle of home county control does not necessarily mean that this principle should be regarded as the main rule; other arguments may show that the principle of host country control should prevail in areas not regulated by this Directive.[9]

The punctual and incomplete nature of the EC rules on advertising has of course caused concern in the Commission. The Commission has very recently adopted a Green Paper on Commercial Communications in the Internal Market.[10] This paper, which discusses future EC policy on this

---

[7] Most consumer protection measures obviously have impliedly a competition aspect as well.

[8] Similar questions arise in relation to control of financial service institutions offering services in other states and are discussed in Chap. 6 section 1B.

[9] See B. Schmitz, 'Advertising and Commercial Communications – Towards a Coherent and Effective EC Policy' (1993) 16 *J.C.P.* 387 at 393–394.

[10] COM(96) 192.

field, defines commercial communications as: 'All forms of communication seeking to promote either products, services or the image of a company or organisation to final consumers and/or distributors.'[11] The Green Paper focuses on the regulation of advertising, direct marketing, sponsorship, sales promotion and public relations. The key findings of the Green Paper are: (i) cross–border commercial communications are growing; (ii) differing national regulations may create obstacles for businesses and problems for consumers; (iii) these divergences could give rise to barriers; (iv) this risk is accentuated by the new services in the Information Society and (v) the availability of information about regulatory measures is becoming more important.[12] The central ethos of the Green Paper seems to be an underlining of the need to remove as far as possible the national barriers to commercial communications within the internal market, with special emphasis on the new needs of the Information Society.

The concrete proposals of the Green Paper are relatively few, as it rather purports to function as a basis for discussion. The Commission has invited comments to the paper which of course can contain among other things views on existing barriers. One may therefore foresee at least a thorough public discussion in the near future concerning the questions analysed in this chapter. Whether this will lead to any legislative results and, in that case, in which direction the law will develop, is too early to predict.

The present chapter deals only with the regulation of advertising. An unfairness standard usually, however, comprises other forms of marketing as well; at least this is the case in Germany and the Nordic countries. The attempts to regulate other forms of problematic marketing are described in the next chapter on trade practices.

B. Product–Specific Rules Excluded

In this chapter the EC rules and principles on advertising which have a more general scope and are applicable to all or most (consumer) products are analysed. As this work focuses primarily on the more general principles of consumer law and as food law anyway is outside the scope of the book, the EC legislation on advertising for certain products, mainly concerning foodstuffs or related products, will not be examined in this context. Of course, in so far as these provisions reflect more general principles or are helpful for understanding the more general rules, they will be briefly mentioned. A very short overview of these product–specific rules will be

---

[11] COM(96) 192, at 1.
[12] COM(96) 192, at 1b.

given here simply in order to provide an outline for the complete picture of EC advertising law.

A relatively large and thorough regulation of the advertising of medicines is effected by the Council Directive 92/28/EEC of 31 March 1992 on the advertising of medicinal products for human use.[13] This Directive affects a large variety of marketing measures, as 'advertising' is given a rather broad definition, including not only advertising through the media, but also 'any form of door–to–door information, canvassing activity or inducement designed to promote the prescription, supply, sale or consumption of medicinal products' (art. 1(3)). It covers advertising to the general public (Ch. II) as well as advertising to health professionals (Ch. III). The rules on advertising to the public include among other rules a prohibition of advertising for certain products, e.g. those which are available on medical prescription only (art. 3(1)), a prohibition of the mentioning of certain therapeutic indications, such as sexually transmitted diseases (art. 3(2)), a statement that the purpose of the message is to be an advertisement should be clear (art. 4(1)(a)) and a list of minimum information to be included in the advertisement (art. 4(1)(b)). There is also, in art. 5, an extensive list of material and claims which the advertisement may not contain, some because of their misleading or excessive character, some because of the risk of damage (e.g. points (a) impression that medical consultation unnecessary; and (i) erroneous self diagnosis) and some because of their improper addressee (point (e) children). The Directive also contains provisions on monitoring of advertising (Ch. IV), according to which 'Member States shall ensure that there are adequate and effective methods to monitor the advertising of medicinal products' (art. 12). These provisions are, according to the preamble, drafted taking into account the corresponding provisions of the Misleading Advertising Directive. There are also restrictions on advertising for medicinal products in the TV Directive (see section 6 below).

Also the advertising for tobacco products has been largely discussed and several proposals on restrictions have been made.[14] No results, however, have been achieved yet, except for a total ban in the TV Directive.

In the area of food law proper there are numerous legislative acts affecting the advertising and marketing of foodstuffs. The following have a general scope:

---

13 OJ 1992 L 113/13 (hereafter the Medicine Advertising Directive).

14 See V. Kendall, *EC Consumer Law*, (Wiley Chancery, 1994) at 173–174. An extensive analysis of the arguments is to be found in N. Reich, 'Rechtsangleichung und Verbraucherschutz – Werbung, Vertragsrecht, Haftung, Vertrieb' (1992) *Verbraucherpolitische Hefte* 197 at 201–203.

–   Council Directive 79/112/EEC of 18 December 1978 on the approximation of the laws of Member States relating to the labelling, presentation and advertising of foodstuffs for sale to the ultimate consumer,[15] which contains a provision forbidding misleading labelling, presentation and advertising (art. 2) as well as detailed rules on obligatory particulars on various labels.
–   Council Directive 90/496/EEC of 24 September 1990 on nutrition labelling for foodstuffs.[16]
–   Council Regulation (EEC) No 2081/92 of 14 July 1992 on the protection of geographical indications and designations of origin for agricultural products and foodstuffs.[17]
–   Council Directive 79/581/EEC of 19 June 1979 on consumer protection in the indication of the prices of foodstuffs.[18]

In addition there is an almost endless number of legislative acts on specific types of foodstuffs, which contain provisions affecting labelling and other aspects of marketing. Although space does not permit that these can even be listed here, one should emphasise that the regulation of labelling is a very important technique in Community consumer policy. This is, however, not very apparent when considering merely the general, non product–specific rules of Community consumer law, and so should be borne in mind.

The special rules on advertising and information in relation to distance selling, consumer credit and timeshare contracts are analysed in the respective chapters below. Labelling and information requirements can be found also in the EC legislation on product safety, described in Chap. 2.

2.   ADVERTISING AND NEGATIVE HARMONISATION

The phenomenon of so called negative harmonisation of European law, that is the ECJ outlawing specific provisions of national law on the basis of the Treaty of Rome, occurs in the present area. In fact this issue is far more important in the field of advertising than when dealing with the law of contract. There are quite a few interesting decisions of the ECJ which should be mentioned in this context. They are worth presenting for two reasons: not

---

[15]   OJ 1979 L33/1 (hereafter the Foodstuffs Marketing Directive). The Directive has been amended several times.
[16]   OJ 1990 L 276/40.
[17]   OJ 1992 L 208/1. See the comments by M. Kolia, 'Monopolising Names of Foodstuffs' (1992) 3 *European Business Law Review* 323.
[18]   OJ 1979 L 158/19; amended 1988: OJ 1988 L 142/23 (hereafter the Foodstuffs Price Indication Directive).

only do they put some – albeit today very vague and unclear – limits on what the national legislator can do in the area, but they also show rather clearly the basic consumer image (consumer protection ideology) which the ECJ tends to use as a starting point in its reasoning on consumer law matters.

The cases in question mainly concern the application of art. 30[19] of the Treaty of Rome on measures having equivalent effect to quantitative restrictions on imports. The Court has in these cases applied the well known *Dassonville*-formula, which brings within the scope of art. 30 all national trading rules which can hinder intra–Community trade 'directly or indirectly, actually or potentially'.[20] It is well known that this gives the ECJ rather broad powers to strike down national laws. A large variety of measures might indirectly and potentially affect trade between the Member States, including national rules on advertising and marketing. The focus of the Court's inquiries has been on the question whether bans or limitations on advertising and marketing *de facto* hamper the access of foreign products to the market in question.[21]

National rules which fall within art. 30 can be held to be inapplicable. It is worth remembering that they can be saved by either (i) art. 36, which allows prohibitions or restrictions on grounds of, *inter alia*, public morality, public policy, the protection of health and life of humans, animals or plants so long as they do not constitute a means of arbitrary discrimination or a disguised restriction on trade, or (ii) in the case of indistinctly applicable rules, if they satisfy one of the mandatory requirements, which include the protection of public health, the fairness of commercial transactions and, most importantly, the defence of the consumer.

In this context it seems worth noting that the outlawing of certain marketing regulations in the cases to be considered, of course, concerns only situations where the regulations in some way affect imported goods. In purely internal matters the national rules may be upheld.[22] As EC law does not forbid a Member State to discriminate against its own citizens, nothing in

---

19 In addition to this provision also art. 59 of the Treaty can be relevant in the advertising context, not only in relation to advertising for services, but also because advertising can be regarded as a service as such, see COM(96) 192 at 5–6, and below at section 6B.

20 *Procureur du Roi v Benoit et Gustave Dassonville*, Case 8/74 [1974] ECR 837 at 852.

21 Reich (1996), *op. cit.*, at 91.

22 See *R. v Secretary of State for Health, ex p. Gallagher et al*, Case C–11/92, [1993] ECR I–3545 (national rule on size of health warning on tobacco products upheld), on which see J. Stapleton, 'Minimum Directives. Do Not Be Misled' (1994) 110 *L.Q.R.* 213. For a discussion in the German context see R. Sack, 'Die kollisions– und Wettbewerbsrechtliche Beurteilung grenzüberschreitender Werbe– und Absatztätigkeit nach deutschem Recht' (1988) *GRUR Int.* 320 at 341–342.

EC law prevents the Member State from retaining its stricter rules for domestic cases and only taking into account art. 30 in cases affecting importation from other parts of the European Union. In practice, however, there would certainly be a pressure towards abolishing such rules for domestic situations as well.

Various types of bans and restrictions on advertising and marketing may come in conflict with art. 30. To start from the obvious, a ban on advertising for a certain (type of) product may of course rather easily form an obstacle to intra–Community trade, if this product is produced in some other Member State. The ECJ has found a national rule forbidding the advertising of strong alcoholic beverages in the media and on streets and highways to fall within art. 30, although in this case the measure was accepted because of public health concerns.[23]

From another angle it is equally clear that national rules on labelling and packaging may have a negative impact on intra–Community trade, if they impliedly demand different labels or design of package in different Member States. Such rules can therefore easily be deemed to conflict with the Treaty of Rome, if they cannot be defended on the basis of the mandatory requirements doctrine or art. 36 of the Treaty. In fact there are a number of cases outlawing national rules on labelling[24] and the obligatory shape of package[25] decided by the ECJ. As many of them deal with foodstuffs and alcohol, and as they do not touch upon central areas of advertising regulation, they will not be analysed further in this context.

Among the decisions on labelling, of more general interest from the point of view of creating an economic (and cultural) Community is the well known case, *Piageme v Peeters*, dealing with rules concerned with the language on

---

23   *Aragonesa de Publicidad Exterior SA et Publivia SAE v Departamento de Sanidad y Seguridad Social de la Generalitat de Cataluña*, Joined Cases C–1/90 and C–176/90 [1991] ECR I–4151.

24   See *Criminal proceedings against Anton Adriaan Fietje*, Case 27/80 [1980] ECR 3839, *Criminal proceedings against De Kikvorsch Groothandel–Import–Export BV*, Case 94/82 [1983] ECR 947. One could here also mention the cases on national rules forbidding the use of certain names for particular products, see as just a few examples, *Commission of the European Communities v Italian Republic*, Case 193/80 [1981] ECR 3019 ('vinegar' should not be restricted to wine–vinegar alone), *Criminal proceedings against Miro BV*, Case 182/84 [1985] ECR 3731 ('genever' should not be restricted to beverages with an alcohol content above 35%), *Proceedings for compulsory reconstruction against Smanor SA*, Case 298/87 [1988] ECR 4489 ('yoghurt' for deep–frozen yoghurt should not be forbidden).

25   See *Walter Rau Lebensmittelwerke v De Smedt PvbA*, Case 261/81 [1982] ECR 3961 (national rules requiring margarine to be marketed in packaging with the shape of a cube).

labels. In this case the ECJ ruled that a national provision instituting an obligation to use exclusively the language of the linguistic region where the goods are marketed is a measure having equivalent effect to a quantitative restriction on imports and therefore prohibited by art. 30.[26] This case has, among other things, led to a Commission communication on the language use in the information of consumers where the fact that this problem has been addressed in various ways in several directives concerning labelling is criticised and an improved consistency of the Community rules in force is recommended.[27]

The problematic nature of the above mentioned national rules in the light of the Treaty of Rome is easy to understand, as an acceptance of the national rules would lead to a need to vary labels or packaging when selling in various parts of the Community. Such changes would have clear cost implications for traders. However, there are also cases dealing with 'pure' advertising rules.[28] Certain national restrictions on advertising methods have, in the practice of the Court, been considered to conflict with art. 30 of the Treaty of Rome.

Two typical examples, both dealing with price information in advertising, should be mentioned. The much–cited *GB–INNO* case concerned a provision in Luxembourg law forbidding the inclusion, in advertisements relating to a special purchase offer, of a statement showing the duration of the offer or the previous price. The Belgian firm, which was not bound by any similar rules in Belgium, used the same marketing strategy in both countries. The Court found the Luxembourg provision – which was similar

---

26 *Piageme and Others v BVBA Peeters*, Case C–369/89 [1991] ECR I 2971. The case can be seen as an attempt to reconcile the requirements of the Foodstuffs Marketing Directive – art. 14 of which requires some particulars to be given in a language easily understood by purchasers – and art. 30 of the Treaty, V. Kendall, *op. cit.*, at 187. See hereto the subsequent case *Piageme and Others v Peeters NV*, Case C–85/94 [1995] ECR I–2955, where the Court interpreted art. 14.

27 Communication from the Commission to the Council and the European Parliament concerning language use in the information of consumers in the Community, COM(93) 456 at 11.

28 Both labelling and advertising were addressed in the food case *SARPP – Société d'application et de recherches en pharmacologie et phytothérapie SARL v Chambre syndicate des raffineurs et conditionneurs de sucre de France and Others*, Case C–241/89 [1990] ECR I–4695; the application to imported artificial sweeteners of national provisions which prohibit any statement in the advertising of such sweeteners alluding to the word 'sugar' or to the properties of sugar which the sweeteners also possess (e.g. 'the taste of sugar without sugar', 'help to avoid excess weight due to sugar' etc.) was precluded by art. 30.

to German rules[29] – to be in conflict with art. 30 of the Treaty and it did not see sufficient arguments justifying it from a consumer protection point of view. The Court noted that the Luxembourg provision would in fact prevent the consumers from receiving relevant information. In this context the Court also expressly stated its view on the basic idea of Community consumer policy: 'under Community law concerning consumer protection the provision of information to the consumer is considered one of the principal requirements.'[30] Consumer organisations have criticised the decision for not clearly seeing the difference between sales promotion and the giving of information;[31] all 'information' is not necessarily to the benefit of the consumer.[32]

A very similar conclusion was drawn in the more recent *Yves Rocher* case. In this case a German rule forbidding eye–catching comparisons between old and new prices for the products of the firm prevented the use of an integrated marketing strategy for companies who distribute mail order catalogues or prospectuses throughout the Community. Therefore this rule was inapplicable according to art. 30 of the Treaty, as it went too far from a consumer protection point of view in outlawing comparisons which were in fact correct.[33] Again the Court seems to assume that information is always advantageous for the consumer, so long as it is true.

However, the Court has not always declined to take into account consumer protection needs as factors justifying special national rules. A greater sensitivity to the needs of all consumers seems to be reflected in the *Oesthoek* case, where a Dutch rule restricting the offer of free gifts as a marketing device was accepted although it forced sellers from other countries to change their marketing strategies. This case is said to reveal 'an acceptance on the part of the Court that the consumer may be unable properly to process information'.[34] Even though the Court also in this case speaks about the protection of consumers through greater market

---

29   H. Piper, 'Zu den Auswirkungen des EG–Binnenmarktes auf das deutsche Recht gegen den unlauteren Wettbewerb' (1992) *Wettbewerb in Recht und Praxis* 685 at 689.

30   *GB–INNO–BM v Confédération du commerce luxembourgeois*, Case C–362/88 [1990] ECR I–667 at 689.

31   Schmitz, *op. cit.*, at 394.

32   Piper, *op. cit.*, at 689.

33   *Schutzverband gegen Unwesen in der Wirtschaft v Yves Rocher GmbH*, Case C–126/91 [1993] ECR I–2381.

34   S. Weatherill, 'The Role of the Informed Consumer in European Community law and Policy' [1994] *Consum.L.J.* 49 at 53.

transparency,[35] it obviously shows less reliance on the consumers' ability actively to use information than the decisions mentioned earlier.

On the basis of these decisions a somewhat vague, but still relatively discernible, picture concerning the possible negative harmonisation of advertising law in the EC began to emerge. All advertising rules which may negatively affect the volume of imports would potentially be caught by art. 30.[36] However, they could be justified by reference to consumer protection, so long as they complied with the principle of proportionality. This required that they go no further than is necessary to provide the protection that was needed. Often this has been interpreted as requiring no more than that the consumer be provided with correct information.

However, the relevance of this practice is now uncertain, since the ECJ changed the direction of the development of Community law in the famous *Keck* decision. In this case the Court introduced the concept of 'selling arrangements' to restrict the applicability of art. 30 of the Treaty. It stated that 'contrary to what has previously been decided' national provisions restricting or prohibiting certain selling arrangements are not to be considered to hinder trade between the Member States within the meaning of *Dassonville*, as long as they are not discriminatory, in law and in fact.[37] The question is, whether advertising is to be treated as a selling arrangement as defined by *Keck*. In this case the scope for negative harmonisation of national rules on advertising would be considerably diminished.

The legal situation after *Keck* does not seem very clear.[38] On the one hand there are cases in which national restrictions on advertising have been treated as selling arrangements and therefore do not fall within the scope of art. 30. In *Hünermund* this was the solution with regard to a German restriction on advertising of pharmaceuticals.[39] The recent decision in the

---

35 *Criminal proceedings against Oesthoek's Uitgeversmattschappij BV*, Case 286/81 [1982] ECR 4575 at 4588.

36 G. Schricker, 'Zur Werberechtspolitik der EG–Liberalisierung und Restriktion im Widerstreit' (1992) *GRUR Int.* 347 at 357.

37 *Bernard Keck and Daniel Mithouard*, Joined Cases C–267/91 and C–268/91 [1993] ECR I–6097.

38 One of the co–authors of this book (Wilhelmsson) has elsewhere, in Finnish, coined the term *Jack–in–the–box–theory of EC law* to refer to the fact that it is virtually impossible to foresee the situations in which the Treaty of Rome–argument can be used against national legislation. The regulation of advertising today seems to be an area where this term is very accurate.

39 *Ruth Hünermund and others v Landesapothekerkammer Baden–Württemberg*, Case C–292/92 [1993] ECR I–6787.

Leclerc–Siplec case points in the same direction.[40] This concerned a French decree prohibiting the distribution sector to advertise on television.[41] On the other hand one may point at the decision in the *Clinique* case, given after *Keck*, where a German measure prohibiting the use of the name 'Clinique' for certain cosmetics – on the basis that the consumers might believe that it was a product with pharmaceutical properties – was deemed to fall under art. 30 and was banned as a barrier to trade which could not be justified.[42]

Parts of what one could mention under the heading regulation of advertising then certainly still fall under art. 30 of the Treaty of Rome, although other parts have been brought outside its sphere of application because of the *Keck* decision. Some hints about how the line between these cases should be drawn are given already by the three cases just mentioned. *Hünermund* and *Leclerc–Siplec* concerned 'pure' advertising provisions, which had no impact on the products themselves; these provisions could therefore easily be classified as selling arrangements. On the other hand it is equally clear that an acceptance of the national restriction in the *Clinique* case would have forced the producer to alter the packages of the product for the German market. As national rules which relate to the product itself in this way always have been especially problematic from the point of view of EC law,[43] it is, perhaps, understandable that the ECJ should wish to apply art. 30 in this case.

Distinguishing between advertising rules which affect the product directly and those which affect its marketing may provide the means to provide a sensible assessment of the consequences of *Keck*. The decisions on labelling and packaging would still be valid,[44] but the 'pure' advertising cases like *GB–Inno*, probably can be questioned after *Keck*. This might also be true for *Yves Rocher*, although the perceived need for a mail order firm to have the same catalogues all over the Community may be used as an argument against employing the *Keck* rule. For consumers, of course, this

---

40   *Société d'Importation Édouard Leclerc–Siplec v TFI Publicité SA and M6 Publicité SA*, Case C–412/93 [1995] ECR I–179.

41   The reason for the decree in this respect was an aim to defend the regional press and pluralism in the mass media.

42   *Verband Sozialer Wettbewerb eV v Clinique Laboratories SNC et Estée Lauder Cosmetics GmbH*, Case C–315/92 [1994] ECR I–317.

43   J. Möllering, 'Das Recht des unlauteren Wettbewerbs in Europa: Eine neue Dimension' (1990) 36 *Wettbewerb in Recht und Praxis* 1 at 12.

44   This is confirmed by the recent case *Verein gegen Unwesen im Handel und Gewerbe Köln eV v Mars GmbH*, Case C–470/93 [1995] ECR I–1923. In this case ice cream bars were lawfully packaged in France with the promotional text '+ 10 %' which, however, was in conflict with German law. The ECJ found that art. 30 prevented the use of the German rules against ice cream bars imported into Germany.

means more freedom for national Governments to develop protective rules. The legal situation is, however, in no way certain. It is relatively impossible to predict exactly how the line will be drawn between cases falling under and cases falling outside the scope of art. 30. In addition, there has been strong criticism of *Keck* in the context of advertising[45] and some have questioned whether the Court in the future will be able to maintain its position in relation to rules on advertising.[46]

In fact, in the Green Paper on Commercial Communications the Commission seems to defend a much stricter censorship of national measures in the area of advertising. There is a proposal for a methodology to deliver a more uniform assessment of the proportionality of such national measures that could be regarded as problematic from the point of view of the internal market.[47]

Whatever the development will be in the future, the described cases from the ECJ at least reveal some traits of the consumer image prevailing in the Court. The consumer is primarily seen as a rational individual capable of understanding and using all the information he is given. The need for provision of information is underlined; correct information of almost any kind is treated as advantageous to the consumer. We here again, in other words, encounter the rational internal–market–consumer as the ideal of EC consumer policy. However, the picture is not completely homogeneous: the *Oesthoek* case puts lesser demands on the abilities of the consumer. Some other cases on marketing, discussed in other chapters, may add some cracks to the homogeneous picture. The *Buet* case could be mentioned as one of the scarce examples of an attitude which takes into account the needs of more vulnerable consumers.[48]

3. MISLEADING ADVERTISING

A. Introduction

The rational consumer needs correct information on which he can base his choices in the market. In view of the image of the consumer which prevails in the Community, it was therefore to be expected that legislative action would be taken in the area of safeguarding the consumer's right to correct information in marketing. The regulation of misleading advertising was one

---

[45] See the statement of Advocate General Jacobs in the *Leclerc–Siplec* case.

[46] F. Wooldridge, 'Article 30 and TV Advertising; the ECJ Judgment in *Leclerc–Siplec*' (1996) *European Business Law Review* 3 at 6.

[47] COM(96) 192 at 33 *et seq.*

[48] See Chap. 5 section 2D.

of the first consumer protection issues to be included in the EC legislative agenda.

The principle according to which misleading advertising is forbidden received its first legislative expression at the EC level within the area of food law. The Foodstuffs Marketing Directive, adopted in 1978, already contains a provision against such advertising. According to art. 2 the labelling and methods used must not be such as could mislead the purchaser to a material degree, particularly as to the characteristics of the foodstuff or by attributing to the foodstuff effects or properties which it does not possess or by suggesting that the foodstuff possesses special characteristics when in fact all similar foodstuffs possess such characteristics. These rules also apply to the advertising of foodstuffs (art. 2(3)(b)).

Even before the adoption of the Foodstuffs Marketing Directive, work had begun on Community legislation concerning misleading and unfair advertising in general. This work has roots going as far back as the 1960s, when deliberations concerning the need for Community rules on unfair competition led to some preliminary research in this field.[49] Later, the focus was shifted from regulation of unfair competition towards consumer protection, and the first consumer protection programme of 1975 expressly mentioned this question.[50] As a consequence of this, the Commission issued its first proposal for a directive concerning misleading and unfair advertising in 1978.[51] The further preparations were cumbersome: there were German interventions accusing the proposal of being too much influenced by English law and English ones seeing it as too German.[52] The idea of such a directive, dealing with unfair and not only misleading advertising, seems to have been especially hard to accept for the United Kingdom, previously not used to a general legal concept of unfair advertising and using self–regulation as the main enforcement mechanism for such matters.[53]

The resistance led to some delay in the preparation of the Directive. Finally, however, in 1984 the Council Directive 84/450/EEC relating to the approximation of the laws, regulations and administrative provisions of the Member States concerning misleading advertising (the Misleading Advertising Directive)[54] was adopted. The Directive was very much watered down in comparison with the original proposal. In this respect it had gone

---

[49]   E. Ulmer, *Das Recht des unlauteren Wettbewerbs in den Mitgliedstaaten der Europäischen Wirtschaftsgemeinschaft*, Band I (C.H. Beck, 1965).

[50]   Preliminary programme of the European Economic Community for a consumer protection and information policy, OJ 1975 C 92/1, items 19, 22 and 23.

[51]   OJ 1978 C 70/4.

[52]   L. Krämer, *EEC Consumer Law*, (Story Scientia, 1986) at 153.

[53]   See Reich (1996), *op. cit.*, at 311 *et seq.*

[54]   OJ 1984 L 250/17.

through the same development as many subsequent consumer protection directives: starting from a relatively far–reaching proposal and ending in a very modest directive.

The most remarkable change was the dropping of the general prohibition in the first proposal concerning unfair advertising. As this concept was given a rather broad definition in that proposal, including, among other things, both certain forms of socially unacceptable advertising, such as advertising which promotes social or religious discrimination or infringes the equality of the sexes, and all kinds of advertising which 'is likely to influence a consumer or the public in general in any... improper manner' (art. 2), it was clearly a major step backwards to remove it from the Directive. As the name of the adopted Directive indicates, it only deals with misleading advertising. No general principle, concerning all media, forbidding unfair advertising is contained in present Community law, although the preamble to the Directive promises harmonisation of national provisions on unfair advertising 'at a second stage' (recital 6). This delimitation of the scope of the Directive seems to reflect very well the prevailing consumer image in the Community. Misleading advertising may distort the function of the assumed rational consumer and should therefore be prohibited. Other forms of unfairness, connected with, for example, suggestive advertising, are likely to be most problematic for more irrational and vulnerable consumers and therefore need not be addressed.[55]

The purpose of the Misleading Advertising Directive is to protect consumers, persons carrying on a trade or business or practising a craft or profession and the interests of the public in general against misleading advertising and the unfair consequences thereof (art. 1). For this purpose, the Directive contains mainly two types of rules. First, there are substantive provisions specifying the extent of the prohibition, that is a definition of misleading advertising (art. 2) as well as a description of the factors which shall be taken into account when determining whether advertising is misleading (art. 3). Second, there are organisational provisions, obliging the Member States to ensure that adequate and effective means exist for the control of misleading advertising. In fact the larger part of the Directive is spent elaborating the details of these procedures (arts 4–6).

The reasons for the Directive, as stated in the preamble, show the usual two sidedness which is typical of most directives in the consumer area. On the one hand the aim is to protect (rational) consumers: 'misleading advertising may cause a consumer to take decisions prejudicial to him when acquiring goods or other property, or using services' (recital 4). On the other hand the concern is expressed about the functioning of the internal market:

---

[55] Of course there is unfair advertising, like advertising which infringes the equality between sexes, which can offend rational as well as less rational consumers.

the differences between the laws of the Member States 'hinder the execution of advertising campaigns beyond national boundaries and thus affect the free circulation of goods and provisions of services' (also recital 4).

Like most consumer protection directives the Misleading Advertising Directive is a minimum directive. It does not preclude the Member States from retaining or adopting provisions ensuring a more extensive protection than the Directive does (art. 7).

As the Directive was rather watered down to a common minimum standard and as its organisational provisions are rather flexible it did not require any large changes of the law in most Member States. Some, like Finland, did not even have to make any amendments at all. On the other hand, in the United Kingdom, where self–regulation previously was the main method of control of advertising, the Directive led to the introduction of authority (back–up) control through the Director General of Fair Trading.[56] The main effect of the Directive is probably a promotion of the authority control systems in the Member States.

B.   Scope

The scope of application of the Directive is defined relatively widely, in two respects. First, it should be emphasised that the Misleading Advertising Directive is not a pure consumer protection measure in the sense that only consumers are protected by its provisions. As mentioned above, according to art. 1 the purpose of the Directive is to protect consumers and persons carrying on a trade or business or practising a craft or profession as well as the interests of the public in general. It is also explicitly stated in art. 4 that the adequate and effective means to control advertising which the Member States are obliged to arrange shall be provided in the interest of consumers as well as competitors and the general public. The relatively narrow consumer concept, typical for many of the EC consumer protection measures, is therefore not relevant in this context, as businesses, professionals and the general public are also to be protected.

Second, the definition of advertising in the Directive is also wide, so wide that one could almost speak about a directive on misleading marketing. According to art. 2(1) 'advertising' means the making of a representation in any form in connection with a trade, business, craft or profession in order to promote the supply of goods or services, including immovable property, rights and obligations. Not only is typical advertising through mass media

---

[56]   See the Control of Misleading Advertisements Regulations 1988 (SI 1988 No 915) and G. Howells and S. Weatherill, *Consumer Protection Law*, (Dartmouth, 1995) at 357–359.

covered by this definition, it also comprises all sorts of representations, as long as they are connected with the purpose of promoting the supply of goods or services.[57] Representations made on the package of the product and in brochures are certainly covered. The same goes, however, also for individual statements made by the seller in connection with the conclusion of the contract. The relevant representation obviously need not be linguistic; a misleading form of a package may be in conflict with the rules of the Directive. According to art. 3 of the Directive, in determining whether advertising is misleading, account shall be taken of all its features. It is also not necessary that the representation directly refers to the goods or services which are promoted, although the characteristics of goods or services as well as the price are emphasised in art. 3 as items concerning which information is especially relevant. Misleading advertising concerning matters such as the business image of the seller is covered, as its ultimate goal certainly is sales promotion. According to art. 3(c) information concerning the nature and attributes of the advertiser should be taken into account when judging whether an advertisement is misleading.

Only such statements as belong to the sphere of political or social discourse fall outside the scope of the Directive. Such statements are not made in order to promote the supply of goods and services. Therefore in an Irish case an advertisement which explained and justified an industrial dispute was considered not to fall within the scope of the Directive.[58]

The field of application of the Directive is general in the sense that no line of business, product or service is excluded. It covers also areas to which specific sectorial legislation applies – it can in this respect be contrasted, favourably, with the General Product Safety Directive. It is clearly stated in the preamble to the Medicine Advertising Directive that this Directive is without prejudice to the application of measures adopted pursuant to the Misleading Advertising Directive (recital 1).

C. What is Misleading?

According to art. 2(2) of the Directive, misleading advertising means:

> 'any advertising which in any way, including its presentation, deceives or is likely to deceive the persons to whom it is addressed or whom it reaches and which, by reason of its deceptive nature, is likely to affect

---

[57] Reich (1996), *op. cit.*, at 313 points out that the purpose, like in German law, is the decisive criterion.

[58] *Dunnes Stores Limited v. Mandate*, [1996] 2 CMLR 120 (Irish Supreme Court).

their economic behaviour or which, for those reasons, injures or is likely to injure a competitor.'

This definition expresses, among other things, the fact that the assessment of whether a representation shall be deemed misleading is freed from any need to prove that anyone was actually misled. It is therefore not necessary to produce consumers or other persons who actually were misled by the advertisement – although this of course often can be a very effective way of convincing the court. It suffices to show that an advertisement is likely to deceive and the judge is free to decide whether the advertisement is of this kind, irrespective of any actual deception.[59] This should make the provision easier to enforce, because time and energies need not be spent tracking down persons who had actually been misled.

Every misleading statement is not, however, necessarily covered by the prohibition in the Directive. The statement should be in some way relevant for the type of recipients. As is stated in the Directive, it should be 'likely to affect their economic behaviour'. A similar idea is expressed in art. 2 of the Foodstuffs Marketing Directive, according to which the methods used must not be such as could mislead the purchaser 'to a material degree'.

The interpretation of the definition of misleading advertising seems clear so far. However, the provision conceals some fundamental differences in approach connected with the consumer images prevailing in the various Member States. The question is, who is the consumer to be protected. Must the advertisement be misleading for the average, normal consumer in order to be condemned, or should one focus rather on how the uneducated or stupid or otherwise weak consumers understand the advertisement? In German law the starting point has rather been the latter; already when 10–20%, sometimes perhaps less, of the consumers are likely to be misled, the advertisement should be forbidden.[60] Also in Nordic law the passive glancer, rather than the active and critical information–seeker, is the dominant consumer image in the regulation of advertising.[61] For a socially–minded consumer law, interested in improving the conditions for the most vulnerable consumers, this seems to be the right starting point. However, the ECJ has chosen another approach, looking more at the reactions of the average consumers (which are perceived as active and rational). This seems to be relatively clearly indicated in the judgment in the *Nissan* case, where the Court had to assess whether the advertising of parallel imported cars as

---

59   Compare, however, the wording of the decision in the *Nissan* case, mentioned below in this section.

60   See Möllering, *op. cit.*, at 10 and Reich (1996), *op. cit.*, at 313.

61   See T. Wilhelmsson, 'Consumer Images in East and West' in H.–W. Micklitz (ed.), *Rechtseinheit oder Rechtsvielfalt in Europa?*, (Nomos, 1996) at 56.

'cheaper' was misleading with regard to the fact that the lower price was to some extent due to these cars having a smaller number of accessories. The Court stated: 'such a claim can only be held misleading if it is established that the decision to buy on the part of *a significant number of consumers* to whom the advertising in question is addressed was made[62] in ignorance' of the said fact.[63]

This view, which is in line with the emphasis on the idea of the rational consumer in Community law, obviously is less favourable for the consumers than the German–Nordic approach, as it leaves the more vulnerable consumers undefended. As the Misleading Advertising Directive is a minimum directive the decision of the ECJ need not affect those more far-reaching national practices.[64] However, a certain pressure from Community law towards lowering the level of protection for vulnerable groups will certainly be felt in practice. There have even been claims put forward that a German judge in the future should follow the Community interpretation of the concept 'misleading' in national law.[65]

In any case the rational consumer perspective is hard to defend in relation to children and other vulnerable groups. Therefore one may assume, like the EFTA Court[66] has done, that 'in considering whether an advertisement is misleading or not, higher standards would normally apply if the advertisement is specifically targeting children'.[67]

In the concept 'false or misleading' lies the claim that a representation – as understood by the average consumer or the vulnerable consumer, as discussed above – does not correspond to reality. In order to call something misleading one therefore has to know relevant facts about reality, i.e. about the product or service advertised. However, in many cases it is not easy to

---

[62] This formulation, that actual misleading should be established, is in direct contradiction with the wording of the Directive, as shown above ('is likely to deceive'), and must be regarded as an error by the ECJ. For a similar criticism, see Piper, *op. cit.*, at 691.

[63] *Complaint against X*, Case C–373/90 [1992] ECR I–131 at 150 (italics added). The result of the case may in spite of this be understandable from a consumer policy point of view, as one may suspect that the prime aim of the Court was to support parallel importers, to the benefit of at least some consumers.

[64] Möllering, *op. cit.*, at 10.

[65] Reich (1996), *op. cit.*, at 316.

[66] This Court, established by the Agreement on the European Economic Area, applies the EC legislation included in the Agreement, like the Misleading Advertising Directive, for that area.

[67] *Forbrukerombudet v Mattel Scandinavia A/S and Lego Norge A/S*, Cases E–8/94 and E–9/94 [1996] 1 CMLR 313 at 330. Of course one may assume that the members of the EFTA Court are strongly influenced by the Nordic approach.

ascertain, without proper testing, whether the qualities promised exist or not. From the point of view of the efficiency of the control, the question of the burden of proof becomes essential in such cases. The 1978 proposal had a clear rule in this respect: when the advertiser makes a factual claim, the burden of proof that his claim is correct shall lie with him (art. 6). However, also in this respect, the Directive was somewhat watered down. The rule is now formulated as a procedural provision: the courts or administrative authorities shall have powers enabling them in civil or administrative proceedings to require the advertiser to furnish evidence as to the accuracy of factual claims in advertising, if, taking into account the legitimate interests of the advertiser and any other party to the proceedings, such a requirement appears appropriate on the basis of the circumstances of the particular case (art. 6). From this rule, however, follows an indirect rule on the burden of proof: the courts or administrative authorities shall have the power to consider factual claims as inaccurate if the evidence demanded is not furnished or is deemed insufficient by the court or administrative authority. This provision of the Directive is not a full–fledged rule on the reversal of the burden of proof, as it operates only if the court actively has required certain information; in addition such a requirement can be made only if it appears appropriate. For other situations the Directive leaves the question of the burden of proof open. From a consumer point of view the original proposal was certainly more advantageous. One could argue, that a business which uses factual statements in advertising without being able to prove their correctness, is acting unfairly simply because it cannot substantiate its claim.[68]

In its Green Paper on Commercial Communications, the Commission has taken notice of the fact that the concept of 'misleading' is interpreted differently in different Member States. This variation in interpretation is said to create 'real barriers to the flow of advertising services'.[69] Whether this may inspire the Community to amend the rules on misleading advertising is too early to predict.

D.   Control and Sanctions

The Misleading Advertising Directive does not only fix the substantive rules to be followed. It also – and this might at least in some countries be the most important effect of the Directive – prescribes a control mechanism to fight misleading advertising. According to art. 4(1) of the Directive, Member

---

[68]   This is the situation in Finland, see T. Wilhelmsson, *Konsumentskyddet i Finland*, (Juristförbundets Förlag, 1989) at 127.

[69]   COM(96) 192 at 22.

States shall ensure that adequate and effective means exist for the control of misleading advertising in the interests of consumers as well as competitors and the general public.[70]

The type of means which should exist is, however, not determined by the Directive. Various administrative or court based judicial means are possible, as long as they can be deemed adequate and effective. The choice is in the main left to national law. The Directive only mentions certain requirements which the control mechanism must fulfil.

The vagueness of the provisions on control is due to the fact that the systems in force were very different in the Member States. A special problem was posed by the UK, whose system was mainly based on self–regulation.[71] The question, whether this could be considered sufficient is addressed by art. 5 of the Directive. Although the Directive, according to the preamble, wants to encourage voluntary control exercised by self–regulatory bodies, because it may avoid recourse to administrative and judicial action, and therefore expressly states that the Directive does not exclude such control, it nevertheless clearly prescribes that such proceedings shall be 'in addition to' court or administrative proceedings (recital 16). The arguments often put forward against self–regulation,[72] such as lack of sufficient sanctions,[73] lack of publicity and the problem of having the business community setting standards for itself, seem to have been given force, insofar as self–regulation is not accepted as the sole means of control.[74] In the United Kingdom the Directive therefore led to the empowerment of the Director General of Fair Trading to institute injunction proceedings before a court.[75]

The adequate and effective means referred to in the Directive shall, according to art. 4(1), include legal provisions under which persons or organisations regarded under national law as having a legitimate interest in prohibiting misleading advertising (like consumer organisations) may take legal action against such advertising or bring such advertising before an

---

[70] See on this provision also below, Chap. 8 section 3.

[71] For a rather positive assessment of the system, see P. Thomson, 'Self–Regulation in Advertising – Some Observations from the Advertising Standards Authority' in G. Woodroffe (ed.), *Consumer Law in the EEC*, (Sweet & Maxwell, 1984).

[72] See T. Wilhelmsson, 'Administrative Procedures for the Control of Marketing Practices – Theoretical Rationale and Perspectives' (1992) 15 *J.C.P.* 159 at 165–166.

[73] Of course there may be methods to combine self–regulation with legal sanctions, see in English law *Director General of Fair Trading v Tobyward Ltd* [1989] 2 All ER 266, where the court granted an injunction with the express aim to 'support the principle of self–regulation'.

[74] According to art. 4(1) the Member States are, however, allowed to require prior recourse to self–regulation before turning to administrative or judicial control.

[75] See Howells and Weatherill, *op. cit.*, (Dartmouth, 1995) at 359.

administrative authority competent either to decide on complaints or to initiate appropriate legal proceedings. This means that the much–discussed question of the independent standing of consumer organisations in court proceedings is treated differently in this Directive than in the comparable Unfair Contract Terms Directive.[76] It is in the present context clear that Member States are not obliged to recognise such standing. It suffices that the organisations can complain to an administrative authority which can initiate the proceedings. The question of cross–border standing of authorities and organisations is dealt with later, in the chapter on access to justice (Chap. 8 section 3).

The minimum sanction against misleading advertising which is required by the Directive is some type of an injunction (art. 4(2)). It must be possible to order the cessation of misleading advertising as well as to prohibit the publication of misleading advertising which has not yet been published.[77]

In addition to this sanction the Directive also mentions the possibility of requiring the publication of a decision granting an injunction and of a corrective statement. However, as the Directive only states that Member States 'may' confer such powers on the courts or administrative authorities, this provision only amounts to a recommendation.

There is also no rule on the contract law consequences of false or misleading advertising. A general rule according to which the information given in advertising normally should become a part of the contract is not expressly included; a provision in the Package Tour Directive, which will be mentioned later, may be seen as a germ to such a principle,[78] which is also evident in some of the provisions of the draft directive on consumer sales.[79] We would support such a principle both to enhance consistency and because of its value as a principle which promotes efficiency in contractual relationships.

---

[76]   See Chap. 3 section 2E(ii).
[77]   Although the drafters of the Directive certainly are right when they state in the Preamble that it 'in certain cases... may be desirable to prohibit misleading advertising even before it is published' (recital 12), such pre–censorship may be seen as problematic in view of the fundamental principle of freedom of speech. For such constitutional reasons Finland has not implemented this detail of the Directive.
[78]   See Chap. 7 section 2C.
[79]   See Chap. 3 section 3.

4. COMPARATIVE ADVERTISING

A. Introduction

Comparative advertising means advertising in which the offer of the advertiser in some respect and in some way is compared[80] to one or more other offers on the market. Such advertising may form an important marketing strategy of a business. In some countries this type of advertising may be one of the principal forms of marketing.[81]

Within the EU comparative advertising plays different roles in Member States, because of great variations in the background legislation. In some countries, like Germany, Italy, Belgium and Luxembourg, comparative advertising is, as a main rule, forbidden. Other countries, however, consider comparative advertising to be acceptable or even useful, and may have various rules on the standards such advertising ought to fulfil.[82] Some countries, like the Nordic states, impose very strict truthfulness and relevance criteria, while in others, like the United Kingdom, courts are reluctant to interfere.[83] It is obvious that such diversity must be inimical to the functioning of the internal market.

The question has therefore even been raised whether the case of comparative advertising is a situation where negative harmonisation rules should apply. One could claim that the principles of the above–mentioned *GB–INNO–case* would imply that countries which forbid comparative advertising could not enforce this prohibition as it is contrary to art. 30.[84] There are, however, in legal writings attempts to distinguish these two situations.[85] Anyway, after *Keck* it seems very unlikely that the ECJ would interfere in such advertising rules. If one wants a harmonisation of the rules on comparative advertising positive legislative measures seem to be the only device.

---

80 The Common Position mentioned below uses the rather wide wording 'any advertising which explicitly or by implication identifies a competitor or goods or services offered by a competitor' (art. 2(2)(a)). This definition in earlier proposals was criticised as being too wide by Schricker, *op. cit.*, at 353.

81 It has been claimed that comparative advertising would amount to as much as half of all advertising in the US, see Schmitz, *op. cit.*, at 403.

82 On the situation in the various Member States see the proposal COM(91) 147 at 13–19 and Th. Bourgoignie, 'Comparative Advertising and the Protection of Consumer Interests in Europe: Reconcile the Irreconcilable?' [1992] *E.Consum.L.J.* 3 at 4–8.

83 See R. G. Lawson 'Comparative Advertising: The Present Position and EEC Proposals' (1991) *Business Law Review* 213.

84 A hint in this direction is given in COM(91) 147 at 7.

85 See Bourgoignie, *op. cit.*, at 14–15.

Such measures have in fact been in preparation for a long time. Already the 1978 proposal for a directive concerning misleading and unfair advertising contained a provision on comparative advertising.[86] As mentioned above this was later dropped from the Misleading Advertising Directive, though the Preamble did promise legislation on this item 'at a second stage... as far as necessary' (recital 6). A new Commission proposal, aiming at an amendment of the Misleading Advertising Directive with rules on comparative advertising, was published in 1991.[87] After the usual stages in the preparation of a new directive[88] the Council in March 1996 adopted the Common Position.[89]

The Commission gives three main reasons for why the rules on comparative advertising should be harmonised. First, there is, of course, the internal market argument: comparative advertising is an important marketing tool and differing rules can complicate the marketing process and the free movement of goods. Second, benefits for the consumers are also expected, as comparative advertising can be useful as a source of information for the consumer. Finally, comparative advertising is seen as a means of stimulating competition.[90]

The aims of the proposed Directive are therefore twofold. Most important is the objective of removing the national prohibitions of comparative advertising and allowing such advertising throughout the Union. In addition it strives to harmonise the standards for such advertising.

The proposed Directive differs from many other directives in the consumer area as its main aim is not to restrict, but to allow certain advertising. In the background to this one again meets the Community law emphasis on information. As just mentioned the Commission has stressed that comparative information is useful and 'can facilitate a rational choice in the market place'.[91] Seen from this point of view it is not surprising that comparative advertising – among all the various forms of marketing – has been chosen for special attention by Community law. The choice seems to fit very well in the information paradigm prevailing in Community consumer law. That is of course only if one really believes that accurate and impartial information can be given through advertising. The proposal for allowing comparative advertising may be criticised – and has in fact been so criticised

---

86   OJ 1978 C 70/4, art. 4.
87   OJ 1991 C 180/1.
88   The amended Commission proposal was published in COM(94) 151.
89   OJ 1996 C 219/14.
90   COM(91) 147 at 6–9.
91   COM(91) 147 at 8.

for only creating confusion between advertising, which will always be incomplete and biased to some extent, and information.[92]

Obviously the aim of removing prohibitions on comparative advertising cannot be achieved by a minimum directive. Therefore the minimum directive clause found in art. 7 of the Misleading Advertising Directive cannot be applied to comparative advertising. Such advertising will be allowed 'under identical conditions in all Member States'.[93] The exact consequences of this solution may, however, be somewhat uncertain, as comparative advertising certainly is affected also by general rules on unfair marketing which are not harmonised in the Community. According to the Common Position the minimum directive clause shall not apply to comparative advertising 'as far as the comparison is concerned' (art. 7(2)). Where is the line to be drawn between rules which merely *affect* comparative advertising – which, at least to some extent, can have a national content – and rules *on* the comparison which have to follow the Directive?

B. Requirements on Comparative Advertising

As the Directive is not approved yet, only an overview of the solutions accepted in the Common Position will be given in this context. The specific details cannot be commented upon at this stage.

The basic idea is, as mentioned above, to amend the Misleading Advertising Directive by introducing rules on comparative advertising. The part of the Misleading Advertising Directive concerning control and sanctions would therefore apply to comparative advertising.

The new provisions of the Directive would also fix the requirements which should be imposed on comparative advertising. In these one can clearly recognise the fact that the rules are based on ideas both of consumer protection and fair competition. From the point of view of consumer protection the following requirements seem especially important:

– The advertisement should not be misleading. Here a reference is made to the general provisions of the Misleading Advertising Directive. However, in practice one should in this area perhaps employ even more stringent criteria than usual, when assessing whether an advertisement is misleading. As comparative advertising, at least in some Member States, is looked upon with suspicion, one should not accept any ambiguity or possibility of misinterpretation to the detriment of the competitor of such advertisements.

---

[92] Bourgoignie, *op. cit.*, at 16–17.
[93] COM(91) 147 at 13.

- The goods or services which are compared should be comparable, that is they should meet the same needs or be intended for the same purpose.
- The comparison should concern material, relevant, verifiable[94] and representative features of the competing offer.
- The comparative advertising should not create confusion in the marketplace.

Some requirements again seem more clearly connected with the purpose of safeguarding fair competition in the market. Into this category would fall the provisions according to which comparative advertising should not discredit or denigrate the competitor or unfairly capitalise on his reputation.

5.   PRICE INFORMATION

A.   Introduction

From the point of view of an information and transparency strategy of consumer protection, it is most important that consumers receive correct and sufficient information concerning the price of products. Prices should be given in a form which makes it easy to compare the offers of various producers. This is the basic idea of the two directives on price indications and their amendments. The need for such rules was acknowledged already in the Preliminary Programme for a consumer protection and information policy of 1975.[95]

In the same way as happened with the regulation of misleading advertising the Community legislator first focused on the food sector when regulating price indications. In 1979 the Council Directive 79/581/EEC on consumer protection in the indication of the prices of foodstuffs was adopted.[96] The Directive contains provisions on the indication of the selling price and the price per unit of measurement of foodstuffs which are to be supplied to the final consumer (art. 1). The obligations always to show the price and, more specifically, to indicate the unit price of certain products are the central elements of the Directive; the latter obligation does not, however, extend to certain foodstuffs pre-packaged in pre-established quantities (art.

---

[94]   This seems to imply a somewhat stricter rule on the burden of proof than concerning misleading advertising in general, see above section 3C.

[95]   OJ 1975 C 92/1, item 35.

[96]   OJ 1979 L 158/19 (hereafter the Foodstuffs Price Indication Directive).

8). In its amended version[97] the Directive is on many points more or less identical with the subsequent Non–Food Price Indication Directive.

The Council Directive 88/314/EEC on consumer protection in the indication of the prices of non–food products was adopted in 1988.[98] This Directive also made mandatory price indication as well as the introduction of mandatory unit pricing for a variety of products the central issues. However, also here there were important exceptions to the latter obligation, concerning products which were sold in certain ranges of nominal quantities (art. 8).

The efficiency of the adopted information and transparency strategy is underlined in the preamble of the Directive. It states that 'indication of the selling price and the unit price of non–food products makes it easier for consumers to compare prices at places of sale... it accordingly increases market transparency and ensures greater protection for consumers' (recital 4).

The system introduced by the Foodstuffs Price Indication Directive and the Non–Food Price Indication Directive proved to be too complicated. The main problems with these Directives were connected with the large number of compulsory or optional exceptions to the obligation of unit pricing in the Directives, relating to predetermined ranges of products. The Directives were based on the idea that standardised Community ranges of quantities could function as an alternative to unit pricing. This complicated structure led to a relatively poor effectiveness of the price indication directives. As the Commission stated in 1995, 'price information availability is still not satisfactory'.[99]

This was due, among other things, to the fact that Member States had taken advantage of the long transition period of seven years for implementing the Directives in relation to pre–packaged products in pre–established quantities (art. 10 of both Directives). In 1995, again, when the transition period was expiring the idea that standardised ranges could be used as an alternative to unit pricing according to the Commission was 'no longer tenable, because of the profound changes which have taken place in the meantime both in production methods and in distribution channels, and because making such a connection would constitute an unreasonable brake on innovation'.[100] Therefore, as several countries indicated difficulties in implementing the Directives the period of implementation was eventually extended by two years.[101]

---

[97]   The Directive was amended in 1988 (OJ 1988 L 142/23) in connection with the adoption of the Non–Food Price Indication Directive.

[98]   OJ 1988 L 142/19 (hereafter the Non–Food Price Indication Directive).

[99]   COM(95) 276 at 4.

[100]   *Ibid.*

[101]   OJ 1995 L 299/11.

Meanwhile the Commission has drafted a proposal for a new directive on consumer protection in the indication of the prices of products offered to consumers.[102] This directive would have a general scope and replace both the Foodstuffs Price Indication Directive and the Non–Food Price Indication Directive. The proposed directive is intended to simplify existing law and emphasise consumers' right to information, by severing the link between consumer information and standardisation of packages. The aim is to have a homogeneous level of price information in the consumer area.[103] The need for a general obligation to indicate both the selling and the unit price is also emphasised in the context of the Economic and Monetary Union; price transparency is said to be a priority in the run–up to this Union.[104]

The proposed general system of unit pricing has led to considerable concern among businesses.[105] However, the drafting of the directive has continued and the adoption procedures have already reached their final stages. In April 1996 the Council reached a political agreement on a common position on the directive.[106] After the Parliament adopted its resolution on the proposal, the Commission adopted an amended proposal in June 1996.[107] The Common Position of the Council was adopted in September 1996.[108]

As it therefore seems that the existing Directives will in many countries never be implemented in full – this is very likely to be the case, even if the proposed directive will not enter into force before the expiry of the prolonged implementation period – and eventually will be repealed, only an overview of the Non–Food Price Indication Directive (the Foodstuffs Price Indication Directive being outside the scope of the book) will be given. On the other hand, as the final fate and details of the proposed new directive are also not clear, it shall also be described very briefly. The Directive and the amended proposal (the Common Position) will be discussed together in the following.

In this context one may finally mention that certain specific rules on price information may be required in the transition to a Monetary Union. It is still being discussed as to whether legislation on mandatory dual pricing is needed in this phase.[109]

---

102   COM(95) 276.

103   COM(95) 276 at 10.

104   COM(95) 276 (recital 111).

105   A. Davis [1995] *Consum.L.J.* CS 43.

106   PRES/96/100, 23 April 1996; [1996] *Consum.L.J.* CS37.

107   COM(96) 264, OJ 1996 C 249/2.

108   OJ 1996 C 333/7.

109   See *Green Paper on the Practical Arrangements for the Introduction of the Single Currency*, COM(95) 333 at 52.

B. Scope

The Non–Food Price Indication Directive (as well as of course the Foodstuffs Price Indication Directive) concerns only 'products'. The same limitation is also to be found in the proposed new directive. This is, in other words, again one example of the preoccupation of Community consumer law with the regulation of products. No general rules on price indications on services exist or are proposed in the Community.

The price indication measures are also limited to the consumer area. The Non–Food Price Indication Directive relates to 'products offered to the final consumer' and expressly excludes 'products bought for the purpose of a trade or commercial activity' as well as 'private sales' (art. 1). There is no doubt that a similar delimitation will be included in the forthcoming directive.[110] The dominating paradigm of consumer law, focusing only on relations between businesses and individual consumers, is clearly reflected in the rules on price indications.

C. Mandatory Price Indications

The price indications directives make price indications on products in the retail sector mandatory. The obligation covers indication of the selling price, that is the price for a given quantity of the product, as well as the unit price, which means the price for one kilogram, one litre, one metre or one square metre (but not the imperial measures in the United Kingdom) of the product.[111] According to the Non–Food Price Indication Directive the obligation to indicate the selling price is general, covering all products within the scope of the Directive, whereas unit pricing is required only in certain

---

[110] In the Common Position the scope is designated by the words 'offered by traders to consumers' (art. 1). The latter concept (then referring to 'final consumers') is in the 1995 explanatory memorandum defined as 'a natural person who is not purchasing in the course of business', COM(95) 276 at 12.

[111] These definitions are taken from the Non–Food Price Indication Directive (art. 2). According to art. 6 Member States may allow the unit price to be expressed also in relation to decimal multiples or fractions of the mentioned units. In the proposed new directive the rule speaks about 'a single unit of quantity which is different from those referred to in Article 2(b), taking into account the nature of the product and the quantities in which it is customarily sold in the Member State concerned'.: OJ 1996 C 333/9, art. 6.

situations (art. 3). The proposed new directive[112] widens the scope of mandatory unit pricing, making it a main rule subject to certain exceptions.

The price indications need not necessarily be fixed to the products themselves. According to art. 4 of the Non–Food Price Indication Directive each Member State may lay down the specific rules for such indication of prices, for example, by means of posters, labels on shelves or on packaging. A similar rule, obligating the Member States to lay down the detailed rules for indicating prices,[113] is included in the proposed new directive (art. 5).

There are also some rules on the clearness and transparency of price indications which are closely related to, though obviously more strict than the general rule forbidding misleading advertising. According to the Non–Food Price Indication Directive the selling price and the unit price must be unambiguous, easily identifiable and clearly legible (art. 4). This provision is also included in the proposed new directive (art. 4).

As already mentioned, the obligation to indicate the unit price is perhaps the most central element, but also the most difficult to implement in the price indication legislation. This obligation covers a narrower area in the existing Directives than in the proposed one. The Non–Food Price Indication Directive prescribes such an obligation for certain products pre–packaged in pre–established quantities, products pre–packaged in variable quantities as well as products sold in bulk (art. 3). This obligation, however, is in addition narrowed down by certain exceptions, the most problematic referring to certain products which are sold in ranges of nominal quantities (art. 8). The Member States are also given the possibility to make exceptions for cases where unit price indication would be meaningless (art. 7) or when it would be excessively burdensome or impracticable for certain small retail businesses (art. 11).

The proposed new directive purports to broaden the obligation to indicate unit price to a general rule for all products (art. 3) and get rid of the idea that standardisation of packages could be an alternative to unit pricing. This change is, among other things, justified by reference to the fact that because of modern computer technology indication of unit prices does not impose significant costs on businesses which in any event have to indicate the selling prices.[114] The obligation to indicate unit prices would not, however, be completely without exceptions. Member States would have the possibility of waiving the obligation for products concerning which unit price

---

[112] The proposed directive is below described in the version of the 1996 Common Position: OJ 1996 C 333/7.

[113] The explanatory memorandum specifically mentions that Member States 'may specify the cases in which it is necessary to label the price of each product individually and those in which it is enough to put a price label on the shelf', COM(95) 276 at 12.

[114] COM(95) 276 at 9.

indication would not be significant because of the product's nature or purpose or would be liable to create confusion (art. 7). A special rule exempting certain small retail businesses is also retained (art. 8). This question, concerning the obligations of small retail shops, seems in the final stages of preparation to have been the most controversial issue of the directive and the Commission will be asked to report on the application of this exemption (art. 13).

6.   TV ADVERTISING

A.   Introduction

In addition to the general rules on advertising and marketing described above there are also EC rules on advertising in a specific medium, television. These sectorial rules cover a much wider range of questions than the rather specifically focused provisions which apply to advertising in all media. In the TV area there is a more complete set of provisions on advertising.

The preparation of the TV advertising rules have not primarily been a consumer protection project. The provisions on advertising are part of a larger set of rules purporting to give a general legislative basis for transfrontier television activities. It is natural that the Community has shown great interest in these questions, since the technique of transfrontier broadcasting has become more advanced. It is obvious that the facilitation of transfrontier broadcasting must be an important objective for institutions which strive at developing Europe into a real Community. With regard to advertising it seems clear that a satellite channel that had to follow all the very different rules prevailing in the Member States could not transmit any advertisements at all.[115]

The work on regulation of transfrontier television was taken up both by the European Community and the Council of Europe. The latter has in March 1989 adopted the European Convention on Transfrontier Television. This Convention contains many rules which strongly resemble those of the TV Directive. As the Convention is not a part of Community law and the Directive in the Community context is the important piece of legislation, the description here will focus on the provisions of the Directive.

The work on a directive in this area within the Community started by a Green Paper on the establishment of the common market for broadcasting, especially by satellite and cable, called *Television Without Frontiers*, which

---

[115] S. Crosby, 'Advertising on Satellite Television', in S. de B. Bate (ed.), *Television by Satellite – Legal Aspects* (ESC Publishing, 1987) at 53.

was published in 1984.[116] The first proposal for a directive was presented in 1986.[117] In only three years this work led to results. The Council Directive 89/552/EEC on the co–ordination of certain provisions laid down by law, regulation or administrative action in Member States concerning the pursuit of television broadcasting activities was adopted in 1989.[118] The provisions on television advertising and sponsorship are contained in Chapter IV of this Directive. These provisions are of three kinds. There are rules, first, on the recognisability of advertising and sponsoring (arts 10 and 17), second, on the content of advertising (arts 12–16), and third, on the placing and amount of advertisements (arts 11 and 18).

The comprehensive character of the TV Directive is reflected in its goals. Its primary objectives are expressed in the preamble according to which 'broadcasts transmitted across frontiers... are one of the ways of pursuing the objectives of the Community'; therefore 'measures should be adopted to permit and ensure the transition from national markets to a common programme production and distribution market and to establish conditions of fair competition without prejudice to the public interest role to be discharged by the television broadcasting services' (recital 3). Only as one minor objective is consumer protection mentioned in the preamble: 'in order to ensure that the interests of consumers as television viewers are fully and properly protected, it is essential for television advertising to be subject to a certain number of minimum rules and standards' (recital 27).

A revision of the rules in this area is underway. In the TV Directive itself there is a provision requiring Commission monitoring of the application of the Directive (art. 26). In 1995 the Commission presented a report on the application of the TV Directive, in combination with a proposal for a directive to amend it.[119] Some of the proposed amendments concerned other parts of the Directive than those dealing with advertising. The amendments proposed in the chapter on advertising mostly relate to the growing phenomenon of so called home shopping and make it clear that home shopping should not be subject to the restrictions concerning the maximum amount of advertising permitted by the Directive.[120] The proposal purported to facilitate such activity. The Commission emphasised that home shopping 'should be encouraged as it is highly valued by consumers'.[121] Recently the Commission has published an amended proposal. The Common Position was

---

[116]   COM(84) 300.

[117]   COM(86) 146, OJ 1986 C 179/4.

[118]   OJ 1989 L 298/23 (hereafter the TV Directive).

[119]   COM(95) 86.

[120]   See COM(95) 86, at 40–42. Such home shopping is also covered by the draft directive on distant selling, see, Chap. 5 section 3.

[121]   COM(95) 86 at 23.

adopted by the Council in July 1996; this version, *inter alia*, makes clear that the advertising rules apply to teleshopping; forbids teleshopping for medicinal products subject to marketing authorisation (art. 14(2); prescribes that teleshopping shall not exhort minors to contract (art. 16(2)); forbids sponsorships by tobacco undertakings (art. 17(2)); and provides special rules on windows devoted to teleshopping broadcasts by a channel not exclusively devoted to teleshopping (art. 18a) as well as for channels exclusively devoted to teleshopping (art. 19).[122]

There also seems to be some uncertainty about the scope of the Directive which is likely to become important as the methods for marketing develop. It is not settled whether the rules of the TV Directive are applicable to advertising on the Internet and other computer advertising.[123] As there are also some important cases concerning TV advertising pending in the ECJ there is a considerable amount of uncertainty in the area at the moment. In the following the focus will be on the relevant provisions of the TV Directive in its present form.

B. Host and Home Country Control

The harmonisation of the rules on TV advertising effected by the TV Directive is not complete, but only partial. Only certain questions are regulated in the Directive and for unregulated questions it is obvious that Member State law still has a role to play. This certainly goes for general Member State advertising rules applicable to advertising in all kinds of media, but there is also room for national provisions specifically focused on TV advertising. In the *Leclerc–Siplec* case a French decree prohibiting the distribution sector to advertise on television was considered not to be contrary to the TV Directive.[124]

In fact the TV Directive is a minimum directive, as the Member States are free to require television broadcasters under their jurisdiction to lay down more detailed or stricter rules in the areas covered by the Directive (art. 3(1)).[125] This minimum character is, expressly in connection to advertising, reaffirmed by the preamble, according to which 'the Member States must maintain the right to set more detailed or stricter rules and in certain

---

[122] OJ 1996 264/52.

[123] A. Vahrenwald, 'The Advertising Law of the European Union' (1996) 18 *E.I.P.R.* 279 at 285.

[124] *Société d'Importation Édouard Leclerc–Siplec v TF1 Publicité SA and M6 Publicité SA*, Case 412/93 [1995] ECR I–179.

[125] See also art. 19 expressly accepting stricter rules for programming time of advertising.

circumstances to lay down different conditions for television broadcasters under their jurisdiction' (recital 27). This freedom of the Member States is not restricted to any significant extent by the general provisions of the Treaty of Rome.[126] The relevant provisions on the freedom to provide services in arts 59 and 60 – TV broadcasting has in the *Debauve* case been classified as falling under the rules of the Treaty relating to services – have not been considered to preclude national rules prohibiting the transmission of advertisements by cable television if those rules are applied without discrimination.[127]

As therefore the rules on TV advertising may vary considerably between the Member States and as, in addition, the efficiency of enforcement also may show considerable variations, it is – in transnational advertising within the European Union – a rather important question from the point of view of the advertiser under which system of rules he has to work and which enforcement agency has the power to control his advertisements. Although these two questions are in principle separate, they are, in practice, tied together; each enforcement agency enforces the rules of its own country.[128] Therefore it usually suffices to distinguish two types of supervision and control. On the one hand supervision of transnational advertising can be effected by the enforcement agency in the transmitting state, applying its rules (home country control), or, on the other hand, it may be subject to the authorities and rules of the receiving state (host country control). The question to be put here is therefore: is advertising under the TV Directive subject to home country or host country control or both?

The Directive has adopted the principle of home country control (art. 2).[129] It is therefore clear that advertisements in, say, TV satellite channels are subject to control by the authorities and rules in the country from which the broadcast is sent. Furthermore, as the Directive in art. 2(2) prescribes that Member States as a rule shall ensure freedom of reception and shall not restrict retransmission on their territory of television broadcasts from other Member States, it seems as if host country control would be excluded. The advertisers could enjoy being controlled by just one authority and one set of rules.

However, this conclusion is not unquestionable. In cases where the home country control is considerably more lenient than the host country control,

---

126   M. Pullen, 'TV Advertising within the EU and EEA' (1996) 7 *Ent.L.R.* 35 at 38–39 seems to argue for a more strict application of the Treaty in this respect.

127   *Procureur du Roi v Marc J.V.C. Debauve and Others*, Case 52/79 [1980] ECR 833.

128   See also art. 2(1) of the TV Directive.

129   The home country control of the Member State concerns all broadcasters 'under its jurisdiction'. On the interpretation of this rule, see *Commission v United Kingdom*, Case C–222/94, judgment of 10 September 1996, not yet published.

the principle of the TV Directive is problematic from a consumer point of view. The principle even invites attempts to circumvent strict national advertising rules, by the use of channels transmitting from other countries. Therefore, one may ask whether, in addition to the home country control prescribed by the Directive, there still is room for some host country control in the interest of the consumers. In fact, as will be described below, this question has recently been put to both the ECJ and the EFTA Court.

There are several arguments which can be relied on in favour of allowing a certain host country control by the authorities in the receiving country. One might argue that the rules on control in the Directive only concern broadcasters, as the aim of the Directive is to facilitate transborder broadcasting.[130] It has not been the purpose to regulate the control of advertisers, and there is no reason to subject TV advertisers to a more lenient control than others such as newspaper advertisers. These reasons point to a general acceptance of a control in the receiving country in relation to the advertiser. In addition one could refer to the argument that circumvention of national law by the help of Community law should be prevented.[131] At least in cases of obvious circumvention host country control should therefore be allowed.

These arguments have not, however, convinced the EFTA Court. In a recent case this Court expressly rejected the arguments just mentioned. This case concerned an action of the Norwegian Consumer Ombudsman against two companies for advertising to children on TV in breach of Norwegian rules. The broadcast was transmitted from the United Kingdom. The Court concluded that the authorities of the receiving state were not allowed to interfere against advertising sent from other Member States, except in the very rare cases explicitly mentioned in art. 2(2) of the TV Directive. As a main rule host country control was excluded. The Court expressly speaks about 'the transmitting State principle' of the Directive.[132]

However, there is a loophole in this conclusion. In its discussion of the relationship between the TV Directive and the Misleading Advertising Directive, the EFTA Court notes that the TV Directive is not intended to prevent a receiving state from prohibiting misleading advertising under the latter Directive; according to the Court the receiving state might even be

---

130 In addition, if the aim would have been a harmonisation of consumer law the Directive should have been adopted on the basis of art. 100a of the Treaty of Rome, instead of the chosen arts 57(2) and 66, see the written observations by the Finnish Government to the EFTA Court of Justice in Case E–5/94 at 4.

131 This argument was mentioned in *J. Knoors v Secretary of State for Economic Affairs*, Case 115/78 [1979] ECR 399 at 410.

132 *Forbrukerombudet v Mattel Scandinavia A/S and Lego Norge A/S*, Cases E–8/94 and E–9/94 [1996] 1 CMLR 313.

better placed to assess whether an advertisement is likely to mislead its receivers.[133] In other words, host country control is back, through this backdoor. This is of course to be welcomed from the consumer point of view. However, as the Misleading Advertising Directive is a minimum directive, it is at the moment rather hard to judge how far this acceptance of host country control reaches.[134]

One may expect the situation to become clearer in the near future, as there are three Swedish cases on this question pending at the ECJ at the moment.[135] The question has also been taken up during the work on amendments of the TV Directive. The European Consumer Law Group has proposed, in a letter to the Commission, a new article to be included in the Directive according to which the host country could take measures against advertisers concerning advertising originating from other Member States, if this is required in the interest of the general good.[136] There is, in other words, some pressure towards clearer and larger possibilities of host country control. Whether this pressure will lead to any result is hard to predict.

C.   Unfair Advertising

There are a number of substantive rules on advertising in the TV Directive which would come under the heading of unfair advertising, in Nordic terminology. Most of these rules are of the kind that could apply as naturally to advertising through other media than television. One could therefore look at the rules on advertising in the TV Directive as a germ to a set of minimum Community principles on unfair advertising.

The effects of advertising are somewhat restricted by the fact that consumers to some extent feel sceptical or defensive against claims made in advertising. From a consumer point of view it is therefore of utmost

---

133   *Ibid.*, at 330.

134   See also criticism by Pullen, *op. cit.*, at 38.

135   *Konsumentombudsmannen v De Agostini (Svenska) Förlag Ab*, Case C–34/95 and *Konsumentombudsmannen v TV–Shop i Sverige AB*, Case C–35/95 and C–36/95. Advocate General Jacobs delivered his opinion in these cases on 17 September 1996. He reaches the same result as the EFTA Court in excluding host country control, but goes further in not even approving the 'loophole' concerning misleading advertising: the TV Directive 'prevents a Member State from taking action against television advertisements broadcast from another Member State which are directed at children or which are allegedly misleading within the meaning of the Misleading Advertising Directive' (para. 87).

136   For discussion of this principle in the context of the financial services directives, see Chap. 6 section 1B.

importance that advertising can be identified as such. This question is dealt with in the International Code of Advertising Practice adopted by the International Chamber of Commerce (the ICC Code) which prescribes that an advertisement shall be clearly distinguishable as such (art. 11). The advertising provisions of the TV Directive start with a rule on the recognisability of advertising. According to art. 10, television advertising shall be readily recognisable as such and kept quite separate from other parts of the programme service by optical and/or acoustic means. In addition it is prescribed, among other things, that advertising shall not use subliminal techniques, and that surreptitious advertising shall be prohibited.

In this context one should also mention the rules on sponsorship in the Directive (art. 17). It is required that sponsored television programmes, among other things, must be clearly identified as such by the name and/or logo of the sponsor at the beginning and/or the end of programmes[137] and must not encourage the purchase or rental of the products or services of the sponsor, by, for example, special promotional references.

There are also provisions on the allowed content of advertising in the TV Directive. These provisions are especially interesting from the point of view of drawing the boundaries around consumer law.[138] The provisions clearly show that supervision of advertising should not only be interested in protecting the consumers in a limited sense, as actors in the marketplace, but should also take an interest in the effects of advertising on the development of our social values in general.[139] In this, again, the TV Directive follows the ICC Code which has adopted this broader view on the assessment of advertising. The provision on protection of social values in advertising in the TV Directive is to be found in art. 12. According to this provision television advertising shall not prejudice respect for human dignity; include any discrimination on grounds of race, sex or nationality; be offensive to religious or political beliefs; or encourage behaviour prejudicial to the protection of the environment.

For self–evident reasons regulators have often paid special interest to advertising directed to children and young persons. Even the ICC Code contains an art. (13) forbidding advertising which can harm children or

---

[137] According to the Commission's view – of doubtful value with regard to the consumer interest – this does not prevent the mentioning of the name and logo of the sponsor also during the programme, COM(95) 86 at 22.

[138] The wide perspective of the TV Directive may of course be explicable by the fact that it is not a consumer protection directive proper.

[139] In Sweden the Market Court has been reluctant to issue injunctions on this basis, in contrast to Finland where the Market Court has forbidden advertising with violent scenes and advertising which has been deemed unacceptable from the point of view of gender discrimination, see Wilhelmsson (1989), *op. cit.*, at 154–158.

young persons or which exploits their credulity or lack of experience. The TV Directive is in line with these requirements.[140] According to art. 16 television advertising is not allowed to cause moral or physical detriment to minors. It shall therefore comply with the following criteria: it shall not directly exhort minors to buy a product or a service by exploiting their inexperience or credulity; it shall not directly encourage minors to persuade their parents or others to purchase the goods or services being advertised; it shall not exploit the special trust minors place in parents, teachers or other persons; and it shall not unreasonably show minors in dangerous situations.

Even stricter measures against television advertising to children could be thought of. In some countries like Greece and Sweden,[141] as well as Norway, such advertising is prohibited during certain hours of the day or altogether. Sweden has tried to promote such a ban in the preparation of the amendments of the TV Directive, but so far with little success.

Irrespective of which standpoint will be taken in the controversy between home and host country control described above, a certain host country control of advertising to children is allowed. The authorities of the receiving state may interfere if a broadcast seriously and gravely infringes the provision forbidding programmes which seriously impair the physical, mental or moral development of minors (arts 2(2)(a) and 22).

Finally the TV Directive contains special provisions on the advertising of certain products. Television advertising for tobacco products (art. 13) and for medicinal products and medical treatment available only on prescription (art. 14)[142] is forbidden. Advertising for alcoholic beverages is allowed, subject to certain criteria (art. 15).

D.   Placement and Quantity of Advertising

The TV Directive also contains provisions on how often the programmes can be interrupted by advertisements, where the advertisements should be placed in the programme and which programmes should not be interrupted by advertisements (art. 11). As these rules primarily seem to be adopted in order to protect the cultural, religious etc. value of the programmes, they will not be described more closely in this context, although they of course have a

---

140   It may also be mentioned here that the Medicine Advertising Directive forbids advertising of medicinal products directed exclusively or principally at children (art. 5(e)). The same goes for TV advertising of alcoholic beverages (TV Directive art. 15(a)).

141   COM(96) 192 at 26.

142   For medicinal products this principle is extended to all media by the Medicine Advertising Directive, art. 3(1).

consumer aspect as well. At least it is clear that they protect the receiver of the broadcast as a consumer of cultural services, but they of course can have indirect protective effects also in a more limited consumer protection sense.[143]

There are also provisions on the allowed quantity of advertising in the TV Directive (art. 18). According to the main rule the amount of advertising shall not exceed 15% of the daily transmission time. In addition the amount of spot advertising within a given one–hour period shall not exceed 20%.[144]

7. ECO–LABEL SCHEME

The core of consumer law concerns the protection of the direct consumer interests when the consumer is acting in the marketplace. However, consumers may be interested in promoting values other than their own short–term interests when taking decisions connected with consumption. Environmental factors, for instance, have considerable relevance in the decision–making of many consumers.[145] Although having different and partly even contradictory starting–points,[146] consumer law and environmental law may come together to protect and promote such consumer attitudes. Both for environmental law and for consumer law it is important that environmentally interested consumers receive sufficient and correct information to be able to make environmentally sound decisions. From an environmental law perspective the focus is, of course, on the consequences for the environment, while consumer law perhaps looks more at the need to protect the consumer's right to correct information as a goal in itself.

One way to convey messages about environmental–friendliness to consumers is to use various kinds of eco–labels, like the German 'Blue Angel' or the Nordic swan. Such labels of official or semi–official character are in use in some countries and in addition businesses may create their own labels. The multitude of labels with varying criteria, if any, for the award, however, rather tend to confuse than to inform the consumer. Therefore there was felt a need for a uniform Community eco–label scheme.

---

143 For example, the prohibition against interrupting children's programmes shorter than 30 minutes by advertising could be read in connection with the general aim to protect children against advertising.

144 According to the Commission this provision applies to 60–minute periods starting on the hour, COM(95) 86 at 22. This is made clear in the new proposal, art. 18(2).

145 See F. Maniet, 'The Eco–label and Consumer Protection in Europe' [1992] *E.Consum.L.J.* 93.

146 Basically the consumer law perspective often seems to evaluate consumption more positively than the environmental law perspective.

The first proposal for such a scheme was published in 1991.[147] The matter proceeded relatively quickly and the Council Regulation (EEC) No 880/92 on a Community eco–label award scheme (the Eco–Label Regulation) was adopted by the next year.[148] This scheme, however, does not purport legally to replace the various national eco–labels and has not succeeded in removing them from the market.

The main purpose of the Regulation relates to the protection of the environment. Eco–label schemes are usually seen primarily as instruments of environmental rather than consumer protection.[149] This is reflected also in the preamble to the Regulation. First is mentioned the 'objectives and principles of the Community's environment policy', highlighting among other things 'the importance of developing a policy towards clean products' (recital 1). Only thereafter, rather as an instrument for achieving these goals, is mentioned the need to provide consumers and users with guidance, which 'can best be achieved by establishing uniform criteria for the award scheme to apply throughout the Community' (recital 6).

The Eco–Label Regulation establishes a Community eco–label award scheme. The dual intention of this scheme is reflected in art. 1 of the Regulation which sets out the objectives of the scheme. First, the focus is on the impact on the environment: the scheme is intended to promote the design, production, marketing and use of products which have a reduced environmental impact during their entire life cycle. Thereafter, as a purpose of its own, is mentioned the intention to provide consumers with better information on the environmental impact of products.

The Community eco–label – a flower with the European stars and an E – can be awarded to products which meet these objectives and are in conformity with Community health, safety and environmental requirements (art. 4). An important point to underline in this context is the holistic nature of the assessment. It is not enough that the product in some respect is more beneficial for the environment, if it is less beneficial in some other way; the product shall have a reduced environmental impact during its entire life–cycle, covering choice of raw materials, manufacturing, distribution, consumption and disposal after use (art. 3(d)).

This global approach focuses on the ecological impact of the product. If this impact is positive the eco–label may be awarded even where the product is not of best possible quality. This is clearly stated in art. 1 according to which the eco–label scheme is intended to work 'without... compromising product or workers' safety or *significantly* affecting the properties which

---

[147]   COM(91) 37, OJ 1991 C 75/23.

[148]   OJ 1992 L 99/1.

[149]   Maniet, *op. cit.*, at 94.

make a product fit for use.'[150] The inclusion of the word 'significantly' has been criticised, as the consumers are said not to have to accept a decrease in quality for ecological reasons.[151] However, the perception of this problem may be different, depending on whether it is looked at from a consumer or an environmental point of view. From the latter perspective a certain quality decrease – at least if it is necessary – seems an acceptable price to pay for an improved ecological soundness. It should of course be underlined that this decrease cannot normally imply a shorter life–span of the product or a need for a use of larger quantities of the product, as such quality factors have a negative impact on the ecological assessment as well.

The more specific conditions for awarding the label shall be defined by product groups (art. 5). A few such norms have already been adopted.[152] They are still, however, very few.

The Eco–Label Regulation of course contains extensive provisions on the procedure for awarding the label. These administrative rules will not be described here. It should only be mentioned that the decision to award an eco–label to a product mainly is in the hands of the Member States. Each Member State designates a body or bodies which are responsible for taking the first decisions on applications for eco–labels.[153] However, in order to achieve uniformity the competent bodies are obliged to notify all decisions to award an eco–label to the Commission. If the Commission produces reasoned objections to the decision, informal consultations to resolve the issue should take place; if these do not lead to agreement the Commission takes the final decision (art. 10).

At this stage it is too early to make an overall evaluation of the Community eco–label scheme; a relatively pessimistic view seems most realistic at this moment. The scheme has not yet become so widely known and generally accepted that its informational value would be indisputable. It rather seems fairly unknown in many quarters. As the scheme is voluntary it does not remove other labels from the market; one could say that at this stage it even adds to the confusion by introducing yet another label in addition to the existing ones. Of course, if the Community eco–label gained wider

---

[150] Italics added.

[151] Maniet, *op. cit.*, at 101.

[152] As examples one may mention Commission Decisions establishing the ecological criteria for the award of the Community eco–label to washing machines, OJ 1993 L 198/35; to dishwashers, OJ 1993 L 198/38; to soil improvers, OJ 1994 L 364/21; to toilet paper, OJ 1994 L 364/24; to kitchen rolls, OJ 1994 L 364/32.

[153] The freedom of the Member States in this respect is limited by a rather self–evident provision (art. 10(2)) that the composition of these bodies should be 'such as to guarantee their independence and neutrality'. They should also be able to apply the Regulation in a consistent manner.

acceptance, the situation would change; the aim of the Regulation, according to the preamble, is only 'to create the conditions for ultimately establishing an effective single environmental label in the Community' (recital 7).

The present informational deficits are hardly relieved much by the fact that a misleading use of labels is, of course, forbidden. This would follow already from the Misleading Advertising Directive, but is underlined by the Eco–Label Regulation itself. According to art. 16(2) any false or misleading advertising or the use of any label or logo which leads to confusion with the Community eco–label is prohibited. This provision, which as it is contained in a regulation is directly applicable,[154] perhaps can make the assessment of the advertising in this area more strict than might otherwise be the case. For instance, pure confusion is a sufficient ground for prohibition according to the Regulation.

Of course, one may also in a more general perspective question the use of eco–labels altogether. If one assumes that most consumption is to some extent harmful for the environment, such labels only help the consumers to get rid of the bad conscience they should have when consuming too much. Be that as it may be, in any case a symbol cannot be really informative about the environmental impact of certain forms of consumption. The function of an eco–label is therefore 'not to inform but to incite a reflex'.[155]

On the other hand the Eco–Label Regulation has at least some positive symbolic value from the point of view of consumer policy. It expresses a larger approach to consumer issues transgressing the narrow focus on the direct consumer interest in consumption. It is a sign of the idea already put forward in the Preliminary Programme for a consumer protection and information policy, according to which the 'consumer is no longer seen merely as a purchaser and user of goods and services for personal, family or group purposes but also as a person concerned with the various facets of society which may affect him either directly or indirectly as a consumer'.[156] As noted in the introduction the Commission has repeatedly stressed the need for integrating consumer policy and other policies of the Community.[157]

---

[154] The Jack–in–the–box image (see *supra* n. 38) again comes to mind. It is not very easy even for lawyers – at least not for continental ones used to a systematically structured legislation – to find a directly applicable rule on advertising at the end of something which is presented as a voluntary scheme!

[155] Maniet, *op. cit.*, at 98.

[156] OJ 1975 C 92/1, item 3.

[157] See Chap. 1 section 3A.

8. CONCLUSIONS

The rules on advertising in Community law very clearly express the information and transparency paradigm prevailing in Community consumer law. The main aim of the provisions is the safeguarding of the right of the consumer to receive correct information, and in some cases his right to receive sufficient information. The consumer is perceived as a rational actor in the marketplace who is interested in and able to take care of his own interests so long as he is well informed.

The basic level is of course the safeguarding of correct information. False or misleading advertising is forbidden. This requirement of Community consumer law has not added much to the substantive law of the Member States.[158]

Community law has also been interested in creating new possibilities for giving information in advertising. Examples of this are the removal of prohibitions against comparative advertising and the introduction of the Community eco–label scheme. Such measures have been criticised for blurring the line between sales promotion and consumer information.

Finally, the most far–reaching intervention within the information paradigm consists of rules making the giving of certain information mandatory. Such rules are introduced concerning price indication, but, as has been noted, they are to a large degree still not effective. In addition, there are many rules on the mandatory information to be given in labelling, especially concerning foodstuffs. As explained in the introduction these product–specific rules could not be described and analysed in this book. The picture of the EC legislation on mandatory information in advertising and marketing is therefore somewhat distorted. Specific and mandatory labelling requirements form an important part of the consumer information policy of the EC.[159] Rules on certain mandatory information are also contained in the Consumer Credit Directive.[160]

In spite of this, even within the information paradigm the achievements of Community law have been fairly modest. In other respects the results are still more meagre. There are no general Community rules on unfair advertising; the fact that the concept of unfair advertising is very vague and has different contents in various Member States does not make the creation

---

[158] Krämer, *op. cit.*, at 161.

[159] This is not to say that those labelling requirements necessarily give the consumer adequate protection. A shopping list approach, offering a large amount of detailed information to the consumer, may lead to the result that the information becomes hard to use in practice.

[160] See Chap. 6 section 2E–F.

of such rules impossible,[161] as the TV Directive illustrates. This Directive contains more extensive regulation of such questions, and it may of course be regarded as a germ to a more general Community legislation. However, this does not mean that the advertising chapter of the TV Directive is very radical as to its contents. As noted above, most of the rules pertaining to the fairness of advertising have their counterparts in the ICC International Code of Advertising Practice, that is in the self–regulatory principles which business has set for itself.

---

[161] Compare Bernitz, *op. cit.*, at 58 who finds the lack of an unfairness standard in the Misleading Advertising Directive understandable for the reason mentioned in the text.

5   Trade Practices

1.   INTRODUCTION

On the market consumers are confronted with a large variety of methods by which businesses attempt to sell their products and services. Advertising, dealt with in the previous chapter, is just one of the tools available. In this chapter the focus is on other selling methods. Somewhat vaguely the heading 'trade practices' is chosen to denote these methods.

There is no general legislation on various kinds of trade practices in the EC law. No rule fixing, for example, a general standard of reasonableness, comparable to the standards in many of the Member States, is laid down in the EC. This is an area which in general terms is left to national law, as long as one respects certain boundaries which may follow from competition law, such as the provisions on the abuse of dominant position. The restrictions on national law in this area based on the Treaty of Rome are not very severe, especially after *Keck*.[1]

This is not to say that the Community has shown no interest in the matter. In the Preliminary Programme of the European Economic Community for a consumer protection and information policy of 1975 one of the needs emphasised was for the protection of consumers against high–pressure selling methods; one of the priority measures was protection against unfair commercial practices, particularly in the area of premium offers and unsolicited goods and services.[2] Again, the Second Programme of the European Economic Community for a consumer protection and information policy 1981 mentioned the continuation of action against unfair commercial practices.[3]

There was some work undertaken on the regulation of premium sales[4] and on the protection of participants in correspondence courses,[5] but these

---

1   See Chap. 4 section 2. The *Buet* case, analysed below in section 2D, which considers a prohibition on canvassing to violate art. 30 of the Treaty, is probably overruled by *Keck*. See also the *Oesthoek* case, discussed in Chap. 4 section 2.

2   OJ 1975 C 92/1, items 19 and 24.

3   OJ 1981 C 133/1, item 30.

4   See L. Krämer, *EEC Consumer Law*, (Story Scientia, 1986) at 147–148.

5   *Ibid.*, at 150–151. Recently a new study on the subject was published by the Commission. See O Remien, *Distance Education and Economic and Consumer Law in the Single Market*, (Office for Official Publications of the European Communities, 1996). The conclusions concerning Community measures are rather modest.

projects were abandoned. The regulation of premium sales were mentioned as a priority in the Preliminary Programme for a consumer protection and information policy. A Commission ordered study of the issue, which was not published, led to strong criticism against the Commission especially from the United Kingdom and the issue was dropped. The reason for the criticism lay in the fact that premium offers are usually legal in the UK and not more or less strictly regulated as is the case in many continental countries. In this area there are in other words still considerable differences between the Member States. A Community measure could have been useful both from the point of view of harmonising rules which affect the functioning of the internal market[6] and with regard to the consumer interest in countries like the UK. However, this is yet another example of the difficulties connected with introducing sufficiently ambitious Community rules concerning questions where the solutions in the Member States are very different.

Some of the Directives presented in other parts of this work can at least partly be seen as reactions against harsh trade practices of businesses working in the area. A good example is the Timeshare Directive, analysed in Chap. 7. These pieces of EC consumer law will not be dealt with in this context. Here the focus is on some measures regulating special forms of selling where the consumer may easily be confronted with unacceptable pressure, lack of choice etc. The EC legislation presented here concerns doorstep selling and distant selling.

Trade practices, like direct marketing, are affected by data protection legislation as well. One should therefore mention the recent Directive of the European Parliament and of the Council 95/46/EC on the protection of individuals with regard to the processing of personal data and on the free movement of such data.[7] This Directive, among other things, gives the data subject the right (i) to object, on request and free of charge, to the processing of personal data relating to him which the controller anticipates being processed for the purposes of direct marketing, (ii) to be informed before personal data is disclosed for the first time to third parties or used on their behalf for the purposes of direct marketing, and (iii) to be expressly offered the right to object free of charge to such disclosures or uses (art. 14). As the rules on data protection are created mainly for reasons other than consumer protection they will not be analysed further in this context.

---

6   As the *Oesthoek* case shows (above Chap. 4 section 2), there fortunately seems to be little room for negative harmonisation here as well. Although restrictive provisions on premium offers in this case were considered to form an obstacle to trade according to art. 30, they were accepted on the grounds of consumer protection.

7   OJ 1995 L 281/31.

2. DOORSTEP SELLING DIRECTIVE

A. Introduction

Doorstep selling, by which is meant selling at the consumer's home or some other comparable places, is problematic from a consumer point of view in several respects. The problems mainly relate to the possible negative influence of the sales method on the consumer's choice. Various kinds of developed sales techniques may be used to put pressure on the consumer, who may find it hard to reject a seller who has entered his home. The consumer also is not in a position to compare the goods or services sold to other offers available on the market and he has little ability to assess the trader, not even on the basis of his business premises. In some cases he might not have the opportunity to examine a sample of the goods before deciding to buy. All these factors easily tend to produce situations where consumers later regret their decisions to purchase and to some extent might even facilitate the selling of low–quality or useless goods.[8]

For such reasons some Member States had introduced special legislation on doorstep selling. The problem therefore attracted the interest of the Community relatively early: it was thought, as is stated in the preamble to the Doorstep Selling Directive, that 'any disparity between such legislation may directly affect the functioning of the common market' (recital 2). The legislation in the area belongs to the first batch of consumer protection directives issued by the EC. The Doorstep Selling Directive, that is the Council Directive 85/577/EEC to protect the consumer in respect of contracts negotiated away from business premises,[9] was adopted in 1985.

The preparation of the Directive started as far back as the 1970s. Doorstep selling was mentioned in the Preliminary Programme for a consumer protection and information policy of 1975.[10] The first proposal for a directive was published relatively soon thereafter, in 1977.[11] The proposal was originally much wider, covering more questions than the adopted Directive. The process of developing the text after the first proposal was characteristic of the watering–down–effect so typical for the preparation of EC consumer law. The rules requiring a certain form of contract and the use of a certain cancellation form were removed, as well as the detailed rules on the effects of cancellation, and insurance contracts were, after intense

---

[8] Such tendencies are to be seen in empirical research in Finland, see T. Wilhelmsson, *Konsumentskyddet i Finland* (Juristförbundets Förlag, 1989) at 213.

[9] OJ 1985 L 372/31.

[10] OJ 1975 C 92/1, item 24.

[11] OJ 1977 C 22/6.

lobbying from the insurance companies,[12] excluded from the scope of the Directive. These are some of the setbacks experienced from the consumer perspective during the preparation of the Directive.

The Directive as it stands only contains a few substantive provisions, aimed at safeguarding consumer choice. The main purpose of the Directive is to give the consumer a cooling–off period. A seven days period is provided for within which he may cancel the contract. All the substantive articles of the Directive are related to this cooling–off measure. These rules are of course mandatory; the consumer may not waive his rights under the Directive (art. 6).

As the content of the Directive is limited to some questions relating to the cooling–off period, it can obviously not be intended to achieve any far-reaching harmonisation in the area, even though its preamble announces that 'it is... necessary to approximate laws in this field' (recital 2). Even concerning the cooling–off period harmonisation is not necessarily reached. The Directive is a minimum Directive, allowing the Member States to adopt or maintain provisions more favourable to consumers (art. 8).

The Doorstep Selling Directive is often implemented through special legislation. In the United Kingdom it is enforced by a special regulation, The Consumer Protection (Cancellation of Contracts Concluded Away from Business Premises) Regulations 1987.[13] In Germany an Act on Cancelling Doorstep and Similar Sales was enacted a month before the Directive![14] In Finland, where the provisions on doorstep selling were contained in a chapter of the Consumer Protection Act, only a few amendments were necessary.[15]

All Member States did not implement the Directive within the prescribed time. Therefore this Directive has given rise to one of the spectacular cases on direct effect of EC directives. In the *Dori* case the ECJ confirmed that directives do not have so called horizontal direct effect. An Italian consumer could therefore not rely on the Directive against a private firm and cancel a doorstep contract, as Italy had not yet implemented the Directive.[16]

---

12   The arguments for this exclusion were, on the one hand the need to continue prevailing contracting practice through commission paid representatives and on the other hand the claim that the consumer friendly practice of putting the insurance cover in force immediately after the conclusion of the contract could not be continued, see e.g. N. Reich, *Europäisches Verbraucherrecht*, (3rd ed., Nomos, 1996) at 358. These arguments do not seem very convincing.

13   S.I. 1987/2117.

14   Gesetz über den Widerruf von Haustürgeschäften und ähnlichen Geschäften 22.1.1986, BGBl. I S. 122. It was, of course, intended to satisfy the demands of the Directive.

15   Act 84/1993.

16   It was later implemented by Decreto Legislativo No 50 of 15 January 1992.

However, the Court tried to comfort the consumer by noting her right to compensation, according to the *Francovich* principle, from the Member State for damages because of non–implementation of a directive.[17] Of course this seems like a rather theoretical comfort. Ms Faccini Dori has to be a very principled person in order to bother to start a new procedure against the Italian state for the value of a correspondence course she bought in 1989.

B. Scope

The paradigmatic example of a doorstep contract is, naturally, a contract concluded in the home of the consumer. The term used for this type of selling in many languages clearly shows this.[18] However, the scope of the Directive is not limited to this situation alone. It covers a broader area, which is defined by art. 1 of the Directive. According to that article the Directive applies to the following two types of situation (here presented not in the order of the Directive, but starting from the more typical situation).

First, the Directive covers contracts concluded – and offers made by the consumer – during a visit by a trader to the consumer's home, to the home of another consumer[19] or to the consumer's place of work. It in other words typically focuses on situations where the consumer is caught in his own milieu, and therefore probably is more susceptible to manipulation than in other places. The Directive does not expressly extend to all selling outside usual business premises, although it does not as a minimum directive prevent such a wider approach. The statement in recital 4 of the preamble that 'this surprise element generally exists not only in contracts made at the doorstep but also in other forms of contract concluded by the trader away from his business premises' does not therefore seem to be clearly reflected in the text of the Directive.[20] A surprise sales contact entered into, for example, in the street does not seem to fall within the scope of the Directive. It is interesting to note, however, that the famous *Dori* case where the direct effect of the Directive was discussed concerned a contract made at Milan Central Railway Station, away from the business premises of the seller.[21] Probably

---

[17] *Paola Faccini Dori v Recreb Srl*, Case C–91/92 [1994] ECR I–3325.

[18] See, for example the German term Haustürgeschäft and the Swedish term hemförsäljning (home selling).

[19] This covers so called home party selling, for which the Tupperware brand first became known.

[20] The words 'under conditions similar to these described in paragraph 1 or paragraph 2' in arts 1(3) and (4) could perhaps be given such a wide interpretation. This does not, however, seem to reflect the function of those paragraphs in their context.

[21] [1994] ECR I–3325 at 3350.

one should not, however, draw any conclusions concerning the scope of the Directive from this case, as this problem was not touched upon in the question which the Italian court referred to the ECJ for a preliminary ruling.

The surprise element and the initiative of the trader are the features which make selling in the homes and workplaces problematic from a consumer's point of view. Therefore it is natural that the Directive covers only such visits by the trader which do not take place at the express request of the consumer.[22] However, even in a case where the consumer requested the visit of the trader, the Directive is applicable under certain conditions, namely if the trader during the visit sells other goods or services than those concerning which the visit was requested.[23]

As the Directive expressly only covers 'visits', offers by telephone are not within its scope, although some Member States include them in their definition of doorstep selling.[24] Telephone selling will, however, be covered by the directive on distant selling, described below.

Second, the Directive also covers certain trips arranged by the trader. The Directive applies if the contract is concluded or the consumer's offer is made during an excursion organised by the trader away from his business premises. Even though the element of surprise here might be lacking and the consumer might even himself have taken the initiative to participate in the trip, such trips are obviously thought to include an element of pressure which justifies the application of the Directive. However, this definition of the scope of the Directive only covers cases where the trader has organised a journey – if he has only invited consumers, for example, to a restaurant, the situation does not fall within the wording of the Directive. It also does not cover excursions taken to the business premises of the trader, to conclude

---

22 As the request should be express, the Directive still covers e.g. a case where the trader has notified the consumer in advance by sending marketing materials indicating he will contact the consumer if this does not especially forbid it, see Finnish Government Bill 218/1992 at 9.

23 For example, if the consumer has requested maintenance of a machine and a new one is installed, the latter contract of sale is not covered by the request, see the Belgian case R.G.8233, No. Rép. 570; [1996] *Consum.L.J.* CS23. Member States may, however, derogate, to a certain extent from this rule by refraining from applying the Directive to contracts for the supply of goods or services having a direct connection with the goods or services concerning which the consumer requested the visit of the trader (art. 3(3)).

24 Like Finland, see Consumer Protection Act 6:1. In Germany the legislation is not completely clear on this point, see P. Ulmer, 'Direktvertrieb und Haustürwiderrufsgesetz – Zivil- und Wettbewerbsrechtliche Probleme' (1986) 32 *Wettbewerb in Recht und Praxis* 445 at 449–450.

contracts there. Excursions to factories and shops ('*Kaffeefahrten*') are therefore not covered.[25]

The Doorstep Selling Directive covers both consumer goods and services.[26] The fact that it is normally not possible to return a service which already has been rendered has not prevented the EC legislator, who has not regulated the consequences of cancellation, to give the Directive such a wide scope. Some types of contracts are, however, expressly excluded from its scope (art. 3). These are most contracts related to immovable property, contracts for the supply of foodstuffs or, in certain cases, other goods intended for current consumption (like newspapers), insurance contracts and contracts for securities. Certain contracts made on the basis of catalogues are also not covered, provided, among other things, that the consumer in these cases is given a contractual right of cancellation. Small purchases, worth less than 60 ECU, may also be excluded by national legislation.

Finally, it should be noted that this Directive is delimited to consumer transactions, using the usual definition of a consumer as a person 'acting for purposes which can be regarded as outside his trade or profession' (art. 2). The well known *Di Pinto* case concerned the application of this definition in the Doorstep Selling Directive.[27] The ECJ decided that this consumer notion should not be extended outside consumers proper and therefore should not be applied to a businessman making an advertising contract to sell his business, although the transaction was not common to him and so could have been said to fall outside his trade or profession.

C. Right of Cancellation

The central rule in the Directive is to be found in art. 5 which regulates the consumer's right of cancellation. This rule is not only of some practical importance for the conduct of doorstep selling business, but it is also of paramount theoretical importance, from the perspective of contract theory. It introduces into EC contract law an institution which for a certain period challenges the traditional doctrine of the immediate binding force of contracts.

The binding force of a doorstep selling contract is, for a certain time, only one-sided. The trader is bound to the contract, but the consumer has the

---

25   On the similar English definition, see G. Howells and S. Weatherill, *Consumer Protection Law*, (Dartmouth, 1995) at 292.

26   The question whether this covers also declarations of suretyship is referred to the ECJ for a preliminary ruling, [1996] *Consum.L.J.* CS40.

27   *Criminal proceedings against Patrice di Pinto*, Case C–361/89 [1991] ECR I–1189; see in more detail, Chap. 1 section 1B.

right to renounce it, thereby becoming released from all his obligations under the contract. The 'cooling–off–period' during which such cancellation may be effected, according to the Directive, has to be at least seven days. It starts to run when the consumer receives from the trader a written notice of his right of cancellation.

This notice is mentioned in art. 4 of the Directive. In order to make the right of cancellation more effective the Directive obliges the traders to give consumers written notice of their right of cancellation. The notice shall be dated, identify the contract and mention the name and address of the person against whom the right may be exercised. The notice shall be given in connection with the conclusion of the contract.[28]

The procedure for using the right of cancellation is left to national law. Obviously, however, the law is expected to accept written notice of cancellation. For such a notice there is an explicit rule in the Directive on the time and transfer risk for sending the notice. For the effect of the right of cancellation it suffices that the notice of cancellation is dispatched to the trader within the cooling–off–period, even if it is received outside this period or, presumably, even if it is never received because it is lost in the post.

The sanctions for non–compliance with the information rule is in only one respect specified by the Directive. As mentioned above the cooling–off–period does not start to run before the notice is given to the consumer. The Directive also – and obviously in addition to the sanction just mentioned – requires the Member States to lay down appropriate consumer protection measures in case the information is not supplied. Various sanctions, like criminal sanctions, injunctions etc. are imaginable. The choice is up to the Member States, as long as the general EC law principle of efficient remedies is taken into account.[29]

D.   Stricter Measures

As noted at the beginning of this section there are in practice several consumer problems connected with doorstep selling. Therefore, in some countries opinions have been expressed according to which doorstep selling as such, at least when it takes places without prior warning or agreement,

---

28   Art. 4 specifies in more detail the moment when the notice should be given in various contracting situations.

29   From this perspective we would venture to suggest that a pure private law sanction, like the complete nullity (unenforceability) of the contract, might not be sufficient. Experience from Finland shows that this does not adequately prevent traders from breaking the information rule, as the buyers do not know about their rights anyway, see Wilhelmsson, *op. cit.*, at 220. Efficiency may require criminal sanctions.

should be considered an unfair trade practice.[30] Legislation forbidding doorstep selling has been introduced in Denmark.[31] Are such stricter measures compatible with Community law?

Looking only at the Doorstep Selling Directive it seems easy to give a positive answer to the question. The Directive is, according to art. 8, a minimum directive, and in the preamble to the Directive prohibitions of doorstep selling are expressly accepted: 'the freedom of Member States to maintain or introduce a total or partial prohibition on the conclusion of contracts away from business premises, inasmuch as they consider this to be in the interest of consumers, must not be affected' (recital 7). However, one also has to take into account the general rules of the Treaty of Rome. From that perspective it does not appear equally clear that all kinds of bans on doorstep selling would be accepted.

The ECJ has made a ruling on this question in the *Buet* case which concerned a French prohibition on canvassing in connection with the sale of educational material.[32] The Court considered this prohibition to form an obstacle to imports in the sense of art. 30, as it deprived the trader concerned from the possibilities of using a method of marketing whereby he realised almost all his sales. However, because of the greater risk of ill-considered purchases in the area in question the prohibition was considered to satisfy the mandatory requirements and was therefore acceptable. The reasons given by the ECJ are astonishingly socially minded given the Court's track record in this area. It stated: 'The potential purchaser often belongs to a category of people who, for one reason or another, are behind with their education and are seeking to catch up. That makes them particularly vulnerable ... '[33]

This case seems to indicate that a total ban on doorstep selling might not be acceptable, as the prohibition must be grounded on more concrete reasons connected with the relevant line of business. However, the situation may have changed after the famous *Keck* decision.[34] The rules on doorstep selling might in the future be treated as such selling arrangements which should not be affected by art. 30. This is, however, by no means certain: one could already mention a more recent case on distant selling where the ECJ found that a prohibition of unsolicited telephone calling, without written permission, to potential customers of investment services constituted a

---

30 See, on the German discussion, Ulmer, *op. cit.*, at 446 *et seq.*

31 See P. B. Madsen, *Markedsret, Bind 2* (2 ed., Jurist– og Ökonomforbundets Forlag, 1993) at 190.

32 *R. Buet and Educational Business Services (EBS) SARL v Ministère public*, Case 382/87 [1989] ECR 1235.

33 *Ibid.*, at 1252.

34 *Criminal proceedings against Bernard Keck and Daniel Mithouard*, Joined Cases C–267/91 and C–268/91 [1993] ECR I–6097.

restriction (although justified in this case) on the freedom to provide services safeguarded in art. 59 of the Treaty.[35] Still, as the case concerned telephone selling from one Member State to another, one should not draw too far-reaching conclusions from it in relation to doorstep selling. The main rule here should be, according to the preamble of the Directive and especially after *Keck*, that national prohibitions of doorstep selling, which simply affect the way goods are sold within national boundaries, are allowed.

E.   Conclusions

The Doorstep Selling Directive only regulates the cooling–off period in doorstep selling. Other problems in relation to this type of trade practice are not dealt with. Even concerning the cooling–off period the Directive mainly limits itself to establishing its existence and length. Most other practical questions, such as the procedure of cancellation (art. 5), the legal effects of cancellation, such as the reimbursement of the price, the return of the goods (art. 7), as well as the consequences of the goods being damaged when in the custody of the consumer, are, without any express reasons, left to national law.[36] Therefore, and as the Directive is a minimum directive, it does not purport to achieve any considerable harmonisation of the law in this area. It just makes one type of consumer protection measure, the right of cancellation, obligatory for the Member States.

One may doubt whether such a measure in practice marks a very important advance in the position of the consumers.[37] Of course it gives the consumer a possibility he would not have without the rules to get acquainted with the product and to rethink the contract. In some cases this measure certainly improves the situation of consumers in a practical way. However, if looked at from a more general perspective the changes may be relatively marginal. In spite of the obligatory cooling–off period one can assume that at least a considerable part of the contracts which consumers would not have made, had they not been under special pressure derived from doorstep

---

35   *Alpine Investments BV v Minister van Financien*, Case C–384/93 [1995] ECR I–1141.

36   The 1977 proposal was somewhat more elaborated in this respect. This proposal contained rules, for example, prescribing an obligatory cancellation form (art. 7), reimbursement of payments and return of the goods at the expense and risk of the trader (art. 8(1)), as well as forbidding the requirement of any payment by the consumer for the use of the goods before cancellation (art. 8(2)), payment of the price before the expiry of the cancellation period (art. 9) and any requirement of payment of compensation for cancellation (art. 11). It also tried to prevent problems following from false statements as to the date of the conclusion of the contract (art. 12).

37   The usefulness of the Directive has been doubted, see L. Krämer, *op. cit.*, at 150.

selling, will remain in force. This may follow from lack of knowledge about the right of cancellation – the information on this right which art. 4 of the Directive requires to be given to the consumers may not be understandable to all consumers. It may also be explained by psychological barriers to cancellation. The consumer can consider a cancellation troublesome, he may dislike the thought of being in a kind of conflict situation with the seller etc. For consumers the length of the cooling–off period, one week, is also relatively short.

The Directive clearly builds on the transparency policy of EC consumer law. It does not affect the content of the contract, but tries to create conditions for market rational behaviour by consumers. From a legal point of view it is, however, radical in the sense that it not only emphasises information before and during contracting, but it in addition seeks to give the consumer some time for rethinking the deal even after it has been made. It thereby makes a theoretically important deviation from the traditional starting points of contract law. As will be noted below, the cooling–off measure has been adopted in certain other directives as well, offering building blocks for discussion of a more general Community law principle of cancellation.[38]

3. DISTANT SELLING[39]

A. Introduction

Distant selling covers a wide range of trading activity. Some forms are fairly traditional, such as mail order catalogues, mail order advertisements in newspapers, personalised direct mailing and door to door distribution of leaflets. These traditional means of distant selling rely on written communication. Increasingly, however, audio–visual techniques have been used to sell at a distance. One particularly prevalent practice in recent times has been telephone selling. This has caused a great deal of concern as it is far more intrusive to receive unwanted telephone calls, which must be answered, than to receive written material which one can choose whether to read or not. More recently the television has been used as a sales medium. Videotext systems allow the customer to view information about products stored in a computer on the television screen and to order using a key pad. Satellite and

---

[38] See Chap. 9 section 2E.

[39] This part of the book is a shortened and rearranged version of G. Howells, 'A Consideration of European Proposals to Regulate Distant Selling' in J. Lonbay (ed.), *Enhancing the Legal Position of the European Consumer*, (BIICL, 1996).

cable television have recently introduced shopping programmes and channels where goods are advertised and consumers phone through their orders.

The rationales for protecting consumers in distant selling contracts are complex. The means of selling at a distance are varied and each technique gives rise to different concerns. Many of them are the same as are expressed in relation to doorstep selling: intrusion of privacy, high pressure selling, impulse buying and lack of knowledge of the product and/or the seller.

These reasons for regulating distant selling all relate to the need to protect consumers. The distant selling industry, however, has an interest of its own in providing adequate consumer protection. Distant selling provides industry with many new avenues to reach potential consumers. It can also be a very cost effective way of doing business, avoiding the expense of High Street showrooms. If the legislative regime is not adequate consumers will not have confidence to use the new methods of trading.

The European Commission also has an interest in promoting confidence in distant selling. In addition to the consumer protection objectives included in the Treaty of European Union, distant selling is a tool by which the market can be integrated. Distant selling allows consumers to purchase anywhere in the Community from the comfort of their own armchair. The development of distant selling, therefore, allows consumers to become active participants in the single market experience. In the context of the single market the need to engender confidence in consumers that they have adequate protection when making contracts with foreign companies is even more apparent than in the domestic context.

Problems in this area attracted the attention of the Community legislature relatively early. In the Second Programme for a consumer protection and information policy a study of 'the use of new data–processing and telecommunications technology' was proposed.[40] In its document to the Council *A New Impetus for Consumer Protection Policy* the Commission specifically commented on the problems of systems, such as videotext which allow orders to be placed from the consumer's home.[41] The matter was also mentioned in the Commission's 1990 action plan[42] which resulted in a draft directive[43] and a Recommendation.[44] An amended draft directive was

---

[40]   OJ 1981 C 133/1, item 33.

[41]   OJ 1986 C 167/1.

[42]   COM(90) 98 at 15.

[43]   OJ 1992 C 156/14; see COM(92) 11.

[44]   Commission Recommendation on codes of practice for the protection of consumers in respect of contracts negotiated at a distance (distance selling), OJ 1992 L 156/21. This recommended trade associations have codes of practice covering dissemination of solicitations for custom; presentation; sales promotion; financial security; the right of withdrawal and knowledge of the code. Regrettably the latest version of the

subsequently issued.[45] A Common Position was finally adopted by the Council on 29 June 1995.[46]

The draft Directive represents a non–excludable minimum level of consumer protection. Art. 14 of the Common Position preserves the right of Member States to introduce or maintain more stringent provisions to ensure a higher level of consumer protection, so long as they are compatible with the Treaty provisions. It is expressly stated that these shall be able to include the prohibition of marketing goods and services by distance contracts; medicinal products are expressly cited as one such category of goods.

B. Scope

The Common Position attempts a definition under which 'distance contract' means any contract concerning goods or services concluded between a supplier and a consumer as a consequence of an organised distance sales or service provision scheme of the supplier, using, for this contract, exclusively one or more means of communication at a distance up to the conclusion of the contract and including the conclusion of the contract itself' (art. 2(1)). In this definition 'means of communication at a distance' are any means used to conclude a contract between a consumer and supplier without the simultaneous physical presence of those parties (art. 2(4)).[47]

Earlier drafts of the Directive had required there be a 'contract solicitation', which was defined as 'any communication at distance, whether public or personalised, including all the necessary elements to enable the recipient to enter directly into a contractual commitment'. Forms of advertising which did not contain all the necessary elements for consumers to enter directly into a contractual relationship were expressly excluded. The intention seemed to be to distinguish situations where consumers could enter directly into a contract following the solicitation, from selling techniques which involved the consumer attending a seminar or other event.[48] The latter selling techniques would also be excluded from the present definition of a

---

Directive, unlike the previous version, does not require Member States to take steps to ensure consumers are informed of the existence and content of these codes of practice.

[45]   See COM(93) 396.

[46]   OJ 1995 C 288/1. The draft Directive is described here as worded in the Common Position. Subsequent amendments have been made by Parliament, see Info–C (1996) VI/1.

[47]   Annex I provides an indicative list of examples of communications at a distance covered by the Directive.

[48]   COM(92) 11 at 17.

distance contract as it requires the means of communication at a distance to be used *exclusively* up to and including the conclusion of the contract itself.

The second draft Directive had also provided that where a contract involves successive acts of performance or a series of separate operations the Directive only applied to the overall contract.[49] Thus, if an order was placed for a set of encyclopaedia to be supplied in parts, the master agreement would have been covered but not the supply of each volume. This exception is not contained in the latest draft, but if the supply is under one contract then the same result would be arrived at.

Art. 3 provides for exemptions from the proposed Directive for contracts concluded by means of automatic vending machines and automatic commercial premises. Contracts concluded with telecommunications operators through the use of public pay–phones are also excluded, to prevent an operator connected call being within the scope of the Directive. Also excluded are contracts for the construction and sale of immovable property and rights therein (other than rental agreements) and contracts concluded at an auction.

The most controversial exclusion is that relating to financial services.[50] A non–exhaustive list of financial services is provided in Annex II. These include investment service, banking services, insurance and reinsurance operations, operations relating to pension funds and services relating to dealings in futures and options. This exclusion creates a serious gap in consumer protection, particularly as financial services are amongst the sectors making most use of distant selling techniques and are certainly areas where consumers traditionally have many complaints. One might expect the number of complaints to increase with the move to less personalised service provision. The Council and Commission propose to review the position, in the light of Article 129a of the Treaty which requires the attainment of a high level of consumer protection, and to suggest specific measures to reinforce consumer protection in particular with regard to insurance, investment services and credit. Ominously, the United Kingdom Government, in response to a similar proposal in an earlier draft, suggested that such a review should only take place at a suitable interval after the directives relating to financial services come into force and if the study shows consumer protection needs strengthening. It was then prepared to accept that appropriate measures should be taken, but what was appropriate should be viewed in the light of the subsidiarity principle, with amendment of the directives being only one possible response. Once again one can foresee the

---

49   COM(93) 396, art. 2.

50   Note Germany, the Netherlands and the United Kingdom had favoured the exclusion of all services.

financial services industries being subjected to soft law, whilst other sectors have to face up to hard law.

There are also certain limited exemptions from the draft Directive (art. 3(2)). Thus contracts for foodstuffs, beverages or other goods intended for current consumption supplied to the home, residence or workplace of consumers by regular roundsmen, e.g. milkmen, are excluded from arts 4–7(2) (i.e. those articles dealing with information and performance requirements and the right of withdrawal). The exclusion from these Articles also applies to contracts for the supply of accommodation, transport, catering and leisure services, where the supplier undertakes, on conclusion of the contract, to provide the services at a specified date or within a specific period. The justifications for this limited exclusion of services with reservation are presumably that it is unfair to impose the risk of withdrawal on suppliers who have already committed themselves on the consumer's behalf and unnecessary to impose information obligations, whilst the rules on performance are obsolete where a date has been fixed.

Additionally there are various specific exclusions from the right of withdrawal which seem sensible to prevent abuse or hardship on the part of the seller (art. 6(3)). These include, unless the parties have agreed otherwise, contracts relating to:

(a) services, where performance has begun with the consumer's agreement within the seven day cancellation period;
(b) goods or services, the price of which is dependent on fluctuations in the financial market which cannot be controlled by the supplier;
(c) goods made to measure or clearly personal or which by reason of their nature cannot be returned or are liable to deteriorate or expire rapidly;
(d) the supply of audio and video recordings, disks and computer software;
(e) the supply of newspapers, periodicals and magazines;
(f) gaming and lottery services.

C. Inertia Selling

Art. 9 of the Common Position requires that Member States take the necessary steps to prohibit the supply of goods or services which have not been ordered beforehand, where such supply involves a demand for payment. They should also exempt the consumer from performance of any consideration in the case of unsolicited supply. The absence of a response from the consumer should not constitute consent.

Earlier drafts had clearly prohibited the supply of goods, not only where purchase was demanded, but also where the consumer was asked to return them, even at no cost. It seems that such cases are intended to be caught by the exemption of the consumer from the performance of any consideration, but this is rather opaque and it is unfortunate that an express provision to this effect has not been retained.

D. Controls on Solicitations

The Common Position states that measures should be taken to ensure that means of communication at a distance can only be used where there is no clear opposition from the consumer (art. 10(2)). This might have been better worded as a prohibition where there is opposition from the consumer; also the adjective 'clear' appears inappropriately restrictive. Any opposition known to the trader should put him on guard that the consumer might not want to be contacted by a particular means of communication. In the explanatory memorandum to its first draft the Commission had noted that five national bodies had met to consider placing schemes like the Mailing Preference Scheme[51] on a Community–wide basis. It would be useful if an obligation was placed on Member States to facilitate the expression by consumers of their opposition to being contacted by distant means of communication.

The Common Position requires prior consent for communication by fax and automatic calling machines (art. 10(1)). The second draft Directive had also required prior consent for communication by electronic mail and telephone. Requiring prior consent for telephone selling would have been a welcome development for many consumers who resent being 'cold called', but would have seriously disrupted the selling practices of many businesses.

E. Information

In good time – a concept which is not specified – prior to the conclusion of any distance contract, the consumer will have to be provided information relating to:

(a)   the identity of the supplier;
(b)   the main characteristics of the goods or services;
(c)   the price of the goods or services, including all taxes;
(d)   delivery costs, where appropriate;
(e)   the arrangements for payment, delivery and performance;
(f)   the right of withdrawal, where appropriate;

---

51   A voluntary scheme operating in the United Kingdom, under which individuals can register if they do not want to receive mailings.

(g) the cost of using the means of communication at a distance, where it is calculated on a basis other than the basic tariff;

(h) the period for which the offer or the price remains valid (art. 4(1)).

Earlier versions of the Directive contained special provisions relating to contract solicitations by television, which included the requirement that the consumer be able to request that the same information be provided in written form if it was not displayed on the screen. The current version of the Directive simply has a general requirement that the information be provided in a clear and comprehensible manner in any way appropriate to the means of communication at a distance used (art. 4(2)). The information must also make clear its commercial purpose and comply with the principles of good faith[52] in commercial transactions and those governing the protection of minors. An earlier version of the Directive had extended this to protect also those who under national law are unable to consent, but under the present version these cases would have to be brought within the general good faith requirement.

Art. 4, above, governs the information which must be provided before the conclusion of the contract. In good time during the performance of the contract and at the latest at the time of delivery, where goods are concerned, most of the same information will have to be confirmed in writing, unless it has already been given to the consumer prior to the conclusion of the contract in writing or in another permanent medium at his disposal (art. 5).

This written confirmation must be accompanied by:

(a) written information on the procedures for exercising the right of withdrawal;[53]

(b) the geographical[54] address of the supplier's place of business to which complaints can be addressed;

(c) information on after–sales service and guarantees; and

(d) conditions of withdrawal from contracts of unspecified duration or for a duration of longer than one year.

The Common Position provides that the use of languages in respect of distant selling contracts is a matter for the competence of the Member States (recital

---

52 The concept 'good faith', rather unfamiliar to common law, has been introduced in the Unfair Contract Terms Directive; see Chap. 3 section 2C(i).

53 This must also be given in respect of contracts for the provision of services, even though the right of withdrawal might be lost if performance begins with the consumer's agreement within the seven day cancellation period.

54 Earlier versions had talked about the 'postal' address. Presumably the change to 'geographical' address is to prevent the use of P.O. Boxes.

8). This perhaps reflects the inability of the Community legislator to resolve the problem of language. Whilst freedom of national governments to impose language requirements may be desirable, at the very least these should contain the rule that as a minimum requirement the information be available in the same language as the solicitation to contract.

Overall the rules on information have been greatly simplified in the latest text. The Common Position could, however, be criticised for failing to specify the consequences if the information provisions are not complied with. Will infringement just result in a regulatory infringement or will there be civil consequences? For some of the obligations it is hard to envisage what the civil consequences could be, but others have interesting possibilities. Thus, if the information does not disclose elements of the price, taxes, delivery costs or the cost of using the means of communication at a distance then these could be made irrecoverable. If the period for which the price is valid is not mentioned then this can be deemed to be open–ended. There is, in fact, a sanction for failing to provide information on the right of withdrawal, as the cancellation period is deferred for up to three months until such information is supplied (art. 6(1)). Leaving the choice of how to ensure the obligation is fulfilled to Member States is likely to lead to an even less harmonised state of regulation than the present unregulated position.

F.   Right of Withdrawal

The motives for allowing a right of withdrawal in the context of distant sales are more complex than in relation to doorstep selling, where the desire is to allow parties a chance for quiet reflection on a contract struck in the heat of the moment. Removing the danger of rash decision–making certainly plays a part in relation to distant selling, especially where the solicitation is by telephone (which may be equated to a personal visit) or an enticing television home shopping feature. This motivation would not explain why the right is extended to mail order sales, for instance, in response to newspaper advertisements or to catalogue sales. Here the policy is far more a desire to give the consumer an opportunity to assure himself of the quality of the goods. Thus, the right of withdrawal can be seen as an extension of the policy of ensuring the consumer makes a fully informed choice. Recital 12 of the Common Position's preamble suggests that the right of withdrawal is indeed motivated by the inability of the consumer to see a product or ascertain a service.

The Common Position provides for a right of withdrawal for any contract negotiated at a distance (art. 6), but there are some exemptions.[55]

---

55   See above, section 3B.

The withdrawal period is seven days. It commences, in the case of products, on receipt of the goods by the consumer, or, in the case of services, from the conclusion of the contract. However, the period only ever begins running once the written confirmation required by art. 5 has been supplied. If this is not supplied then the calculation of the withdrawal period can be deferred for up to three months.

The consequences of withdrawal are not altogether clear. Art. 6(1) provides that the consumer can withdraw from the contract without penalty and without giving any reason. Presumably without penalty means not only that there should be no additional penalty, but also that the consumer should be freed from obligations under the original contract. It might also be possible to construe this as also placing the cost of returning the goods on the trader as otherwise the consumer would be penalised for exercising his right of withdrawal.[56]

Art. 6(2) states that where withdrawal has been affected then sums paid should be reimbursed by the supplier as soon as possible. Where goods were bought on credit then the credit contract will be cancelled when the consumer withdraws from the supply contract if the credit was supplied by the supplier or a third party who had a prior agreement with the supplier (art. 6(4)). Member States are left to determine the detailed rules for the cancellation of credit agreements.

G. Performance

Earlier versions of the draft Directive had provided that, if no time limit was stipulated, performance must begin no later than thirty days after the order is received. There was, however, no way of the consumer knowing for sure when the order was received. This has been improved on in the latest provision, found in art. 7(1) of the Common Position, which allows for a maximum period of thirty days from the day following that on which the consumer forwarded his or her order to the supplier (although it is not clear why it does not simply say thirty–one days from when the consumer forwarded his or her order!). The parties continue to be free to specify another period.

Where a supplier defaults because of the unavailability of goods or services ordered, then the consumer must be informed and be able to obtain a refund as soon as possible in respect of sums paid out (art. 7(2)). Member States are given the option of permitting, under certain conditions, the supplier to supply the consumer with equivalent goods or services, without this being regarded as equivalent to inertia selling (art. 7(3)). In this case the

---

56   See discussion in section 3G below.

cost of returning the goods is said to fall on the supplier. This might cause one to conclude that in other circumstances the consumer must bear the cost of returning goods after exercising the right of withdrawal. However, this would be rather unfair, especially if the reason was that the consumer was disappointed with their quality. It is better to see the costs involved in goods being returned as part of the costs of this form of trading which should be borne by the trader.

H.   Access to Justice

Access to justice has two elements. First, there are questions relating to the burden of proof; second, there is the question of the provision of a forum in which disputes can be heard and the related matter of whom should have the right of standing.

The Common Position seeks to improve the position of a consumer, who under traditional legal rules must prove his case on the balance of probabilities. This is a particular problem in distant selling where the usual written evidence of transactions may be lacking. Thus, the consumer is to be given the right to request cancellation of a payment when a fraudulent use is made of his payment card in distance contracts covered by the Directive (art. 8). The consumer is to be recredited with such sums or else have them returned. Earlier versions had stated that this provision on recrediting was without prejudice to any claim for damages in the event of an operation being disputed improperly. Although no longer expressly stated this is self evidently still the position. Thus, there is in effect a reversal of the burden of proof. In addition Member States may expressly place the burden on the supplier to provide proof that the necessary prior information and written confirmation has been provided, that time limits were complied with and that any necessary consent of the consumer has been obtained (art. 11(3)(a)).

Enforcement of private law rights is problematic. The Common Position requires that Member States ensure adequate and effective means exist to enforce compliance with the Directive in the interests of consumers (earlier versions had also referred to the interests of competitors) (art. 11(1)). In particular, Member States should take the necessary measures to ensure, when they are able to, that suppliers and operators of means of communication cease practices which do not comply with the Directive (art. 11(3)(b)).[57]

---

57   This could usefully also allow action to be taken against trade associations, if, for example, they sponsor codes of practice which are found to breach the Directive.

The Common Position envisages giving a right of action to public bodies or their representatives or consumer organisations, having a legitimate interest under national law in protecting consumers to take action before the courts or before the competent administrative bodies (art. 11(2)). Although not using identical wording this seems to follow the approach of the Misleading Advertising Directive and would only require that consumer organisations be allowed to complain to administrative authorities. It would not require that they have direct access to the courts. This is not therefore likely to give rise to the same debates as to whether consumer organisations should have the right to seek injunctions as surrounds the implementation of art. 7 of the Unfair Contract Terms Directive.[58] The question of cross-border standing of authorities and organisations is dealt with in Chap. 8 section 3.

A great deal of law enforcement in this area is undertaken by self-regulatory bodies. Member States may add recourse to such bodies as a means of ensuring compliance with the Directive (art. 11(4)), but it seems implicit that such recourse should be additional to and not instead of court procedures. This provision is, however, worded rather opaquely.

I. Conclusions

Distant selling provides an opportunity for consumers to be active participants in the Single Market. It offers great opportunities for businesses and consumers, but also many potential pitfalls for consumers. If consumers are to be persuaded to take advantage of the new opportunities they will have to have confidence that this sector of commerce is well regulated. The draft Directive on distant selling provides a starting point for such regulation.

This Directive is strongly connected with the transparency policy of EC consumer law, with important provisions on information and withdrawal. Much of what was said on the Doorstep Selling Directive in this respect holds true also concerning the proposed Directive on distant selling.[59]

Many important questions have also been left unregulated, such as who carries the risk of damage to or destruction of the goods during the cancellation period. The most serious omission seems to be the lack of mandatory protection of pre–payments.[60] There is a very real danger to customers' money in distant sales where money is required as a pre–payment.

---

[58] See Chap. 3 section 2E(ii)

[59] See above, section 2E.

[60] The lack of such protection is also mentioned by H.W. Micklitz, 'Der Vorschlag für eine Richtlinie des Rates über den Verbraucherschutz bei Vertragsabschlüssen im Fernabsatz' (1993) 8 *Verbraucher und Recht* 129 at 138.

The danger may consist of fraud, as there is the possibility that rogues advertise non–existent goods or services, but also there is the risk of insolvency. The risk of the supplier going insolvent is inherent in every transaction requiring a pre–payment, but is exacerbated where consumers do not always have a good knowledge of the nature of the business they are dealing with, as is frequently the case in distant sales.

This important matter was not dealt with in the first draft Directive. Instead the non–binding Recommendation proposed that Codes of Practice should cover arrangements to ensure the reimbursement of payments made by customers at the time of placing an order. The present draft Directive makes no provision at all to protect pre–payments. This is a massive gap in consumer protection. If consumers are to be persuaded to send money abroad they need to be assured that there are safeguards in place to protect their money.

4.   GENERAL CONCLUSIONS

EC regulation of trade practices has tended to concentrate on certain types of selling method which are open to abuse. In the Single Market context the promotion of a well regulated and thriving distant selling industry obviously has great relevance because of its potential to allow consumers to derive concrete benefits from the new freedom to trade and buy across national boundaries.

There is no general fair trading obligation in EC law. Possibly such a concept would be too ambitious to introduce into EC law at present. However it would not be too onerous to set up an information exchange system so that enforcement authorities were required to inform the Commission and thereby other Member States of serious trading malpractices (and this could include matters relating to advertising) affecting consumers in their territory. Authorities in the Member States could then learn from one another's experiences as many (mal)practices are likely to be replicated throughout the Community.[61] The RAPEX system for dangerous products might be cited as a precedent for such a system.

In addition it should be possible for EC law to require that national rules on fair trading apply not only to practices which harm domestic consumers, but also cover practices which harm any of the Community's consumers. National authorities should be given responsibility for protecting the interests

---

61   The value of such information is made clear by the existence of an international forum for the exchange of experiences by enforcement agencies which they have established on their own initiative, see I. Edwards, 'Le réseau international de contrôle des pratiques commerciales' [1993] *R.E.D.C.* 135.

of consumers wherever they reside within the Community. Subsequently it may be possible to fix minimum fair trading requirements which national laws would have to satisfy.

6 Financial Services

1. INTRODUCTION

A. General Structure

This chapter's title – financial services – is in fact somewhat misleading as we do not intend to look at all the details of EC financial services law as they impact upon the consumer. That would be too ambitious a task for the space available.[1] The boundaries of consumer law as a discipline are not clear, and nowhere is this more obvious than in the financial services field. We have therefore had to be selective in the materials we cover.

Consumer credit law is usually seen as being within the core of consumer law as a subject and we have followed this approach giving extensive treatment to the Consumer Credit Directives. The section on methods of payment is included, partly because of their practical significance within the single market context and also because they provide useful case studies of the ineffectiveness of 'soft law'. Finally bankruptcy measures are mentioned as they are likely to be a live topic on the Commission's future agenda and also highlight fundamental questions about the nature and values of the EC's consumer policy. We realise this chapter is somewhat eclectic in content, but hope the reader appreciates our good intentions in the selection of material.

B. Financial Service Regulation

Although we do not intend to look in detail at financial services regulation there is no doubting that it is a matter of vital consumer concern. Many recent scandals – BCCI, Barings Bank and Barlow Clowes to name but a few of the more high profile disasters – bear witness to the consumer interest in the general probity of the financial services sector and its prudential regulation. We therefore think it is important to comment on the general thrust of financial services regulation policy at the EC level and in particular to consider its possible impact on consumer protection, especially in relation to national contract law. We will largely limit our comments to the banking directives. This approach should suffice to illustrate our general points and

---

[1] Instead the reader may wish to consult the forthcoming books in this series on *EC Banking Law*, (A. Arora and X. Favre–Bulle) and *EC Insurance Law*, (A. McGee).

provides the best fit with the rest of this chapter. This is also the area in which the impact of the free movement measures on consumer protection is currently being most closely scrutinised by the EC.

The basic principle underpinning the Second Banking Directive[2] is 'home country' control. This means that the supervision of credit institutions is undertaken by the country in which their Head Office is based, even if they provide services or establish branches in other Member States. The scheme depends upon putting in place minimum requirements across Europe and the development of confidence in the effectiveness of the regulatory authorities in other Member States so that faith can be placed in a system of mutual recognition. The consumer should benefit in terms of wider choice, greater competition and hence presumably better value for money.[3]

There are also clear dangers for consumers. One obvious danger is that a 'race to the bottom' begins with financial service companies moving to locate in the state with the most liberal regime. However, we would wish to focus our attention on the danger that the 'home country' control principle could have the potential to regulate not only the condition under which credit institutions operate, but also the contract law which governs the transactions they conclude. We would seek to draw a distinction between home authority supervision of the business operation and host country control of the contracts concluded, especially as we shall see that the EC regulation on consumer credit contracts is far from complete or satisfactory (see section 2 below).

First, it is necessary to outline the structures which the Second Banking Directive puts in place to allow the host Member State to monitor the behaviour on its territory of a credit institution authorised and supervised by the authorities of another Member State. Here it is important to determine whether the company has established a branch or is simply providing services in the state.[4] Establishment and provision of services are covered by different Treaty provisions (arts 52–58 and arts 59–66 respectively) and generally EC law provides for greater controls by the host state when

---

2   Second Council Directive 89/646/EEC on the Co–ordination of Laws, Regulations and Administrative Provisions Relating to the Taking up and Pursuit of the Business of Credit Institutions and amending Directive 77/780/EEC: OJ 1989 L 386/1.

3   However, it has been noted that consumers have had some difficulties in obtaining financial services when it is they who have pro–actively chosen to purchase from a company based in another Member State: see the Green Paper, *Financial Services: Meeting Consumers' Expectations*, IP/96/432.

4   See draft Commission Communication, *Freedom to Provide Services and the Interest of the General Good in the Second Banking Directive*: OJ 1995 C 291/7. This contains a useful discussion of what amount to the provision of a service or establishment and the difficulties of distinguishing between them.

establishment is involved. This is reflected in the notification obligations contained in the Second Banking Directive.

If a credit institution wishes to establish a branch in another Member State it must notify its home country authority (art. 19). This notification should within three months be passed on to the authorities of the host state in which the business intends to establish. Then, within two months, the host authorities must prepare for supervision of the credit institution in accordance with art. 21 (see below). If necessary they should indicate the conditions under which, in the interest of the general good, those activities must be carried on in the host state. The question of which matters are in the 'general good' is contentious and will be returned to shortly. For now it is sufficient to note that the Commission does not see this provision as requiring that the credit institution need be informed of all such provisions or that the institution is relieved of the obligation to comply with provisions of which it was not informed.[5] The credit institution cannot commence its activities in the host state until these notification procedures have been completed.

By contrast, if a credit institution wishes merely to provide services in another state for the first time, art. 20 provides that it shall notify its home authority who must forward the notification to the host authority within a month. There is, however, no standstill period during which the service cannot be offered in the host state.

Art. 21 lists some of the powers which host authorities retain against branches operating in its territory. Periodic reports can be required for statistical purposes and information can be required to enable them to fulfil their responsibilities in relation to liquidity, monetary policies and the covering of risks arising out of open positions on financial markets (see arts 14(2)(3)). The authorities can require institutions to put an end to practices which breach the Directive. If this request is not complied with, they can inform the institution's home authority and then as a last resort take measures themselves to prevent or punish further irregularities and prevent that institution from initiating further transactions within its territory. In emergencies precautionary measures can be adopted without having to go through the above procedures.

All of the above is said not to 'affect the power of host Member States to take appropriate measures to prevent or to punish irregularities committed within their territories which are contrary to the legal rules they have adopted on the interest of the general good' (art. 21(5)). This provision applies equally both to where branches have been established and to where services are being provided from another state. A crucial question is which national

---

5   *Ibid.*, at 14–15.

rules are protected by this proviso: does it, for instance, require that all national rules on consumer credit have to be complied with?

The Commission is attempting to grapple with these questions in its recent draft Communication.[6] It notes that the 'general good' principle seems to reflect the case law of the ECJ which provides that the fundamental principle of freedom to provide services 'may be limited only by provisions which are justified by imperative reasons relating to the public interest'.[7] The restriction that national laws must be in the general good is likely to impact more in the context of the right of establishment in relation to which the ECJ has viewed the Treaty provisions as only prohibiting discriminatory treatment. Admittedly, this position has changed recently in relation to professional qualifications, where the Court has recognised that even some non–discriminatory measures may be liable to hamper or make less attractive the exercise of basic Treaty freedoms and so could only be justified if they 'pursued a legitimate objective compatible with the Treaty and justified by urgent reasons of general interest'.[8] Member States still seem to be free, however, to impose their own rules on the conduct of businesses which are established within their territory, but in the banking sector they can now only do this to the extent that it is in the 'general good'.

Certain principles can be derived from the case law as to what amounts to measures for the 'general good'.[9] They should be non–discriminatory, or else they would have to satisfy art. 56(1) which provides that the rules on the right of establishment should not prevent special treatment of foreign nationals on the grounds of public policy, public security or public health. The measures should also be in the interest of the general good and be objectively necessary. They should be proportionate to the objective pursued; this may mean that measures acceptable in the context of establishment are not necessary in the context of service provision. They must not be covered by equivalent rules in the state where the provider is established nor be subject to harmonised Community rules.

National consumer credit laws can offer higher protection than the EC Directives and are unlikely to be found to breach the principle of free movement.[10] The ECJ has already rejected challenges to insurance laws based on free movement arguments[11] and this approach is likely to be strengthened following the *Keck* decision. On the other hand, the Commission argues that if the Rome Convention on the law applicable to contractual

---

6   *Ibid.*
7   *Säger v Deenmeyer*, Case C–76/90, [1991] ECR I–4221 at 4244.
8   *Kraus v Land Baden–Württenberg*, Case C–19/92 [1993] ECR I–1663 at 1697.
9   See discussion in OJ 1995 C 291/7, *op. cit.*, at 15.
10   See Chap. 3 section 1.
11   *Commission v Federal Republic of Germany*, Case 205/84 [1986] ECR 3755.

obligations[12] leads to the law of the host country applying then this should only be applied if either it does not constitute an obstacle to mutual recognition or it is in the general good.[13] The Commission does note that, in the case of consumer protection then the host country legislation may either in whole or in part, come under the interest of the general good. If any consumer protection measures fell outside the general good there would be a dual standard with some national rules applying to domestic businesses but not to those supervised by other Member States.

We would prefer a different approach to be taken which would differentiate between the public law supervisory powers which are the main concern of the Second Banking Directive and the laws governing the resulting contracts which are the province of Consumer Credit Directives. The latter should be a matter for the host country. This seems the correct approach as the Consumer Credit Directives permit Member States to offer more protection than is required by them. Our approach would also have the advantage of ensuring that all consumers contracting in the same state receive the same protection whether using a domestic credit institution or one from another state.[14] Of course many of these problems would disappear if the 'general good' requirement was interpreted very broadly as there are few consumer credit protection measures which have not been introduced for the sake of the 'general good'.

Some difficult problems would of course still remain. For instance, should an authority in the home state take account of breaches of the law of another Member State even if these would not be breaches in the home state? Such questions could be particularly pertinent when exercising licensing powers.

---

12   See, Chap. 8 section 2C(i)(a).

13   OJ 1995 C291/7, *op cit.*, at 19.

14   We are heartened in this approach by the knowledge that in the insurance directives the standard situation is that the applicable law is that of the country where the risk is located, i.e. usually the country where the policy–holder is resident; see A. McGee, 'The Single Market in Insurance' in G. Howells (ed.), *European Business Law*, (Dartmouth, 1996) at 229 who points out that these generally consumer friendly provisions are to some extent undermined by certain rules allowing for the choice of other systems.

2.   CONSUMER CREDIT DIRECTIVE

A.   Introduction

Credit is common place in the modern consumer society. No longer is resort to credit viewed as a sign of failure, but rather as a necessary means of securing consumer durables or an acceptable way of managing the household budget. However, as a consequence of the expansion of the credit market in the 1980s and the recession which followed, the amount of over-indebtedness has increased throughout Europe. This phenomenon has not only been caused by macro–economic catastrophes, but also by the irresponsible over promotion of credit. Often this has been targeted at poor and vulnerable consumers, who are least able to resist the temptation of the 'have now pay later' inducements of the credit companies. To date the EC has not addressed the fundamental questions relating to the ethics of the credit market, but has been satisfied with a consumer protection policy based on informing the consumer and providing some minimal protection against the worst abuses.

The *Preliminary Programme of the European Economic Community for a consumer protection and information policy* cited protection of the consumer's economic interests as one of the five basic rights; particularly it sought to protect consumers from harsh credit conditions with a priority being the harmonisation of the general conditions of consumer credit.[15] The first proposal for a Directive on consumer credit was made in 1979.[16] After wide ranging consultations a more adventurous proposal was made in 1984.[17] But the final measure was watered down because at that time the measure had to be adopted under art. 100 with its unanimity requirement.[18] Left out of the final version were, *inter alia*, provisions for cooling–off periods and the joint and several liability of connected lenders. The complicated and sensitive matter of arriving at a common method of calculating the annual percentage rate was left over to a later directive which

---

15   OJ 1975 C 92/1 at 6.

16   OJ 1979 C 80/4.

17   OJ 1984 OJ C 183/4.

18   Council Directive 87/102/EEC for the approximation of the laws, regulations and administrative provisions of the Member States concerning consumer credit: OJ 1987 L42/48. On which see E.P. Latham, 'The EEC Consumer Credit Directive' (1987) 84 *Law Soc. Gaz.* 3331 and 3494, also published as 'Disposition communautaire relative au crédit à la consommation: la directive 87/102/CEE de 22 Décembre 1986', [1988] *R.M.C.* 219. On the directive as amended see F. Domont–Naert, *Consommateurs Défavorisés: Crédit et Endettement*, (Story Scienta, 1992) Ch. 2, N. Reich, *Europäisches Verbraucherschutzrecht* (3rd ed., Nomos, 1996) at 360–4 and V. Kendall, *EC Consumer Law*, (Wiley Chancery, 1995) at 93–97.

amended Directive 87/102.[19] It is also relevant to note that the Directive was developed during a period when the impact of new technology and, in particular the growth in importance of the credit card, had not been fully appreciated.[20]

Directive 87/102 entered into force on 1 January 1990. Art. 17 requires the Commission to produce a report on its working every five years. The first report provides a very interesting history of the implementation of the Directive and consideration of future Commission action in this area.[21]

One of the interesting conclusions of that report is that Member States have drawn extensively upon the minimal harmonisation clause in art. 15 which permits them to retain or adopt more stringent provisions. This produces an irony. The main motivation for the Directive was harmonisation to reduce distortions in competition and to even out differences which affected the volume and nature of credit sought and thereby influenced the free movement of goods and services (recitals 2 and 3). Widespread use of the minimal harmonisation clause conflicts with the dominant justification for the Directive.

Protecting consumers against unfair credit terms was mentioned (recital 5), but the main benefits to consumers were viewed in terms of the greater choice available as creditors supplied credit aCross–Borders and consumers gained confidence to shop around the common market for credit (recital 4). The Directive seems to have been used as a floor of rights and an impetus for further reforms to protect consumers in national legislation. This may indicate that the competition and internal market bases for Community action were never very serious justifications and possibly supports the move to establish a clearer autonomous foundation for consumer policy. It also illustrates the benefits of even weak EC legislative activity if it can be used as a spark for national reforms.

The impetus a directive can give for more far reaching domestic reforms are, however, likely to be most significant in those states which already enjoy high levels of consumer protection. The effect is likely to be to accentuate the differences between Member States. Ironically, this may actually produce a

---

19 Council Directive 90/88/EEC amending Directive 87/102/EEC for the approximation of the laws, regulations and administrative provisions of the Member States concerning consumer credit: OJ 1990 L61/14. We will refer to articles of Directive 87/102, as amended by this Directive.

20 Specific Community rules on payment cards are also being developed, see section 3B, below.

21 Report on the operation of Directive 87/102/EEC for the approximation of the laws, regulations and administrative provisions of the Member States concerning consumer credit: COM(95) 117.

situation in which internal market concerns do require and justify harmonisation.

Hopefully, EC laws can have a ratchet effect. By setting minimum standards and promoting internal debates within states, the hope must be that over time the consensus level for harmonised EC laws can be raised. It is possible to view the Consumer Credit Directives and the Commission's recent proposals for reform as working to this model.

The question of the direct effects of the Consumer Credit Directive has recently been before the ECJ.[22] The case concerned the attempt by a Spanish citizen to rely upon the connected lending provisions in the Directive (see section 2I(iii) below) to justify ceasing to make repayments on a loan which had partly financed a failed holiday contract. She had to rely on the direct effect of the Directive, as Spain had not implemented these provisions. The ECJ, however, held to its firm line of refusing to allow Directives to have horizontal direct effects. This case illustrates the hardship which such a rule can lead to. The consumer ought to have had the right to withhold payments; the finance company would have been aware of its imminent obligations under the Directive and yet was allowed to escape liability because of the failure of the Member State to comply with binding legal obligations. Mrs Blasquez Rivero might have a claim under the *Francovich* principle against the Spanish Government, but this would most likely be complex to try to enforce.

B.   Scope

The Directive has a broad scope applying to all credit agreements entered into by consumers and creditors. Credit agreements are broadly defined to include deferred payments, loans or other similar financial accommodations (art. 1(2)(c)).[23] The Directive therefore follows the trend of modern consumer credit legislation by regulating the substance and not the form of the agreement. Consumer is given the familiar definition 'of a natural person acting for purposes which can be regarded as outside his trade or profession' (art. 1(2)(a)).[24] Creditor means a natural or legal person, or a group of such

---

22   *El Cortes Ingles SA v Christina Blasquez Rivera*, Case C–192/94, see A. Davis, [1996] *Consum.L.J.* CS31.

23   But services or utilities paid for by instalments are not included.

24   This Community law concept of the consumer is likely to be narrowly interpreted, see Chap. 1 section 1B; but many Member States have given it a broader meaning in their implementing legislation. However, the United Kingdom has used it as an excuse to suggest removing all business lending from the detailed controls of its Consumer Credit Act 1974 (individuals including partnerships will still be subject to

persons, who grants credit in the course of his trade, business or profession (art. 1(2)(b)).There is no requirement that his business be that of lending, or even that he customarily provides credit; the provisions of the Directive would also seem to apply to a one off transaction.

C. Exemptions

(i) Value of the Credit

The Directive does not apply to credit agreements of less than 200 ECU or more than 20,000 ECU (art. 2(1)(f)). The lower limit excludes contracts for small values where the formalities required by the Directive are considered excessive, although one might question whether consumers should not retain some protection. A sensible compromise might be to disapply in respect of credit for small amounts those aspects of the Directive which impose positive obligations on the creditor, whilst retaining the other controls on creditor behaviour.

The upper limit was imposed because 'credit agreements for large amounts tend to differ from the usual consumer credit agreements' (recital 14). Presumably, it is thought that such consumers are more likely and/or more able to look after their own interests. Neither of these assumptions are substantiated and the result is that those who need to borrow most receive least protection!! The Commission has expressed a preference for the removal of this limitation.[25]

(ii) Hire

Hire agreements are excluded, except where the title will ultimately pass to the hirer (art. 2(1)(b)). This exclusion is both poorly drafted and inappropriate.[26] As drafted, it is uncertain whether hire–purchase contracts are exempt. Under these agreements it is not clear whether title will pass until the consumer exercises an option to purchase, even if this is usually a formality.

---

licensing controls): see *Consumer Credit Deregulation*, (Office of Fair Trading, 1994) at 29–30.

[25] COM(95)117 at 48.

[26] Latham, *op. cit.*, at 3334 suggests the provision would have been 'better left in the Commission's original wording, i.e., simply "hiring agreement"', with national courts being left to decide if the agreement was merely for hiring or was actually for credit.

More fundamental is the criticism that hirers need a protective framework. Hired goods frequently have only a limited value at the end of the hire period and so hiring often performs a similar economic function to buying on credit. The Commission has proposed removing this exemption.[27]

(iii) Purpose of Loan

Agreements are exempt if intended primarily for the purpose of acquiring or retaining property rights in land or in an existing or projected building (art. 2(1)(a)). Other credit agreements secured by mortgage on immovable property are also exempt from art. 1a and arts 4–12 of the Directive.

The exclusion of property contracts is typically found in consumer credit legislation, since in many countries such contracts tend to be entered into after legal advice and there is a need for certainty in property law matters. This is not, however, the position in all countries and in Finland, for instance, the rules have been explicitly made applicable to housing credit.

Therefore, although many of the most serious consumer debt problems stem from mortgage debt or secured loans, there is no effective Community regulation of these problems. The Commission has recognised this gap in consumer protection and is looking into the need for a Directive relating to mortgage credit.[28]

Art. 2(1)(a) also exempts credit agreements intended to renovate or improve buildings. This exemption is harder to justify and indeed the Commission is looking to extend the Directive to cover loans for building work, provided they are not secured by a mortgage.

(iv) Interest Charged

Free credit, i.e. where there are no interest or other charges, is exempt (art. 2(1)(c)). It is hard to justify the blanket exemption of interest free credit from all the provisions of the Directive, including, for example, those regulating the right to recover possession.

Indeed there is a broader question about the ethics of free credit when it is usually offered as part of a contract to supply goods or services and is obviously taken into account when calculating their price. However, unless one insists on a clear separation between supplier and creditor, there is always a risk of cross subsidisation between the cost of credit and the price of the goods. This cross–subsidisation can occur, whatever the interest rate,

---

[27]   COM(95)117 at 43.
[28]   *Ibid.*

and therefore a particular prohibition on interest free credit may be inappropriate. However, in some Member States, like Finland, it is forbidden to market interest free credit and in France consumers can insist on a reduction in the cash price if goods are offered with free credit.[29] By contrast, in the United Kingdom the description 'interest free credit' has been held to be misleading when a discount is available for cash.[30] In any event, free credit offers should not be unregulated. The danger that the lure of interest free credit might cause consumers to overextend themselves can perhaps be best addressed by imposing prudent lending obligations on creditors (see section 2E, below).

Member States may, in consultation with the Commission, exempt credit agreements granted at rates below those prevailing in the market and not offered to the public generally (art. 2(2)). This is one of many instances where the Directive grants Member States a discretion and thereby undermines the harmonisation goal. The Commission reports that the Dutch law contains such an exemption and the German and Irish laws exclude such contracts made between employer and employee. In Belgium law certain low interest loans made for social purposes by non–profit organisations can be exempted by the executive from certain provisions.[31] No mention is made in the report of the United Kingdom, yet it exempts loans not exceeding 13%, or, if higher, one per cent above base rate, but there is no requirement that these be not available to the general public.[32] This would seem to breach the Directive. The fact that it is not commented upon in the Commission report either points to a weakness in the Commission's monitoring of Member State's laws, or an acceptance that it complies with the spirit if not the letter of the Directive.

(v) Repayment Period

Credit agreements under which no interest is charged provided the consumer agrees to repay the credit agreement in a single payment are exempt (art. 2(1)(d)).This would exempt charge cards, like American Express, where the balance is payable in full. In the United Kingdom, at least, there is a move towards offering high earner 'gold cards' where the balance is debited from

---

29 See art. L311–6 of the French *Code de la Consommation* which requires this discount to be indicated in any advertisements. Such advertisements for interest free credit are only allowed in France at the point of sale.

30 See *Metsoja v Norman Pitt & Co. Ltd.* (1989) 153 *J.P.* 485.

31 COM(95)117 at 49.

32 Reg. 4, Consumer Credit (Exempt Agreements) Order 1989, S.I. 1989/869.

the current account each month. Although it depends upon the exact contract terms, these are likely to be exempt.

Credit agreements will also be exempt if they have to be repaid either within three months or, by a maximum of four repayments, within 12 months (art. 2(1)(g)). This exemption can be justified by the desire to exclude typical consumer transactions which are not credit agreements in the true sense, such as the weekly payment of the newspaper bill. The simple exclusion of loans of less than three months' duration is harder to justify, given that loans by moneylenders to low income families could easily be for small amounts over short periods and these are the very type of loan which need close supervision.[33]

(vi)   Overdrafts

Advances on current accounts granted by credit or financial institutions are exempt (art. 2(1)(e)). This does not apply to credit card accounts, which again leaves the status of 'gold card' accounts somewhat ambiguous.

Art. 6, however, applies to overdrafts which are exempted. This requires that, at or before the time the contract is concluded, the consumer be informed of any credit limit, annual rate of interest, applicable charges (and how these might be amended) and the procedure for terminating the agreement and that this information be confirmed in writing. Consumers must be informed of any change in the annual rate of interest or charges when they occur, possibly in their statements. Where overdrafts can arise by tacit agreement then the consumer shall be informed of the annual rate of interest, charges and any amendments if the overdraft lasts for more than three months.

(vii)   Authentic Acts

Member States are given the option of exempting authentic acts signed before a notary or judge from the provisions in arts 6–12 of the Directive.

---

[33]   It might be argued that these are the loans which need least formalities in order to keep the administrative costs down, but this is unconvincing given the vulnerable position of low income consumers: see K. Rowlingson, *Moneylenders and their Clients*, (Policy Studies Institute, 1994).

D.   Advertising and Marketing

Art. 3 is the only provision in the Directive dealing with advertising, or for that matter credit marketing.[34] It requires that a statement of the annual percentage rate of charge (by representative example, if no other means are practicable) be provided whenever an advertisement or offer displayed at business premises indicates the rate of interest or any other figures relating to the cost of credit.

The annual percentage rate ('APR') is seen as an important means of enabling consumers to compare interest rates; by taking account of various variables it seeks to provide a 'true' indication of the cost of credit. We will discuss this concept in more detail below, after noting that it is also a key feature of the information which must be included in the credit contract.

In fact credit advertising is more strictly regulated in most Member States. This is because of the significant impact advertising can have on consumers. Certainly there is widespread concern about advertising aimed at young people and the Commission is considering preparing a code of conduct on this matter.[35] However, there are other problematic types of advertising, such as that which is targeted at those who already have significant debt problems. Although some marketing practices might in the first instance be dealt with by codes of practice, on the whole we would prefer such matters to be dealt with by legislation. Some practices, such as mailing credit offers to minors should be prohibited. If these practices persist then the courts should be able to take them into account whenever the creditor is trying to enforce the resulting agreement.

The courts should not be restricted to considering advertising, but should also be able to take into account the general marketing ethics of credit companies. One might have expected the Directive to have imposed some controls on the marketing of credit. For instance, in the United Kingdom the canvassing of money loans off trade premises is prohibited. This seems a sensible rule – preventing consumers being tempted to take on such loans too easily in the comfort of their home – which could well be exported.

The first draft of the Directive had prohibited unsolicited visits to consumers at the home, workplace or elsewhere. The amended proposal did not prohibit such visits, but made any contract concluded as a result subject to a seven day cooling off period. The final proposal contains no such provision, although it does include any cooling–off period as one of the terms which Member States may require to be included in written agreements. Of

---

34   Privacy matters are dealt with in Parliament and Council Directive 95/46 on the protection of individuals with regard to the processing of personal data and the free movement of such data: OJ 1995 L 281/31.

35   COM(95) 117 at 51.

course many credit contracts concluded off business premises will be covered by the Doorstep Selling Directive.[36] Many Member States also provide cooling off periods for certain credit contracts. There would seem to be a need to harmonise these and co–ordinate them with the provisions of the Doorstep Selling Directive. The Commission has announced its intention to study these issues.[37]

The policy justifications for having a cooling–off period are the same as for doorstep selling – preventing the consumer from being taken by surprise and allowing him to reflect on his decision. Cancellation is a legal technique which takes the information approach to consumer protection seriously, by requiring the consumer to have time to reflect on the information and, if he so desires, to make use of it by withdrawing from the contract. It is also a legal technique which challenges the traditional principle that contracts are final once they have been concluded. However, the weakness of the principle is that it requires the consumer to take positive steps to unravel the contract, usually within a short space of time. The consumer may not do this because of ignorance of his rights (even if they are stated in the contract); or lack of knowledge of how to exercise them (providing a cancellation notice which simply has to be returned may partially reduce this problem); or because he does not want to upset or offend his supplier. Also the consequences of the contract may only become apparent to consumers once the cooling–off period has expired. For instance, consumers only really feel the burden of a credit contract once they have started to repay it.

E.   Information

In contrast to the rather radical approach to consumer information which underpins cancellation rights, art. 4 is premised upon a traditional rather staid approach to consumer information built around providing consumers with a written copy of the agreement. Unlike in the original draft of the Directive, there is no requirement that the consumer should have signed the agreement and so the principal purpose of the provision must be as a record for reference in future disputes. Even if the agreement is presented for signature, this is unlikely to yield significant benefits for consumers since they are unlikely to read it in detail, never mind challenge, terms of a contract placed in front of them for signature.

Art. 4 requires the written agreement to include a statement of the APR and the conditions under which it can be amended. Where this rate cannot be stated then adequate information should be given, including, at least, the

---

36   See Chap. 5 section 2.
37   COM(95) 117 at 76.

annual rate of interest and the conditions under which it can be amended. Since Directive 90/88 amended the original Directive, it must also state the amount, number and frequency or dates of repayments, and the total of interest and other charges. In addition those elements of the total cost of credit which are not taken into account when calculating the APR (other than those relating to breach of contract) must be indicated.

All the other essential terms must be included in the written agreement. It would be desirable if there were a common European interpretation of which terms are essential, but agreement could not be reached on this point.[38] It is left to Member States to decide what is essential. Annex 1 attempts to promote some harmony by providing illustrations of the terms for various types of agreement which Member States may consider as essential and which they may require to be included.

In its recent report on the operation of the Directive, the Commission has floated a rather more radical conception of the creditor's duty to inform.[39] This includes a requirement that the consumer be informed of all aspects of the credit agreement, including what the creditor believes to be the consumer's optimum type and amount of credit given the consumer's financial circumstances (this is balanced by an obligation on the consumer to provide relevant information). The creditor should then only make an offer of an amount which he is reasonably sure the consumer will be able to repay. The penalty will be the court's power to waive all or part of the interest on arrears and to reduce the consumer's liabilities for the cash price of goods or services or the amount borrowed. This principle is said to be derived from Belgian law, although the report notes that French courts can take notice of the information available to the creditor and similar reforms are being mooted in Norway and Sweden.[40]

Such a duty could have an important role to play as a useful counterpart to cancellation rights in creating a legal structure which takes the need to inform the consumer seriously. Indeed it goes beyond simply informing the consumer and introduces a co-operative ethic into consumer contracting. Intriguingly the Commissions report states:

---

[38] See Latham, *op. cit.*, at 3494.

[39] COM(95) 117 at 52–53.

[40] The United Kingdom Government has also accepted the Director–General of Fair Trading's recommendation that 'the lender's care and responsibility in making the loan, including steps taken to find out and check the borrower's creditworthiness and ability to meet the full terms of the agreement' should be one of the factors considered when assessing whether there is an unjust credit transaction (which would replace the present concept of the extortionate credit bargain): see *Unjust Credit Transactions*, (Office of Fair Trading, 1991).

'These standards of behaviour are not exclusive to credit providers but are expected of all professionals.'[41]

There must be some limits to this. For instance, consumers should in the main be responsible for choosing their own cars, white goods, clothes furniture etc. But for more sophisticated products such as pensions, insurance, even heating systems, security systems etc. the consumer does rely on the professional to guide him. This new principle would place the onus on certain suppliers to appreciate that they are being relied upon and to take positive steps to fulfil those expectations. Subject to these limitations this would seem to be an interesting principle to develop further.

F.   Annual Percentage Rate

Cancellation rights and creditor's duties to assess the needs of consumers are possible future developments which suggest that an approach based on information provision might be made relevant to the needs of many consumers. For the moment, however, the Directive is premised on a policy of information provision which only assists the active information seeker. The centrepiece of this is the APR.

The APR is an attempt to show the true cost of credit in a manner which makes it possible meaningfully to compare the cost of different credit offers. Formally it is defined as the total cost of credit to the consumer (i.e. all costs, including interest and other charges, which the consumer has to pay for the credit, art. 1(2)(d)) expressed as an annual percentage of the amount of the credit granted (art. 1(2)(e)). The APR is the equivalent, on an annual basis, to the present value of all commitments (loans, repayments and charges), future or existing, agreed by the creditor and the borrower. It must be calculated in accordance with a mathematical formula, set out in Annex II of the Directive (art. 1a(1)).

Attempts to harmonise the manner in which Member States calculate the APR have been problematic. So much so that in Directive 87/102 this matter had to be left to the discretion of the Member States. In 1988 the Commission proposed the adoption of a common mathematical formula for calculating the rate, but did not specify which elements of the cost should be taken into account.[42] Eventually Directive 90/88 was adopted. This amended Directive 87/102[43] by inserting both the mathematical formula for the APR, with four worked examples, a set of assumptions which may be used to

---

41   COM(95) 117 at 52.

42   OJ 1988 C 155/10.

43   See art. 1a and Annexes II and III to Directive 87/102.

calculate the APR and a list of charges which should be excluded when calculating the total cost of the credit (see art. 1a and Annexes II and III).

However, final agreement could still not be reached on a common mathematical formula. Therefore Member States which already used a different formula were allowed to retain this so long as only one formula was used in their territory (art. 1a(5)). In addition Member States which imposed maximum interest rate ceiling by reference to APRs, but did not take account of certain charges included within the Directive's definition of the APR, were granted the right to continue to exclude such charges for those transactions provided the consumer is informed of such amounts in the agreement and advertising, in accordance with art. 3 (art. 1a(3)).

The Council was supposed to take a decision by 1 January 1996 leading to the adoption of a single mathematical formula. This has been delayed because of the process of enlargement and the Commission has signalled that the transitional period has been impliedly extended. However, a report on the operation of Directive 90/88 proposed amendments to the consumer credit directives to effect this change,[44] and a draft directive has recently been published.[45]

Although the elements of costs to be included in or excluded from the calculation of the APR are not to be amended, the Commission does foresee the introduction of a common mathematical formula in the same form as currently used in the Directive. This would require changes in practice in Finland, France and Germany, although the report points out that national deviations 'do not derive from mathematical origins, but rather from differences in the assumptions applied to the calculations in certain Member States'.[46] A consequence of this would be the removal of the transitional concessions found in arts 1a(3) and 1a(5), although the former relating to maximum ceilings on interest rates has not actually been invoked by any state.

The Commission also proposes that a symbol be required to be shown alongside the APR so that it is recognisable in cross border transactions.[47] Familiar national wording would be retained rather than a European term be imposed for the APR. This ensures that the effort that has been expended on raising consumer awareness of certain terms at the national level is not

---

[44] *Report on the Operation of Directive 90/88*, COM(96) 79.

[45] Proposal for a European Parliament and Council Directive amending Directive 87/102/EEC (as amended by Directive 90/88/EEC) relating to the approximation of the laws, regulations and administrative provisions of Member States concerning consumer credit: OJ 1996 C 235/39.

[46] *Ibid.*, at 5–6.

[47] The symbol is of 12 stars in a circle around a % sign.

wasted. Certain other technical and linguistic amendments to the directives are also proposed.

There is no doubt that the mathematics and politics[48] which lie behind the APR figure are baffling. One only has to read the relatively well set out comparison of the EC, French and German methods of calculation in the recent Commission report to break out into a cold sweat at the memory of school algebra. The technicalities baffle experts in the field, therefore can the figure be of any relevance to the ordinary consumer? The answer is yes. Ordinary consumers do not need to know the nuances of how the figure is arrived at so long as they can comprehend that this is a useful comparator by which to assess competing credit offers. Certainly it is more useful than a flat interest rate figure. However, because it is an artificially constructed figure it will take a lot more consumer education before the mass of consumers are able to handle it confidently.[49] Consumer confidence in the term in cross–border transactions will be easier to establish once a common formula has been agreed upon.

G.   Repossession

One of the most serious dangers for consumers purchasing goods on credit is the threat of repossession. They might have to forfeit goods for which they have paid a considerable amount of the purchase price, possibly be left with continuing credit commitments and at best hope to recover the low price for which many repossessed goods are sold on the open market.

Earlier drafts of the Directive had provided that on repossession the credit agreement was void or terminated. Art. 7 of the final version simply leaves it to the Member States to 'lay down the conditions under which goods may be repossessed, in particular if the consumer has not given his consent'.[50] The only normative obligation on Member States is to ensure

---

48   These relate to which elements should be included in the calculation and to which contracts it should be applied to – for instance the rules do not normally apply to bank overdrafts.

49   In a survey conducted by one of the present authors only a little over three quarters of debtors had heard of the term APR and only 1 in 7 of those could be regarded as having a reasonable understanding of what it meant: see I. Crow, G. Howells and M. Moroney, 'Credit and Debt: Choices for Poorer Consumer' in G. Howells, I. Crow and M. Moroney (eds), *Aspects of Credit and Debt*, (Sweet & Maxwell, 1993).

50   The question of consent is problematic, particularly if it is sought when the consumer is vulnerable, equally if it is included as a standard term in the original contract the consent cannot be considered to be meaningful.

that, if the creditor takes possession, the repossession should not entail unjust enrichment.

The lack of a Community approach to the consequences of repossession reflects the weakness of the Directive in failing to address the fundamental imbalance between creditor and debtor. The second draft of the Directive had included a provision that goods could not be recovered without a court order where one–third of the credit price of the goods had been repaid; repossession in breach of this rule would have led to the agreement being terminated, release from all liabilities under the agreement and the consumer being entitled to recover all sums paid under the agreement. Such a rule would have addressed one of the worst abuses of creditor power and given a powerful remedy, which would certainly affect creditor behaviour.

Repossession is not the only potential threat facing consumers in financial difficulty. A missed payment may, for instance, make all sums owed fall due. Effective consumer protection requires supervision of all actions of the creditor which impose potentially onerous conditions on the consumer.

H. Early Repayment

The consumer is entitled to discharge his obligations under the credit agreement before the time fixed by the agreement (art. 8). He is then entitled to an equitable reduction in the total charge for credit. The rules for calculating this reduction are to be laid down by the Member States. There are disparities between the way the Member States calculate the rebates.

I. Liability of a Third Party Creditor

(i) *Assignment*

Art. 9 provides that where a creditor's rights are assigned to a third party, the consumer shall be entitled to plead any defence available against the creditor. This will include the right of set off if this is permitted in the Member State concerned. As the rules of the Directive are mandatory (art. 14), this provision requires, *inter alia*, that so–called 'cut–off' clauses, limiting the defences available against the assignee, are not effective.

(ii) Negotiable Instruments

Many of the rights of consumers under sale and credit law could be evaded if consumers were required to provide a negotiable instrument which could be presented or transferred to a third party without being subject to any of the defences available under the original credit sale. In the original drafts of the Directive the Commission had wanted to prohibit the use of negotiable instruments in such circumstances. This went too far for some Member States. Art. 10 therefore simply requires Member States, which permit (a) payment by bills of exchange including promissory notes, and (b) security by bills of exchange, including promissory notes and cheques, to ensure consumers are protected.

In many countries, such as the Nordic states, such negotiable instruments are forbidden in consumer transactions. In Member States where this is not the case, art. 10 seems to require the availability of defences in spite of the negotiable instrument, in line with the main rule in art. 9. However, as art. 10 is very loosely worded, other solutions might also be allowed.

(iii) Connected Lender Liability

Art. 11(1) provides that the existence of a credit agreement shall not affect the rights of the consumer against the supplier of goods and services. Art. 11(2) is more interesting, for it introduces the concept of connected lender liability. This principle means that where goods are sold on credit and the seller and creditor are connected then the consumer should be able to exercise rights against the creditor as well as the seller if the goods are not supplied, only supplied in part or are not in conformity. The rationale behind this is that the creditor is in a form of joint venture with the supplier and should not be able simply to walk away should things go wrong. Also the reputation of a creditor may have convinced consumers that the suppliers they work in tandem with must be reputable. Moreover, the ability of the consumer to withhold payment from the creditor is a very important weapon when negotiating with suppliers. Creditors have the potential to exert a positive control over the behaviour of suppliers they work with.

There are, however, several problems of principle and drafting with art. 11(2). The original drafts of the Directive had followed the approach of s.75 of the United Kingdom's Consumer Credit Act 1974 and made the creditor and supplier jointly and severally liable. Under the final version, the consumer must have pursued his remedies against the supplier and failed to obtain satisfaction before he can address the creditor. This is unsatisfactory.[51] It forces the consumer to keep repaying the credit whilst he is in dispute with the supplier and probably not able to enjoy the goods. It removes one of the means by which many disputes are settled, namely pressure exerted by the creditor on the supplier to resolve the consumer's dispute. It also creates uncertainty as to how far the consumer has to go in pursuing the supplier before he can turn his attention to the creditor.

Liability arises when 'the grantor of credit and the supplier of goods or services have a pre–existing agreement whereunder credit is made available exclusively by that grantor of credit to customers of that supplier for the acquisition of goods or services from that supplier'. This causes particular problems in connection with credit cards. The notion of pre–existing agreement is fundamental to the reason why the creditor can be made responsible for the supplier. Problems arise in the credit card context where the creditor and supplier do not have a direct agreement, but rather are connected because they are part of a network, such as Visa/Mastercard. The requirement of exclusivity is also problematic since credit cards can be used at many network outlets.

There are differences between credit card companies and other forms of connected lender, but we do not accept that credit card companies should be exempt from connected lender liability. Credit cards can be used at so many outlets that it is hard to see consumers viewing the credit card companies as working in a hand and glove relationship with the seller in the same way as, say, a car dealer and a finance company work together. On the other hand we assume credit card companies do make some checks on the outlets they permit to use their facilities. Moreover the value of making the credit card company liable is the ease with which it allows consumers access to justice, for all a consumer has to do is dispute an amount on his bill. The liability of credit card companies, especially for debts incurred in foreign countries, is currently being hotly debated in the United Kingdom.[52] Making the credit card companies the insurer of the supplier is one means by which the risk of contracting in an increasingly distant market place can be reduced. This is a particularly important consideration in the context of encouraging consumers to shop across national borders.

The burden on connected lenders is in any event limited as the above rules do not apply to individual transactions of less than 200 ECU (of course the Directive does not apply if the credit is more than 20,000 ECU). However, there is some confusion by what is meant by 'transaction': Does it mean that the cash price, amount of credit, or combination of both of these, must be less than 200 ECU? Presumably it is not the amount of credit,

---

51   Latham, *op. cit.*, at 3495 explains that this was due to implacable Dutch resistance to the principle of joint and several liability.

52   See for instance, *Connected Lender Liability*, (Office of Fair Trading, 1994).

because in that event the Directive would not apply in any event by virtue of the exemption for credit agreements of less than 200 ECU which is found in art. 2(1)(f).

It would seem that connected lender liability would not attach to a set of small purchases whose individual values are less than 200 ECU, but whose combined total exceeds that figure. This interpretation is based on the use of the term *individual* transaction. However, if the items were typically sold together and had been separated simply to avoid the rules then connected lender liability should apply. The more difficult case is where goods are commonly bought together, but can also customarily be purchased individually. The Directive provides no clear answer to this problem, but one might suggest that if goods which formed part of a set or unit were purchased on the same occasion then they should be treated as forming one transaction.

Member States are left free to decide to what extent and under what conditions the remedies resulting from connected lender liability shall be exercisable. Thus it is unclear whether consumers will be restricted to a claim for the amount of credit advanced or whether consequential damages will also be available.

J.   Enforcement

Member States must provide one of the following means of ensuring the Directive is given effect to:

- requiring official authorisation for persons offering credit or offering to arrange credit;[53]
- ensuring persons granting or arranging credit are subject to inspection or official monitoring by an institution or official body;
- promoting the establishment of bodies to receive complaints and to provide consumers with information and advice.

Although the first two options can be viewed as alternative methods of monitoring credit institutions, it is hard to see how a complaints and advice body can perform the same function as a monitoring body. Thankfully all Member States have adopted, at least, one of the first two options. The Commission is considering whether the wording of art. 12 should be amended to make it mandatory for Member States to create bodies

---

53   Member States may provide that authorisation is not required of someone authorised under the banking co-ordination Directives.

authorised to receive consumer complaints.[54] This must be a step forward in ensuring consumers have access to justice. However, it is not clear whether such complaints' bodies need have a role in providing consumers with remedies or if the information they receive is simply to be used to better regulate the market.

One must be concerned that the Commission reports that an answer which recurred in relation to its questionnaire survey of the Member States regarding the Consumer Credit Directives was 'the Ministry has no information on the way in which these provisions are enforced in practice'.[55] This may simply be the result of the questionnaire landing on the wrong desk, or it may fuel fears that there is a wide difference between the consumer law in books and in practice.

K. Controls on Evasion

Art. 14(1) requires that Member States ensure that credit agreements cannot derogate from the provisions of the Directive as implemented in national law. Art. 14(2) goes on to provide that they should further ensure that these provisions can not be circumvented by the way in which agreements are formulated. It particularly mentions the technique of distributing the amount of credit over several agreements so as to evade regulation as one device which should be thwarted.

L. Usury

It is obvious from the above that the Consumer Credit Directives do not cover all aspects of the debtor–creditor relationship. Without listing all the matters not covered, it is worthwhile mentioning one important aspect – usury. This is worth highlighting, because the Commission has indicated that they want a debate at the Community level about usury laws and suggest that following economic and monetary union such rules should apply at the Community level.

Usury laws tend to follow two approaches: either they strike down high interest rates because of the unconscionable way in which they have been concluded or they impose a more normative control by fixing interest rate ceilings.[56] The Commission suggests that laying down maximum rates is the

---

[54]   COM(95) 117 at 61.

[55]   *Ibid.*, at 4

[56]   See G. Howells, 'Controlling Unjust Credit Transactions: Lessons from a Comparative Analysis' in Howells, Crow and Moroney (eds), *op. cit.*, and 'Seeking

most effective approach. This would be rather interventionist. It would also be out of line with the approach taken in the Unfair Contract Terms Directive which excludes from review the core provisions.[57] It is, however, a welcome recognition of the need to take the interests of disadvantaged consumers into account.

M. Conclusions

The Commission's report on the operation of Directive 87/102 gives one the impression that it realises the deficiencies of the present EC law. The Consumer Credit Directives as presently drafted impose relatively few controls on credit contracts or the behaviour of creditors. They are based on an information strategy of providing consumers with information on contract terms so that they can be efficient market players. Interesting ideas are certainly on the agenda, such as cancellation rights and interest rate ceilings. However, one suspects that it will be a slow process for agreement to be reached on even the matters the Commission itself recognises need to be addressed. Nevertheless the Commission is helping to resolve these problems by laying down some fundamental rules and occasioning debate and reforms at the national and EC level. It must still be seen if the Consumer Credit Directives conform to the ratchet model described in section 2A, above, under which their implementation raises consciousness of issues at the national level, which may in time be transformed into higher minimum standards at the European level.

3. METHODS OF PAYMENT[58]

A. Introduction

If the single market is to become a reality for consumers then they need to have reasonably priced efficient means of paying for goods in other Member States. The easiest means of achieving this is by the use of payment cards which are transportable and can be used by the consumer when travelling abroad or when ordering at a distance. However, it should also be a

---

Social Justice for Poor Consumers in Credit Markets' in *Consumer Law in the Global Economy*, I. Ramsay (ed.) (Dartmouth, forthcoming).

57 See Chap. 3 section 2B(ii).

58 These issues are also considered by A. Arora and X. Favre–Bulle, 'The Single European Market and the Banking Sector' in G. Howells (ed.), *European Business Law*, (Dartmouth, 1996) and in their forthcoming book in this series.

relatively simple operation for consumers to transfer funds from their account to that of the supplier in another state.

A feature of regulation in this area, at least until recently, has been the Commission's preference for 'soft law' solutions. Thus, the Commission has favoured proceeding by way of non–binding Recommendations. These Recommendations in turn proceeded on the assumption that many of the goals would be achieved by self–regulatory systems. The reasons for favouring a soft law approach seem to be partly a desire to require existing systems to be altered as little as possible – a policy which is underpinned in more recent times by the subsidiarity principle. In addition, however, there has been a reluctance to legislate and thereby impose detailed rules at a time when the technology associated with payment systems is still developing for fear that the legislative framework may impede practical advances.

However, the Commission has become frustrated by the industry's lack of progress and is now proposing a Directive on Cross–Border credit transfers. Payment cards remain subject to only non–binding recommendations. However, the recommendations are not necessarily without any legal status. The ECJ has stated that they should be taken into account by national judges[59] and there is even a recorded instance of a French court holding a bank liable in damages to one of its customers based on the Payment Systems Recommendation.[60] We will first consider the EC rules relating to payment cards before moving on to consider the law relating to Cross–Border transfers.

B. Payment Cards

(i) *Electronic Payment Recommendation*

The first Community initiative in this area was *Commission Recommendation 87/598/EEC on a European Code of Conduct relating to electronic payment*.[61] One of the objectives of this recommendation was to afford consumers security and convenience when using new, electronic means of payment. It also contained some provisions on contract formation and transparency as well as privacy. Thus contracts with consumers had to be in writing (in the official language(s) of the Member State in which it was concluded) and be the result of a prior application by the consumer. It

---

59   *Salvatore Grimaldi v Fonds des maladies professionnelles*, Case 322/88 [1989] ECR
      4407.
60   Tribunal d'instance de Juvisy sur Orge, 27 April 1990, n. 51/90, Marand/Credit
      Lyonnais, cited in Arora and Favre–Bulle, *op. cit.*, at note 29.
61   OJ 1987 L 365/72.

provided that contracts should set out the general and specific conditions and required conditions relating to termination to be stated in the contract and brought to the notice of the other party.

It provided that the scale of charges should be determined in a transparent manner and take account of actual costs or risks. This seemed to be a surprising attempt to constrain the freedom to contract, but it was not likely to be a major constraint as the next clause reasserted the principle that all conditions are freely negotiable provided they are in conformity with the law and clearly stipulated in the contract. Thus freedom of contract remained the guiding principle outside the question of charges which had to relate to actual costs and risks.

The Recommendation required that privacy be protected when information is transmitted to the trader's bank at the time of payment and subsequently to the issuer. Information should be strictly limited to that which is normal for cheques and transfers. Also electronic payments were said to be irreversible. Any orders given were irrevocable and it was not possible to countermand them. There was no provision for consumers to be able to challenge payment orders, although it did state the (too?) general principle that problems with protecting information and security should be openly acknowledged and cleared up.

In truth, however, this measure was more concerned with ensuring systems were inter-operable and that traders had fair access to them than with consumer protection matters. The impact of this measure on consumer protection does not seem to have been great and has largely been superseded by the Payment Systems Recommendation.

(ii) *Payment Systems Recommendation*

Consumer protection aspects were addressed more directly in *Commission Recommendation 88/590/EEC concerning payment systems, and in particular the relationship between cardholder and card issuer.*[62] Interestingly the preamble mentioned not only that contract terms in Member States were divergent, but also that in some cases they were disadvantageous to the consumer (recital 6). This represents a rather clear autonomous consumer protection motivation for EC intervention, albeit by a means of non-binding act.

The Payment Systems Recommendation applies to a wider range of payment systems than the Electronic Payment Recommendation, which was

---

[62]   OJ 1988 L 317/55. See generally, X. Thunis, 'The Second European Recommendation Concerning Payment Systems: New Obligations for Card Issuers?' [1992] 3 *J.I.B.L.* 101.

restricted to electronic payments by cards. This later Recommendation covers electronic payment by card, but also non–electronic payment by card (other than when the card is simply to guarantee a cheque), electronic payment made without a card (e.g. home banking) and matters connected to the withdrawal of banknotes or deposits made at cash dispensing or automatic teller machines. On the whole it improves upon the provisions in the Electronic Payment Recommendation both regarding the clarity and content of obligations. It covers a wider range of issues of concern to the consumer, such as liability for unauthorised use of the card, the burden of proof in relation to unauthorised fund transfers and responsibility for non or defective execution of transfers.

Payment devices can only be provided in response to an application from the consumer.[63] Each issuer of payment devices must draw up full and fair contract terms. The contract must be in writing, in a form which is easy to read and use easily understandable words. A novel feature is that the contract must be in the language or languages which are ordinarily used for such or similar purposes in the regions where the contract terms are offered. This is an interesting intermediate position, falling short of necessarily requiring all Member State languages to be used, but ensuring that a language appropriate to the context is used. Contract terms cannot be altered without agreement, but this is to be inferred if a payment device continues to be used after notice of an alteration has been received.[64]

The contract must specify the basis of the calculation of charges including interest. Unlike in the Electronic Payment Recommendation, there is, perhaps regrettably, no exhortation to take into account actual costs and risks. It must state whether debiting and crediting will be instantaneous, and if not the period within which this will be done, and when any invoices will be sent out.

The consumer is under obligations to take all reasonable steps to keep safe the payment device and means of using it (e.g. PIN). He must not record the PIN or other means of using the device on the payment device or anything kept with it. The issuer or a central agency should be notified

---

63   We use the phrase consumer for ease of comprehension, but the Recommendation refers to 'contracting holder'.

64   The mere fact that the consumer has not terminated the contract within a certain period after notification of the modification, without having actually used the device, does not fulfil the Recommendation's requirements concerning silent acceptance. Such a rule is, however, included in the code of conduct adopted by European card issuers, see Thunis, *op. cit.*, at 104 who seems to accept this rule.

without undue delay (a) of the loss, theft or copying of the payment device[65] or the means to enable it to be used, (b) the recording of any unauthorised transactions, and (c) any error or irregularity in the issuer's maintenance of the account. These last two obligations require the consumer to check his records. It is unclear whether failure to notify precludes the consumer from redress or indeed how the question of whether there has been undue delay will be interpreted.

The contract must provide that there will be no liability for use of the payment device after notification of its loss etc. Liability prior to notification is to be limited to 150 ECU.[66] However, these restrictions on liability do not apply where the consumer has been fraudulent or extremely negligent, although even in these cases the issuer is obliged to take all action open to him to stop any further use of the payment device. Whilst one can accept that the fraudulent consumer might not deserve protection it might seem unfair to penalise the careless consumer, even if he is extremely negligent.[67] After notification the consumer is not liable for damage caused by use of the card. But this extinction of liability can be denied even where the consumer has not been extremely negligent, for it seems to be a pre–requisite[68] that the consumer has fulfilled his obligations, mentioned above, to safeguard the device and means to access it and to notify losses and irregularities.[69] This seems to be too onerous on the consumer. A better approach is that adopted by the United Kingdom's Consumer Credit Act 1974 which only denies relief to a consumer where the misuse arose from his giving possession of a credit token to another and even then liability ends when there is notification that it is likely to be misused. This is one clear example where the risks of new

---

65   Issuers must have means for consumers to notify such events day and night, although company specific cards need only have this facility during the issuer's hours of business.

66   This limitation of liability *before* notification was a novel concept in some Member States, such as Belgium, see Thunis, *op. cit.*, at 109.

67   As the Recommendation uses the word 'extremely' negligent, this might indicate a higher threshold than the usual legal term 'grossly' negligent; in which case the criticism in the text may lose some of its force.

68   We say seems to be a pre–requisite for although para. 4.2 of the Annex states that these conditions shall be included in the terms of contract, no mention is made of these pre–conditions in para. 8.2 which contains the main rule extinguishing liability after notification.

69   These restrictions do not apply to the 150 ECU limit. Is therefore the careless, but not extremely negligent, consumer to be subject to a 150 ECU limit for payments made prior to notification, but to be wholly liable for uses made of the payment device thereafter?

technologies should not be unfairly placed on the inexperienced or naive consumer.

Payment device issuers must have internal record keeping arrangements which are sufficient to enable operations to be traced and for errors to be rectified. Consumers are entitled to be given a record of operations instantaneously or shortly after they have been completed. In an important consumer protection provision the Recommendation provides that in any dispute relating to liability for an unauthorised electronic fund transfer, the burden of proof shall be on the issuer to show that the operation was accurately recorded and entered into the accounts and was not affected by technical breakdown or other deficiency. This is a welcome recognition of the need to protect consumers from the risks inherent in the use of new technology. However, it has been suggested that this improvement may well be more theoretical than practical as issuers will often be able to produce elements of proof and the courts have been reluctant to question the reliability of issuer's systems.[70]

The issuer of the payment device is liable for the non–execution or defective execution of an operation, even if the device used is not under his direct or exclusive control. Liability is limited to the amount of the unexecuted or defectively executed operation. The issuer is also liable for operations not authorised by the consumer, subject to what has been mentioned above concerning liability for misuse. In such cases liability extends to the amount needed to put the consumer into the position he was in before the unauthorised operation. Questions of any further financial consequences are subject to the national law applicable to the contract between the issuer and the consumer. At least some of the risks created by the use of new technology are placed on the issuer, who is most able to control them.

Follow up surveys have seemed to suggest that the Payment Systems Recommendation has not been fully implemented in practice.[71] Indeed the European credit–sector associations have adopted their own *Code of best practice of the European banking industry on credit–based payment systems*, which is similar to the Payment Systems Recommendation, but less protective of the consumer. In 1991 the Commission sponsored industry manned Committee on Commerce and Distribution adopted a Code limited to

---

[70]   Thunis, *op. cit.*, at 107.

[71]   See C. Knobbout–Bethlem, *A survey of the implementation of the EC recommendation concerning payment systems*, (BEUC, 1990) and J. Mitchell and W. Thomas, *Payment card terms and conditions in the European Union, A survey of the implementation of European Commission Recommendation 88/590/EEC on payment systems*, (International Consumer Policy Bureau, 1995).

cards issued by traders which was also less consumer friendly.[72] The Commission shows signs of weariness at the lack of effectiveness of these private codes of conduct and seems to be in the process of reviewing the Payment Systems Recommendation and is likely to propose two new Recommendations – one concerning cards and the other dealing with other means of payment. The Commission may even consider proposing a directive. If it does so it will mirror the trend that can be seen in the European regulation of cross–border transfers.

C.   Cross–Border Transfers

(i)   Cross–Border Transfers Recommendation

Commission Recommendation 90/109/EEC on the transparency of banking conditions relating to cross–border financial transactions[73] set out six principles aimed at increasing transparency; clarifying which party is to bear the costs; setting out a time scale within which action will be taken and promoting complaint procedures. In summary the six principles involved:

- provision of easily understandable and readily available information;
- giving a transaction statement setting out commission fees, charges and exchange rates;
- providing information on who will bear the fees and charges as well as provisions to ensure the transferor can choose to bear all such charges;
- requiring each intermediary institution to deal with a transfer order within two working days;
- obliging the transferee's institution to complete its obligations by the day following receipt of funds;
- the establishment of complaints machinery, including an eventual referral to an independent body

Subsequently the Commission issued a number of reports on this topic[74] and undertook a number of surveys on the implementation of the Recommendation as well as the *European banking industry guidelines on customer information on cross–border remote payment.* It was clear that

---

[72]   *Code of conduct concerning payment systems, and in particular the relationship between cardholders and company–specific card–issuers.*

[73]   OJ 1990 L 67/39

[74]   *Making payments in the internal market,* COM(90) 447 and *Easier cross–border payments: breaking down the barriers,* SEC(92) 621, *Transparence et Qualité d'Execution des Paiements Transfrontaliers,* SEC(93) 1968/5.

self regulation was not effective enough by itself and so a Directive was proposed.[75]

(ii) Draft Directive on Cross–Border Transfers

The proposed Directive would be minimal in character and set out to fulfil the principles of the Cross–Border Transfers Recommendation (recital 8). It would apply to cross–border credit transfers of less than 50,000 ECU. Two key definitions are – 'originator' – the natural or legal person who orders the making of a cross–border credit transfer; and 'beneficiary' – the final recipient of the transfer when it is made available in an account to which he has access (arts 2(h) and(i)).

The Directive proposes that financial institutions be under a duty to provide prescribed information both prior to a cross–border transfer and subsequent to such a transfer. Such information must be in a readily comprehensible form and should be in writing, although this is stated to include, where appropriate, information supplied by electronic means.

Art. 3 provides that actual or prospective customers must have available to them an indication of both the time needed for a cross–border transfer to be effected (with the point in time from when that period runs being clearly indicated) and an indication of the time taken to credit a beneficiary's account when funds are received from such a transfer. The manner of calculating commission and charges, including where appropriate rates, together with any value date and an indication of the reference exchange rates used, must also be provided, along with an indication of the complaint and redress procedures available and means of accessing them. One might criticise the use of the term 'indication' to qualify some of these obligations as being rather vague and encouraging imprecision.

Unless the customer expressly forgoes his right, art. 4 requires he shall be supplied subsequent to the execution or receipt of a cross–border credit transfer with a statement containing a reference enabling him to identify the transfer, the original amount, the amount of charges and commission fees payable, any value date applied and any exchange rate used. Where the originator specified that the beneficiary should bear part or all of the charges, then the beneficiary's own institution should inform him of this.

---

[75] See proposal for a European Parliament and Council Directive on cross–border transfers at OJ 1994 C 360/13, amended proposal at OJ 1995 C 199/16; common position at OJ 1995 C 353/52 with latest amendments found at COM(96) 172. We will refer to the latest version. The Commission has also issued a Notice on the application of the EC competition rules to cross–border credit transfers: OJ 1995 C 251/3.

By art. 5, an institution, unless not wishing to deal with a customer, must at his request give an undertaking concerning the time needed for executing the transfer, the commission fees and charges payable, apart from those relating to the exchange rate.

These pre–contractual information provisions are weak. Art. 3 contains a requirement to provide very general indicative information and this only has to be made available and need not be automatically supplied. Art. 5 requires more precise information, but this must be expressly requested by the consumer. Few consumers are likely to make such specific requests. It could have usefully been provided that such information should always be given when a consumer makes an enquiry or places an order. This could then have been a firm benchmark against which the subsequent obligations of the institution might be judged. In this respect it is important to appreciate that the value of information may not simply be to inform decision–making, but it may also serve as a record of what was agreed which can be referred to when subsequent disputes arise.

Art. 6 imposes obligations relating to the time taken for transfers. The originating institution shall execute the transfer within an agreed time. Where this is not complied with, or if there is no agreed time, then, at the end of the fifth day following the date of the acceptance of the transfer order, the originating institution becomes liable to pay the beneficiary institution compensation (art. 6(1)).[76] This compensation is based on the reference rate of interest (established in accordance with rules laid down by Member States) calculated for the period running from the end of the agreed time, or, in default, the end of the fifth banking day following acceptance of the order until the date the funds are credited to the beneficiary. This compensation is payable to the beneficiary's institution, not the beneficiary.

The beneficiary's right to compensation is triggered by a different event than delay on the part of the originating institution. The beneficiary institution must make funds available within any agreed time limit, and failing any agreed date by the end of the banking business day following the day when funds were credited to it (art. 6(2)). Interest is to be calculated by applying the reference rate of interest from the agreed time limit, or default limit, until the date funds are credited to the beneficiary's account. Thus the proposed Directive appears to create the possibility of the beneficiary's institution being compensated for delays in transferring money to it, but only becoming liable itself to the beneficiary once it has received funds. These compensation obligations do not, in any event, apply if it can be established that the delay was attributable to the originator or beneficiary.

---

[76] Similar obligations are placed on intermediary institutions to compensate the institution from which the order originated.

Art. 7 provides a welcome recognition of the need for cross–border transfers to be made in such a way that the beneficiary can receive the full amount without deductions. It requires the originating, any intermediary, and the beneficiary's institution to execute the credit transfer for the full amount unless the originator has specified that the costs of the transfer are to be borne wholly or partly by the beneficiary. Nevertheless, the beneficiary's institution can levy an administration charge in accordance with relevant rules and customs, so long as it is not used as a way of avoiding the obligation to transfer the full amount. Earlier drafts of the Directive had usefully included the rule that such charges should not be higher than those applied to a domestic credit transfer. If the originating or intermediary institution has breached this obligation then, when requested by the originator, the originating institution is under a duty to credit the beneficiary with the amount deducted, free from all deductions and at its own cost. Commendably, the originating institution takes responsibility for the errors of intermediaries.[77] Where the failure to execute the order in accordance with the originator's instructions was caused by the beneficiary's institution then it shall be liable to credit the beneficiary, at its own cost, with any sum wrongly deducted.

If a cross–border transfer order has been accepted, but the beneficiary institution has not been credited with that amount, then art. 8 provides that the originating institution is liable to credit the originator with the amount of the transfer (up to 20,000 ECU), interest calculated using the reference interest rate on the amount from the date of the transfer order to the date of the re–crediting, plus any charges paid by the originator. These obligations must be fulfilled within 14 banking business days of a request from the originator, such request not being made until the time limit set out in art. 6 for completing the transfer has lapsed. However, the obligations do not apply if, in the meantime, funds have been credited to the beneficiary. Thus in practice the provision is likely merely to provide a mechanism for spurring the institution to fulfil its obligations. The obligation to re–credit does not apply if the transfer was not completed because of an error or omission in the originator's instructions or because of non–execution by an intermediary expressly chosen by the originator.[78] In this instance, the originating institution and the others involved shall endeavour as far as possible to refund the amount, but would not seem to be obliged to refund charges and

---

[77] Intermediaries in breach of art. 7 are under a duty to credit amounts deducted to either the originating institution or, if that institution so requests, the beneficiary.

[78] In this situation it is not made clear that the chosen institution should bear a responsibility towards the originator.

interest accruing and may deduct the costs of recovery.[79] Where the reason why the transfer was not completed was non–execution by an intermediary chosen by the beneficiary's institution, then this latter party is the one obliged to make funds corresponding to the amount of the transfer available to the beneficiary.

It should be noted that there is a general *force majeure* defence to all obligations laid down in the Directive (art. 9). The concept of *force majeure* is considered in more detail in the tourism chapter (see Chap. 7 section 2E(ii)).

Member States must ensure that 'adequate and appropriate complaints and redress procedures [are.....] available to afford the consumer better protection, using existing procedures where available' (art. 10). It will be remembered that the Cross–Border Transfers Recommendation had required there be an independent body to whom consumers could complain; it had listed the following as examples of bodies which might be competent to hear such appeals – ministerial departments, central banks, a specialist body, such as an Ombudsman, or a contact committee comprising bank representatives and users. A similar range of bodies could be called upon to fulfil the Directive's obligation in relation to dispute resolution. The fact that the task may be taken on by different bodies in Member States can be seen as a legitimate expression of national traditions and preferences. What is important is that those procedures are adequate and effective and that consumers know to whom they can complain.

D.   Conclusions

Despite the impending Directive on cross–border transfers, self regulation remains important for other payment systems. The evidence of practice in this area has not tended to support the view that 'soft law' can be an effective method of consumer protection. It may be now that the Commission has proven its willingness to regulate in one area that self regulation will work in the others, but this supports the cynic's view that effective self–regulation is adopted by industry as the lesser of two evils when faced with the prospect of legislation, rather than for its intrinsic merit.

This is unfortunate, for within the present context voluntary codes could have a role to play in developing, for instance, how industry can best meet its obligation to provide its customers with readily comprehensible written

---

79   Intermediary institutions have similar obligations to refund their instructing institution if transfers have not been made. Where the transfer was not completed because of an error or omission of the instructing institution then the intermediary must endeavour as far as possible to refund the amount.

information on conditions for Cross–Border transfers. The mistake in this area has been to use soft law as a source of obligations and not as a means of building upon and giving practical content to legally enforceable obligations. However, once the need for a legally binding regulation is recognised, soft law ought not to be jettisoned entirely for it can play an important supplementary role and allow regulation to be framed in a manner which leaves scope for alterations over time.

4. BANKRUPTCY

The development of the 'credit society' has been, on the whole, a positive development for consumers, giving them greater choice and control over their financial planning. It does, however, pose dangers to consumers. There is a need to balance greater access to credit with controls against its over-promotion, which can lead to the over–indebtedness of consumers. When indebtedness becomes over–indebtedness this has consequences for the individual consumers, the creditors and society as a whole.

Increased over–indebtedness can be detected as a phenomenon affecting many EC Member States in recent years.[80] In part this is due to the credit boom of the late 1980s which has widely been recognised as being fuelled by imprudent lending practices. However, sharp falls in house values in many countries and the general economic recession are also seen as contributing factors.

It is interesting that many of the explanations for indebtedness based on empirical research concentrate of social and economic phenomena (often involving a change of circumstance such as the debtor becoming unemployed, falling ill or having a relationship breakdown) rather than blaming the individuals for their own plight.[81] This is helping to change social attitudes, so that just as credit is now socially respectable, so too debt

---

[80] See the statistical survey in Chap. 1 of N. Huls *et al.*, *Over–indebtedness of Consumers in the EC Member States: Facts and Search for Solutions*, (Story Scientia, 1994).

[81] See, in the UK, Dept. of Trade and Industry, *Surveys Carried out for the Committee on Consumer Credit*, (H.M.S.O., 1971), cited in R. Cranston, *Consumers and the Law*, (2 ed. Weidenfeld and Nicolson, 1984) at 205 and R. Berthoud and E. Kempson, *Credit and Debt*, (Policy Studies Institute, 1992); in Germany, K. Holzscheck, G. Hörmann and J. Daviter, *Praxis des Konsumentenkredits in der Bundesrepublik Deutschland*, (Bundesanzeiger, 1982). See also U. Reifner and J. Ford (eds), *Banking for People*, (de Gruyter, 1992), Chap. 31 *et seq.*, with national reports from several European Countries. A similar pattern is found and in the USA, D. Caplovitz, *Consumers in Trouble*, (Free Press, 1974).

is increasingly seen as the result of social or personal misfortune rather than individual fault. As credit is becoming an increasing feature of our society it is being recognised that over–indebtedness is an inevitable by–product. Ill health, unemployment, house price collapses, business failure, marriage break–up etc. are all conditions which may cause credit which was manageable when taken out to become an intolerable burden. More problematic is the appreciation that some individuals will simply drift into a situation where they are over–committed. This can be seen as often being just as much related to credit marketing practices as to individual weakness or irresponsibility. What is clear is that some of the myths surrounding bankruptcy seem to have been exposed.[82] Thus it is no longer tenable to see all debt as the fault of individuals who deserve to be punished or to suggest that there are numerous devious consumers seeking to use bankruptcy laws to escape their obligations.

Indeed some level of bankruptcy can be taken as an indicator of a healthy society as it shows that people have confidence to take on credit burdens and also take out credit for entrepreneurial reasons (many individual debtors are in reality small businesses, who have not been able to take advantage of limited liability). Perhaps, for this reason, and also because to some extent bankruptcy laws act as a surrogate for a welfare state, bankruptcy laws have always been more liberal in the United States. In fact the consumer market society benefits if debtors can be recycled and put back on to the market as soon as possible.

American consumers have a favourable choice between two bankruptcy plans. Chap. 7 of the US Bankruptcy Code allows them to liquidate their property in return for an immediate discharge of most debts, whilst Chap. 13 provides for a repayment plan over three to five years which leads to the 'super–discharge' of virtually all debts. The consumer is free to choose Chap. 7 if he has no property, but a reasonable income, and Chap. 13 if he has a low income, but plenty of property.[83] It is perhaps, not surprising that, with the welfare state being rolled back in Europe and individualism becoming a dominant philosophy, bankruptcy laws should become a topic of debate and legal reform in Europe. Although European conditions may not justify the replication of US bankruptcy laws, nevertheless the philosophy behind them and some of the principles such as the 'fresh start' are clearly becoming features on the European legal and social landscape.

Procedures to allow bankrupts to discharge their debts without necessarily repaying them in full have been a feature of United Kingdom law

---

[82]   See the influential survey of US debtors in T. Sullivan, E. Warren, J. Westbrook, *As We Forgive Our Debtors*, (Oxford UP, 1989).

[83]   See N, Huls, 'American Influences on European Consumer Bankruptcy Law' (1992) 15 *J.C.P.* 125.

for some time. On continental Europe, however, the traditional concept of the sanctity of contract held sway until recently. Contracts could become a permanent shackle from which debtors were in practice unable to free themselves. This was of course intolerable for the individual, but also did not benefit society which had to meet the social costs of indebtedness, such as marriage break–up, ill health etc. and the fact the individual had little incentive to improve his economic performance. Ironically creditors also suffered as debtors had no incentive to co–operate with them and frequently competition arose among creditors for the debtor's assets. Realisation of the need for a consumer bankruptcy scheme has seen a spate of legislative activity in several Member States in recent years.[84]

In 1992 the Council asked the Commission to propose measures to create consumer confidence in the single market and recommended as one of the priorities 'examination of the question of excessive consumer indebtedness'.[85] The Commission commissioned a study which proposed the adoption of a Consumer Financial Services Marketing Directive.[86]

Despite having a rather contrived structure to mimic that of the General Product Safety Directive, there is much in this proposal which we would welcome. In the first place, it proposes that there be a general transparency obligation on suppliers of financial services and intermediaries only to place transparent financial products on the market and suggests the Community might want to establish codes of practice to improve transparency. Although the proposal is still vague as to what transparency should entail – does it for instance go so far as to require positive counselling? – it is certainly a proposal which sits easily with our call for a more radical information strategy. It is also relevant to the bankruptcy issue, as it could remove the one avoidable cause of bankruptcy, i.e. the over–promotion of consumer credit.

The remainder of the proposals relate more directly to bankruptcy law, or as they prefer to call it, to avoid stigmatisation, debt settlement. A central policy would be the requirement that Member States ensure debt counselling services are available. In some countries debt counsellors have become highly efficient and provided much practical benefit and the Commission could usefully promote such services throughout the Community. The proposal then goes on to suggest that these debt counsellors should be encouraged to propose debt settlement plans, but that also judicial procedures should be established which can lead to discharge of the debtor's

---

[84] An annex to COM(95) 117 lists the debt arrangement schemes in Europe.

[85] Council Resolution on Future Priorities for the Development of Consumer Protection Policy: OJ 1992 C 186/1.

[86] See, N. Huls *et al.*, *op. cit.* and N. Huls, 'Towards a European Approach to Over-indebtedness of Consumers' (1993) 16 *J.C.P.* 215.

obligations after no more than four years. It is also suggested that the laws on exemptions be modernised so that a fresh look is taken at what part of a debtor's assets and income are protected. In order not to make the new procedures a haven for the devious it is proposed that they should only be available to debtors who have acted in good faith and a discharge should not be granted within six years of a previous discharge.

Although the adoption of such a directive remains but a distant hope, the Commission is certainly taking the question of over–indebtedness seriously. It raised the topic in its recent review of the Consumer Credit Directive,[87] even though the topic need not have been broached in that context. Its tone is still, however, rather tentative. It still talks about examining the application of Member States' laws and the disparities they produce in credit markets. It says it will examine the need for European intervention but with an eye on the principles of subsidiarity, consumer protection and free movement. It also talks of looking at what non–regulatory mechanisms might be proposed. Certainly soft law solutions look the most likely route in the short term.

An internal market dimension can be seen in the bankruptcy situation, but only indirectly. Bankruptcy laws do not create any direct barriers to trade, but can lead to distortions in competition if debts are more difficult to enforce in some states than others. As consumers become more active in the single market and 'collect' debts from different countries the advantages of a common European bankruptcy procedure may become more obvious.

However, in the short term the motivation for a European bankruptcy regime will be inspired more by consumer protection than market integration motives. The lack of a strong internal market dimension will make it difficult for the Commission to have binding legislation adopted given the current fashions for deregulation and limited Community intervention, under the guise of the subsidiarity principle. Also the knock–on consequences for national property laws of any bankruptcy regime will act as a brake on the adoption of binding EC legislation. Whether a European bankruptcy regime does finally emerge will be a good test of the extent to which an autonomous EC consumer protection policy has been developed which shows respect for the interests of vulnerable consumers.

5. CONCLUSIONS

One of the themes of this work is the lack of EC regulation of services compared to products. It is perhaps, therefore, surprising that there is enough material to warrant a chapter on financial services – the service sector which is usually most successful at shielding itself from regulation. However, this

---

87 COM(95) 117 at 93–6.

should not lead one to conclude that the EC has been a particularly vigorous regulator of financial services in the past.

What regulation there is has been the result of the need to address very real consumer problems which have either been emphasised or created by the establishment of the internal market. Financial institutions have benefited from rules which make it easier for them to provide services or establish themselves in other Member States and rules on consumer credit are seen as a necessary counterbalance. Equally rules on Cross–Border payment systems are necessary if consumers are to be able to participate in the internal market.

The nature of the EC regulation to date has not been very onerous. We have seen that the Consumer Credit Directive is rather unambitious and tends to rely upon fairly formal traditional information disclosure provisions. The regulation of payment systems has been until recently based on rather ineffective non–binding acts, whilst EC regulation of bankruptcy is still in the first phase of discussion.

There are signs in that the Commission wishes to develop more substantive consumer rights in the financial services field. For instance, it has opened up a debate on cooling–off periods in consumer credit contracts, duties to counsel potential debtors, usury provisions and bankruptcy reform. These could be cited as examples of a possibly more radical Community approach to consumer protection in the financial services sector.

However, in Chap. 5 section 3, we saw the ability of the financial services sector to have itself excluded from the Distant Selling Directive, with no guarantee that equivalent provisions would be included in sectoral directives. This illustrates the difficulties ahead if effective consumer protection regulation of financial services is to be achieved.

One important development will, however, require future financial services regulation. When Monetary Union is achieved, and the 'euro' single currency is a reality, consumers will need to have their interests taken into account.[88] Consumers will want to ensure, *inter alia*, that they do not lose out when the exchange to 'euros' is made; that their position under existing contracts is secured; that they are able to use the new currency effectively (possibly through dual pricing) and that they do not incur greater bank charges, particularly during the transitional period when old and new currencies will both be circulating. Such measures are essential if consumers are to have confidence in the new currency.[89]

---

[88] See J. Allix, 'Consumers and the Single Currency: Legal Problems' [1996] *Consum.L.J.* forthcoming.

[89] The first Commission analysis of the effects of the EMU on consumers and their need of protection is presented in the *Green Paper on the Practical Arrangements for the Introduction of the Single Currency*, COM(95) 333 at 48 *et seq.* The preponderant

Effective financial services regulation is essential if consumers are to have confidence to take advantage of the internal market. The financial service industry is playing a dangerous game if it resists legitimate attempts to provide an effective framework for consumer protection.

---

part of the proposals mainly deal with consumer information and cover areas other than financial services.

7 Tourism

1. INTRODUCTION

One of the fundamental freedoms of the European Union is the free movement of persons. Tourism is one manifestation of this freedom. Tourism may also be considered important for the creation of closer ties between the citizens of the Member States. For these reasons alone one would expect an interest in tourism from the side of the Union. In addition, and perhaps as a still more important reason, there is the economic weight of the tourism industry in Europe. As is noted in the preamble to the Package Travel Directive 'tourism plays an increasingly important role in the economies of the Member States' (recital 7).

The regulation of tourism came on to the agenda of the European Community in the beginning of the 1980s. In 1982 the Commission issued the first guidelines for a Community policy on tourism. Already in these 1982 guidelines, Community rules on package tours were foreseen.[1]

Tourists are consumers. In a Community policy on tourism, consumer protection therefore has a natural place. The mention of consumer protection measures in tourism policy is not surprising. Broadly speaking most parts of EC consumer law have as one of their purposes to protect consumers as tourists. As we noted in the introduction to this work, the harmonisation of consumer law in the EC is partly justified by the aim of promoting the cross-border activities of consumers in the internal market. Such cross-border purchases often take place in connection with tourism. It is therefore natural to look at, for example, the general rules on credit cards or on unfair contract terms also as complementing the Community's tourism policy.[2]

In this chapter of the book, however, a more narrow perspective will be adopted. Here the focus is on Community legislation directly regulating tourism services. The most important directive in this area is Council Directive 90/314/EEC on package travel, package holidays and package

---

[1] Initial guidelines for a Community policy on tourism, Bulletin of the European Communities, Supplement 4/82 at 6.

[2] See the European Parliament Resolution on a Community Tourism Policy: OJ 1991 C 183/74, items 95 and 96. The tourism policy is of course also linked with environmental policy – one could as an example mention the policy of easing the congestion around the Mediterranean – but this does not come to the fore in the materials dealt with in this chapter. See also on this link the Resolution on a Community Tourism Policy, items P, 28, 32, 37 and 38.

tours (the Package Travel Directive).[3] Partly connected with this Directive is Council Regulation (EEC) No 295/91 establishing common rules for a denied–boarding compensation system in scheduled air transport (the Overbooking Regulation).[4] Some other regulations on air traffic services which might be, in part, based on consumer policy goals will not be dealt with here.[5] The various kinds of measures adopted in the field of transportation law are also not considered here.[6]

There is also a Council recommendation on fire safety in existing hotels.[7] As the practical impact of this non–binding instrument seems to be small, and as it mainly consists of technical guidelines concerning escape routes, construction features, coverings and decorations, electric lighting, heating, ventilation systems, fire–fighting, alarm and alerting equipment, and safety instructions, it will not be analysed further.

Another type of service connected with tourism is regulated by the newly adopted Directive 94/47/EC of the European Parliament and the Council on the protection of purchasers in respect of certain aspects of contracts relating to the purchase of the right to use immovable properties on a timeshare basis (the Timeshare Directive).[8] This has practical significance for an increasing problem facing consumers who are persuaded to enter such contracts when on holiday and is considered below.

---

[3]   OJ 1990 L 158/59.

[4]   OJ 1991 L 36/5.

[5]   See Council Regulation (EEC) No 2342/90 of 24 July 1990 on fares for scheduled air services: OJ 1990 L 217/1 and Council Regulation (EEC) No 2299/89 of 24 July 1989 on a code of conduct for computerised reservation systems: OJ 1989 L 220/1, amended OJ 1993 L 278/1.

[6]   See V. Kendall, *EC Consumer Law*, (Wiley Chancery, 1994) at 257 *et seq.* as well as the proposed Regulation on common rules for the international carriage of passengers by coach and bus: OJ 1989 C 31/9 and the Proposal for a Council Regulation (EC) on air carrier liability in case of accidents: COM(95) 724. The latter project has already reached its final legislative stages. In September 1996 the European Parliament approved the proposal, subject to a series of amendments. See European Parliament, Minutes of the sitting of 17 September 1996, PE 252.048, PV 36.

[7]   OJ 1986 L 384/60.

[8]   OJ 1994 L 280/83.

2. PACKAGE TRAVEL DIRECTIVE

A. Introduction

As already mentioned, legislation on package tours was envisaged in the 1982 guidelines for a Community policy on tourism. The first proposal for a directive on the subject was published in 1988.[9] After this the preparation of the Directive proceeded relatively expeditiously: the Package Travel Directive was adopted in 1990. Although the Parliament proposed a large number of amendments to the proposals,[10] this did not have any considerable effect on the content of the Directive. The Package Travel Directive offers a very good example of the weak role of the Parliament in the EC legislative process, at least at that time. It also exemplifies the typical watering down–development during its preparation.[11]

The Directive contains three kinds of provisions. First, there are rules on marketing and the pre–contractual duty to give information. These provisions aim at increasing transparency, and are supplemented by a rule on the minimum information content of the contract. Second, the bulk of the rules in the Directive are of a contractual nature. The Package Travel Directive is certainly the most detailed attempt to regulate a part of contract law in the consumer area so far adopted at the EC level. Third, there is a rule on the obligation of the organiser or retailer to provide sufficient security for the refund of money paid over and the repatriation of the consumer.

As is the case with most consumer law measures in the EC, consumer protection is not the only purpose of the Directive. In fact internal market reasons are strongly emphasised in the preamble to the Directive. It is noted that 'one of the main objectives of the Community is to complete the internal market, of which the tourist sector is an essential part' (recital 1) and that the disparities in national laws concerning package tours give rise to obstacles to the freedom to provide services and distortions of competition which should be removed by the Directive (recital 2). The drafters of the Directive hope – perhaps, somewhat unrealistically – that 'the package travel industry in Member States would be stimulated to greater growth and productivity if at least a minimum of common rules were adopted in order to give it a Community dimension' (recital 7). The harmonisation of the law is thought to encourage especially the active internal market consumer; as the existing 'disparities in the rules... are a disincentive to consumers in one Member State from buying packages in another Member State' (recital 8).

---

9   OJ 1988 C 96/5.
10 OJ 1989 C 69/102 and OJ 1990 C 149/86.
11 See K. Tonner, 'Die EG–Richtlinie über Pauschalreisen' (1990) *Europäische Zeitschrift für Wirtschaftsrecht* 409 at 411.

The Directive does not, however, seek a total harmonisation of the rules in this area. The Directive is expressed to be only a minimum directive, allowing the Member States to use more stringent provisions to protect the consumer (art. 8).

As will be noted later, the harmonisation even of the minimum level of protection has not been very successful, as many rules of the Directive can be and have been interpreted in different ways in different Member States. The form of implementation also varies significantly.[12] In the United Kingdom the implementation has taken place through specific regulations which in many parts follow the wording of the Directive very closely.[13] The more common way to implement the Directive, however, has been to redraft the material more thoroughly and adopt specific legislation on package tours according to national legislative traditions.[14] It has also been possible to include the rules in the national civil code, as has been done in the Netherlands[15] and in Germany.[16]

B. Scope

The Directive does not cover all activities of travel agencies and other travel organisers. It is specifically delimited to deal with 'packages' only. According to art. 2(1) a package is a pre–arranged combination of at least two elements sold or offered at an inclusive price; the possible elements being transport, accommodation and other tourist services, if they account for a significant proportion of the package.[17]

---

12 A description of the implementation of the Directive in the then Member States is given in A. de León Arce, *Contratos de Consumo Intracomunitarios*, (Eurolex, 1995) at 226 *et seq.* The implementing legislation in Germany is analysed in K. Tonner, *Der Reisevertrag*, (Luchterhand, 1995) and in Austria in W. Graziani–Weiss, *Reiserecht in Österreich*, (Verlag Österreich, 1995).

13 The Package Travel, Package Holidays and Package Tours Regulations 1992, S.I. 1992/3288.

14 See in France Loi n° 92–645 du 13 Julliet 1992 fixant les conditions d'exercice des activités relatives à l'organisation et à la vente des voyages ou de séjours. In the Nordic Member States specific Package Tours Acts (which are not similar) have been adopted: see Acts 472/1993 (Denmark), 1079/1994 (Finland) and 1992:1672 (Sweden).

15 A new Chap. 7A of Book 7 of the Civil Code, see Act 689/1992.

16 *Bürgerliches Gestezbuch*, art. 651(a)–(l). See Tonner (1995), *op. cit.*

17 This definition corresponds, in spite of a different terminology, to the definition in art. 1(2) of the Brussels International Convention on Travel Contracts of April 23,

The central idea here is that only combinations of the elements mentioned are covered by the Directive. A pure contract of transportation is outside its scope, as well as, for example, the leasing of a holiday cottage.[18] It suffices that two of the three elements are present.[19] There may therefore be a 'package tour' even though no element of transportation is included. A combination of accommodation and other significant tourist services would be covered by the Directive.[20] These other services should obviously not include things that are usually performed in connection with transport or accommodation. Breakfast offered together with accommodation does most certainly not constitute a 'package' and the same can probably also be said about the offering of sheets and cleaning as part of the lease of a holiday cottage.[21]

The combination should be pre-arranged in order to form a package. If a consumer plans his journey himself and turns to a travel agency to have his air tickets and hotel accommodation arranged according to his wishes, this does not constitute a package tour even though the travel agency may charge him for both on the same invoice.

The service should have a minimum duration in order to be caught by the Directive. The Directive is only applicable when the service covers a period of more than twenty-four hours or includes overnight accommodation. A pre-arranged one day trip, for example, to a cultural event is therefore not covered.[22]

Even though the growth and importance of cross-border tourism is one of the reasons for the Directive, this is not reflected in its scope of application. A purely national package tour with all services offered in the country of the consumer would be covered.

1970, see S. Zunarelli, 'Package Travel Contracts: Remarks on the European Community Legislation' (1994) 17 *Fordham International Law Journal* 489 at 491.

18 N. Reich, *Europäisches Verbraucherrecht*, (3rd ed., Nomos, 1996) at 365.

19 The famous letter of the then President of the British Board of Trade, Mr. Heseltine, explaining that a combination of a ferry transport and a cottage lease was outside the scope of the Directive therefore was clearly wrong, see D. Grant and S. Mason, *Holiday Law*, (Sweet & Maxwell, 1995) at 35.

20 S. Storm, 'Harmonisation of the Legislation of EC Member States on Consumer Protection Regarding Package Holidays: Analysis of the Community Package Holiday Directive 1990, with Particular Reference to Scandinavian Law' [1992] *E.Consum.L.J.* 189 at 190.

21 In Austrian implementation the latter situation has been treated as a 'package', see criticism by W. Schuhmacher & M. Tüchler, 'Das österreichische Reiserecht nach Umsetzung der Pauschalreiserichtlinie' (1995) 10 *Verbraucher und Recht* 418 at 419.

22 Storm, *op. cit.*, at 190 *et seq.*

The Directive is a consumer protection directive and it therefore focuses on the relationship between a consumer and an enterprise.[23] However, the Directive is not limited to this relationship in a narrow sense, but covers a somewhat larger area. It has a wider scope of application in two respects. First, not only packages offered by businesses or enterprises *stricto sensu* are covered. All persons who, other than occasionally, organise and sell packages are treated as 'organizers' (art. 2(2)). Packages put together by groups such as cultural or sporting associations and sold to their members on a non–profit basis would therefore fall within the Directive, so long as this does not happen purely occasionally.[24] For the 'retailer', as defined in art. 2(3), there is even no requirement concerning repeated activity; even an occasional retailer is covered, so long as there is a non–occasional organiser behind him. Second, the consumer concept of the Package Travel Directive is wider than usual. According to art. 2(4), a consumer means a person who takes or agrees to take the package or any person on whose behalf the purchase of the package is made or to whom the package is transferred. As there is no delimitation relating to the trade or profession of the buyer of the tour, the Directive covers not only consumers proper but also businessmen buying a business trip.[25]

C.   Information and Transparency

As is typical of EC consumer law measures, one centre of gravity of the Directive relates to information and transparency. The natural basic rule is the truthfulness requirement. According to art. 3(1) any descriptive matter concerning a package, its price and other conditions must not contain any misleading information. This provision can be seen as one reflection of the general truthfulness principle contained in the Misleading Advertising Directive. As such it is therefore rather self–evident. More interesting is the question of the legal consequences. In general these are not spelt out in the Directive; one would therefore have to resort to the Community law principle of effective remedies.[26] The remedies required according to the Misleading

---

23   See above Chap. 1 section 1B.

24   Storm, *op. cit.*, at 191. This seems to be a response to the criticism by the Economic and Social Committee of an earlier proposed definition: 'the person who *in the course of his business* organises the package', see OJ 1989 C 102/27 at 28.

25   Storm, *op. cit.*, at 191 and Schuhmacher & Tüchler, *op. cit.*, at 418.

26   See for example, *Von Colson & Kamann v. Land Nordrhein–Westfalen*, Case 14/83 [1984] ECR 1891, *M.H. Marshall v Southampton and South West Area Health Authority*, Case C–271/91 [1993] ECR I–4367 and *Commission v Denmark*, Case 143/83 [1985] ECR 427.

Advertising Directive would seem, in general, to be sufficient. However, it is interesting to note that the Package Travel Directive does in certain cases expressly attach contract law sanctions to the information provided. Information given in a brochure is, according to art. 3(2), usually binding on the organiser or retailer. Only if changes in the particulars have been clearly communicated to the consumer – and this obviously means specific information to the individual consumer and not merely information in general advertisements etc. – before the conclusion of the contract does this contractually binding effect not arise.[27] This rule on contractual consequences of misleading information in the brochure may be seen as a germ to a more general principle on the contractually binding effect of marketing information.[28]

The transparency policy is not satisfied only by rules on truthfulness of the information which the organiser and retailer happen to give. The Directive also contains provisions which oblige the organiser or retailer to give certain information.

Package tours are usually sold with the help of brochures. If such a brochure is made available to the consumer, it shall in a legible, comprehensible and adequate way indicate the price and certain specified information on the destination, transport, accommodation, meals, passport and visa requirements, health formalities and payment plan as well as the required minimum number of participants and the deadline for informing the consumer of cancellation in case this number is not reached (art. 3(2)). It should be noted that this information is obligatory only if a brochure is used. The provision does not oblige the organiser or retailer to provide any brochure if he does not want to do so. In this sense the described obligation to give information is not an absolute one.

There are however also rules on the obligation to give information which cannot be escaped. Art. 4(1) contains a very extensive list of which the organiser or retailer must give to the consumer. The information shall be given in writing or any other appropriate form. Some of this information, such as passport and visa requirements and health formalities, is to be given before the contract is concluded. Other information, for example, that concerning the particulars of the transport, the local representative, agency or at least an emergency contact, the possibility to contact minors on the tour and possible insurance, should be given in good time before the start of the journey. The latter information requirement is therefore not, as most

---

27   The Directive further qualifies this rule by the requirement that 'the brochure shall expressly state so'. Taking into account the fact that the parties can always agree on changes, it is difficult to perceive the contract law significance of this qualification.

28   T. Wilhelmsson, *Social Contract Law and European Integration*, (Dartmouth, 1995) at 130.

transparency rules, aimed at giving the consumer tools for a rational decision–making concerning the contract, but it rather relates to practical measures to be taken by the consumer before the journey, that is it has to do with the performance of the contract.

As 'consumer' according to art. 2(4) also covers a person to whom the package is transferred – that is each new member of the group – the organiser or retailer may be obliged to give the above–mentioned information several times.[29]

Finally, there are provisions affecting transparency in contracting and the information content of the contract (art. 4(2)). All the terms of the contract have to be communicated to the consumer before the conclusion of the contract. These terms have to be set out in writing 'or such other form as is comprehensible and accessible to the consumer'; as the latter expression in the preamble has been given the formulation 'such other documentary form as... ' (recital 12), it is obvious that purely oral communication is not sufficient. In addition to the communication of the terms the consumer should also receive a copy of them; this copy might, however, be given after the conclusion of the contract.[30] Its role is therefore as a point of reference for the consumer should a dispute arise.

It should be emphasised that 'contract terms' do not only refer to the standard form conditions used by the enterprise, but also to the particulars of the contract. In fact the Directive obliges the contracting enterprise to include certain elements in the contract which are listed in an Annex to the Directive. This list largely repeats in a more detailed form most of the above–mentioned elements of information which should be given in the brochure or before the start of the journey. Some new items are, however, included, such as the price and an indication of the possibility of price revisions, an indication of the periods within which the consumer must complain and, if relevant, any special requirements of the consumer as well as excursions and other services included.

It should be noted that the Directive does not directly prescribe that the contract should be made in writing.[31] It only requires that the consumer should receive written documentation of the terms. It aims at securing that the consumer gets a document (or documents) containing a relatively large amount of information concerning the package and its terms. Whether this is actually called the contract document or, say, a booking document is not important. Therefore the consequence of non–compliance with this requirement of form is not necessarily that the contract is void. Such a

---

29 J. Meyer and S. Kubis, 'Pauschalreiserecht in Europa' (1993) 92 *Zeitschrift für Vergleichende Rechtswissenchaft* 179 at 209.

30 See *ibid.*, at 208.

31 *Ibid.*, at 208.

sanction may of course be prescribed in national law,[32] but various public law sanctions are possible as well. There is also nothing in the Directive which prescribes that the written terms should be conclusive; if the consumer can show that the oral contract was more favourable to him, this contract may, depending on the content of national law, prevail.

Finally, there is an exception to the obligation of strict adherence to the information requirements of the Directive. These requirements shall not preclude the conclusion of last–minute reservations or contracts.

D. Consumer's Right to Transfer

Usually, in most legal systems, a debtor cannot put another person in his place. Travel organisers therefore have not been obliged to accept changes of participants in the package tours. This can be unreasonable with respect to a consumer who cannot participate in a tour he has contracted for, but who wants to send someone else instead. In order to prevent such unreasonableness the Directive contains a rule on the consumer's right to transfer his booking (art. 4(3)).

The consumer has the right to effect such a transfer when he 'is prevented from proceeding with the package'. This should not be interpreted as any strong precondition for the right to transfer; usually the consumer should not be asked to produce cumbersome proof as to why he cannot participate. This interpretation is based on the fact that the requirement in an earlier proposal that the consumer should have been prevented from proceeding for serious reasons has been dropped.[33]

The transfer can only be made to a consumer who satisfies the conditions for the package, for example, concerning health formalities etc.[34] The organiser or retailer may charge for the additional costs arising from the transfer. The traditional contract law principle of non–transference of the burden of contracts is upheld in so far as the transferor and transferee are held jointly and severally liable for payment to the organiser or retailer.

---

[32] See the UK Package Travel, Package Holidays and Package Tours Regulations 1992, reg. 9(3) which make it an implied condition that the requirements are complied with.

[33] According to the 1988 Proposal (art. 4(3)), the consumer had the right to transfer only if he was prevented from proceeding with the package 'for serious reasons'. This was criticised by the Economic and Social Committee, OJ 1989 C 102/27 at 2.4.1.

[34] Storm, *op. cit.*, at 194. Even age might be relevant: a youngster may perhaps not be allowed to participate in a trip for retired persons, see Schuhmacher & Tüchler, *op. cit.*, at 422.

E.   Variation

(i)   The Right to Vary the Contract

Several provisions of the Directive are designated to protect the consumer against unwarranted changes in the contract after it has been concluded. This reflects the principle of *pacta sunt servanda*.

One of the most essential terms, the change of which consumers should be protected against, is the agreement on the price. Price revision is expressly regulated in art. 4(4). Such price revision is of course possible only if it is foreseen in the contract. However, not all kinds of price revision clauses are permitted. In order to be valid such a clause has to fulfil the following conditions: (a) it has to provide for both upward and downward revision,[35] (b) it has to state precisely how the revised price is to be calculated, and (c) it may only allow for variations in transportation costs, certain dues, taxes or fees and exchange rates. Price increases are not allowed during a twenty day period prior to the departure date.

It is not clear to what extent the Directive seeks to regulate the right of the organiser to vary other terms of the contract. The provisions in arts 4(5)–(6) on significant changes of essential terms, including the price, expressly only regulate the effects of such changes and do not address the question, whether the opportunity to make alterations should be considered a right of the organiser or whether such an alteration should be looked upon as a breach of contract. Therefore this point of the Directive has been systematised in various ways. Some understand the provision as giving the organiser a right to change the contract without these changes being regarded as breaches of contract; only the consequences expressly enumerated in the Directive, described below, would follow.[36] Others are of the opinion that only an express clause in the contract on the right to make alterations makes it possible not to regard alterations as breaches.[37] Finally some read the Directive, as it prescribes relatively wide sanctions in case of alterations, as classifying all significant alterations as breaches of contract, whether or not the contract contained an express clause on the right to make changes.[38]

---

[35] Although the Directive uses the word 'or' between upward and downward, only this interpretation makes it understandable why the directions of the changes are expressly mentioned.

[36] In this vein see the implementation in France and the Netherlands, J. Bärlund, 'Matkanjärjestäjän vastuu suhteessa matkustajaan EY:n matkapakettidirektiivin mukaan' in T. Wilhelmsson & K. Kaukonen (eds), *Euroopan integraatio ja sosiaalinen sopimusoikeus* (Lakimiesliiton Kustannus, 1993) at 327.

[37] Storm, *op. cit.*, at 195.

[38] Meyer and Kubis, *op. cit.*, at 210.

However, one should not read into the Directive more than what it contains. It is clear that the Directive prescribes certain legal consequences – analysed below – in case of significant alterations and that these remedies may be used by the consumer irrespective of whether the contract contained an alteration clause or not.[39] Nothing more is required by the Directive in this respect. It is for national law to decide the often primarily metaphysical question of the classification of these rules,[40] as well as questions relating to whether other remedies are given to the consumer and if these should depend upon whether the organiser had reserved a right to vary the contract.

(ii) Consequences of Alterations Before Departure

There are provisions in the Directive concerning the situation that the 'organiser finds that before the departure he is constrained to alter significantly any of the essential terms, such as the price' (art. 4(5)). There are two conditions which should be fulfilled for the rule to apply.[41] First, the change should concern an essential term; the Directive mentions the price, but also the destination, mode of transportation, time of departure and return etc. are certainly essential in this sense.[42] Second, the alteration should be significant; earlier proposals had suggested that a 10% price rise should be considered a significant change.[43] On the other hand one might assume that a few hours alteration of the time of departure or return in a week's package is hardly significant. As one of the consequences of the changes regulated in this provision is the consumer's right of withdrawal, one can see a clear parallel between the requirement of significant change of an essential term

---

39 Bärlund, *op. cit.*, at 326.

40 Compare, however, what is said on insignificant changes in section E(ii), below.

41 In fact one could see the requirement that the organiser is 'constrained' to alter the terms as a third prerequisite. However, as it is hard to imagine that the consumer could be given less protection in a case where the organiser changes the contract without being constrained to do so than when he is forced to do it, the minimum level of protection prescribed in arts 4(5)–(6) should obviously cover both situations.

42 The first two examples are picked from the Danish proposal for implementing legislation, Betænkning nr. 1240 at 171, and the third from the Finnish Government Bill 237/1992 at 22.

43 OJ 1988 C 96/7, art. 4(5)(a). See also Tonner (1990), *op. cit.*, at 410 and K. Tonner, *Reiserecht in Europa*, (Luchterhand, 1992) at 266, as well as Schuhmacher & Tüchler, *op. cit.*, at 420. In German legislation a 5% rule has been adopted (*Bürgerliches Gesetzbuch* art. 651(4)).

and the principle that avoidance of a contract requires fundamental breach which is upheld in many countries.[44]

Slight alterations and alterations of non–essential terms are not regulated by this rule. This means that if such changes are allowed by the contract they cannot be condemned on the basis of this Directive.[45] If the alterations are not foreseen in the contract, such an alteration might be regarded as a breach of contract[46] and the liability rules of art. 5 would apply.[47]

If the organiser makes a significant alteration of an essential term the consumer must, firstly, have the right to take a decision on the future of the contract. He should be able to choose, whether to withdraw from the contract without penalty or to accept the alteration (art. (5)). These are the alternatives required by the Directive. The Directive does not demand that the consumer retains any right to insist on specific performance of the original terms.

If the consumer withdraws from the contract or if the organiser decides to cancel the contract (which is of course the ultimate form of alteration) for any reason other than the fault of the consumer, the consumer is again given a choice by the Directive (art. 4(6)). On the one hand he has the right to demand a substitute package from the organiser or retailer, if they are able to offer such a substitute. It is not expressly stated in the Directive, but presumably the offeror has no right to extra charges even though the substitute is of higher quality than the original package; the right to a substitute package could otherwise easily be circumvented.[48] If the substitute package is of less value than the original package the consumer should be refunded the difference in price. On the other hand, if the consumer does not wish to take a substitute package he can claim repayment, as soon as possible, of all sums paid by him under the contract.

If the consumer does not use any package, he also has the right to compensation for non–performance. This compensation should be awarded 'if appropriate'. This expression probably refers to rules requiring some (economic or perhaps also non–pecuniary) loss as a prerequisite of compensation. This liability is strict and there are no specific restrictions of

---

44   See United Nations Convention on Contracts for the International Sale of Goods (1980), arts 49 and 64.

45   They might under certain circumstances be forbidden on the basis of the Unfair Contract Terms Directive, see its Annex points (j) and (k), see Chap. 3 section C(iv).

46   Compare, however, above in section E(i), one of the interpretations of art. 4(5) according to which it gives the organiser the right to alter the contract.

47   Bärlund, *op. cit.*, at 331.

48   On this point, however, the implementing legislation in the Member States contains various solutions; Bärlund, *op. cit.*, at 334 *et seq*. Storm, *op. cit.*, at 195 presumes that the consumer must pay the difference if he chooses a package of higher quality.

liability when the consumer withdraws from the contract. Where the contract is cancelled by the organiser or retailer the starting point again is strict liability. Here the Directive, however, mentions two exceptions: there is no liability for damages, firstly, if the cancellation is due to the fact that the minimum number of participants mentioned in the package description is not reached, and, secondly, if the cancellation, excluding overbooking, is for reasons of *force majeure*.

Force majeure is here defined as 'unusual and unforeseeable circumstances beyond the control of the party by whom it is pleaded, the consequences of which could not have been avoided even if all due care had been exercised'. (art. 4(6)(ii)). The concept of *force majeure* in Community law has been defined in a number of decisions of the ECJ in the area of agricultural law.[49] However, these decisions do not necessarily affect the interpretation of the concept of *force majeure* in the Package Travel Directive,[50] even though they may be of some relevance. It will be interesting to see how this concept will be applied, as the concrete content of *force majeure* is not the same in all Member States. Certainly the rule is stricter[51] than the 'control liability' of the international sales convention.[52] This provides that any kind of impediment beyond the control of the party may lead to exemption, whereas the Directive accepts only 'unusual and unforeseeable circumstances' as grounds for avoiding liability.

---

[49] See Wilhelmsson, *op. cit.*, at 50.

[50] See the case *An Bord Bainne Co-operative Ltd v Intervention Board for Agricultural Produce*, Case C–124/92 [1993] ECR I–5061, 3 CMLR 856 at 877: 'it must be borne in mind that the Court has consistently held that, since the concept of *force majeure* does not have the same scope in the various spheres of application of Community law, its meaning must be determined by reference to the legal context in which it is to operate.' Compare, however, the more generalising attitude in Commission notice C(88)1696 concerning '*force majeure* in European agricultural law', OJ 1988 C 259/10: 'The aim of this notice is to ensure transparency and consistency in the application of the *force majeure* clause in European law, and particularly in agriculture.'

[51] Bärlund, *op. cit.*, at 343, who in spite of this considers the control liability (granting exemption for all kinds of impediments beyond the control of the party) adopted in the Swedish and Danish implementation sufficient to fulfil the minimum requirements of the Directive. Compare, however, Storm, *op. cit.*, at 195, who for some reason considers the control liability to be stricter.

[52] United Nations Convention on Contracts for the International Sale of Goods (1980), art. 79.

F.   Protection Against Breach of Contract

The Package Travel Directive does not contain any general regulation of the consequences of breach of contract by the organiser or retailer. Only certain situations and remedies are regulated, with the remainder being left to national law.

(i)   Who is Liable?

Art. 5(1) requires Member States to ensure that the organiser and/or retailer is liable to the consumer for the proper performance of the contract, both when the obligations are to be performed by that party himself or by other suppliers. However, this rule does not specify any remedies. It is only concerned with who should be liable for the breach. Its main idea is to prevent the defence that the organiser and/or retailer should not be liable because the breach was due to an independent supplier. The organiser and/or retailer are made liable for the performance of such suppliers.

However, even this limited function of designating the right subject of liability is not performed properly by the provision. The words 'organiser and/or retailer party' are not completely clear. Do they leave it to the Member States or the parties to make the choice? Is it always only the contracting party who is obliged to carry the liability, although he could be a not very solvent retailer? Or should one advocate a more consumer friendly solution and claim that only joint and several liability of the organiser and retailer fulfils the aims of the Directive?[53]

(ii)   Non–Provision of Significant Proportion of Services

Only for a certain type of breaches of contract – in addition to the rules on variation described above – does the Directive prescribe specific remedies. Art. 4(7) concerns the situation where, after departure, a significant proportion of the services is not provided or the organiser perceives that he will not be able to procure such a proportion of the services. This provision only deals with the partial, but significant non–performance of the contract, leaving the consequences of poor performance outside the scope of the rule. One may of course question the practicality of such a distinction.

---

53   See Zunarelli, *op. cit.*, at 499 *et seq.*

In the cases covered by the rule the organiser is obliged to make suitable alternative arrangements. If this is not possible[54] or if the alternative arrangements are not accepted by the consumer for good reasons, the organiser shall provide the consumer with equivalent transport back to the return–point. No extra cost may be charged to the consumer for these arrangements.

In both cases the organiser is also liable to pay compensation to the consumer. This liability arises 'where appropriate'. It is unclear whether this provision contains an independent liability rule of a rather strict character or whether it only is intended to refer to the general rule on liability for damages in art. 5(2), mentioned below.[55]

(iii) Liability for Damages

Only for the remedy of damages does the Directive contain a more generally applicable rule, not limited to certain specific situations (art. 5(2)). This has not, however, produced sufficient clarity as to the liability of the organiser or retailer of a package tour. The liability rules of the Directive are fuzzy and insufficient in several respects.

The complex and sometimes conflicting liability rules in the Directive seem hard to understand. In addition to the main rule in art. 5(2), described below, there is the special rule on compensation in case of variations in art. 4(6)[56] which does not contain all the exempting circumstances mentioned in the main rule. Still more confusion is added to the liability soup by the unsolved question just mentioned, regarding whether art. 4(7) contains an independent liability rule.

The basic liability rule in art. 5(2) regulates the consumer's right to damages resulting from both the failure to perform and improper performance of the contract. In such cases the organiser and/or retailer shall be liable, unless the breach of contract 'is attributable neither to any fault of theirs nor to that of another supplier of services, because' the failures are attributable to the consumer or to a third party, or are attributable to *force majeure* (as defined in art. 4(6), described above) 'or to an event which the

---

54 Of course, if the organiser does not provide alternative arrangements, although he could, the consumer should also have the right to demand return transport, Bärlund, *op. cit.*, at 351 *et seq.*

55 Bärlund, *op. cit.*, at 355 *et seq.* finds arguments for the second alternative, but mentions the opposite interpretation in the Swedish Act. Storm, *op. cit.*, at 196 reads the Directive according to the first alternative, as she expressly denies the possibility of the organiser pleading *force majeure* to avoid payment of compensation.

56 Above, section E(ii).

organiser and/or retailer or the supplier of services, even with all due care, could not foresee or forestall'.

This rule leaves room for different interpretations. Some Member States, like Germany, have implemented the provision as a negligence rule, with a reversed burden of proof, while others interpret it as a strict liability rule, admitting exemption only in case of *force majeure* and certain other situations.[57] The difficulties in the interpretation of the Directive stems from its contradictory wording. The negligence principle seems to be expressed in the first part of the paragraph, by the word 'fault':[58] 'the organiser and/or retailer is/are liable unless such failure to perform or improper performance is attributable neither to any fault of theirs not to that of another supplier of services, because – the failures... are attributable to... '. Also in the preamble the negligence principle seems to be taken for granted, for it states liability occurs, 'unless the defects in the performance of the contract are attributable neither to any fault of theirs nor to that of another supplier of services' (recital 18). Still, a closer reading reveals that this is not necessarily a question of normal negligence liability with a reversed burden of proof. The exemption is qualified by the word 'because'. This indicates that the exemption in fact covers only the three cases enumerated after this word: namely the failures are attributable to the consumer, to a third party or due to a case of *force majeure* and certain comparable situations. What one is speaking about here therefore seems to be a kind of strict liability with an exception for *force majeure* etc.[59]

The Directive also has taken into account the fact that it regulates an area partly covered by international conventions, such as those on transportation and hotel keeping. The Member States may, according to the Directive, allow compensation to be limited in accordance with the international conventions governing such services. In other situations, contractual limitations of liability are only allowed to a limited extent. Such limitations are not permitted at all with respect to personal injury. For other damages the Member States may allow compensation to be limited under the contract, provided the limitation is not unreasonable. Again, this provision leaves room for interpretation. It is not clear whether it allows exemption clauses concerning the grounds for liability or whether it only deals with a

---

57   An overview of the very different solutions is given by Bärlund, *op. cit.*, at 360 *et seq.*

58   The French version uses the word 'faute' and the German 'Verschulden'.

59   See Bärlund, *op. cit.*, at 364 *et seq.* and Zunarelli, *op. cit.*, at 498. Compare, however, N. Reich, 'From Contract to Trade Practices Law: Protection of Consumers' Economic Interests by the EC' in T. Wilhelmsson (ed.), *Perspectives of Critical Contract Law*, (Dartmouth, 1993) at 90.

possible limitation of the amount of the damage. The interpretation varies from country to country.[60]

Liability might be limited by art. 5(4) which concerns the obligation of the consumer to communicate any failure in the performance of a contract to the counterparty 'at the earliest opportunity'. This provision seems rather harsh towards consumers, at least if the quoted words concerning the time for giving the required notice are taken literally.[61] However, again there is lack of clarity as to the legal consequences of this rule. It is not expressly stated, and therefore not certain, that a consumer who does not comply with this obligation should lose his right to compensation.[62] Anyway it should be noted that this obligation of the consumer must be stated clearly and explicitly in the contract and that the contract, according to point (b) of the Annex of the Directive, has to mention the periods within which the consumer must make his complaint. If these rules are not followed, the organiser or retailer obviously cannot rely on the lack of proper communication from the consumer concerning the failure.

G. Protection Against Insolvency

As package tours are usually paid in advance, and are often relatively expensive, the insolvency of the organiser or retailer before or during the tour may cause considerable losses and expenses for the consumer. Therefore the Directive contains a provision on financial security. According to art. 7 the organiser and/or retailer party to the contract shall provide sufficient evidence of security for the refund of money paid over and for the repatriation of the consumer in the event of insolvency.

The form of security is left to the choice of the Member States. Both various kinds of funds as well as insurance cover are acceptable,[63] so long as they provide sufficient security. In order to be efficient this rule ought to be interpreted to require some form of authority supervision of the package tour business.[64] This requirement could be founded on the Community law principle of effective remedies.

---

[60] A comparison is made by Bärlund, *op. cit.*, at 367 *et seq.*

[61] See H.P. Lehofer, 'Minimum Implementation of Minimum D0irectives? Consumer Protection in Austria in the Context of European Integration' (1994) 17 *J.C.P.* 3 at 17 who criticises the placing of such an obligation on the consumer at all.

[62] Storm, *op. cit.*, at 197.

[63] Storm, *op. cit.*, at 198, Reich, *op. cit*, at 366, and Tonner (1990), *op. cit.*, *at* 411.

[64] Reich, *op. cit.*, at 366. Compare Meyer and Kubis, *op. cit.*, at 214 who stress that the Directive does not demand any control system.

Finally, it should be mentioned that the security requirement is typically a provision the non–implementation of which can lead to Member State liability on the basis of the Francovich–principle. This question has been largely discussed in German doctrine[65] and the ECJ has recently, in a case against the German Government, stated that consumers have such a right.[66]

H.   Conclusions

The above presentation has shown that the Package Travel Directive is rather unclear and unsystematic. Many of its provisions leave room for different interpretations. In a study concerned only with the liability rules of the Directive, Johan Bärlund has found many such points which have led to large variations in the implementation of the Directive in different countries. His study also shows that no Member State has been able to avoid conflicts with the Directive in its implementation – except those who have implemented the Directive word by word, where, however, the problems of understanding the Directive have been transferred to the courts or others applying the Directive and to consumers seeking support from it.[67]

When one adds to this the fact that the Directive does not strive at a more complete regulation of the area (it does not deal with many questions, for example those concerning remedies for breach of contract) and that it is a minimum directive, it is quite clear that the level of harmonisation achieved by the Directive is relatively low. The protection afforded to the consumer of package tours may still vary a lot in different Member States, in spite of the Directive.

Of course the existence of a harmonised minimum protection is of some value for the consumers. The Directive has led to the adoption of new legislation in the Member States, which certainly at least in some respects has improved the position of consumers. In some Member States the improvements have been considerable.

---

65   See E.R. Führich, 'Gemeinschaftsrechtliche Staatshaftung wegen verspäteter Umsetzung der EG–Pauschalreise–Richtlinie' (1993) 4 *Europäische Zeitschrift für Wirtschaftsrecht* 725, D.–E. Khan, 'Staatshaftung für verpfuschten Urlaub?' (1993) *Neue Juristische Wochenschrift* 2646, M. Schimke, 'Zur Haftung der Bundesrepublik Deutschland gegenüber Bürgern wegen Nichtumsetzung der EG–Richtlinie über Pauschalreisen' (1993) 4 *Europäische Zeitschrift für Wirtschaftsrecht* 698 and K. Tonner, 'Staatshaftung wegen verspäteter Umsetzung der EG–Pauschalreise–Richtlinie' (1993) 14 *Zeitschrift für Wirtschaftsrecht ZIP* 1205.

66   *Erich Dillenkofer et al. v Germany*, Joined Cases C–178/94, C–179/94, C–189/94 and C–190/94, [1996] ALL ER (EC) 917.

67   Bärlund, *op. cit.*

3.   OVERBOOKING REGULATION

In some situations the Overbooking Regulation is applicable concurrently with the Package Travel Directive. This enactment, which as a regulation is directly applicable in the Member States without any implementation measures, establishes common rules for a denied–boarding compensation system in scheduled air transport. The Regulation, which, according to the preamble, has been issued for 'the protection of the interests of air transport users' (recital 2), establishes common minimum rules applicable where passengers with a valid ticket and a confirmed reservation are denied access to an overbooked scheduled flight (art. 1).

The scope of the Regulation, like the Package Travel Directive, is broader than being a pure consumer protection measure. The Regulation does not cover only consumers proper. It consequently speaks about 'passengers' instead of 'consumers'. It therefore clearly covers business travel as well as tourist travel. Only when the passenger is travelling free of charge or at reduced fares not available directly or indirectly to the public does the denied–boarding compensation scheme of the Regulation not apply (art. 7).

The Regulation gives the passenger certain rights in the event of boarding being denied because of overbooking (art. 4). In such a situation the passenger shall have the choice between reimbursement of the cost of the ticket, re–routing at the earliest opportunity or re–routing at a later date at the passenger's convenience. In addition the passenger also has a right to compensation, irrespective of which choice he makes. A minimum compensation shall be paid to the passenger immediately after boarding has been denied. This compensation is standardised: ECU 150 for flights up to 3500 km and ECU 300 for flights of more than 3500 km, with a possibility of 50% reduction of this figure for certain slight delays. The compensation also need not exceed the price of the ticket. In addition the air carrier shall offer the passenger free of charge telephone/telex/fax expenses, meals and refreshments and possibly hotel accommodation (art. 6).

The Regulation applies to all scheduled flights. If boarding is denied on such a flight sold as part of a package tour, both the Overbooking Regulation and the Package Travel Directive apply. In such a case the air carrier shall pay the standardised compensation mentioned above to the tour operator who in turn is obliged to pass on these sums to the passengers (art. 5). The communication expenses, meals and accommodation mentioned in art. 6 should, however, obviously be offered by the air carrier directly to the consumer of the package tour.[68]

---

68   This seems to follow from the order of the articles in the Overbooking Regulation.

In order to make the handling of an overbooking situation transparent the air carrier is obliged to establish rules for boarding in the event of an overbooked flight, which shall be notified to the Member State and the Commission and be available to the public (art. 3). These rules have to include a certain social element: 'the air carrier should take into consideration the interests of passengers who must be given boarding priority for legitimate reasons, such as handicapped persons and unaccompanied children.'

The need for the Overbooking Regulation must be seen against the background that many air carriers almost regularly overbook some flights, to counterbalance the no–show phenomenon. In most cases this balancing works, but overbooking situations are bound to arise relatively regularly. It is obviously in the interest of the air carriers to have a standardised and easily applicable compensation scheme to use in such cases. The foreseen compensation is rather modest, taking into account that it is a question of breach of contract which might in some cases be regarded as intentional. Of course the fact that the Regulation only establishes 'minimum rules' makes it possible to use any more favourable compensation rules which might exist in national law.[69] The air carrier cannot usually make it a precondition for paying the standardised compensation according to the Directive that the passenger should give up his right to further compensation (art. 9).[70]

4.　TIMESHARE DIRECTIVE

A.　Introduction

Timesharing is a relatively recent way of arranging holiday accommodation. It is an arrangement which gives the purchaser the right, on payment of a global price, repeatedly to use one or more immovable properties for a certain period of the year. Such timesharing is in practice used mostly in the area of holiday accommodation, to create rights in holiday apartments or holiday houses.

---

[69]　It is not settled whether the liability provisions on delay in the Warsaw Convention of 1929 on International Carriage by Air are applicable to non–performance (overbooking can be seen as a case of non–performance) and practice is different in different countries, L. Sisula–Tulokas, 'Dröjsmålsskador vid passagerartransport' (Suomen Lakimiesliiton Kustannus, 1985) at 148 *et seq.*

[70]　This he was obliged to do in the previously used voluntary Denied Boarding Compensation–scheme recommended by the Civil Aeronautics Board and the Association of European Airlines.

The EC legislation concerning timesharing was introduced relatively rapidly. The first proposal was published in 1992.[71] After little more than two years, in October 1994, the Timeshare Directive was adopted. The Directive has not, however, entered into force yet. The Member States have been given a 30 month period from the publication of the Directive to implement it (by 29 April, 1997).

As most Member States did not have any specific legislation on timesharing the Directive will result in new enactments. In the UK the relatively recent Timeshare Act 1992 is proposed to be replaced by new regulations.[72] Of course it is also possible to add these rules to a civil code, as will be done in Holland.[73]

In its adopted version the Directive contains only two kinds of substantive provisions. First, like in much Community consumer protection legislation, there are rules on information and transparency in the pre-contractual stage as well as in the contract. Second, also in line with some other Directives, a right of withdrawal for the consumer is introduced in this field. The consumer's rights under the Directive cannot be excluded by the contract (art. 8).

The 1992 proposal contained a much wider palette of rules, among other things on guarantees to be given by the vendor. The cancellation period was also considerably shortened during the preparation of the Directive, from 28 days for timeshares abroad in the 1992 proposal, to 10 days in the adopted Directive. The Timeshare Directive is therefore again another good example of a consumer protection measure which has been clearly watered down during the preparation process.

The reasons for the Directive are not spelled out clearly in the Directive itself. Of course the preamble starts with the usual reference to internal market considerations: the disparities between national legislation on timeshare contracts 'are likely to create barriers to the proper operation of the internal market and distortions of competition and lead to the compartmentalisation of national markets' (recital 1). Therefore the aim of the Directive 'is to establish a minimum basis of common rules on such matters which will make it possible to ensure that the internal market operates properly and will thereby protect purchasers' (recital 2). No far-reaching harmonisation of the rules on timesharing is attempted. The preamble concedes that the legal nature of the timeshare rights varies

---

71 OJ 1992 C 222/5.

72 Department of Trade and Industry, *Implementation of the EC Directive on Timeshare (94/47/EC), A Consultation Paper*, February 1996.

73 The Bill on timeshare (No. 24449), submitted to the Parliament in October 1995, proposes the insertion of these rules into Book 7, Section 10A of the Dutch Civil Code, see C. Joustra, [1996] *Consum.L.J.* CS24.

considerably from one Member State to another, and notes that no harmonisation is implied in the Directive in this respect (recital 3). Also, as is expressly noted in the preamble, the Directive 'is not designated to regulate the extent to which contracts for the use of one or more immovable properties on a timeshare basis may be concluded in Member States' (recital 4). Possible restrictions on the use of timeshare contracts of certain types, concerning certain property, in certain areas etc. are left to be regulated by the Member States.

The reasons why consumers are thought to need special protection in this area are connected with the advertising and selling practices prevailing on the timeshare market. The vendors often use very aggressive sales techniques and the advertising material is in many cases misleading or incomplete and fails to give the consumer a correct picture of the right he will acquire and his actual possibilities to resell his timeshare.[74] To this one could add the fact that timeshares in practice are expensive, both in comparison with package travel and in relation to the value of the property in question.[75]

As already mentioned only a minimum protection is established by the Timeshare Directive. Like most consumer protection directives this Directive is a minimum directive, which shall not prevent the Member States from having more favourable rules as regards the protection of purchasers (art. 11).

B.   Scope

The ways in which timeshare rights are legally constructed vary a lot in different parts of Europe. The Directive does not aim at any harmonisation in this respect. Art. 1 states that the Member States shall remain competent *inter alia* for the determination of the legal nature of the rights covered by the Directive.

However, it has been considered important that the Directive covers all forms of timeshare arrangements, irrespective of what legal form they have been given. The definition of a timeshare contract in the Directive is therefore rather wide: it covers 'any contract or group of contracts concluded for at least three years under which, directly or indirectly, on payment of a certain global price,[76] a real property right or any other right relating to the use of one or more immovable properties for a specified or specifiable period of the

---

[74]   COM(92) 220 at 39.

[75]   See G. Mäsch, 'Die Time–Sharing–Richtlinie' (1995) 6 *Europäische Zeitschrift für Wirtschaftsrecht* 8 at 9.

[76]   This prerequisite is intended to distinguish a timeshare contract from a tenancy agreement, see the preamble to the Directive (recital 5).

year, which may not be less than one week, is established or is the subject of a transfer or an undertaking to transfer' (art. 2). The Directive, by using the expression 'directly or indirectly', is applicable to all the three main forms of timeshare arrangements:[77] (i) the property law based timeshare, where the purchaser is given a shared right of ownership or some other property right in the object, (ii) the contractual form of timeshare, where the purchaser has a right of use based on contract, and (iii) the form of timeshare using the law of associations and companies, where the right of the purchaser is based on membership.[78] All these forms are covered, as long as the temporal prerequisites in the definition are fulfilled: the contract should be of long-term duration, concluded for a minimum period of three years, and the yearly right to use the object should not be less than one week.

As the right of use, according to the above definition, may relate not only to one, but also to several immovable properties, it seems clear that the Directive covers so called flexible timesharing. This is a form of timesharing which is not tied to a specific apartment or house, but gives the purchaser the right to use for a certain period yearly an object of his choice, for example any property belonging to the stock of his association or company. Admittedly, some of the provisions of the Directive, such as those tying their applicability to the place of the object (arts 4 and 9), cannot be applied according to their wording to flexible timesharing.[79]

The Directive only applies to timeshares in immovable property, defined as 'any building or part of a building for use as accommodation' (art. 2). In the light of this wording one may doubt the correctness of the Commission's view that pleasure boats, mobile homes and moorings would be covered by the Directive.[80]

Finally, the Timeshare Directive is a consumer protection measure, and delimited accordingly. The purchaser is defined as any natural person who acts 'for purposes which may be regarded as being outwith his professional capacity'. Although the Directive does not use exactly the same phrase as many of the previous consumer protection directives ('primarily outside his trade or profession'),[81] the content of the limitation seems to be the same.

---

[77] See M. Martinek, 'Das Teilzeiteigentum an Immobilien in der Europäischen Union' (1994) *Zeitschrift für Europäisches Privatrecht* 470 at 480 *et seq.*

[78] In this perspective one may criticise some of the terminology of the Directive, such as 'vendor' and 'purchaser', for giving the impression that only property based timeshare is covered, c.f. the criticism against the 1992 proposal by Martinek, *ibid.* at 491.

[79] Mäsch, *op. cit.*, at 14.

[80] COM(92) 220 at 44.

[81] See above Chap. 1 section 1B.

C.   Information and Transparency

(i)   *Precontractual Information*

Like much EC consumer legislation, the Timeshare Directive emphasises information requirements. The vendor must provide any person requesting information on the immovable property or properties with a document containing certain information (art. 3). The provision concerns only information to be given to persons who make a request for it. It does therefore not pose any obligation for the vendor to give certain information to the public in general, for example in his advertising. At this stage only information about the right to get information is obligatory.

The document envisaged in art. 3 shall contain a general description of the property or properties. In addition it shall include information on a relatively wide range of particulars mentioned in the Annex to the Directive. These include certain information on the parties, on the nature of the offered right, on the property, on the services offered, on the common facilities, on maintenance and repairs, on the price, costs and charges, and on the right of cancellation. The Directive does not prescribe any specific form for the document,[82] but it is subject to relatively detailed language requirements, described below. The Directive seeks to improve the consumer's knowledge of the existence of such a document by a provision according to which any advertising referring to the immovable property concerned shall indicate the possibility of obtaining the document and where it may be obtained (art. 3(3)).

As mentioned before 'any person' requesting information has the right to obtain this document. On this point the Directive goes further than the 1992 Proposal according to which the obligation to provide a document would exist only in relation to 'any potential purchaser'. One may doubt, however, whether the new wording really can be taken literally. Should the vendor – and for what reason? – really be obliged to give a document to a person with whom he is under no circumstances willing to make a contract?[83]

On the other hand one should construe the term 'requesting' widely. The request does not have to refer to the document; any request for any sort of information concerning the timeshare should trigger the obligation to provide the document.

The time when the document should be given to a possible purchaser is not regulated in the Directive. The content of art. 3 clearly indicates that it has to be given at the latest when the contract is concluded. However, in order to have any effects on the contracting behaviour of the consumer it

---

[82]   COM(92) 220 at 45.
[83]   Mäsch, *op. cit.*, at 11 *et seq.*

should be provided earlier, before the contract is actually made. As no such requirement is stated one may legitimately doubt the efficiency of the provision.

The document to be given to the potential purchaser has certain contractual effects. At least the obligatory information in the document[84] shall become a part of any contract which is concluded. From the point of view of the consumer who does not necessarily know the content of the Annex to an EC directive it seems hard to defend the limitation only to obligatory information. It would have been better to resort to the more general principle on the contractually binding effect of marketing information (as has been done in the Package Travel Directive with respect to the information in the brochure). Such a more general binding effect of the document is mentioned in the preamble.[85] In fact such a broader reading also seems to be implied in the rule on variations also contained in art. 3(2). According to this only changes resulting from circumstances beyond the vendor's control may be made to the information provided in the document, unless the parties expressly agree otherwise. This provision is not limited to cover only the obligatory information.

These contract law provisions can function as a sanction against false or misleading information. What then are the sanctions, if the vendor does not follow the rules requiring a document to be provided containing certain information? This is left to the Member States to decide. The Directive only requires that there should be some sanctions: according to art. 10 the Member States shall make provision in their legislation for the consequences of non–compliance with the Directive. This might imply the need for criminal sanctions or comparable penalties.[86]

(ii) The Form of Contract

An obligatory form is prescribed for the timeshare contract. It shall, according to art. 4, be made in writing. From art. 5 as well as from the Annex point (m) it is to be inferred that this requirement includes the need for both parties to sign the contract.

The contract has to contain at least all the rather numerous items (points a–m) mentioned in the Annex to the Directive. These are the items which must already have been mentioned in any precontractual document – which

---

[84] Art. 3(2): 'all the information... which must be provided...'.

[85] See recital 7 'whereas the information therein must constitute part of the contract...'.

[86] In COM(92) 220 at 46 the provision – which was identical with the one adopted in this respect – is interpreted to mean that 'National legislation must make provision for penalties...'.

means that some consumers shall have written information on these items twice[87] – and some additional items which can be determined at this stage, concerning for instance dates and periods of use of the property, the possibility to join an exchange and resale scheme and the date and place of signature. The contract should also contain a clause limiting the costs, charges or obligations of the purchaser to those specified in the contract (Annex (j)). The language requirements of the contract are dealt with below.

The sanctions for the contract not including the prescribed items are of two kinds. First, if certain of the items are lacking, this will lead to a prolongation of the period of cancellation, as described below. Second, the rule on penalties mentioned above in connection with the precontractual document are also applicable in this context. There is no requirement in the Directive that contracts which are not made in the prescribed form should be regarded as void; such a consequence is of course perfectly possible on the basis of national law.

(iii) Language

As timeshare contracts are in most cases transborder contracts the problem of language can frequently occur. The Directive therefore contains, in art. 4, strict provisions on the language of both the precontractual document and the contract itself.

The main rule leaves the purchaser with an option as to the language of the precontractual document and the contract. He may usually choose between the language (one of the languages) of the Member State in which he is resident and the language (one of the languages) of the Member State of which he is national. As to the language of the contract, the Member State in which the purchaser is resident may, however, require the use of this language. The rules only cover languages which are official languages of the Community.

The *ratio* of these rules is of course to ensure that the information really reaches the consumer in a language he understands. In addition to these rules there is, however, still one, rather curious, rule on the language of the contract in the Directive. In addition to the contract in the language mentioned above the vendor must provide the purchaser with a certified translation of the contract in the language (one of the languages) of the Member State in which the immovable property is situated. The idea of this provision is, according to the preamble, to have documentation for the

---

[87]   It is hard to imagine that a consumer concluding a timeshare contract has not requested any information beforehand; such a request triggers the obligation to provide the precontractual document.

purposes of formalities in the Member State of the property (recital 10). In addition such a translation seems to be useful because the country of the property in many cases may be the country where legal proceedings concerning the property will take place.

D. Cancellation

A timeshare contract is often a relatively complicated arrangement and in many cases made after a rather short deliberation by the purchaser. Therefore, according to the preamble, 'to give the purchaser the chance to realise more fully what his obligations and rights under the contract are' he should be granted a right of withdrawal or cancellation (recital 11). The rule on the consumer's right of cancellation may be regarded as the key provision of the whole Directive (art. 5).

The consumer shall have the right to cancel the contract without giving any reason. The period of cancellation is ten days and it starts running when both parties have signed the contract or a preliminary binding contract.

The period is prolonged, if the contract does not include certain of the items listed above which it is required to contain. The Directive prescribes that there will be a three month period within which the vendor can provide the necessary information – in writing, one may assume, although it is not clearly stated – with the consequence that the ten day period starts to run from when the information is supplied to the consumer. If no such additional information is given, the ten day period starts to run at the expiry of the three months period. What this rather funnily structured and complicated–looking provision in other word says is that the period of cancellation is three months and ten days(!) if the required information is not given.

The required information includes information on the right to cancel (Annex, point (l)). It has to mention the addressee of the cancellation and the arrangements under which a letter of cancellation has to be sent, as well as some other information. In this way the Directive seeks to guarantee that the consumer has sufficient knowledge of his right.

The procedure for cancellation is not specified in the Directive.[88] The purchaser shall notify the relevant person 'by means which can be proved in accordance with national law in accordance with procedures specified in the contract' (art. 5(2)). It is therefore left to national law to decide matters such as whether a registered letter is required.[89] If there are specific provisions of this kind in national law their content should be mentioned in the information described above. If the notification is made in writing it is deemed to have

---

[88] The notification need not even be in writing, see art. 5(2): 'if it is in writing.'

[89] Mäsch, *op. cit.*, at 12. In the 1992 proposal (art. 7(3)) a registered letter was required.

been made in time, if it is dispatched before the deadline expires, even if it is not (or indeed could not have been) received by the addressee within the cancellation period.

The economic consequences of cancellation are spelt out in the Directive. The purchaser can only be obliged to pay certain expenses for possible legal formalities which have to be completed within the ten day period, provided they are expressly mentioned in the contract (art. 5(3)). If the purchaser cancels within the longer three months period, in cases where he did not receive the proper paperwork, not even these expenses can be placed on him (art. 5(4)). The question of payments from the vendor to the purchaser in case of withdrawal, on the other hand, should not arise at all, if the Directive is followed. The Member States shall prohibit any advance payments by the purchaser before the end of the withdrawal period (art. 6). Obviously if any money had been handed over in breach of these provisions it would be recoverable.

The right of cancellation should also be effective when the contract is covered by a credit agreement. In this case the purchaser should also be able to cancel the credit agreement without any penalty. These rules cover both the obvious situation that the vendor himself has granted the credit and also credit from a third party, if the credit is granted on the basis of an agreement between the third party and the vendor (art. 7). Credit which the purchaser has arranged for himself is outside this rule.

The procedure for cancelling the credit agreement is not prescribed by the Directive. Member States are required to lay down the detailed arrangements. One need not necessarily require the purchaser to make separate notification to the third party creditor within the cooling–off period, if he cancels the timeshare.

E.   Applicable Law

Like some other directives in the area of consumer law, the Timeshare Directive contains a provision on applicable law (art. 9). This is important as the consumer protection provision in art. 5 of the Rome Convention on the Law Applicable to Contractual Obligations does not cover timeshare contracts.[90] The provision in the Directive is thought to prevent the risk of circumvention of the protection by the help of rules on applicable law.[91] It seems that it tries to solve some of the problems connected with the fact that timeshare contracts often are made subject to the laws of offshore

---

[90]   Mäsch, *op. cit.*, at 13.
[91]   COM(92) 220 at 46.

jurisdictions like the Channel Islands and Isle of Man.[92] According to the Directive the Member States should 'ensure that, whatever the law applicable may be, the purchaser is not deprived of the protection afforded by this Directive, if the immovable property concerned is situated within the territory of a Member State'.

The provision is restricted to timeshares on property situated within the Member States. The Directive does not require – but it does of course not prevent either – any protection in cases where the timeshare property is situated outside the Community, even when the timeshare was advertised in the country of the purchaser (a Member State) and the contract was concluded there.[93] In the case of so called flexible timeshare, where the right of the purchaser comprises several optional properties, it is probably sufficient that one property is on the territory of a Member State for the protection of art. 9 to come into play.

The *ratio* of the provision is of course to preserve the minimum protection of the Directive in cases where applicable law would be the one of a non–Member State. However, the provision is not limited in this way; it expressly comes into play, 'whatever the law applicable may be'. Therefore, it seems, it should also cover the situation where the applicable law is the law of a Member State which has not implemented the Directive.

Art. 9 does not regulate how the mandatory minimum protection shall be effected. The Member States need not resort to rules on applicable law as such, but may uphold the minimum mandatory requirements of the Directive in the environment of a foreign law.[94]

F.   Conclusions

The very strong emphasis on a transparency strategy in the Directive has already been underlined. Information and cooling–off are the means by which the Community legislator wants to counteract the aggressive sales techniques which was one of the motivations for the Directive. It remains to be seen whether these means are sufficient to achieve such a goal. One may also wonder whether the information requirements have been carried too far to fulfil their functions; so much information should, according to the Annex, be given to the consumer that there seems to be a real danger of the consumer drowning in it.

---

[92]   N. Downes, 'A Quest for "Transparency" in the Spanish Timeshare Market. What Will EU Directive 94/47 Bring?' (1995) 18 *J.C.P.* 433 at 444.

[93]   Compare the more far–reaching provisions in the 1992 proposal, OJ 1992 C 222/5, art. 9.

[94]   See also Mäsch, *op. cit.*, at 13.

The most important provision of the Directive is of course that on cancellation. Here the shortening of the period of cancellation from 28 to 10 days is regrettable from the consumer viewpoint.[95] As timeshare contracts are often made abroad, typically during holiday trips, the consumer in these cases has very little time to consult a lawyer or some other expert in his own country before making up his mind. In many cases he might even have no such opportunity, as ordinary package holidays often last two weeks.

The transparency strategy of the Directive is directed mainly against aggressive sales techniques. There are of course many other problematic questions connected with the timeshare business which are not addressed by the Directive. In the future, for instance, the supervision of the running of the timeshare properties may become a more important question for consumers.[96]

Still the Directive obviously brings about at least some improvement of the position of the purchaser in the Community. In most Member States there was no existing specific legislation on timeshare contracts.[97] The Directive certainly introduces new rules in the area. This, however, is not only in the interest of the consumers. As the timeshare business has a rather bad reputation in many countries, responsible representatives of the line of business have also been eager to have some legislation to clear up the situation.[98]

---

[95]   In the UK, where the cancellation period according to the Timeshare Act has been 14 days, market research by the timeshare industry is claimed to show that although most cancellations occur during the first days of the cancellation period, there is a 'final burst of cancellations during the last 3–4 days', DTI Consultation Paper, *op. cit.*, item 38. At least some of these cancellations might not have been made, had the cancellation period been 10 days.

[96]   Downes, *op. cit.*, at 446 *et seq.*

[97]   See COM(92) 220 at 20 *et seq.*

[98]   See N. Jäckel, 'Referententwurf zur Umsetzung der EG–Richlinie über den Erwerb von Teilzeitnutzungsrechten an Immobilien' (1995) 10 *Verbraucher und Recht* 265 at 267 and K. Sorsa, *Time–share liiketoiminnan sääntelystä* (Publications of the Turku School of Economics and Business Administration, 1994) at 149.

8 Access to Justice

1. GENERAL ISSUES

A. Introduction

All the consumer rights provided by the EC legislation described in the previous chapters will count for nothing if they cannot be effectively enforced. This chapter is about the ways in which EC and national consumer law can be made available to Europe's citizens – in other words the access to justice question. This may be achieved by individuals or groups of consumers seeking redress or it may take the form of regulatory control.

B. Individual Redress

Relying on individual redress mechanisms to ensure consumer protection is problematic, even in the domestic context. Consumers are often not aware of their rights and so redress simply does not occur. Even if they realise they have a legal claim they may not know how to go about establishing it. Legal advice from traditional lawyers may be less than satisfactory[1] and funding for consumer advice centres is poor in many parts of the European Union. The biggest inhibitor to consumer redress is, however, the fact that it often does not make sense for consumers to pursue their claim because of the relatively small amounts involved. Costs to the consumer comprise not only court or arbitrator fees and lawyers' bills (which are avoided by some more modern redress schemes for small claims), but most significantly the time which they have to invest in pursuing the claim.

Businesses also have structural advantages in litigation. Not only do they often have greater resources, including skilled lawyers who specialise in this area, but they can also play a long term strategic game. This allows them to choose which cases to settle and which to fight, thereby attempting to prevent

---

[1] Research by Macaulay suggests that lawyers tend to be more sympathetic to business defendants than to consumers whom they often view as 'freaks': S. Macaulay, 'Lawyers and consumer protection laws' (1979) 14 *Law and Soc. Rev.* 115. One also doubts whether many general practitioners have a detailed knowledge of consumer laws.

unhelpful precedents arising and encouraging courts to confirm rules which are favourable to them.[2]

The domestic problems facing consumers are aggravated in the cross–border context where consumers have to litigate in the courts of another Member State or the law of a foreign country is applicable. Consumers are less likely to know their legal rights or have the confidence to pursue them. Even if they know of rights derived from EC directives, these are implemented by national rules and form part of a national legal environment with its own culture, rules and procedures.

Language can be a problem in cross–border disputes. This may require the services of a lawyer in circumstances where one could be dispensed with at the national level. Finding a competent foreign lawyer may be problematic in itself. If the consumer needs to travel to a foreign country to press a claim, then in most cases litigation will simply not be worth the effort. The Commission has presented estimates that the average litigation costs for a 2,000 ECU intra–community claim are 2,500 ECU, with in many states a large proportion of this being unrecoverable even if the consumer wins.[3]

On the positive side one might suggest that as European Union citizens have 15 jurisdictions to litigate in they may be able to use decisions in one state as arguments for similar advances in the others, at least where the rights derive from the same EC laws. Equally, however, business will be able to pass the benefits on of any national decisions favourable to itself, and the business community is likely to be better organised than consumers to publicise favourable decisions.

C. Collective Regulation

As individual consumers frequently lack the motivation and/or means to bring cases to courts or other dispute resolution fora, the regulation of the marketplace is often left to public officials. They may perform a number of functions which control trade practices and regulate the quality and safety of goods and services. They may issue licenses which are needed before trading is possible or keep registers so that enforcement is easier to effect. They may undertake pre–market and post–market controls and have powers to remove dangerous goods, prohibit misleading practices or tackle rogue traders. The extent to which a state relies on public authorities to perform these functions depends upon its legal and political culture. It is well known, for instance, that in the US the ability of regulators to control enterprises is widely

---

2 See M. Galanter, 'Why the "Haves" Come out Ahead: Speculations on the Limits of Legal Change' (1974) 9 *Law and Soc. Rev.* 95.

3 COM(96) 13 at 9–10.

doubted, and this, in part, explains why they have such strong product liability laws which are frequently invoked. By contrast, in many Northern European countries public regulators play a major role in consumer policy, with the Nordic Ombudsmen or the United Kingdom's Director–General of Fair Trading and network of Trading Standards Officers being prime examples. Particularly in Southern Europe, however, there is less of a tradition of effective public regulation of the market place.

Some of the rules of EC law clearly envisage enforcement by regulatory authorities and/or the involvement of consumer groups in bringing test cases. The main thrust of these provisions is to prevent harm by removing dangerous products, unfair contract terms, misleading advertisements, unfair trade practices etc. before they affect consumers. Compensation for individual consumers harmed by these practices is typically not the objective of such controls. However, we see no reason why in principal consumers should not benefit from the involvement of public agencies to make civil claims easier. Agencies might be permitted to assist consumers obtain individual redress, perhaps by negotiating on their behalf or bringing test cases.[4] Of course any such approach would have to be seen as part of a strategy which made best use of limited public resources, and so there could be no automatic right of consumers to be assisted by the public authorities. In fact the Finnish Ombudsman has had a very positive, if limited, experience in using his powers under s.2 of the Consumer Ombudsman Act.[5] This permits him with the authorisation of a consumer, to bring a case if the issue has a precedent value or the business has not complied with a decision of the consumer complaint board.

We shall note, below, the potential problems of using public controls to regulate practices emanating in one state but causing harm in another.

---

[4]   The Australian Consumer and Competition Commission has the right to support consumers with product liability claims and this power is perceived as being unproblematic. This is an example of a public authority assisting consumers to obtain redress even where no public law regulation has necessarily been breached. Piggy-backing a civil claim on to the back of a regulatory infringement either as part of a judgment or settlement negotiation would seem to be even less problematic. However, the United Kingdom's Office of Fair Trading backed away from favouring a General Duty to Trade Fairly, because in part, it believed it was too ambitious to seek both to improve standards and redress in the same measure; among the matters discussed was the objection to using public funds to finance individual redress and the loss of impartiality on the part of regulators which this new role might entail: see, *Trading Malpractices*, (Office of Fair Trading, 1990).

[5]   1978/40. See in more detail T. Wilhelmsson, 'Le droit de la Consommation Finlandais et le modèle nordique de Protection de Consommateur' [1989] *R.E.D.C.* 265.

Nevertheless we shall suggest that such forms of 'public' controls can offer a very realistic chance of assisting with cross–border consumer problems.

D.   The National and European Levels

(i)   *The National Level*

In previous chapters, we have seen that EC consumer law has often had just as great an impact on domestic consumer problems as on those which are unique to the single market context. Therefore the EC can have a role to play in encouraging access to justice for consumers at the national level through, for instance, the development of simplified small claims procedures, alternative dispute resolution and group or class actions. The EC can also promote the effective public regulation of the market place at the national level.

Making consumer redress easier to obtain within the domestic legal systems of the Member States and raising the effectiveness of national authorities responsible for the administration of consumer laws should have the knock on effect of assisting consumers with cross–border complaints and creating confidence in the single market. Such measures can therefore be seen as having an internal market aspect. However, they also represent an autonomous consumer protection philosophy. Assuring effective means of redress is also in keeping with the general Community principle which requires effective remedies to be available for breaches of EC law.

(ii)   *Cross–border Disputes*

Discussion of the access to justice question at the EC level has, however, focused more on ways of resolving cross–border disputes than with introducing general reforms. This may be partly because it is impolitic to raise the sensitive topic of EC interference with domestic legal procedures at a time when subsidiarity is the dominant principle. However, there is also an urgent need from an internal market perspective to address the particular problems of access to justice raised by cross–border purchases. It is fundamental to consumer confidence in the single market that consumers have confidence that matters can be put right and abuses stopped throughout the Community. Also, whereas substantive legal improvements benefit both the domestic and cross–border consumer, improved access to justice within Member States may not assist cross–border consumers greatly if the particular problems they face remain unaddressed.

There are several ways in which European consumers can become entangled in cross–border disputes. Sometimes this can occur without consumers even having to leave their own country. They may, for instance be sold, in their home state, products and services by firms based in other Member States. This is becoming increasingly common with the growth of distance selling within the Community. Local sales may also be effected by enterprises from other Member States. Traditionally overseas manufacturers have been the ones who entered foreign markets, but recently several European retailers have expanded into other Member States (e.g. Aldi, Ikea, Netto). The sales contracts will usually be governed by the domestic law of the state where the sale was made. However, we have seen that, at least in the financial services sector, businesses trading in other Member States are governed by home country controls rather than those of the host state in which they are trading. In the context of distant selling from one state to another there is the added complication of there being no local intermediary against whom claims and enforcement action can be directed. Product liability claims may also have to be made against foreign businesses, as the liability of the importer attaches to the importer of the goods into the European Union.

As business and tourist travel increases within the European Union, consumer problems relating to goods and services purchased abroad will take on a greater significance. Occasionally the foreign trip will be organised by an enterprise with a view to securing a sale; for example, a trip organised to a French vineyard. More typically consumers will simply avail themselves of goods and services as an incident of being in a foreign country. Almost certainly they will have to use hotels and restaurants and may often make use of personal services such as hairdressers; in emergencies they may need to call on the services of local garage mechanics, doctors etc. Many souvenirs are often brought home from trips abroad. Local purchases of food and clothing will frequently be made either out of necessity or because of their local character or advantageous pricing.

Tourists frequently return home with stories of the great bargains they found in the local resorts they visited. If the single market becomes a reality for consumers there should be greater opportunities for taking advantage of differential pricing within the Union. We have already noted that one way for this to happen is for retailers to set up in other states. But the Commission's aim is also to make Europe's consumers more active cross–frontier shoppers. For example, many UK consumers would be happy to pay the lower prices for cars which apply in many other European countries. In some respects the purchase of a car is relatively unproblematic from a single market viewpoint (if all the customs formalities and tax rules are sorted out), since it represents a major financial outlay with the possible savings justifying the cost of travelling to another state. It can also be readily transported back home.

Many consumer white and brown goods are, however, rather bulky and any savings are unlikely to justify a journey to the other side of the Union. This is not to say that bargains cannot be found. For example, many Danish consumers buy televisions from Germany where they are a lot cheaper. This example, however, reflects the fact that any large scale active cross–border consumerism is likely to be restricted to those consumers who live in border regions. Thus Dutch Maastricht consumers, for instance, who have Belgium and Germany within easy reach, are more likely to be able to take pro–active advantage of the single market, than are consumers in Lapland or Rhodes. Most European consumers will have to rely on developments in new technology and the increased use of distant selling techniques if they are to be able to gain the full advantages of the single market from the comfort of their own home.

Although many consumer transactions will continue to be made close to home, it is clear that in the future there will be more cross–border consumer transactions within Europe than there have been in the past. Predictably some of these transactions will give rise to consumer complaints. Domestic consumer complaints give rise to many access to justice problems, but the cross–border dimension provides an additional complication.

E.   Our Approach

In the following discussion we divide our treatment of the topic between those rules which seek to provide individual redress and those which seek to improve the general trading conditions through regulatory powers and/or the use of injunctive procedures. This division is useful, although it is also somewhat artificial. Individual claims should have an impact on trader behaviour and regulatory or collective actions can also provide for individual redress. We will see that the EC's most concrete proposals in this area are to improve collective procedures in cross–frontier disputes. Individual redress across borders is seen as being more problematic. Nevertheless national reforms aimed at improving individual consumer access to justice will indirectly benefit the cross–border shopper and are a legitimate matter of interest for the EC.[6]

First, however we set the scene by looking at the involvement of the EC in this field to date. We look at how the general principles of EC law impact

---

6   See M. Goyens, 'EC Policy with Regard to Consumer Redress' [1995] *Consum.L.J.* 35 at 36 who argues that as the Green Paper on Access to Justice was pre–Maastricht it had to be limited to cross–border problems, but that 'A more global approach would have been far more consistent with the new approach towards EC consumer policy, as contained in art. 129a'.

on the access to justice debate, before moving on to preview the Commission's recent Green Paper and subsequent concrete follow–up proposals, which are discussed in more detail later in the chapter.

F.   EC Law

(i)   General Principles

There is at present very little EC law on the access to justice question outside the realm of private international law (which is discussed in section 2C). However, the impact of general principles of EC law should not be overlooked. The *Francovich* case, as well as imposing state liability, also reiterated that Community rules would only be fully effective if individuals can obtain redress and that providing this was an obligation of Member States based on art. 5 of the Treaty. The decision goes on to make it clear that this requires not merely providing effective remedies, as well as substantive rights, but also the means of enforcing them. The ECJ states:

> 'In the absence of Community legislation, it is for the internal legal order of each Member State to designate the competent courts and lay down the detailed procedural rules for legal proceedings intended fully to safeguard the rights which individuals derive from Community law....
>
> the substantive *and procedural conditions* [our emphasis] for reparation of loss and damage laid down by the national law of the Member States must not be less favourable than those relating to similar domestic claims and must not be so framed as to make it virtually impossible or excessively difficult to obtain reparation...'[7]

Legal process matters therefore remain within the competence of Member States. The reference to procedural conditions, presumably was intended to refer to private law matters such as notice between the parties. Yet, one could argue that the principle is broad enough to encompass procedural rules related to access to the court system. Thus it could be argued that the principle of non–discrimination in access to justice is enshrined in EC law, although Member States retain the right to determine the means of securing redress within their territory. Strictly such a principle would seem to be limited to access to the courts and tribunals over which Member States have control. It would therefore exclude many of the alternative dispute settlement

---

7   *Francovich and Others v Italian State,* Cases C–6/90 and C9/90) [1991] ECR I–
     5357, at paras 42–3.

institutions which are becoming an ever more common feature of consumer redress. However, where a state relies upon private bodies to secure access to justice, then it would seem necessary that it should ensure that these procedures were available to all European citizens.

As well as non–discrimination the ECJ imposes some controls on the form of redress systems. Admittedly these are not very demanding being phrased in negative terms (i.e. they should not be 'virtually impossible', 'excessively difficult') rather than positive ones (e.g. 'easily accessible', 'efficient' etc.).' The *Francovich* judgment was concerned with individual redress, but the philosophy lying behind it – 'the obligation to nullify the unlawful consequences of a breach of Community law'[8] – would mean that similar principles should underpin access to and the effectiveness of regulatory controls.

Of course it would be little use having access to a legal system which offered meagre remedies. Consumers would not be satisfied, nor businesses deterred, by inadequate damages or public authorities with inadequate powers to counter misdemeanours. The ECJ has thus developed an effective remedies principle under which national measures implementing EC directives must be 'sufficiently effective to achieve the objectives of the Directive and should be capable of being effectively relied upon before their national courts'.[9] Damages should be adequate to make good in full any loss and damage.[10] In relation to public law remedies the jurisprudence is less well developed, but presumably the remedies must be sufficient to reduce the impact of any infringement so far as possible and to prevent future harm. It has even been suggested that it might require public law measures to be given private law sanctions, such as damages.[11]

(ii) Competence

We shall see that the measures currently being proposed in this field are based on the jurisdiction afforded by art. 100a of the Treaty, which relates to the internal market dimension of the problem. However, we have commented that the problem also has an autonomous consumer protection dimension which could support measures being taken under art. 129a(1)(b) to support and supplement the policies of Member States to protect the health, safety

---

8   *Ibid.*, at para. 36.

9   *Marshall v Southampton AHA (No. 2)*, Case 271/91 [1993] 3 C.M.L.R. 293 at para. 22.

10   *Ibid.*, at para. 26.

11   See T. Wilhelmsson, *Social Contract Law and European Integration*, (Dartmouth, 1995) at 48–49.

and economic interests of consumers. The one question mark over the Community's competence to regulate access to justice matters by virtue of these provisions, might be whether such questions are not more appropriately regulated under that pillar of the Maastricht Treaty which makes provision for co–operation in the fields of justice and home affairs (art. K). The consequence of this would be that measures would have to be decided upon unanimously by Council (art. K4(3)). Art. K1 provides that judicial co–operation in civil matters should be regarded as a matter of common interest, but as the consumer access to justice question goes far beyond judicial co–operation it can perhaps continue to be seen as best treated under the main Treaty provisions.

(iii) Green Paper on Access to Justice

As early as 1975 the Council of the EC had recognised the right of consumers to proper redress by means of swift, effective and inexpensive procedures as one of five categories of fundamental consumer rights.[12] This problem has been alluded to subsequently by Community institutions on several occasions. Notably, a Commission Communication in 1985 affirmed the aim that 'consumers throughout the Community enjoy a broadly similar standard of redress'.[13] In 1987 the European Parliament passed a resolution[14] and the Commission issued a supplementary communication[15] on the topic. Central to both 1987 documents was the idea of consumer organisations having the right to bring actions. We shall see this idea has become a central plank of the EC's approach to consumer access to justice.

The establishment of the single market has given impetus to the development of a European strategy for consumer access to justice. The Sutherland Committee on meeting the challenge of the internal market recommended that the effective protection of consumers' rights be given 'rapid consideration'.[16] The Commission responded with a Green Paper entitled *Access of Consumers to Justice and the Settlement of Consumer*

---

[12] Council resolution of 14 April 1975 on a preliminary programme of the European Economic Community for a consumer protection and information policy: OJ 1975 C92/1.

[13] COM(84) 692 at XVI.

[14] OJ 1987 C 99/203.

[15] COM(87) 210.

[16] Recommendation No. 22.

Disputes in the Single Market,[17] in which it tried to encourage debate on consumers' access to justice. The Green Paper sees access to justice as a way of ensuring that the rhetoric of a 'People's Europe' is made a reality for consumers. The latest three year action plan of the EC foresaw appropriate action being taken in response to the Green Paper.[18] The Commission has subsequently issued a proposal for a directive relating to injunctions for the protection of consumers' interests[19] and an *action plan on consumer access to justice and the settlement of consumer disputes in the internal market*.[20] The Green Paper and these follow up documents will be referred at appropriate points throughout the remainder of this chapter.

2.   INDIVIDUAL DISPUTES

A.   Introduction

The emphasis of the Green Paper was placed on collective redress. Some commentators subsequently suggested ways in which EC rules could enhance individual redress, but these tended to concentrate on the improvement of national systems.[21] It has already been commented that improved access to justice at the national level is a legitimate goal in its own right for the EC to strive towards and that this will indirectly ease the burden of consumers with cross–border disputes. The Green Paper did, however, raise a number of issues related to the resolution of individual disputes and it is to be hoped that this will generate reflection at the national level which will in turn bring about improvements. The academic writings on the Directive may be seen as part of a process in which EC initiatives act as a spur for national reforms.

---

17   COM(93) 576: see discussion of the Green Paper in the special issue of the *Consumer Law Journal* devoted to Access to Justice in the light of the Green Paper [1995] *Consum.L.J.* 1–39.

18   *Priorities for Consumer Policy, 1996–98*, COM(95) 519.

19   Proposal for a European Parliament and Council Directive on the co–ordination of the laws, regulations and administrative provisions of Member States relating to injunctions for the protection of consumers' interests: COM(95) 712.

20   COM(96) 13.

21   K. Viitanen, 'Consumer Redress' [1995] *Consum.L.J.* 6 suggests a public board for consumer complaints should have to be established in every state; W. Jacobs and C. Joustra, 'Consumer Redress from a Comparative Perspective' [1995] *Consum.L.J.* 16 see a role for the EC in establishing minimum standards with which court procedures have to comply to facilitate access to justice for consumers and ensuring that due process is guaranteed in alternative dispute resolution.

We have already seen that practical problems make it particularly difficult to ensure individual cross–border consumer disputes can be successfully litigated. In the past ambitious schemes have been vaguely mooted, involving the establishment of a special court apparatus for such disputes or giving the Commission a role in assuring claims are enforced against entities outside the consumer's home state. These were not taken very seriously. This may have been partly because the problem was not perceived as being sufficiently serious to justify such measures, but also probably because of the technical difficulties which such reforms would give rise to. The proposed action plan suggests some tentative, but potentially useful, developments to assist individuals in resolving cross–border disputes.

B. Action Plan

The *Access to Justice* Green Paper seemed largely to avoid proposing practical ways of resolving individual cross–border disputes. Collective action was clearly seen as a more promising and practical way forward. However, the follow up *action plan on consumer access to justice and the settlement of consumer disputes in the internal market*[22] is more innovative. It proposes several possible means for improving opportunities to resolve cross–border disputes.

Noting the rise of out of court procedures it proposes the establishment of a structure ensuring minimum criteria for extra–judicial procedures for dealing with intra–Community disputes. A Commission Recommendation is promised in the near future on this topic.[23] Such alternative dispute resolution (ADR) procedures are viewed as additional to court redress and should be available to the parties on a voluntary basis. The criteria such scheme would have to fulfil would relate to impartiality, effectiveness and adequacy as well as requirements that they inform the consumer of the decision in his own language, do not deprive him of mandatory rules of law of the country in which he resides and do not permit non–negotiated terms which deprive the consumer of the right to bring the case before a court which has jurisdiction. A further useful suggestion is that a central PO Box be created to which consumer complaints could be sent and forwarded to the correct ADR institution in the appropriate Member State.

The Commission is more cautious about attempting to harmonise court procedures, although it does suggest it might be possible to reach a

---

22   COM(96) 13.
23   It should be remembered that both the Cross Border Transfer Recommendation and the draft directive on cross–border credit transfers have provisions aimed at ensuring there is machinery to settle intra–Community disputes: see Chap. 6 section 3C.

consensus on a monetary ceiling for 'small claims'. This would be relevant in relation to a harmonised European form (available in the eleven official languages of the Union) which it hopes to introduce to facilitate dialogue between the parties to consumer disputes. This would be filled out by the claimant in the language of his country of residence and then translated into the language of the addressee of the complaint by bodies to be notified by each Member State. If agreement between the parties is not possible and resolution by extra–judicial procedures not practical, the form is forwarded to the competent authorities to investigate the background and subject of the complaint and to identify the parties. It is not clear whether the competent authorities means the courts or an administrative body, nor what happens once they have completed their investigations. Does this, for instance, mean that in the final analysis individual justice cannot be guaranteed and the matter can simply be reported to the regulatory authorities. Clearly, this concept although welcome in principle, needs to be further developed. Furthermore, the scheme is quite sensibly to be tested for a three year observation period in a small number of cross–border regions before coming into general use.

A *Guide to Legal Aid in the European Union* is to be available at consumer information points.[24] Legal aid is the key to whether many consumer disputes are resolved. The guide should be of assistance when consumers want to take advantage of national dispute resolution mechanisms in other Member States.

The action plan stops short of proposing a Community collective action procedure. However it does suggest that procedures be developed for consolidating related actions, although the cases would remain individual cases and not form a class action as such. In order to encourage the use of out–of–court procedures it is suggested that this procedure might only be available where either out–of–court mechanisms are not available or have been tried and failed. In this context a comparison is drawn with art. 22 para. 3 of the Brussels Convention which allows related actions to be consolidated when they have been commenced in courts in different Contracting States. It is unclear whether the use of this analogy is meant to suggest that the proposed related action procedure would also only be available in such circumstances, or whether it would also be available for purely domestic cases. Probably the reference to the Brussels Convention was simply to show a precedent for such a procedure and should not be taken as a basis for limiting the scope of the procedure.

---

24   It is already available on the Internet and will be sent free of charge to solicitors, courts, local and regional information agencies and consumer associations so that they can pass it on to consumers.

C. Private International Law

(i) Choice of Law

Choice of law rules are not necessarily part of the access to justice debate, but in the consumer area it is convenient to consider them in this context. If the consumer knows he can rely on his national law, or at least the mandatory consumer protection rules of that legal system he may be more confident in bringing claims, even if this means litigating in another state. These rules also help to ensure that protective consumer protection measures are not negated by choice of law clauses which choose legal systems which are unfavourable to the consumer.

(a) Contract

In contract, the Rome Convention on the Law Applicable to Contractual Obligations 1980 sets out two basic principles. First, where the parties have made a choice of law, this will generally be respected (art. 3(1)). This represents a freedom of contract philosophy which runs counter to the needs of consumer protection, for consumers will typically be unable to challenge choice of law clauses found in standard form contracts.[25] The other basic principle is also in practice rather consumer unfriendly. It provides that where no choice of law has been made, the contract will be governed by the country with which it is most closely connected (art. 4(1)). Art. 4(2) presumes that the contract is most closely connected:

> 'with the country where the party who is to effect the performance which is characteristic of the contract has, at the time of the conclusion of the contract, his habitual residence, or in the case of a body corporate or unincorporate, its central administration. However, if the contract is entered into in the course of that party's trade or profession, that country shall be the country in which the principal place of business is situated or, where under the terms of the contract the performance is to be effected through a place of business other than the principal place of business, the country in which that other place of business is situated.'

As the characteristic of a consumer contract is the supply of goods and services then in most cases the governing law will be that of the supplier's

---

25 See N. Misita, 'Toward "Consumer Law Proper"' in T. Wilhelmsson and K. Kaukonen (eds), *Euroopan integraatio ja sosiaalinen sopimusoikeus*, (Lakimiesliiton Kustannus, 1993).

state, unless the performance is effected through another place of business, which may or may not be in the same jurisdiction as the consumer.

Art. 5 counterbalances the generally unwelcome impact of the general principles by granting some special protection to consumers, but only in limited circumstances. The consumer contracts to which art. 5 applies are 'contracts the object of which is the supply of goods or services to a person ("the consumer") for a purpose which can be regarded as being outside his trade or profession, or a contract for the provision of credit for that object' (art. 5(1)).

This definition throws up several difficult questions of interpretation. Some of these are addressed, although not necessarily fully answered, in the Giuliano–Lagarde Report.[26] For instance, what is the position of goods and services bought for both work and domestic purposes? The Giuliano–Lagarde Report suggests that art. 5 will only apply if the person acts primarily outside work or trade,[27] but in many cases it will be difficult to determine a consumer's intention. More worryingly the report goes on to suggest that consumers will not benefit from art. 5 even if they are acting primarily outside their trade or profession if the other part did not reasonably know this.[28] Whilst there might be some justice in applying the rule to the example cited in the report – ordering goods on professional paper – the test ought not to be whether the trader had reasonably known the buyer's purpose, but rather whether the buyer's conduct or representations were such that he should be stopped from claiming the protection afforded by art. 5.

It is also unclear whether the other party must be acting in the course of his trade or business. The majority in the Giuliano–Lagarde Report thought that 'normally' this would have to be the case,[29] but there was clearly some disagreement and the use of the word normally simply reformulates the question with a different emphasis. Moreover, a consumer should be able to rely on art. 5 even if the seller is acting outside the course of his trade or business where the consumer reasonably assumed him to be acting within it, especially where the seller had led him to this belief.[30] This would be particularly important if the sale must be of the type of goods or services usually supplied in that trade or business, rather than covering any sale

---

26   This is an experts' report given a special status by its publication in the Official Journal of the Community: OJ 1980 C 282/1. This report's special status is referred to in s.3(3)(a) of the UK's Contracts (Applicable Law) Act 1990, which provides that it may be considered when interpreting the Convention.

27   *Ibid.* at 23.

28   *Ibid.*

29   *Ibid.*

30   See L. Collins, *Dicey and Morris, The Conflict of Laws*, (Sweet & Maxwell, 1993) at 1288.

which is integral to the running of the business even if that sort of sale was not the usual purpose of the business (for example, a lawyer selling a second hand computer). It is not clear which interpretation applies in this context.

For art. 5 to apply one of the three conditions outlined in art. 5(2) must also be satisfied; these are where:

(i) In the country of the consumer's habitual residence, the conclusion of the contract was preceded by a specific invitation or by advertising and the consumer had taken in that country all the steps necessary on his part for the conclusion of the contract.

   The fact the invitation must be specific suggests that it must be individually addressed. Therefore it should be fairly easy to determine whether the letter, phone call or approach was made to a consumer in the country of his habitual residence.

   It is unclear, however, whether it is sufficient for an advertisement to have reached the consumer in his country of habitual residence, or whether it must have been targeted at him in that country. The Giuliano–Lagarde Report seems to favour the latter interpretation, but this seems untenable as it leaves unaffected traders who advertise in media which they know circulate throughout Europe. Rather than restricting the scope to those advertisements targeted at a specific market, the provisions of art. 5 should apply unless it would be unusual for a consumer in that country to come across the advertisement; for example, where someone buys a foreign imported newspaper.

   The second limb of this condition is phrased in terms of taking all the steps necessary to conclude the contract in order to avoid legal technicalities concerning the place where a contract is concluded. The Convention is based on the place where the factual steps were taken, regardless of where they are deemed to have had legal consequences.

(ii) The other party or his agent received the consumer's order in the country where the consumer is habitually resident.

   It seems that 'agent' is intended to cover all parties acting for the trader and a strict legal relationship of principal and agent does not need to exist.

(iii) In the case of sale of goods contracts, the consumer travelled from the country of his habitual residence to another country and the consumer's journey was arranged by the seller for the purpose of inducing the consumer to buy.

   This covers shopping trips where a trader in one country organises transport for consumers in another country. It would also seem broad enough to cover 'duty free' trips which intend to induce the consumer to buy *en route*.[31] The seller does not have to provide transport personally so long as he has made arrangements with a transportation company. This provision is limited to sales of goods presumably as this type of shopping expedition is most frequently related to goods; but there is no reason why it could not be extended to a trip organised, say, to a beauty salon in another Member State where the owner is trying to tempt guests to use his services.

Art. 5 does not apply to a contract of carriage or a contract for services which are to be supplied to the consumer exclusively in a country other than that in which he is habitually resident (art. 5(4)). However, this exclusion does not apply to contracts which offer travel and accommodation for an inclusive price (art. 5(5)). Thus package travel contracts are included within the scope of art. 5.

For consumer contracts which fall within art. 5, a choice of law clause cannot deprive the consumer of the protection afforded to him by the 'mandatory rules' of the law of the country in which he is habitually resident (art. 5(2)). These are defined as rules of law in the consumer's country which cannot be derogated from by contract (art. 3(3)). Presumably this only covers rules relating to consumer protection.

The chosen law would remain applicable to the extent that it did not conflict with mandatory rules. It may be possible for a chosen law to actually be more favourable to the consumer than the mandatory rules. In this case the consumer could not be said to be being 'deprived' of his mandatory rules and should be able to rely on the chosen law.[32] It may be possible for a consumer to have more than one country of habitual residence. However, we do not see this as leading to the situation where there are more than one set of mandatory rules, as the three conditions for the application of art. 5, set out above, are each linked to actions in a specific country of habitual residence. If the law did provide for there to be more than one set of mandatory rules we would prefer the consumer to be able to choose which state's laws should apply.[33]

---

31 See Misita, *op. cit.*, at 254.

32 See Collins, *op. cit.*, at 1291 which seems to suggest, correctly, that the consumer should not be able to rely cumulatively on both his rights under the chosen and mandatory law. Mixing and matching of legal rules is not permitted. The chosen law must at least provide the minimum protection required by the mandatory rules of the consumer's country of habitual residence. Above this level it can impose such conditions as it wishes.

33 C.f. R. Plender, *The European Contracts Convention*, (Sweet & Maxwell, 1991) at 132 who sees this as a potential problem to be resolved in favour of the habitual residence having the closest relationship to the contract and its performance.

Consumer contracts within art. 5, which contain no choice of law clause, will be governed by the law of the country in which the consumer has his or her habitual residence.

If a consumer enters into a contract, but the contract does not fall within art. 5 there may still be situations when the 'mandatory rules' apply. For instance, the mandatory rules of a country will apply if all the other elements relevant to the situation at the time of the choice are only connected with that country (art. 3(3)).

In addition art. 7(1) permits the mandatory rules of a country with which the situation has a close connection to be applied; in deciding whether to give effect to the mandatory rules regard shall be had to their nature and purpose and to the consequences of their application or non–application. The United Kingdom objected to this provision and has made a reservation so that it does not apply in the United Kingdom.

Mandatory rules of the forum which are said to apply whatever the applicable law remain valid (art. 7(2)). This preserves, *inter alia*, rules found in some directives which seek to prevent the evasion of EC law by clauses making the law of a non–Member State applicable (art. 7(2)).[34]

(b) Tort

There is no equivalent of the Rome Convention governing choice of law in tort law. Instead each state has its own rules of private international law. There is a Hague Convention on the Law Applicable to Products Liability 1973, but this has only been ratified by four Member States.

(ii) Jurisdiction

One of the most effective means of helping to ensure consumers can secure redress is by making it possible for them to be able to litigate close to home. There are two principal means of achieving this. Rules of private international law can be used to give jurisdiction to the consumer's legal system, or the range of defendants can be extended to include some who are in the consumer's home state.

---

[34] See for instance art. 6(2) of the Unfair Terms in Consumer Contracts Directive; discussed at Chap. 3 section 2F.

(a) Brussels Convention

The Brussels Convention on Jurisdiction and the Enforcement of Judgments in Civil and Commercial Matters 1968[35] contains some general rules on jurisdiction as well as some which are particularly aimed at protecting consumers. The basic principle behind the Convention is that defendants domiciled in a Contracting State should be sued in the courts of that State (art. 2). The Convention then goes on to make certain generally applicable exceptions to this basic rule which allow defendants to be sued in courts in other contracting States. Those of particular relevance to consumers allow actions to be taken:

(i)   in matters relating to a contract, in the courts for the place of performance of the obligation in question (art. 5(1));

(ii) in matters relating to tort, in the courts where the harmful event occurred (art. 5(3)); and

(iii) as regards a dispute arising out of the operation of a branch, agency or other establishment, in the courts for the place in which the branch, agency or other establishment is situated (art. 5(5)); this applies even if the other party is domiciled outside a contracting state (art. 13).

The above exceptions could still leave the consumer having to litigate in foreign courts. Another set of provisions have more overt consumer protectionist intentions (arts 13–15). These rules apply to consumer contracts, which are defined as contracts which a person enters 'for a purpose which can be regarded as being outside his trade or profession' (art. 13). The contract must be for the sale of goods on instalment credit terms; for loans repayable by instalments, or any other form of credit, made to finance the sale of goods; or any other contract for the supply of goods or services. In addition, if the protective provisions are to apply, in the state of the consumer's domicile the conclusion of the contract must have been preceded by a specific invitation addressed to him or by advertising (art. 13), and the consumer must have taken in that state the steps necessary for the conclusion of the contract.[36] Transport contracts are, however, excluded from this provision.

If a dispute arises in relation to a consumer contract covered by this special jurisdiction, the consumer can bring an action in either the state where the defendant is domiciled or in the courts of a Contracting State in which he is domiciled (art. 14). Also actions can only be brought against

---

[35]   See amended text, at OJ 1990 C 189/2.

[36]   See discussion of the similar wording found in the Rome Convention, see above section 2C(i)(a).

consumers in the courts of the Contracting State in which the consumer is domiciled (art. 14).

Any jurisdiction agreement will only be recognised if it was entered into after the dispute arose; or allows the consumer to bring proceedings in courts other than those specified in the scheme; or is made between parties domiciled or habitually resident in the same Contracting State and confers jurisdiction on the courts of that state provided that the agreement is not contrary to the law of that state (art. 15).

Nevertheless, these provisions may still leave consumers having to litigate in foreign legal systems. For instance, whenever they purchase goods or services for cash in another state on their own initiative.

(b)   Range of defendants

It is worth noting at this stage that an alternative means of ensuring the consumer can bring the action in his own state is to provide him with a defendant who is based in his own state. Some EC consumer law show a pleasing recognition of the value of rules which have this effect, but unfortunately the approaches adopted so far have been *ad hoc* and sometimes frustrated by the contradictory desire to portray Europe as a fully functioning single market (so that it is deemed adequate to provide a defendant anywhere within the Union).

For instance, we saw how the Product Liability Directive extended the potential range of defendants beyond the producer/manufacturer.[37] Making suppliers jointly and severally liable would have done a great deal to assure consumers had a defendant in their own jurisdiction, but supplier liability is easily avoided by informing the consumer of the identity of their own supplier or the producer/importer. Classification of 'own-branders' as producers does give some consumers a defendant close to home in many circumstances. Moreover, the need to make the importer as well as the producer liable is recognised, but the importer to whom liability attaches is the first importer into the EC. This may still leave the consumer having to sue a party based on the other side of Europe. By way of contrast, the General Product Safety Directive directs the authorities to take measures against the most appropriate person, including 'in particular the party responsible for the first stage of distribution on the national market'.[38] A similar rule where consumer redress was available would be a major advance in consumer protection.

---

[37]   Art. 3, see Chap. 2 section 3C.
[38]   Art. 6(2)(b), see Chap. 2 section 4E(vi).

(iii) Enforcement

Art. 31 of the Brussels Convention permits the enforcement of judgments made in one Contracting State by courts in another Contracting State on application by an interested party. However, the Sutherland Report on meeting the challenge of the internal market expressed doubts about the effectiveness of the Convention, as in practice it seemed courts in Member States refused to execute orders made in other states on public interest grounds. Another weakness was seen as being that it did not apply to decisions taken by administrative bodies rather than courts of law. However, for most consumers such nuances will be irrelevant, since having to seek enforcement of a judgment in a foreign country will be as daunting a prospect as having to litigate there.

(iv) Assessment of Private International Law as a Method of Consumer Protection

Private international law is a 'second best' method of consumer protection. It gives consumers a limited amount of confidence to become active players in the single market by guaranteeing that in certain situations they will retain mandatory protection afforded by their home state and/or will be able to litigate close to home. However, these rights are only granted for specific categories of consumer claims. The private international law approach is not therefore a substitute for positive harmonisation.[39]

It also runs counter to the idea that European consumers should have rights by virtue of their citizenship of the European Union. Private international law rules concerning the choice of law favour consumers from countries with protective consumer laws. Consumers from these countries carry their protective mandatory laws with them wherever they shop in the Union. Consumers from countries with few protective rights are likely to gain little for their mandatory laws will generally be no more beneficial than those of the country where the purchase was made. Indeed the rules of private international law can even be seen as a cause of inequity between consumers in rich and poor countries. As consumer laws tend to be less protective in the poorer countries of the Union, consumers from those countries will gain little from these rules, but the cost of the additional rights provided to visitors from the richer states of the Union (who tend to have the more protective consumer laws) will have to be met in the price paid by all consumers in countries with weak consumer laws. Of course, in practice, the

---

[39]   In similar vein see P.B. Madsen, 'Commercial Guarantees in Consumer Contracts' [1995] *Consum.L.J.* 149 at 150–1.

costs involved are likely to be small and should not be invoked as a reason why consumers should not be granted rights by means of choice of law rules. Nevertheless, it does favour increased harmonisation of consumer law as a means of providing a sound basic level of consumer protection throughout Europe.

Norbert Reich makes the interesting suggestion that there should be a Community conflict rule based on art. 5 of the Treaty which would require the judge of the forum to allow foreign consumers the benefit of secondary EC law even if it had not been properly implemented in the state whose law was applicable.[40] This would in effect circumvent the rule against giving directives horizontal effects. It will give consumers confidence to shop in other Member States with the security that they are assured a minimum level of EC law derived protection.

Private international law rules do nothing, of course, for the purely domestic consumer. We have even seen how the application of rules of private international law can force consumers in countries with poor consumer protection laws to subsidise consumers from countries with strong consumer laws. The choice of law inequalities result from differences in substantive law rules; but the most dramatic differences in the practical amount of consumer protection enjoyed by consumers in the various Member States in the Community results from the different opportunities for access to justice. It is to these, essentially domestic issues which we now turn our attention, bearing in mind that effective national solutions which are open to all Community citizens can in themselves assist in the resolution of disputes which have a cross–border character.

D. Advice

Although traditional lawyers may be of limited utility in solving the structural problems facing consumers seeking justice,[41] there are still times when consumers will require a lawyer's assistance in resolving individual claims. This will be particularly true in cross–border claims when the services of a lawyer will often be necessary, even if not formally required. The Commission's Green Paper argues that legal aid eligibility rules neglect this point, by failing to recognise that persons, who are capable of bringing a claim personally in their national courts or financing a domestic claim, may

---

40 N. Reich, 'Competition Between Legal Orders: A New Paradigm of EC Law' (1992) 29 *C.M.L.Rev.* 861 at 882.

41 See I. Ramsay, 'Consumer Redress Mechanisms for Poor Quality and Defective Products' (1981) 31 *U.T.L.J.* 117.

not be able to cope with the extra complexity and costs of cross–border litigation.[42]

The Green Paper also notes that the legal aid conditions vary between Member States. Differences arise as to eligibility (level of income/capital, importance of claim and chance of success); scope of coverage;[43] and whether the consumer can choose his lawyer. The *Conseil des barreaux de la Communauté européenne* was commissioned to research the Member States' legal aid laws. However, harmonisation seems a very distant prospect with the best that can be hoped for being that consumers can be informed of the legal assistance available in other Member States and be granted equal access. In the transfrontier context the Green Paper makes the novel suggestion that consideration be given to making non–profit making associations (including consumer associations) eligible for legal aid.[44] However, this must be seen in the light of the Commission's proposal for injunctive procedures for cross–border disputes.

Of course consumer advice need not be given solely by lawyers, at least not lawyers working on a traditional fee basis. This fact is well evidenced by the strong networks of debt counsellors working within Europe. The United Kingdom has a national network of consumer advice bureaux where trained volunteers provide advice. Germany has Government funded Verbraucherzentrale, whilst in the Nordic countries the public complaints boards will assist consumers as well as eventually handing down non–binding judgments and in Finland there are also municipal consumer advisers. However, in many countries of the Union there is little provision for consumer advice.

The Commission has sponsored some pilot schemes to try to provide impetus for new means of assisting consumers. For instance, it funded a scheme in Liège, Belgium (based on a scheme launched by the Paris bar in 1981) whereby a centre of consumer law specialists was established. These lawyers work for a flat rate, below standard charges, for consumer claims up to a ceiling of 75,000 BF. In Greece, whose legal aid was described by the Green Paper as the least developed, legal advice bureaux were established in four cities to provide consumers with information, mediation and conciliation and to institute legal proceedings when the general interest was at stake.

The Commission has also been active in promoting pilot schemes which address particular cross–border concerns. Thus it has encouraged co–operation between consumer organisations in frontier regions so that they

---

42   Green Paper, *op. cit.*, at 69.

43   Notable, in the light of our subsequent discussion of the increasing importance of ADR, is the lack of availability of legal aid for most such schemes.

44   Green Paper, *op. cit.*, at 68.

become familiar with 'the "foreign" law which applies across the border'.[45] Also debt advisers have been supported in their attempts to devise common computer programmes which can assist in creating debt repayment plans. However, outside these specific instances one suspects it is very difficult for a consumer to obtain sound advice if his complaint relates to goods or services bought in another Member State. Indeed the Nordic consumer complaint boards will not assist consumers in bringing claims abroad.

Many consumer disputes are, of course, resolved by consumers themselves. Consumer education and information are therefore very important so that consumers know of and are able to assert their rights. In this field the EC has issued some non–binding acts aimed mainly at children,[46] but not exclusively so.[47] The Commission publishes literature on European consumer rights and even sponsors television programmes explaining these rights, yet the primary responsibility for consumer education and information remains with the Member States.

E. Simplified Court Procedures

The Green Paper notes that there is a trend towards simplified court procedures and that in all Member States disputes below a certain value can be brought by means of simplified procedures which provide easy means of initiating a claim, do not require a lawyer's assistance and usually involve a conciliation procedure, which is often mandatory. However, the upper limit for these proceedings varies greatly from 645 ECU in Ireland to 66, 836 ECU in Denmark. Only in Ireland is the procedure solely available to consumers and not businesses. This leads some to criticise such procedures for effectively being a streamlined method of bringing consumers before the courts as defendants. Whilst not supporting this objection entirely,[48] one might criticise the German system of *Mahnbescheid* where the court approves claims automatically and places the onus of the defendant to appeal against the summary notice. Many consumers may be frightened by receiving

---

45 Green Paper, *op. cit.*, at 85.

46 See Council Resolutions on consumer education in primary and secondary schools of 1986 (OJ 1986 C 184/21) and 1989 (COM (89) 17) and Commission communication on Community information and awareness campaign on child safety (COM(87) 211).

47 Council Resolution of 9.11 1995 on consumer education and information, not yet published.

48 After all consumers are the ones who directly or indirectly bear the costs of debt recovery proceedings and so also benefit if the costs involved can be reduced.

a court demand and may not be able to handle the psychological or intellectual demands required to appeal.[49]

The Green Paper appears on the whole to be content to describe the moves towards simplified court procedures for small claims and to approve the general principle that 'the cost of a procedure (court costs, lawyer's fees, expert's fees) should not be out of proportion to the value at issue'.[50] One statement made in the Green Paper should not be left without comment, however. After noting the role which conciliation plays in many simplified procedures, the Green Paper expresses a preference for such conciliation to be undertaken by the judge who may eventually hand down the judgment. It argues that this increases the likelihood of success as his credibility is underpinned by his independent and impartial status. Although conciliation by a judge is certainly better than conciliation by a trade association it is not necessarily advantageous that it be undertaken by the same judge as will deliver the final verdict. Involvement in conciliation might make it inappropriate for a judge to decide the case if he learns too much about it during the negotiation process. At least this is the case from the common law tradition under which judges are not supposed to investigate the facts, but rather decide upon such evidence as is placed before them in accordance with the strict rules of evidence. Civilian judges may be less concerned that the judge plays an investigative role during the conciliation stage and becomes familiar with the whole background to the problem, but there must be a risk that the parties may not be truly open with him at the conciliation stage for fear of revealing too much of their hand. Nevertheless, small claims procedures are an attempt to provide affordable justice and so practical constraints may require the same judge to be both conciliator and arbitrator. Certainly a multiplication of the times consumers need to attend court to obtain justice is not in their interest.

One matter which is not mentioned in the Green Paper is the possibility that in small claims the court could decide the case upon its substantial merits, with technical legal defences being ignored. This is not currently the position in any European legal system. Possibly, however, the civilian tradition, because of the discretion it confers on the judge with respect to the application of the written law to particular facts and the ability of civilian judges to appeal to principles of justice, has less instances of technical defences preventing substantive justice than does the common law. A rule that small claims should be decided on the substantial merits and justice of the case and not be bound by the strict legal position does operate in

---

49   See H. Koch, 'Consumer Dispute Resolution – A Plea for the Improvement of Civil Procedure Rules in Germany and European Perspectives' [1995] *Consum.L.J.* 29 who cites the objection rate as being only between 3–5%.

50   Green Paper, *op. cit.*, at 56.

Australia and New Zealand.[51] Such a rule could usefully be introduced into European legal systems. Consumers should not be bound by technical aspects of the law far removed from the substantive merits of the case. As the amounts involved are by definition 'small', this should not cause undue hardship to commercial defendants, who have in any event no substantive defence. A broader lesson, can, perhaps, also be learned; for although European legal culture is rich, experience from elsewhere should not be ignored. In particular it is too narrow to limit discussion of the common law world to just the United Kingdom and Ireland.

F. Alternative Dispute Resolution

The Green Paper notes the trend towards out–of–court procedures. In particular it notes the diversity of such procedures. Some are alternatives to courts (e.g. arbitration schemes); others precede litigation (e.g. conciliation/mediation); whilst others complement litigation (e.g. schemes where decisions are only binding on businesses). Although the Nordic countries have Consumer Complaints Boards which are publicly run,[52] many alternative dispute mechanisms are run by private bodies. The Green Paper comments on the need for consumer organisations to be involved if private schemes are to be trusted by consumers.[53] It also remarks that the independence (or at least impartiality) of the new 'judges' in out–of–court procedures might be questioned. It makes the interesting suggestion of establishing minimum conditions which a body must satisfy before it can label itself as an 'Ombudsman'. It suggests that the minimum conditions to be fulfilled to obtain the 'ombudsman label' could be discussed by consumer organisations and the professional sectors, possibly under the aegis of the Commission.[54] The result should be to give consumers confidence in using such bodies in other Member States. This is particularly important in the single market context, for if consumers have problems assessing the value of a dispute settlement mechanism in their home state, the problems are compounded when faced by a foreign procedure with which they are likely to be less familiar and which operates in a foreign legal culture. The United Kingdom Ombudsman Association has recently been renamed the British and

---

51 See C.N. Yin and R. Cranston, 'Small Claims Tribunals in Australia' and A. Frame, 'Fundamental Elements of the Small Claims Tribunal System in New Zealand' in *Small Claims Courts*, C. Whelan (ed.), (Clarendon Press, 1990).

52 See K. Viitanen, 'The Scandinavian Public Complaint Boards' *Consum.L.J.*, forthcoming.

53 Green Paper, *op. cit.*, at 58.

54 Green Paper, *op. cit.*, at 83.

Irish Ombudsman Association, and possibly a similar organisation could be placed on a European wide scale. Members must be ombudsmen of schemes which live up to the key criteria of independence, fairness, effectiveness and accessibility.[55]

Although the term 'ombudsman' is in vogue, other out–of–court schemes should not be ignored. Dialogue on minimum conditions for other arbitration/conciliation/mediation schemes should be encouraged together with some means of alerting consumers to schemes which meet these criteria or suppressing those which do not.

G. Class/group Actions

The Green Paper is rather thin on discussion of class/group actions. This is surprising given that this has, in the recent past, been the subject of a conference and publication sponsored by the Commission.[56] Certainly there is no suggestion of a move to impose a common European class action procedure, with the action plan being content to promote some form of consolidation of related actions.

No European state has a fully fledged class action procedure along the lines of the US procedure which allows non–parties to be bound by the litigation. However, the possibility of groups of consumers being allowed to litigate their common cause in the same action is increasingly being recognised in Member States. This is important not merely because it can make litigation more affordable, but also because it allows the collective dimension of the problem to be highlighted. Such procedures are relatively unproblematic from the consumer perspective so long as they are based on consent. In determining whether this should be developed into a class action which can require consumers to be bound by the decisions of the majority as to choice of representative, acceptance of settlement etc., one should, perhaps, distinguish between large scale personal injury claims (where the stakes are high for individuals and so they should be able to retain some control over the litigation) and smaller economic loss claims (which are unlikely to be litigated except for under a streamlined class action procedure).

Only France knows of an action based on harm to the general consumer interest, rather than an action based on the sum of individual claims, and

---

55 See W. Jacobs, 'United Kingdom Ombudsmen in Financial Services' in *Developments in Consumer Redress*, (Office of Fair Trading, 1996) at 30–31.

56 See Th. Bourgoignie (ed.), *Group Actions and Consumer Protection*, (Story Scientia, 1992).

even that is circumscribed by many conditions.[57] In relation to claims for small amounts or where, as in France, the damage is to the general consumer body, it may be futile, or even impossible, to award individual damages. Of course, an injunction might be possible to prevent future harm, but an award of damages might also be desirable. They could usefully be paid to consumer organisations to support their work on behalf of the collective consumer interest. There is a precedent for this in European law as Rover agreed to pay £1M to the UK's Consumers' Association for consumer research into cars in lieu of a fine when it was found to breach EC competition law.[58] Such an action could be particularly useful in the Community context where a practice affects a widely spread number of Community citizens.

H. Conclusions

There is a possible contradiction in the trends emerging with respect to individual access to justice. The ordinary courts are beginning to be receptive to collective claims by consumers, but at the same time the forum for consumer disputes is moving away from traditional court settlement to simplified court procedures or ADR procedures. It is important that these ADR mechanisms are also exposed to class/group actions. In these contexts the practical advantages of group litigation (i.e. lower costs) are not needed so much as the symbolic and political impact of class/group actions. This is important to counteract the perceived danger that while the new procedures may be more effective in resolving individual problems they do little to assist the general development of the law, as they simply hide away consumer concerns.

Group/class actions even more than individual claims have a dual role of resolving disputes and developing the law and practice. They highlight the overlap between redress mechanisms and the techniques used to promote general business standards, to which we now turn our attention.

---

[57] Art. 421–1 Consumer Code; discussed in J. Calais–Auloy and F. Steinmetz, *Droit de la consommation*, 4th ed. (Dalloz, 1996) at 475.

[58] See *The Independent*, 17 November 1993 at 2.

3.   THE COLLECTIVE DIMENSION

A.   Public Authorities

One of the greatest practical benefits arising from some Directives – notably the Consumer Credit Directive and the General Product Safety Directive – are the obligations they impose to establish authorities responsible for the surveillance of relevant markets and practices. In some Southern European countries, such as Greece, this has led to the establishment for the first time of state institutions responsible for consumer welfare.

The long term practical significance of this should not be underestimated, even if in the short term such bodies appear relatively impotent. Public officials have as much an educative role as a regulatory one. The presence of a Government agency can ensure publicity for consumer laws and increase the chance of compliance by business. Of course there are limitations. Such bodies tend to be under resourced and hopelessly overworked and so the threat of regulatory action will often be weak. Even when offences are detected such agencies usually prefer to negotiate than prosecute. Public officials cannot usually be openly partisan towards consumers[59] and must bear in mind political realities and in some cases even political orders. This can encourage light enforcement. However, the 'neutral' position of public authorities and the connections they have with those wielding political power can also increase the respect with which they are held by business and therefore encourage compliance.

One complication in the European context is that the rules public authorities enforce are criminal in nature in some countries, whilst in others they have a distinct status within administrative law. Often the nature of the sanctions being imposed – especially if they are penal – requires the official's powers to be tightly drawn. The opportunities for using public enforcement actions as a means of obtaining individual redress are quite limited in most European countries.

European laws have not only encouraged the establishment of public authorities. They have also promoted new means of intervention by such authorities. This is evidenced by the Misleading Advertising Directive, the Unfair Contract Terms Directive and the draft Distant Selling Directive as well as the recent draft directive relating to injunctions for the protection of consumers' interests. These all foresee public authorities having a role in seeking injunctions against breaches of the Directives. This approach is

---

59   The Nordic Ombudsmen (with the exception of the Danish Consumer Ombudsman) are an exception to this general statement, see T. Wilhelmsson, 'Administrative Procedures for the Control of Marketing Practices – Theoretical Rationale and Perspectives' (1992) 15 *J.C.P.* 159.

considered in more detail below, but first the role of consumer organisations is addressed because there is some debate as to who can best represent the consumer interest – public officials or consumer organisations.

B. Consumer Organisations

In some European countries, notably France and Germany, there is a tradition of consumer organisations having the right to bring actions to protect the general consumer interest. This typically leads to an injunction being awarded, but there is no reason why damages could not be awarded, and we have already noted that such damages could be used as a source of revenue for consumer protection work.

One problem is establishing which consumer organisations are sufficiently representative of the consumer interest. The representativity question should not be too severe an obstacle, since adjudication on the merits of the case still remains in the hands of a third party adjudicator. Nevertheless, some argue that industry needs to be protected from frivolous claims from minority groups unrepresentative of the general body of consumers.[60] In France this is achieved by official authorisation of national groups by the Ministry and local groups by the prefect, who judge associations by the three criteria fixed by the decree of 6 May 1988, namely their age (at least one year), evidence of effective and public work defending the public and the size of their membership (at least 10,000 for national associations).[61] In Germany consumer associations can under the General Conditions of Contract Act 1976 bring cases for an injunction or withdrawal of an unfair term if they have legal capacity, have the task of safeguarding the interests of consumers through information and advice provided they have organisations in this line of affairs or at least 75 natural persons as members. Similar criteria are used under the Unfair Competition Act 1909, as modified, which allows consumer groups to complain about unfair trade practices. In Germany the status of a consumer organisation will be assessed by the courts on a case by case basis. The Nordic countries grant consumer groups – without control or qualification – the right of action, but it is rarely used because they are usually content to leave matters to the consumer

---

60 Of course costs rulings can perform this function to a limited degree. Greece allows the court to dissolve consumer groups bringing frivolous claims for emotional distress: see A. Vamvoukas, 'Consumer Law in Greece – the State of Play' [1996] *Consum.L.J.* 7 at 9.

61 Calais–Auloy and Steinmetz, *op. cit.*, at 475.

ombudsman.[62] Dutch consumer organisations are similarly allowed access within any prior control. The experience of these countries suggests that any Community rule on the representivity of consumer groups should not be too severe and should allow for more generous national rules.

Granting consumer groups standing is of great symbolic value, underlining the collective dimension of consumer problems and causing business to take consumer organisations seriously. These gains are still tangible even if the practice of consumer associations is not to bring many cases, usually because they do not have the resources to be continually litigating. The United Kingdom refuses to give such powers to its consumer organisations, preferring instead to rely on the Director–General of Fair Trading to represent the consumer interest. Whatever the validity of the United Kingdom's legal position as regards this policy with respect of its implementation of the Unfair Contract Terms Directive (see Chap. 3 section 2E(ii)), nevertheless we regret the lack of a formal right of standing for United Kingdom consumer groups. If the Director–General of Fair Trading acts effectively there should be little need for consumers to take direct action, but the threat of such action may be an incentive for business to come to an accommodation acceptable to consumers. One suspects the objections of the United Kingdom lie not so much in the fear of radical action by consumer groups, but rather with the desire not to create a precedent which could be followed by more radical environmental groups.

C.   Draft Directive on Injunctions for the Protection of Consumers' Interests[63]

(i)   Background

In this section we focus on the most concrete proposal the Commission has made to improve the effective enforcement of EC consumer laws; namely the draft Directive on Injunctions for the Protection of Consumers' Interests. The problem which this initiative seeks to address is how to control an enterprise which in one Member State undertakes activities which harm consumers in another state. The authorities in the state where the enterprise is based may have little incentive, or even legal power[64] to take action; whilst authorities

---

62   J. Tala, 'Soft law as a Method for Consumer Protection and Consumer Influence' (1987) 10 *JCP* 341 at 352 says that Norway is the country where this power has been used most often and then only 10 times, all unsuccessfully.

63   COM(95) 712.

64   For instance, the UK's Director–General of Fair Trading's powers to take action against rogue traders only relates to conduct 'which is detrimental to the interests of

in the consumer's state may not be able to bring claims in their own courts against this type of behaviour (even if they can do so, as in the Nordic countries, it is hard to enforce injunctions against a foreign defendant) and they may not be recognised by the courts of the enterprise's host state.[65]

We have seen that the use of injunction powers to prevent infringements of EC law was first introduced in the Misleading Advertising Directive (see Chap. 4 section 3D). It was also included in the Unfair Contract Terms Directive (see Chap. 3 section 2E(ii)) and will be included as an option in the Distant Selling Directive (see Chap. 5 section 3H). The first controversial matter relating to these powers was whether consumer organisations should be able to seek injunctive relief directly or whether Member States could insist that the power be exercised by a public authority. This is currently the subject matter of a preliminary reference to the ECJ from a judicial review brought by the UK Consumers' Association against the UK implementation of the Unfair Contract Terms Directive (see Chap. 3 section 2E(ii)).

There was no suggestion under the Misleading Advertising Directive or the Unfair Contract Terms Directive of persons or organisations having the right of standing in other Member States. Under an earlier draft of the Distant Selling Directive it had been proposed that:

> 'Each Member State shall confer upon professional organisations and consumer organisations in the event of infringement of measures adopted pursuant to this Directive, the same rights to act under the same conditions as those applicable to organisations in that Member State.'[66]

This novel measure was omitted from the final proposal, presumably because the broader issue was being taken up in the Green Paper on Access to Justice.

The Green Paper noted that many supervisory powers were irrelevant in cross–border situations, but rejected the idea of a Community regulator. Instead, it proposed either (i) minimum harmonisation of actions for injunction i.e. a Community procedure which is available to national regulators accompanied by mutual recognition of the right to bring

---

consumers *in the United Kingdom*', s.34(1)(a) of the Fair Trading Act 1973 (italics added).

[65] For further discussion of the difficulties of bringing cross–border consumer complaints, see H. Micklitz, 'Cross–Border Consumer Conflicts – A French–German Experience' (1993) 16 *J.C.P.* 411, who discusses the problems a German consumer association had bringing an action against a German company that was mail–shooting French consumers and also a German company which was targeting German tourists on holiday in Spain.

[66] See CONSOM 67, art. 11(2)(b).

proceedings by organisations in other Member States, or (ii) continuation of existing national procedures (without harmonising them) but with mutual recognition of *locus standi*. We shall see that the draft Directive seems to favour the former solution.

The Green Paper stated that the subsidiarity principle required Member States to define the criteria for capacity to bring such actions. It seemed to suggest, however, that this did not mean actually setting the criteria (which would presumably be something like, 'bodies representing the interest injured by an unlawful commercial practice'), but rather the means by which these criteria are established (for example administrative procedure or court practice). In truth the thinking behind the Green Paper was rather difficult to follow. It seemed to recognise the problem of reconciling the principle of free movement of injunctions with the desire of some states to restrict the right of action to public officials and not allow consumer groups to bring such cases. However, it failed to suggest any coherent solution. The proposed directive shows evidence of a clearer grasp of the issues and goes some way to provide a workable framework for cross–border collective actions.

(ii)   The Draft Directive[67]

The purpose of this Directive is to introduce a common injunction procedure for a whole raft of EC directives. There are also special procedures to allow for action with respect to intra–Community infringements.

(a)   Scope
The scope of the proposed Directive is limited to infringements of certain EC derived laws (art. 1(2)). These are listed in an annex as the directives relating to Misleading Advertising; Doorstep Selling; Consumer Credit; Television Broadcasting; Package Travel; Medicine Advertising; Unfair Contract Terms; Timeshares and the proposed directive on Distant Selling. The limitation to infringements of certain directives can be criticised as unnecessary and unnatural. The limitation means that, for example, misleading advertising can be attacked in this way, but other forms of wrongful advertising cannot. As the directives are minimum directives, one might also encounter difficult questions as to whether there was an infringement of the directive or only of more far reaching national implementing legislation. From a more systematic point of view one might

---

67   For a rather critical assessment of the draft directive, see G. Bethlem and C. Joustra, 'The draft Consumer Injunctions Directive' *Consum.L.J.*, forthcoming.

claim that as the choice of areas for EC regulation is rather unprincipled any procedural solution based upon it will also be unprincipled.

The Directive requires that the relevant directive have been transposed into the legal order of the Member States. Thus an injunction could be denied if a state had failed to implement a directive. Furthermore a literal reading of the present draft could require that it have been introduced into all Member States, but this would certainly be a very strange interpretation. One is tempted to conclude with Bethlem and Joustra that breach of the underlying directive should be sufficient, at least after the period laid down for its adoption.[68]

Bethlem and Joustra also raise the issue of whether the Directive only applies to cross–border disputes or can also be used in purely domestic disputes. There is nothing on the face of the Directive to limit its scope to intra–community disputes. The explanatory memorandum does, however, state that 'the proposed measure will be strictly limited to whatever is strictly necessary to remedy the consequences of the two problems discussed above' (namely the mutual recognition of entities qualified to protect the collective interest and the need to demonstrate breach of a domestic law).[69] However, many EC laws have been justified by the need to alleviate problems related to cross–border transactions, but have also applied to domestic matters and unless the contrary is expressed in the Directive one should also assume that to be the case with the present directive. This would have the practical consequence that the injunction procedure would be available for a wider range of matters in domestic law than is presently the case, that the penalty for failing to adhere to an injunction would apply in domestic matters (see below) and presumably that a consumer could choose an entity in another Member State to represent his interests. This would be an example of competition between legal orders.

(b) Injunction action

Whereas the earlier directives which had included an injunction action procedure had been silent on the form the remedies should take, art. 2 of the draft Directive specifies them. Member States should designate a court or competent authority which can:

---

[68] *Ibid.;* this has parallels with Reich's suggestion that there should be a Community conflict rule to protect the minimum level of protection which should be afforded by EC Directives, see section 2C(iv). Bethlem and Joustra would also prefer the injunction procedure to be available for breach of any EC consumer law provision and not be limited to specific directives.

[69] COM(95) 712 at 7.

(a)   enjoin, at very short notice. and where appropriate by summary proceedings the cessation or prohibition of an act that is part of the infringement (i.e. an injunction). Member States can require prior notification be given to the defendant (art. 5);

(b)   where appropriate, take the necessary measures to rectify the effects of the infringement, including publication of the decision;

(c)   order the losing party to pay the plaintiff a fixed amount per day (or other amount fixed by national legislation) if the decision is not implemented within the specified time limit. This is not compensation to the injured party, as the plaintiff will be a national authority/consumer organisation. Neither is it a levy to help assist with future consumer interest litigation as the amount is only payable if the defendant is dilatory in complying with any judgment. Rather it is intended as a means of ensuring compliance with decisions. Such a penalty order is familiar to France and the Benelux countries, but would be novel in many other Member States.

It has been suggested that the courts could profitably be given the power to grant declaratory relief in collective actions.[70] If the issue of liability was settled in a collective action then questions of individual compensation could be settled subsequently. At present, however, the draft Directive seems more concerned with stopping harmful practices than with providing redress for harm caused by them in the past.

Art. 2(2) provides that where on the basis of applicable conventions the action is brought in a Member State other than the one whose legislation has allegedly been infringed, then the competent authority shall take the same measures as apply to infringements of national legislation. This seems to be an example of the non–discrimination principle. It seems to be limited to remedies rather than substantive provisions. Thus, if, say, a breach of the law implementing Directive X in Member State A is brought in State B, then as its law is implementing the same directive all the measures it could use against breach of its national law should be available for a breach of the law of State A. In principle there could still be a problem if the law as implemented in state A only covered harm to consumers in state A. Art. 2(2) cannot amend the substantive law of the Member States; but such laws should properly be interpreted as protecting all the Community's consumers.

---

[70]   Bethlem and Joustra, *op. cit.*

(c) Qualified entities

According to art. 3 the right of action can be exercised by any body or organisation which, according to national law, has a legitimate interest to ensure that the laws referred to in the annex are complied with. It goes on to provide that this can be:

'(a) an independent public body, specifically responsible for protecting consumer interests, in countries in which such bodies exists; and/or
(b) organisations with a legitimate interest in protecting consumer interests, as well as representative organisations of firms or federations of firms, in accordance with the criteria laid down by their national law.'

This clearly seems to leave it to the Member States to decide whether the power should be exercised by a public authority or a consumer organisation, or both.[71] Member States should draw up a list of the entities they recognise and communicate this to the Commission who will publish it in the C series of the Official Journal. This recognition is to be based on national law criteria. Thus Member States are free to maintain their own criteria. Recognised bodies receive a certificate of their qualification to act. This would seem to require a change of practice in some countries, such as Germany, which allow courts to recognise consumer organisations on an *ad hoc* basis, without a central registration system as exists in France. Bethlem and Joustra suggest that there is no need to make the possession of such a certificate a mandatory requirement, rather such a certificate could simply have a probative value easing access to the courts of other Member States.[72]

(d) Intra–Community infringements

The certificate establishing that an entity is recognised is important for intra–Community infringements. Art. 4(1) provides that on presentation of this document a qualified entity, whose interests are affected by an infringement originating in another Member State, shall be able to seize the court or competent authority in that state. Thus in principle the United Kingdom would have to allow access to consumer groups recognised by other Member States as having the right of action.

However, this principle is tempered by art. 4(2), which allows Member States the freedom to provide that direct seizure can only be invoked after the qualified entity has first been seized of the matter and has had a reasonable time within which to react. This means that in practice a foreign consumer

---

[71] Perhaps this will weaken the case of the Consumers' Association that they should have standing under the Unfair Contract Terms Directive, see Chap. 3 section 2E(ii).

[72] Bethlem and Joustra, *op. cit.*

organisation would have to inform the Director–General of Fair Trading and could only act in the United Kingdom courts if the Director–General had failed to act. However, a difficult problem might arise if the Director–General had failed to act for what he believed to be legitimate reasons. Would the foreign entity still be entitled to take a direct action or must it first seek judicial review of the national entity's decision? The text of the proposal seems to support the first alternative, as it does not qualify the right to act after a reasonable time.

These provisions attempt to strike a balance between preserving national traditions and yet ensuring adequate protection in the cross–border context. They could be viewed as a sound application of the subsidiarity principle by preserving national enforcement traditions. However, we see nothing threatening in the principle of consumer organisations (even those from other Member States) having the power to seek injunctions. It is to be hoped that experience of the use of such powers in other Member States will convince the UK Government to extend this right to its own consumer organisations.

Bethlem and Joustra note that the proposal is based on the assumption that it is desirable to bring an action in the country from which the harm originates, whereas there may be many advantages in bringing the action in the state where the harm was caused. Such advantages might be related to language, familiarity with procedures etc.[73] The Brussels Convention could then in some cases be used to enforce the judgment in the state of the defendant's domicile.[74] This would require the applicable law to cover harm caused to consumers in other Member States than that from which the harmful act originated. Although this could, as has been mentioned, be implied from general principles of EC law, nevertheless the eventual directive could usefully include a provision clarifying this point.

D.   Conclusions

If the market is to work efficiently and fairly consumer protection laws need to be complied with. For many of the reasons we have already mentioned, consumers cannot be relied upon to impose discipline on traders by seeking redress for every infringement. Indeed some infringements do not have an easily identifiable victim (e.g. distasteful advertising)[75] or need to be removed before harm can be inflicted (e.g. dangerous products). It is therefore important to have public authorities responsible for ensuring

---

[73]   Bethlem and Joustra, *op. cit.*

[74]   However, the Convention is probably not applicable to the administrative and criminal sanctions which are usually involved in these cases.

[75]   A matter which is not, however, the subject of EC law to date.

consumer laws are complied with. Although many Member States already had such agencies, the requirements in some EC directives to establish such bodies and to give them effective powers has been an important development in some countries.

However, relying solely on Government control can also be dangerous, especially when resources are scarce and the prevalent political theory favours light regulation. Therefore, allowing consumer organisations the right to take a collective action is an important symbolic signal that consumers can have confidence in the market. It is to be welcomed that EC law allows for the collective protection of the consumer interest, and irritating that it has to tolerate the resistance of some states to the involvement of consumer organisations in the process of market regulation.

The value of collective action is even more evident in relation to cross–border disputes where individual redress is extremely problematic. The proposed directive attempts to resolve the problem of rights of standing concerning cross–border complaints.

Two weaknesses can, however, be detected in the current EC procedures for collective redress. First, collective regulation need not be completely divorced from individual redress. Collective actions can provide assistance or even be the means through which individual damages are recovered. In some cases damages may, however, be more appropriately paid to the consumer collective rather than to individual consumers. There are, however, no measures permitting individual claims to be settled as part of enforcement proceedings or actions for injunctions. Such possibilities might be one way of making it easier to seek redress in cross–border disputes.

Second, the present injunction procedures are linked to specific directives. In some Member States it is possible to take action against any conduct which is unfair or harmful to consumers. We suggest that EC consumer law has developed to the stage where such broadly framed powers could be adopted. Failing that, it should be possible to ensure that the scope of such national laws of that nature as do exist extend to conduct which is undertaken or causes harm anywhere in the Community. Thus conduct should be caught if it is unlawful in either the state where the trader is based or undertakes the relevant activity or the state where the consumer lives. Persons and organisations in those countries should have access to each others' courts subject to the intra–Community provisions in the draft directive.

4.   GENERAL CONCLUSIONS

Access to justice and effective enforcement of consumer laws are two essential prerequisites for a healthy consumer protection policy. They ensure that consumer laws are not just window dressing, but provide real protection for consumers. A legal system which provides paper rights without the machinery to deliver them could expose consumers to increased dangers if they behave in the expectation that the law will protect them from certain risks. However, consumers can also be quick to apprehend when the law fails to function properly. This brings disrespect for the law and undermines its authority. Either way it is clear that laws should be applied and enforced.

In resolving individual disputes consumers need quick, cheap and independent foras in which to resolve disputes. ADR and small claims procedures can meet these criteria. However, the adoption of these alternatives to traditional court procedures should not be at the price of individual complaints being hushed up. Decisions should be publicly available and be used to raise trading standards and educate industry. Systems for reporting and learning from these type of disputes need to be established. Furthermore the temptation to see such claims as isolated aberrations should be controlled by opening up these types of dispute resolution system to collective actions either in the form of class actions or injunction proceedings brought by public authorities or consumer groups.

Cross–border disputes bring added complications. Resolving individual cross–border disputes can be made easier, by measures such as those included in the Commission's action plan, but it is always going to be difficult for individuals to bring such cases successfully because of practical difficulties. However, promoting co–operation between enforcement authorities[76] and the new injunctive powers given to authorities and consumer organisations should help to prevent cross–border sales being used as a means of circumventing EC regulation. Increasing the means of redress at the national level and promoting the competence of national authorities will also have indirect benefits for resolving or removing cross–border problems.

Access to justice and enforcement practices are phenomena closely linked to legal culture. Expectations should not be too high that by simply enacting a few legal requirements the EC will be able to change that culture so that overnight all legal systems become consumer friendly and enforcement authorities become vigilant in their monitoring of traders and vigorous in their enforcement practices. However, EC laws have the potential to achieve at least some changes in that culture. The presence of new enforcement authorities or new means of redress may not bring change immediately, but the introduction of new institutions may provide mechanisms through which changes in legal culture can be fostered. Learning

---

[76]   There is an international network of consumer protection authorities, see I. Edwards, 'Le réseau international de contrôle des pratiques commerciales' [1993] *R.E.D.C.* 135. and of European product safety authorities (Prosafe).

from best practice in Europe can also help to improve consumer redress and enforcement within national systems.

The Commission is to be commended for having made consumer access to justice one of its top priorities. Inevitably, perhaps, its concrete proposals have focused on attempting to improve the machinery for settling intra–Community disputes. Yet the need to reform domestic redress systems should not be ignored if consumer protection is to be seen as an autonomous base for Community action.

Many national legal systems ignored for a long time the needs of consumers to have access to justice and to have effective agencies with the means to prevent them being harmed. It is to be hoped that the Green Paper represents a signal that the Commission wants to address these serious issues. The very real problems faced by consumers with cross–border disputes should not lead the Commission to overlook the fact that many consumers with domestic disputes are let down by their legal system and their consumer protection authorities. The Commission has a long way to go if it wishes to turn many of the nice sentiments it made in its Green Paper into practical results.

Finally it should be appreciated that even access to justice by itself is not sufficient. Consumers can find themselves with a judgment in their favour, but be unable to enforce it. Equally regulators can find it hard to apply rules to traders who change their line of business, identity and/or location. These practical enforcement problems are not widely enough appreciated at the national level. The same problems exist, sometimes in even more acute form, with regard to intra–Community disputes and should be put on the Commission's agenda.

9   Conclusions

1.   INTERNAL MARKET AND CONSUMER POLICY

A.   Internal Market Policy as Basis for Consumer Law

The purpose of harmonising interventionist norms in the European Community is connected with the fundamental tasks of the Community. One may therefore assume the aims to be connected primarily with the goal of market integration. For instance, in relation to contract law it has been claimed that Community law approaches the subject of regulation from the point of view of economic efficiency and not of social justice.[1] As noted above (in Chap. 1 section 2) the legal basis for Community consumer policy was, at least before Maastricht, clearly tied to internal market considerations.

Looking at the reasons for the consumer law directives as stated in their preambles, internal market considerations appear as very central grounds justifying the measures. The preambles usually start by presenting some reasons of this kind. A closer analysis reveals three types of internal market considerations used to justify consumer law measures:

(i)   Varying consumer protection measures in the Member States are claimed to create barriers to trade within the internal market. It is not surprising that, for example, the preamble of the General Product Safety Directive begins with a reference to the internal market as an area with free movement of goods etc., noting that disparities between Member State legislation in the area are liable to create barriers to trade (recitals 1 and 2). These kinds of deliberations, however, are not confined to product–related measures. Also behind the harmonisation of advertising rules one encounters the same kind of reasons. The Misleading Advertising Directive is justified, *inter alia*, with reference to the fact that the differences between the laws of the Member States 'hinder the execution of advertising campaigns beyond national boundaries' (recital 4). Even divergences in contract law are seen as having effects as barriers to trade. Thus according to the preamble of the Package Travel Directive 'the establishment of common rules on packages will contribute... to the achievement of a common market in services, thus

---

[1]   See the illustrative figure in P.B. Madsen, 'Scandinavian contract law within the EEC' in T. Wilhelmsson (ed.), *Perspectives of Critical Contract Law*, (Dartmouth, 1993) at 113.

enabling operators established in one Member State to offer their services in other Member States...' (recital 3).

(ii) Variations in domestic laws are said to distort competition between enterprises from different Member States. References to this reason are commonplace in the consumer law directives. Even the Unfair Contract Terms Directive begins by noting the many disparities between the domestic laws relating to the terms of contract and underlining 'the result that the national markets for the sale of goods and services to consumers differ from each other and that distortions of competition may arise amongst the sellers and suppliers, notably when they sell and supply in other Member States' (recital 2).

(iii) Lack of harmonisation of consumer protection measures is also considered to hamper the activity of the consumers in the internal market. Again in the words of the Unfair Contract Terms Directive 'consumers do not know the rules of law which, in Member States other than their own, govern contracts for the sale of goods or services... lack of awareness [of which] may deter them from direct transactions for the purchase of goods or services in another Member State...' (recital 5).

Whereas the first two reasons view harmonised consumer protection measures as a necessary incident of the internal market from the producers' and suppliers' perspective, the third considers consumer protection from the consumers' perspective. The idea is that Community law should at least provide a floor of rights throughout the Community so that the confidence of consumers in the internal market is increased. This would, according to this argument, promote cross border shopping and selling.

Even though these kinds of internal market deliberations are often presented as the primary ones, they do not always appear very convincing. In some cases, directly related to the design of products, such as technical product safety matters, it is of course obvious that variations in Member State laws may have a direct negative impact on the creation of the internal market. In other cases, however, one may seriously doubt whether in reality differences in national laws will have a significant impact on inter–state trade. For instance, one may legitimately question whether the variations in the rules concerning contract terms really have such cost effects that they are substantial barriers to trade or affect competition.[2] Similarly, it does not seem very likely that variations in these rules influence to any significant

---

2   H.J. Bunte 'Gedanken zur Rechtsharmonisierung in der EG auf dem Gebiet der missbräuchlichen Klauseln in Verbraucherverträgen' in P. Löffelmann & H. Korbion (eds), *Festschrift für Horst Locher zum 65 Geburtstag*, (Werner – Verlag, 1990) at 328.

extent the decisions of consumers – who usually do not even know about these rules in their national law – to buy at home or abroad.

The emphasis on internal market reasons is explicable on 'constitutional' grounds. As shown in Chap. 1 section 2, there was no basis for an independent consumer policy in the Treaty of Rome, before the Treaty of Maastricht. Measures in this field therefore had to be justified with reference to internal market considerations. The question to what extent the real motives for the measures have been oriented towards the internal market requires further analysis.

Before proceeding to analyse that question, one should draw attention to the fact that different kinds of internal market considerations clearly are behind some measures of Community consumer law. Obviously the increase in cross–border shopping and transacting brings forth specific consumer problems which do not exist or have less importance in purely national settings. It would seem very natural for Community law to focus precisely on these kinds of problems. In fact a part of the materials analysed in this book has certainly been created in order to address problems in connection with cross–border activities. As examples one could mention not only the consumer rules in the 1968 Brussels Jurisdiction Convention and the 1980 Rome Convention on Applicable Law as well as the private international law provisions in the Unfair Contract Terms Directive and the Timeshare Directive, but also measures like the TV Directive and the Cross Border Transfers Recommendation (and proposed directive). Much of the discussion on access to justice concerns cross–border situations as well. Also the substantive rules on timeshare as well as those on distant selling are certainly explicable by the large frequency of cross–border contracts in these contexts, although they are not limited to only cross–border situations.

Internal market reasons of this kind, however, cannot justify but a part of Community consumer legislation. The majority of the measures described in this book certainly are related to and apply to problems which in most cases appear in purely national settings. The thought of a dual system, with the cross–border relationships regulated by Community law and the national ones by pure Member State law, has never received any great support. Even directives which focus on cross–border relations, like the ones on timeshare and distant selling, clearly cover domestic relationships as well. The reference to the need for regulating cross–border consumer problems does therefore not give any sufficient answer to the question concerning the relation between internal market and consumer policy. One is still faced with the question of whether there has been room for an autonomous Community consumer policy with a larger scope, having consumer protection as its primary purpose.

B.   Autonomous Consumer Policy

The fundamental aim of European Community consumer law – to create harmonised conditions of competition in the internal market – does not prevent it from having consumer protection aims as well. One may speak about a Janus–faced regulation, on the one hand seeking to create the internal market, and on the other hand pursuing protective goals.[3] It is clear that internal market aspects of Community consumer law cannot be separated out from the consumer protection concerns which are also addressed in European measures.

It is self–evident that such rules which strive to harmonise – not deregulate – existing national consumer protection legislation will by necessity contain a protective element derived from the national laws of Member States. In this sense European Community consumer law obviously provides for consumer protection. The question is, however, whether Community consumer law goes further than this. Are there any signs of a consumer policy in the Community which would aim at improving the position of the consumers, beyond what is required by the internal market based harmonisation of existing national legislation? One could speak about an autonomous Community consumer policy, autonomous in relation to internal market considerations.

The various consumer protection programmes of the European Community clearly point at an ambition to create an autonomous Community consumer policy. Certain consumer rights are identified and the priorities for the measures by which these rights are to be safeguarded are defined. These programmes are also regularly referred to in the preambles of the consumer protection directives, when the need for creating such protection is underlined. So, for example, the preamble of the Unfair Contract Terms Directive, after presenting the internal market justifications for the measure, continues by mentioning that 'the two Community programmes for a consumer protection and information policy underlined the importance of safeguarding consumers in the matter of unfair terms of contract...' (recital 8).

The constitutional basis for an autonomous consumer policy has, as mentioned earlier, been created by the Treaty of Maastricht, which expressly mentions the development of consumer policy as one of the aims of the Community (art. 3(s)). The Treaty thereby 'liberates pursuit of the consumer interest from the constraints of enforced linkage to internal market policy'.[4] Of course the principle of subsidiarity, also contained in the Treaty of

---

[3]   N. Reich, *Europäisches Verbraucherrecht*, (3rd ed., Nomos, 1996) at 56.

[4]   H.–W. Micklitz and S. Weatherill, 'Consumer Policy in the European Community: before and after Maastricht' (1993) 16 *J.C.P.* 285 at 299.

Maastricht, may on the other hand pull in another direction. One could claim that this principle would lead Community consumer policy to focus primarily on the cross–border problems mentioned in the previous section and leave consumer policy concerning domestic relations mainly in the hands of the Member States. In fact subsidiarity has been used as an argument against some Community involvement in consumer policy[5] and it will remain a relevant argument on the agenda also in the future. However, the subsidiarity argument has not prevented important directives, like the Unfair Contract Terms Directive, from being adopted after Maastricht. The European Parliament has also in a Resolution on the subsidiarity principle underlined that 'securing the highest level of... consumer protection should be the prime criterion' when the Community institutions make decisions on competencies.[6] Subsidiarity therefore does not seem to hinder the development of an autonomous Community consumer policy, even though it emphasises the need for co–operation and mutual influence with national consumer policies. One might say that the subsidiarity principle underlines the idea of shared responsibility, between the Community and the Member States, for consumer policy in the Community.[7] The proposal put forward later in this section concerning the role of Community consumer policy as an engine for internal reforms, in an interplay with national law, is well in line with such an understanding of the subsidiarity principle.

The rapidly growing amount of Community legal materials on consumer law has given rise to opinions among legal scholars according to which one already could speak about the existence of a Community body of consumer law – an *acquis communautaire de consommation* – with its own principles and approaches.[8] The leading principle of this Community consumer law would be the principle of the best possible consumer protection, supplemented by the principles of minimum harmonisation and efficient legal protection.[9]

This is, of course, a normative view, based on the relevant passages of the Treaty which mention a high level of consumer protection as an express goal (arts 100a and 129a). It is another question whether there have been *de*

---

5   After Maastricht the German government issued a list of measures in the consumer law area which should be dropped because of the principle of subsidiarity. The list is published in *Verbraucher und Recht* 1/1993.

6   Resolution A3–0380/92, Subsidiarity, environment and consumer protection, OJ 1993 C 42/40.

7   Micklitz & Weatherill, *op. cit.*, at 315.

8   N. Reich, *Europäisches Verbraucherschutzrecht*, (Nomos, 1993) at 398. In the new edition (Reich, *op. cit.*, 1996), however, this chapter is dropped.

9   N. Reich, 'Zur Theorie des Europäischen Verbraucherrechtes' (1994) 2 *Zeitschrift für Europäisches Privatrecht* 381 at 382.

facto attempts to pursue an autonomous and active consumer policy. In this context it can be noted that many of the directives have been strongly watered down during the process of preparation. What has started as a relatively radical proposal for improving the position of the consumers throughout the Community has frequently ended up as a much more modest act of harmonisation.[10] However, it is clear that many of the directives have improved the position of the consumers – sometimes even considerably – in at least some countries.[11] Even in advanced consumer protection countries, such as the Nordic states, one can record several improvements.[12] It should also be borne in mind that most consumer protection directives are minimum directives, which only prescribe a minimum level of consumer rights and do not compel those countries which have rules more advantageous to consumers to lower their level of protection. Therefore, one may safely say, as a general statement, that Community consumer law has achieved at least some improvement in the position of the consumers within the Community.

However, an autonomous Community consumer policy cannot, and should not, function in the same way as national consumer policy. The role of Community consumer policy could perhaps be seen not primarily as a producer of a new system of rights, but rather as an engine for internal reforms, especially in countries where consumer protection has been less developed. In more developed settings the fact that a directive has brought a certain problem area on the agenda may also inspire Member State legislators to further reforms in the area, as, for example, the section on the Consumer Credit Directive has shown.[13] Community consumer policy functions in an interplay with Member State consumer policy, at its best

---

10   The preparatory works of the Doorstep Selling Directive, the Misleading Advertising Directive, the Consumer Credit Directive, the Package Travel Directive and the Unfair Contract Terms Directive illustrate this very well. The section on sale of consumer goods (Chap. 3 section 3) is also instructive in this respect.

11   As an example one could mention the effect of the Unfair Contract Terms Directive on English law. See the Department of Trade and Industry's consultation document, *Implementation of the EC Directive on Unfair Terms in Consumer Contracts (93/13/EEC)* (DTI, 1993): 'The main effect of the Directive will be to introduce for the first time a general concept of fairness into the UK law of contract.'

12   See T. Wilhelmsson, *Social Contract Law and European Integration*, (Dartmouth, 1995) Ch. 4.

13   Certainly the Timeshare Directive has in many countries introduced this topic on to the legislative agenda, in some of them leading to further reforms than required by the Directive. This is not to say that this is a good example of Community law setting new and advanced priorities for the national legislators; one may question whether the – undoubtedly existing – problems in connection with timesharing really are among the most important ones to be regulated in the Community.

promoting it, at its worst functioning as a, not legal but factual, brake against independent national developments.

Some commentators have talked about a shift from a narrow economic concept of the 'common market' to that of a 'social Europe'.[14] It is certainly an exaggeration to claim that this transformation has been fully completed, but at least at the level of Community ideology there is a great deal of talk about the need for a Community with a social face. If such a claim is really to be taken seriously then there will have to be more emphasis placed on a Community consumer policy which is not bound to internal market considerations and which promotes, not brakes the development in the area.

Such an autonomous Community consumer policy has to produce a Community–wide floor of minimum consumer rights which are also efficiently protected in cross–border situations. Not only should this floor prevent a 'race to the bottom' of consumer legislation in the Member States, but it should be put on a high (the best possible) level and it should be constantly reviewed in order to achieve improvements and new inputs in the interplay between Community and Member State policy. The leading procedural principle of Community action should be the attempt to uphold the momentum of development by introducing new themes on the agenda of this interplay. The development of possible substantive principles for an autonomous Community consumer policy, such as a radical transparency principle and a legitimate expectations principle, are discussed in the following sections.

Such a consumer policy should not be confined to the narrow focus of promoting only the direct safety and economic interests of the consumers. As shown by the Eco–Label Regulation there is a need for playing on a larger field of policy. The advertising rules in the TV Directive, interested in the effects of advertising on our social values in general, in a similar way transgress the boundaries of 'pure' consumer law.[15] Similar needs can be encountered also elsewhere; for example, the Community consumer law rules concerning tourism may be criticised for not having taken into account the environmental problems connected with mass tourism. One should in other words take seriously the idea, which was already put forward in the Preliminary Programme for a consumer protection and information policy, that the 'consumer is no longer seen merely as a purchaser and user of goods and services for personal, family or group purposes but also as a person

---

14   Reich (1993), *op. cit.*, at 393 *et seq.*

15   This is not to say that these rules are very radical as to their content. As shown in Chap. 4 section 6 they merely seem to reflect the self–regulatory principles which business has set for itself.

concerned with the various facets of society which may affect him either directly or indirectly as a consumer'.[16]

2.   CHOICE AND TRANSPARENCY

A.   Starting Points

Community law, based on the four well–known basic freedoms, takes as one of its starting–points the promotion of the freedom of choice of Community citizens. It has been said that the realisation of the internal market of the Community is based on the 'rational–choice' model.[17] It is not therefore surprising that consumer choice is a central idea in Community consumer law. It is possible to talk of a consumer's 'right to participate more actively in the process of market integration'.[18]

The consumer choice–ideology is visible in many ways in the Community legal material. We have already noted that one of the express grounds for harmonising Member State consumer legislation is the promotion of the active engagement of the consumers in the internal market by facilitating cross–border consumer transactions, thereby widening the area of consumer choice. As shown below, much of the positive harmonisation measures can also best be understood in the light of a consumer–choice approach. In addition this ideology is emphasised in the practice of the ECJ.[19] In the application of the rules concerning barriers to trade in the Treaty of Rome, the Court, on the basis of the proportionality principle of Community law, has frequently found rules on information to offer sufficient consumer protection, thereby outlawing the substantive norms which were the subject of challenge in the cases.[20] The ECJ has also

---

16   OJ 1975 C 92/1, item 3. As noted in Chap. 1 section 3A, the Community has underlined the need for integrating consumer policy in the other policies of the Community.

17   H.–W. Micklitz 'Organisierte Rechtsdurchsetzung im Binnenmarkt' (1992) 75 *Kritische Vierteljahresschrift für Gesetzgebung und Rechtswissenschaft* 172 at 178.

18   Micklitz & Weatherill, *op. cit.*, at 287.

19   See S. Weatherill, 'The Role of the Informed Consumer in European Community Law and Policy' (1994) 2 *Consum.L.J.* 49.

20   See the famous Cassis de Dijon–case, *Rewe–Zentral AG v Bundesmonopol-verwaltung für Branntwein*, Case 120/78 [1979] ECR 649 at 664, as well as *Criminal proceedings against Herbert Gilli and Paul Andres*, Case 788/79 [1980] ECR 2071 at 2078, *Commission of the European Communities v Italian Republic*, Case 193/80 [1981] ECR 3019 at 3036, *Commission of the European Communities v Federal Republic of Germany*, Case 178/84 [1987] ECR 1227 at 1271 and *3 Glocken GmbH*

expressly, with reference to the consumer protection programmes of the Community, stated that 'under Community law concerning consumer protection the provision of information to the consumer is considered one of the principal requirements'.[21] Other cases also seem to indicate a rather strong assumption of the Court that information is always advantageous for the consumer, as long as it is true.[22]

The proposals for regulating comparative advertising, aiming *inter alia* at liberating such advertising throughout the Community, show a similar belief in the usefulness of all kinds of correct information. In the words of the Commission, comparative information 'can facilitate a rational choice'.[23]

The consumer policy of the Community is, in other words, to a large extent based on an information strategy. Duties of traders to give information are emphasised. The strategy implies a requirement of transparency. Communications given to consumers should be clear and understandable.

Again, of course Community consumer policy does not build on any completely coherent approach; to some extent it recognises the limits of a strategy basically requiring the consumers to protect themselves and the need to protect consumers through collective choices. There are elements of substantive regulation directly aiming at improving the behaviour of the enterprises in the marketplace, regulating the supply rather than, as information rules do, the demand. Most important in this respect is certainly the vast group of rules dealing with the physical safety of the consumer. Although there is an information element also in the safety definitions of the Product Liability Directive and the General Product Safety Directive one may confidently state that these directives, and other measures in the safety area, go much further than just providing the consumer with information to take care of his own safety. In the safety area, which has been a central focal point for Community consumer policy, the information strategy has not been the dominant philosophy.

Also in other areas, but to a lesser degree, one can find examples of substantive rules applicable without regard to the flow of information to the consumer. Many of the provisions of the Package Travel Directive and the Unfair Contract Terms Directive are of this nature, although the latter by virtue of its basic approach of excluding from its scope contracts which are individually negotiated, is very much building on traditional contractual and market–rational ideas concerning informed consent. Still, in spite of these

---

and *Gertraud Kritzinger v USL Centro–Sud and Provincia autonoma di Bolzano,* Case 407/85 [1988] ECR 4233 at 4281.

21 *GB–INNO–BM v Confédération du commerce luxemburgeois,* Case C–362/88 [1990] ECR 667 at 689.

22 See Chap. 4 section 2.

23 COM(91) 147 at 8.

counter–examples, by and large information and transparency seem to be the dominant policies in Community consumer law. We will look more closely at the ways in which the information and transparency strategy is coming to the fore in the materials analysed in this book.

B.   Truthfulness Requirement

The minimum requirement when speaking about an information and transparency strategy is obviously the requirement that the information which is given to the consumer should be correct and not misleading. This principle is self–evident in most developed legal systems. In spite of this, the Community legislator has found it necessary to acknowledge this principle in several consumer law directives.

The principle of truthfulness is confirmed in directives forbidding misleading advertising. Such a directive, which also contained more detailed rules on specific forms of misleading advertising, was first issued in relation to the marketing of foodstuffs.[24] The Community law on misleading advertising later received a more general sphere of application in the Misleading Advertising Directive. This required the Member States to create adequate and effective means to prevent misleading advertising, but it did not prescribe any private law sanctions to be attached to the information given. During the preparation of the Unfair Contract Terms Directive, a proposal was made in the European Parliament to include a provision on the binding nature of advertising.[25] This suggestion was not accepted, but a first step in this direction can be detected in art. 3 of the Package Travel Directive which provides that the information given in a brochure is binding on the organiser or retailer unless otherwise agreed. The draft Directive on consumer sales will also allow advertising to be taken into account when assessing whether goods are satisfactory and in order to determine the conditions of any commercial guarantee.

C.   Obligations to Give Information

For an effective information strategy it is not sufficient merely to demand truthfulness of the information the trader happens to give. There should also be rules which require that certain information be given. The stress on such information duties is evident in several consumer protection directives. These

---

24   See art. 2 of the Foodstuffs Marketing Directive.
25   See European Parliament, Session documents A3–0091/91, Report of the Committee on Legal Affairs and Citizens' Rights, at 10.

directives emphasise the significance of information to consumers regarding the quality and price of the object of the contract.

This emphasis on information is perhaps most clearly to be seen in the Consumer Credit Directive and the subsequent amendments relating to the disclosure and calculation of the annual percentage rate (APR). The detailed rules of these directives regulate the information to be given to the consumer concerning the cost of the credit. This information should be contained in any advertisement or any offer displayed at the business premises of the person offering the credit which indicates the rate of interest (art. 3). The Second Consumer Credit Directive gives quite detailed rules on the calculation of the effective APR. Against this background it is understandable that it has been stated that in the case of consumer credit, consumer protection in the Community has 'principally meant informing'.[26]

Demands for information to be given are also contained in the Foodstuffs Price Indication Directive and in the Non–Food Price Indication Directive. These directives lay down some Community ground rules concerning the minimum content of price information. In addition the Foodstuffs Marketing Directive makes compulsory the inclusion of certain other matters on the labels of foodstuffs (art. 3). The Council has stated that labelling should fulfil the following requirements: it should be comprehensive, distinctive, relevant, transparent, verifiable and practicable.[27]

One could cite other examples of the Community law duty to provide information. Noteworthy is the extensive list of information which should be given to the consumer under the Package Travel Directive (art. 4). This Directive also prescribes the obligatory minimum content of a brochure concerning the package, if such a brochure is made available to the consumer (art. 3). In the Timeshare Directive an obligation to provide any person requesting information on the immovable property or properties with a document containing certain information is put on the vendor (art. 3). Provisions like these make it possible to speak about a Community consumer law principle concerning a duty of the trader to give sufficient information to the consumer. Of course in practice this obligation to provide information can be rather passive, as, in the provisions cited above, there is no explicit duty placed on the trader to explain the information to the consumer. The intended impact of the information may even fail to materialise because of an overload of detail in the documents.

---

[26] N. Reich, 'From Contract to Trade Practices Law: Protection of Consumers' Economic Interests by the EC' in Wilhelmsson (ed.), *op. cit.*, at 85.

[27] Council resolution of 5 April 1993 on future action on the labelling of products in the interest of the consumer: OJ 1993 C 110/1.

D.   Transparency and Language of Contract Terms

The requirements concerning transparency in the context of contract terms means that consumers should receive such information concerning the content of the contract that it is possible for them to understand their commitments. This principle places certain demands on the person drafting contract terms. Such a requirement is stated in general terms by art. 5 of the Unfair Contract Terms Directive, which expressly provides that the written terms of contract given to the consumer must always be drafted in plain and intelligible language. The Payment Systems Recommendation focuses on both formulation and presentation by requiring the terms of the contract to be expressed in easily understandable words and in so clear a form that they are easy to read (annex, point 3(2)).

A special dimension of the demand for understandable contract terms in the Community setting concerns the language of the contract. However, this problem is not addressed by the Unfair Contract Terms Directive. Other rules of Community consumer law may have an impact on the question; these are, however, relatively heterogeneous and inconsistent. This goes for the language requirements in some directives concerning labelling.[28] There is a provision on language in the Timeshare Directive, which is rather consumer–friendly: the contract should be drawn up in at least the official Community language of the Member State in which the purchaser resides, or, if he so wishes, in the language of the Member State of which he is a national (art. 4). Alternatively, one may focus primarily on regions rather than states. For instance, under the Payment Systems Recommendation the terms of contract must be expressed in the language or languages which are ordinarily used for such or similar purposes in the regions where the terms of contract are offered (annex, point 3(2)). On the basis of these heterogeneous provisions it is not easy to state conclusively any general solution to the language problem – although the alternative offered by the Timeshare Directive of course seems tempting from a consumer point of view. The problem may even be solved by the rules of private international law which may, however, lead to

---

28   See Communication from the Commission to the Council and the European Parliament concerning language use in the information of consumers in the Community, COM(93) 456 at 3. The communication which recommends, *inter alia*, improved consistency of the Community rules in force (at 11) was given after the decision of the ECJ in *Groupement des Producteurs, Importateurs et Agents Generaux d'Eaux Minerales Etrangeres (Piageme) v Peeters*, Case C–369/89 [1993] 3 CMLR 725, where the Court found that a national obligation on labelling which exclusively demands the use of the language of the linguistic region and does not allow the purchaser to be informed by other measures, violates art. 30 of the Treaty of Rome.

results in conflict with the transparency requirement in cases where a law other than that of the consumer's state is applicable to the contract.[29]

Community contract law emphasises transparency instead of substantive regulation. The best expression of this is the limitation of the scope of the fairness principle in art. 4(2) of the Unfair Contract Terms Directive. This provision states that the assessment of the unfair nature of the terms shall relate neither to the definition of the main subject matter of the contract nor to the adequacy of the price or remuneration. These central terms of the contract, determining the contractual balance, may only be the subject of intervention if they are not in plain, intelligible language. One may therefore claim that the Directive 'does not require consumer contracts to be substantively fair, but it does require them to be clear'.[30]

The transparency requirement of the Unfair Contract Terms Directive expressly regulates the drafting of contract terms. In addition, claims have been put forward that the Directive indirectly also demands that the standard terms be handed over to the consumer.[31]

E. Right of Cancellation

The rules on information and transparency focus on the pre–contractual stage. They aim at facilitating rational consumer choice when contracts are made. Another method for strengthening the possibilities of a real choice on the part of the consumer is the granting to the consumer of a right of cancellation (withdrawal). This method has been used in several pieces of Community legislation.

This right of cancellation was included in the first directive on consumer contract law, that is the Doorstep Selling Directive. Under art. 5 of that Directive, the consumer has the right to renounce the contract, which must be exercised within a cooling–off period of not less than seven days. A similar right of cancellation is also included in the proposal for a Directive on distant selling. The Third Life Assurance Directive grants the consumer a cooling–off period of 14–30 days. The cooling–off period in the Timeshare Directive is ten days.

Consistency in EC law might be enhanced by the adoption of more standardised cooling–off periods. There might be policy justifications for choosing different periods in different contexts, but these are not spelt out in

---

29   See Reich (1996), *op. cit.*, at 346 who assumes that the language requirement then would follow the law applicable to the contract. He does not, however, himself accept that solution.

30   H. Collins, 'Good Faith in European Contract Law' (1994) 14 *O.J.L.S.* 229 at 238.

31   See Chap. 3 section 2D(ii).

the recitals to the various directives. Cancellation rules are altogether lacking in the legislation on consumer credit where they might be most badly needed.

The rules on cancellation bring the information and transparency strategy of the Community to a, at least in theory, more radical level. They transgress the traditional starting point of contract law according to which contracts are binding as soon as they are made. They could therefore be seen as one of the first signs of a post–Welfare State reflexive and procedural orientation of consumer law.[32] As they provide an informal way of reacting against sales pressure and insufficient transparency they certainly can have a practical impact as well, at least for the active consumers. One should not, however, overemphasise this impact, as lack of knowledge, psychological barriers, lack of time etc. can undermine the use of the right of cancellation.

As mentioned below, the growing amount of cancellation rules in Community law has made the time ripe for discussing the birth of a more general Community law principle of cancellation. Perhaps one could already discuss the possible emergence of a new post–welfarist contract model in the consumer law area in which the main rule (subject of course to numerous exceptions) would not be the immediate binding force of contracts, but rather the existence of a cooling–off possibility for consumers.

F.   Ecological Information

It should finally be mentioned that information strategies may be used for other purposes than protecting the consumer. For instance, they have also been used as an ecological device. The Eco–Label Regulation is intended to promote the design, production, marketing and use of products which have a reduced environmental impact during their entire life cycle and to provide consumers with better information on the environmental impact of products. The success of the eco–label award scheme has, however, so far been limited.

G.   Perspectives

Consumer choice, information and transparency are central elements of the consumer protection measures introduced so far by the Community. Also in the plans for future development of consumer protection the importance of consumer information is stressed.[33] The information paradigm will have an

---

32   Wilhelmsson (1995), *op. cit.*, at 189.

33   See, Communication from the Commission, Priorities for Consumer Policy 1996–1998, COM(95) 519, item 1. On a more concrete level one could mention the plans to

important position in the future of Community consumer law. It may be mentioned that the policy of the Commission concerning consumer problems connected with the transition to Monetary Union is still based strongly on an information strategy.[34]

From the consumer's point of view there are dangers as well as new opportunities connected with this paradigm. The information strategy is static and traditional, strongly tied to market considerations and thereby perhaps preventing creative development of other strategies which are needed. It may be employed in a negative manner, to prevent or slow down the creation of substantive consumer protection in Member State legislation as well as at Community level. There might even be direct deregulation through negative harmonisation measures prescribed by the ECJ, with information provision replacing domestic regulation. Thankfully, the examples of this are relatively few in the field of consumer law and the *Keck* principle should further restrict the possibilities to resort to negative harmonisation. However, the development towards a stronger emphasis on information may be problematic as a policy in the long run, if it affects the ways of thinking in the Member States and impedes the national development of consumer law.

The problems connected with an information strategy are obvious. The information may not reach the consumer. He may have difficulties in understanding and using the given information. He may not even find it worthwhile to make use of the information, considering the relatively small advantages it may bring. These kinds of problems seem to accumulate in the most disadvantaged groups of consumers. The consumers who would need the information most, that is the poor and uneducated consumers, seem to have the least possibilities of using it. Studies, for example, concerning truth–in–lending regulation clearly show such results. The improvement of the interest awareness, if any, because of such regulation seems to be concentrated in upper income groups.[35] Credit shopping induced by such regulation also seems to occur to a greater extent among higher income groups.[36] Disclosure regulation in practice benefits the rich more than the poor.

The regulation of information also lacks relevance, if the consumer in practice does not have any alternatives. Information that a cheap product is

---

create greater transparency in labelling in the Council resolution of 5 April 1993, *op. cit.*

[34] *Green Paper on the practical arrangements for the introduction of the single currency*, COM(95) 333.

[35] W.C. Whitford, 'The Functions of Disclosure Regulation in Consumer Transactions' (1973) *Wisconsin Law Rev.* 400 at 414.

[36] *Ibid.*, at 420.

of inferior quality than a corresponding more expensive one does not help a consumer very much if he needs the product but cannot afford to buy the more expensive one. Truth–in–lending regulation does not assist a consumer who has only one available source of credit. The poorer the consumer is the less alternatives he usually has.

There is a certain awareness of the problems connected with an information strategy in the Community. In the Commission's Priorities for Consumer Policy 1996–1998 it is stressed that information supply alone is not a sufficient measure from the point of view of the needs of consumers, and that it should be complemented by targeted consumer education from early school days.[37] However, as the prime responsibility for education rests with the Member States this goal is more likely to remain an empty aspiration than to lead to real results. In any case, education cannot extinguish the differences in ability to use information between well–off and disadvantaged consumers.

One strategy employed to make information more efficient is the use of labels which provide easily digestible information to consumers about the product or service. The CE mark is the most widely known label signalling conformity with technical standards.[38] The use of a common mark throughout Europe means that, in theory at least, it can be recognised by all European citizens, even the illiterate. The dangers in this approach are that consumers rely too heavily on the symbol which may not cover all aspects of the product or tell the consumer too much about the quality of the goods or services other than that minimum EC requirements have been met. The CE mark may also be awarded on the basis of different application of the criteria throughout the Community. As more aspects of a product become relevant to consumer choice (such as the environment, guarantees etc.) more labels are created with the result that consumers can become more confused than assisted by their presence. One may also wonder whether weak consumers really have any idea about what the CE mark means, yet alone the other more refined marks. Nevertheless, as a long term consumer education strategy it might be seen as being more profitable to raise awareness about a symbol rather than to educate all consumers about the complicated aspects of the product which have to be satisfied to be awarded, say, a CE mark.

However, there also seems to be a certain potential for more radical positive developments to arise out of the strong emphasis on transparency in Community consumer law. One might use the provisions described above to

---

37   COM(95) 519 at 5.

38   See Council Decision of 22 July 1993 concerning the modules for the various phases of the conformity assessment procedures and the rules for the affixing and use of the CE conformity marking, which are intended to be used in the technical harmonisation directives: OJ 1993 L 220/23.

further the evolution of rather far–reaching information principles.[39] Such a radical transparency principle could contain elements of the following kind:[40]

(i)   a radical obligation of the stronger party to inform the weaker party on facts with relevance for the contract;

(ii) a corresponding obligation to acquaint the weaker party with the content of the contract; this obligation would not only require clear wording of the contract in a language which the weaker party understands and the availability and handing–over of the contract terms, but it may also imply actively explaining[41] and educating consumers about the content of the contract, and

(iii) finally, the development of a more general principle of cancellation.

As an ordinary information strategy usually does not satisfactorily reach disadvantaged consumers, the obligations actively to explain and educate should be underlined, if one desires to achieve outcomes which are more socially balanced. However, the practical impact of such obligations may be questioned. The difficulty in producing significant practical changes in behaviour illustrates the problematic nature of an information strategy, from the point of view of weak consumers.

3.   THE CONSUMER IMAGE

The consumer definition in Community law, like the corresponding definitions in many of the Member States, is relatively abstract, in the sense that all consumers are protected by Community consumer law, irrespective of their actual strength or weakness. It is usually not relevant to ask whether the consumer belongs to some group of especially disadvantaged or weak consumers. All consumers are treated alike.

However, in the minds of the creators of a consumer policy this abstract consumer has to receive some flesh and blood. Consumer policy is guided by consumer images which mirror certain perceptions of reality. Understandings

---

39   Thoughts in this direction are expressed by Hans–W. Micklitz, who uses an active legal strategic approach to develop a general principle of Community law concerning the right to information and knowledge to further the interests of consumers, see Micklitz, *op. cit.*, 178 *et seq.*

40   See Wilhelmsson (1995), *op. cit.*, at 146 *et seq.*

41   N. Reich, 'Verbraucherschutzaspekte der AGB–Banken' in N. Horn (ed.), *Die AGB–Banken 1993*, (Walter de Gruyter, 1994) at 56 *et seq.* interprets the Unfair Contract Terms Directive to contain an obligation to explain the content of the contract terms to customers who are not well acquainted with the language of the contract.

about the behaviour and needs of consumers form the basis for various consumer protection strategies. The measures chosen reflect the consumer images prevailing among the decision makers.[42]

The dominant image of Community consumer law already follows from what was said about consumer choice and transparency. As information is a central device of Community consumer policy one could claim that the consumer image dominating in the Community is a well–informed and well–to–be–informed consumer – the active internal–market–consumer[43] – who can and should decide on his or her own affairs at his or her own risk.[44] The stress on the active and critical approach of the consumer is seen in several decisions of the ECJ relating to information requirements in various contexts.

The emphasis on labelling and information in many of the negative harmonisation cases (in which substantive regulation was outlawed in favour of information provisions) clearly presupposes a consumer who really makes efforts to read the information on labels and make use of other information offered. The consumer image of the Court does not seem to be of the hasty and relatively uncritical consumer who just throws a fast glance at advertisements and other written materials, but rather the Court supposes a critical and attentive consumer who makes use of all the information offered.[45]

The emphasis on transparency also shows a preference for the information–seeking consumer. For example, the requirement in the Unfair Contract Terms Directive that contract terms should be written in a plain, intelligible language can only be relevant for consumers who really make an effort to read their standard form conditions. The dominant consumer image in Community consumer law is therefore the active and critical information–seeker. Many of the Community consumer measures are built on this perception of consumer behaviour.

Rules based on such an image are, as already noted, more suited to the needs of relatively strong consumers, who at least have the ability to act in the way presupposed. The special needs of weak consumers can easily be overlooked in such a model.

---

42   See in more detail, T. Wilhelmsson, 'Consumer Images in East and West' in H.–W. Micklitz (ed.), *Rechtseinheit oder Rechtsvielfalt in Europa? Rolle und Funktion des Verbraucherrechts in der EG und den MOE–Staaten*, (Nomos, 1996).

43   C. Joerges & G. Brüggemeier, 'Europäisierung des Vertragsrechts und Haftungsrechts' in P.–C. Müller–Graff (ed.), *Gemeinsames Privatrecht in der Europäischen Gemeinschaft*, (Nomos, 1993) at 260.

44   P. Hommelhoff, 'Zivilrecht unter dem Einfluss Europäischer Rechtsangleichung' (1992) 192 *Archiv für die civilistische Praxis* 71 at 93 *et seq.*

45   A.H. Meyer, 'Das Verbraucherleitbild des Europäische Gerichtshofs – Abkehr vom flüchtigen Verbraucher' (1993) 39 *Wettbewerb in Recht und Praxis* 215 at 224.

One could to some extent interpret the rules to take the needs of weak consumers into account. For example, the requirement concerning plain, intelligible language in the Unfair Contract Terms Directive need not focus on what the average consumer would consider intelligible, but could be applied with reference to the understanding of 'the naive and inexperienced consumer'.[46] Such interpretations, although commendable from a social point of view, may, however, not be accepted by the ECJ. At least when judging whether an advertisement could be considered misleading under the Misleading Advertising Directive, the Court has expressly stated that an advertisement was misleading only if it was demonstrated that a significant number of consumers to whom the advertisement was addressed were misled by it.[47] The statement shows little understanding for the information needs of the most vulnerable consumer groups.[48]

Anyway, even an information strategy which focused on the naive and inexperienced consumers would probably not satisfy many of their needs for protection. An information strategy, even if it takes special note of the understanding of naive and inexperienced consumers, is still insufficient with regard to the needs of such consumers.

The approach of Community law regarding the consumer image – just as on many other points – is not completely consistent. There are decisions of the ECJ in which the Court seems to be less confident about the active and critical attitude of consumers. In one case the Court upheld national rules prohibiting the marketing device of offering free gifts,[49] which 'reveals an acceptance on the part of the Court that the consumer may be unable properly to process information'.[50]

Exceptionally the Court has also referred to the special needs of weak consumers when applying the rules on barriers to trade. In a much–cited case, *Buet*,[51] a French prohibition on canvassing in connection with the sale

---

[46] Collins, *op. cit.*, at 248.

[47] *Criminal proceedings against 'X' (re Nissan cars)*, Case 373/90 [1992] ECR I–131.

[48] It might, however, be in line with internal market considerations. At least N. Reich, *Privatrecht und Verbraucherschutz in der Europäischen Union*, (Zentrum für Europäisches Wirtschaftsrecht, 1995) at 15 claims that the goal of the internal market cannot be achieved without a certain portion of consumers being misled. This might be, and probably is, a factual consequence of the free flow of goods, services and information, but it is hard to see why it would have to be accepted as a normative starting point.

[49] *Criminal proceedings against Oesthoek's Uitgeversmattschappij BV*, Case 286/81 [1982] ECR 4575.

[50] Weatherill, *op. cit.*, at 53.

[51] *R. Buet and Educational Business Services (EBS) SARL v Ministère Public*, Case 382/87 [1989] ECR 1235.

of educational material was considered to satisfy the mandatory requirements and thereby be acceptable, even though it formed an obstacle to trade in the sense of art. 30 of the Treaty of Rome. One of the reasons the Court gave for permitting the prohibition expressly referred to the special weakness of the type of consumers at whom the product was aimed: 'The potential purchaser often belongs to a category of people who, for one reason or another, are behind with their education and are seeking to catch up. That makes them particularly vulnerable... .'[52] It is also noteworthy that when assessing the safety of products the General Product Safety Directive requires that 'the categories of consumers at serious risk when using the product, in particular children' be taken into account (art. 2).

In summary, therefore, even though the bulk of the Community consumer law material illustrates a strong belief in the consumer as an active and critical information–seeker, there are a few instances which express other consumer images more concerned with the needs of weak and vulnerable consumer groups. A consumer strategy which is genuinely interested in promoting the protection of those groups – not only the poor and ignorant but also other groups with special needs, such as the young, old, handicapped, minority groups, etc. – should emphasise these aspects of Community consumer law. The radical transparency and information strategy described at the end of the preceding section obviously presupposes such an emphasis. It focuses precisely on the need for explanation and education of 'the naive and inexperienced consumer'.

Here it should be pointed out that substantive rules alone, even if they recognised the special needs of weak and vulnerable consumers, would never be sufficient to protect such consumer groups. All private law (that is individual) protective mechanisms which require some form of a reaction by the individual consumer in order to become effective – a consumer who buys defective goods but does not react in any way does not receive any protection – will most certainly be used more often by the more affluent and better educated consumers. People whose ability to perceive their problems in legal terms is limited and who do not have sufficient knowledge about the protective mechanisms cannot be expected to use such mechanisms very frequently. Therefore there is a need for collective mechanisms, such as administrative supervision of matters such as marketing and product safety, which may benefit the whole consumer collective, including its most disadvantaged parts. Of course the value of such measures for the weak consumers is to a large extent dependent upon the actual practice of those using the collective measures. They must take the interests of the poor and disadvantaged into account when applying the provisions and in drawing up their priorities for action. If a consumer is so disadvantaged that he cannot

---

[52]   *Ibid.*, at 1252.

participate at all in the consumption of the goods or services which an administrative measure is concerned with then he will also, of course, not benefit from the measure.

Community consumer law to some, albeit not very radical, extent promotes collective regulation. The General Product Safety Directive, the Unfair Contract Terms Directive and the Misleading Advertising Directive all require such measures. The preparation of new rules regarding access to justice also focus on the collective injunction procedures. In this way Community law at least requires and recognises the need for mechanisms protecting the whole consumer collective. It does not, however, guarantee that the use of these mechanisms, by national authorities and organisations, takes into account the problems which are especially important for weak consumers. In spite of this, a strategy which promotes various kinds of collective measures is certainly needed, if the Community consumer policy is to serve all, and not only the well–to–do citizens of the Union.

Finally, weak consumers might be assisted by anti–discrimination rules, forbidding, for example, the offer of worse contract terms to or the refusal to deal with certain consumers because of race, gender, language etc.[53] Still more radical in this respect would be an equality strategy to fight the phenomenon of 'the poor pay more'[54] questioning the fact that less wealthy applicants for credit are offered credit under worse terms than the terms offered to people in a better economic situation. However, the consumer law material discussed in this book does not offer much fuel for such anti–discrimination and equality strategies. Of course one may seek an impetus in this area from the relatively strong equality elements present in other parts of Community law: the prohibitions on discrimination between citizens of the different Member States, the legislation on equality between men and women and the competition law prohibition against discrimination between contract partners. On this basis one might even attempt to build a general principle of equality and anti–discrimination in European private law.[55] However, in spite of this, the equality perspective is certainly lacking as an active and essential element in the consumer policy of the Community. Also in this

---

53 This problem is especially acute in connection with insurance. In the insurance society (see on this concept F. Ewald, *L'Etat Providence*, (Grasset, 1986)), the calculus of probability which includes reference also to personal qualities of the involved gains central importance. Insurance classification becomes offensive in its unproblematic use of gender, place and race (J. Simon, 'The Ideological Practices of Actuarial Practice' (1988) 22 *Law & Soc. Rev.* 772 at 794). As Nick Huls claims, society moves 'From class struggle to classification', N. Huls, 'Critical Insurance Law' in Wilhelmsson (ed.), *op. cit.*, at 155.

54 D. Caplovitz, *The Poor Pay More*, (The Free Press, 1963).

55 See Wilhelmsson (1995), *op. cit.*, at 203 *et seq.*

respect Community consumer law of today has forgotten the weak and the vulnerable consumers.

4.   LEGITIMATE EXPECTATIONS

It has been suggested that the 'legitimate expectations' concept could be seen as a general principle of Community consumer law.[56] The idea which lies behind this is that consumers purchasing anywhere in the Community should expect goods and services to be of a quality and safety which they are entitled to expect and contract terms should not surprise them. In this sense the principle underpins another contemporary aspiration of Community consumer policy, namely the promotion of the confident consumer – one who is happy to be an active internal market consumer because he has confidence in his legal security wherever he purchases within the Community.[57]

It is possible to find several EC rules which seem to reflect the principle of legitimate expectations. The following are some examples:

- the defectiveness standard in the Product Liability Directive which requires products to 'provide the safety which a person is entitled to expect' (art. 6(1));
- the requirement in the General Product Safety Directive that products do not 'present any risk or only the minimum risks compatible with the product's use, considered as acceptable and consistent with a high level of protection' (art. 2(b));
- the good faith concept in the Unfair Contract Terms Directive, both because the preamble talks about taking the legitimate interests of the other party into account (recital 16) and because the annex of indicatively unfair terms covers terms which run counter to the legitimate expectations of consumers;[58]

---

[56]   H.–W. Micklitz, 'Principles of Justice in Private Law within the European Union' in E. Paasivirta and K. Rissanen (eds), *Principles of Justice and the Law of the European Union*, (Helsinki University Institute of International Economic Law, 1995) at 284 *et seq*. This thesis was, in the same work, supported by one of the present authors, see T. Wilhelmsson, 'The Principle of Legitimate Expectations as a Basic Principle of Community Private Law'.

[57]   See S. Weatherill, 'The Evolution of European Consumer Law and Policy: From Well Informed Consumer to Confident Consumer' in H.–W. Micklitz (ed.), *op. cit.*

[58]   See Wilhelmsson in Paasivirta and Rissanen (eds), *op. cit.*, at 330 *et seq.*, who classifies them as terms which run counter to the principles of autonomy, responsibility for contractual performance, freedom, fair consequences of breach of contract and access to justice.

- the Green Paper on Consumer Guarantees went so far as to suggest that 'the notion of failure to meet the consumer's legitimate expectations would seem well suited to the role [of determining the scope of the legal guarantee]'.[59] Although legitimate expectations are not found on the face of the draft Directive, the principle can be seen to underlie the principle of conformity with the contract of sale (art. 2);
- the notion of misleading advertising in the Misleading Advertising Directive (art. 2(2));
- generally the various rights to cancel consumer contracts (as they allow consumers time to reflect on agreements and remove themselves from them if, *inter alia*, they do not meet up to their expectations).

The legitimate expectations concept is said to have both subjective and objective elements. The subjective element is the expectations generated by consumers. This is, however, controlled by what is 'legitimate', so that the courts can decide what burden it is reasonable to place on traders. The answer to what are the legitimate expectations of consumers is therefore the outcome of a careful balancing of interests.

This does not, however, simply involve a conflict between consumers on one side and traders on the other. Different traders may advocate varying standards depending upon their individual sense of what their sector should offer consumers which may be influenced by the type of consumers to whom they market their goods and services. Certainly there is no set of expectations common to all consumers. Expectations vary between consumer groups, for example rich/poor consumer, vulnerable/strong consumer, the rash consumer glancer/the cautious consumer, risk taker/risk adverse consumer etc.

Perhaps the most problematic differences in expectations in the single market context might be those generated by the different consumer cultures which exist in the Member States. In the short term diversity in the national application of the legitimate expectation principle (in the form of the open-textured norms set out above) might be tolerated as an escape valve to permit gradual acceptance of the Europeanisation of consumer law. However, it should not be seen as a wholly legitimate manifestation of the subsidiarity principle, for there is the danger that over time the *de lege* harmonisation process will be undermined by the *de facto* differential operation of the supposedly harmonised rules. In time not only must the same principles be included in the legal system of each Member States but they must take on the same common meaning, if harmonisation is to be meaningful.[60]

---

[59] COM(93) 509 at 85.

[60] As to whether this is possible see discussion in Chap. 1 section 4C.

The legitimate expectation principle, in its various manifestations in open–textured general clauses, can be seen as an example of reflexive law. By this is meant the creation of procedures through which the interests of various groups can be taken into account.[61] Although this theory of law sees social self–regulation as an ideal, it provides that where there are 'interaction deficiencies' between the parties the law should simulate the process of social self–regulation by the use of general clauses such as 'good faith.'[62]

Of course, what the use of general clauses does in practice is to transfer the forum for the resolution of these conflicts from the democratic legislative process to the courts, albeit with the caveat that court judgments ought to be guided by the values which underlie the general clauses. We shall see, below, that the advocates of reflexive law are rather sceptical about the value of legislative interventions as a means of assuring welfarist goals. However, the appeal of general clauses as an alternative to detailed regulation, may be strongest in civilian countries, such as Germany and the Nordic countries, where there have been positive experiences of general clauses being used creatively by the judges to introduce principles of fairness into the law. By contrast, in the United Kingdom the common law has a presumption that statutes do not alter the common law and this results in a tendency to construe them restrictively. There are also examples of English judges reading common law rules (which are of course based on the traditional principle of freedom of contract) into statutory norms.[63]

Perhaps the most difficult question concerning the legitimate expectations principle is the status and function which should be ascribed to it. It can of course simply be viewed as a heuristic tool to analyse and explain the principles of EC consumer law. This would treat it as a descriptive rather than a normative concept. It could also be seen as a political principle against which to assess the content of legal rules and to highlight inadequacies in EC consumer law. One of the present authors has used legitimate expectations as a critical concept to challenge the validity of the exclusion of the core terms from an assessment of their fairness under the Unfair Contract Terms Directive.[64] One could also argue that the lack of EC regulation of matters such as after–sales service, unfair advertising and the distant selling of financial services etc. runs counter to the legitimate expectations of consumers. Here the need to satisfy the legitimate

---

61   See G. Teubner, 'Substantive and Reflexive Elements in Modern Law' (1983) 17 Law & Soc Rev 239.

62   *Ibid.*, at 277–8.

63   See for example, the study by one of the authors into the interpretation by the courts of the extortionate credit bargain provisions, L. Bently and G. Howells, 'Judicial Treatment of Extortionate Credit Bargains' [1989] Conveyancer 164.

64   Wilhelmsson in Paasivirta and Rissanen (eds), *op. cit.*, at 334 *et seq.*

expectations of consumers is viewed as an essentially political argument, although one rooted in a sense of justice.

A more complex debate concerns whether the principle of legitimate expectations, if established, has any independent normative juridical value. In other words is the legitimate expectations principle a rule which consumers can demand their legal system respects? A difference between the civilian and common law traditions might be discernible in this respect. The civilian tradition places emphasis on the role of doctrine in distilling principles. These principles, if not independent legal rules, are at least used as a valid means of concretising the application of legal norms. Thus, for instance, the civilian lawyer would be able openly to take into account the principle of legitimate expectations when applying principles like good faith.

The role of principles is more opaque in the common law. It is true that in administrative law the principle of legitimate expectations has become accepted, partly through the medium of EC law, but that was on the basis of express statements of the principle by the judges.[65] It is also true that Dworkin has argued that in hard cases – which would cover all the problematic applications of general clauses with which we are presently concerned – judges should be guided by principles.[66] Legitimate expectations could be seen as one such principle. However, this theory, although influential is still controversial, and moreover its aim is to suggest how common law judges ought to (and in some cases do) take decisions. There is no positive legal rule which accepts juridical principles as binding legal norms.

The ECJ may be receptive to the technique of using principles as guides to the concrete content of general phrases.[67] It is to be hoped that the Court makes express its reliance on principles such as that of the legitimate expectations of the consumer. Only if it is transparent in its adoption of the legitimate expectation principle can it be hoped that this worthy principle will be given equal weight in all Member States whatever their legal traditions. Whether legal cultures in all Member States would be able to adapt to this approach is a larger question than we can adequately address in this context (see discussion in Chap. 1 section 4C), but it is encouraging to see how many judges throughout the Member States are becoming aware of the need for a particular approach when applying and interpreting EC derived legal rules.

---

65 See on the impact in English law, C.F. Forsyth, 'The Provenance and Protection of Legitimate Expectations' (1988) *Camb.L.J.* 232.

66 See especially, R. Dworkin, *Taking Rights Seriously*, (Duckworth, 1978) and *Law's Empire*, (Fontana, 1986).

67 See S. Weatherill, 'Prospects for the Development of European Private Law through "Europeanisation" in the European Court – the Case of the Directive on Unfair Terms' (1995) 5 *E.R.P.L.* 307.

5.   GOODS AND SERVICES

At several points in this work it has been remarked that EC consumer law offers greater protection to the consumer of goods than services. However, this statement must be qualified. It is only true of certain areas of EC consumer law. In the area of advertising, marketing practices and the control of contract terms many of the EC rules apply equally to both goods and services. Although even in this context services are sometimes neglected, for instance the Non–Food Price Indication Directive does not apply to services.[68]

Of course the financial service sector has managed to have itself excluded from some, but not all, of these provisions. Financial services are subject to specific EC directives, although the consumer protection content of these is rather weak. We have also described in detail the EC regulation of two service sectors, consumer credit (Chap. 6) and tourism (Chap. 7). Again the content of EC rules in these areas is mainly concerned with advertising, marketing and contract terms.

Therefore EC law does not leave unregulated the provision of services. What the EC (and many national) legislators have been reluctant to do is to impose general rules fixing standards on service providers. This is true both in the context of safety and quality. The possible arguments for the EC failing to provide such rules have already been considered in the context of service safety (Chap. 2 section 2C). We do not intend to repeat that debate, but want to reiterate our conclusions that services should and can be regulated by EC law and to place these conclusions in a wider context than just safety regulation.

Moreover, we would point out that even if the EC wishes to be shy of establishing rules fixing the standard of services, there are still some EC rules which apply to goods which could easily be extended to services. For instance, in the proposed Directive on consumer sales (see Chap. 3 section 3), even if the EC did not want to extend the rules on conformity to services, there is no reason why guarantees offered by the supplier of services should not be subject to the rules in art. 5 governing their form, legal effect and requiring that they provide the consumer with something additional to his legal rights.

The argument that consumer services do not have a significant internal market dimension and therefore EC regulation is not justified, is not tenable for several reasons. First, service providers are increasingly selling either across borders or from within the borders of other Member States. The 'home country' control principle requires that minimum levels of consumer

---

[68]   See Chap. 4 section 5B.

protection be guaranteed. Second, some consumers may actively seek out service suppliers in other states, usually for specialist services; but more significantly, any consumer who visits another Member State will be *forced* to use local services. One can choose which state's goods to buy, but when visiting other states local services must be used. Third, some services carried out in one Member State may have effects in another state if consumers or their goods migrate there. Indeed the existence of many EC consumer rules which do apply equally to goods and services suggests that the argument that there is a lack of internal market effects in relation to services is not a viable explanation for the gaps in consumer protection relating to services. Indeed, if we are right in suggesting that there should be a shift away from an internal market to an autonomous consumer protection basis to EC consumer law then this excuse would disappear entirely. The real objection to EC regulation of service standards seems to be the impossibility of fixing the level at which they should be pitched.

It is easy to make a theoretical distinction between goods which can have ascertainable standard characteristics and services which are more individualistic and can produce idiosyncratic outcomes. This has resulted in different legal regimes being applied to goods and service. The different principles are, perhaps, best encapsulated in the French terms distinguishing between *obligations de resultat* (for goods) and *obligations de moyens* (for services). However, even besides the technical point, that it can sometimes be difficult to decide whether something is goods or a service (which in itself suggests the distinction is rather artificial), this legal distinction in liability regimes ignores the real nature of many contemporary consumer services. Many such services are, if not 'mass produced', at least standardised and consumers expect guaranteed outcomes from service provision in the same way as they expect goods to have certain qualities and characteristics. The onus should be on particular sectors to make out a strong case for their exemption from general regulation of consumer services.

If a distinction is to be drawn between goods and services, it is probably not in relation to civil liability or a general safety standard. Defectiveness standards and the rules on conformity could be applied to services with little difficulty as they have within them a discretion to take the circumstances of the case into account. Rather the difference in approach will be with respect of those rules which regulate the detailed quality and safety characteristics of services. Instead of controlling a finished product, service regulation would have in the main to be concerned with the elements involved in the supply of the service. Whereas product standards can demand final products comply with certain composition and design rules, for services the emphasis would have to be on ensuring the service supplier had the appropriate means to provide the service, even if the result could not be guaranteed. Relevant factors for service providers might therefore be whether staff were adequately qualified and trained or if equipment and premises were satisfactory.

Of course one of the obstacles to imposing general horizontal rules on service providers is the range of services which would be caught. Consumer service providers range from cleaners to gynaecologists! However, there is no real difference between this and the position with respect to products. After all a ginger beer bottle and a supersonic jet are quite different objects, but have to comply with the same general rules on quality and safety. Of course more complex products may have many additional rules and standards with which they need to comply. The same should be true of services. Specific rules should be in addition to horizontal legislation.

It is interesting to note that recent research carried out by MORI (a market research organisation) for the United Kingdom's Institute of Trading Standards Administration found that 'consumers were particularly concerned about areas outside the tradition remit of the trading standards service – for example, financial services, health care, legal services and the utilities'.[69] In response to these 'new' consumer concerns, a range of initiatives have been adopted which seek to assist consumers with problems and to give them confidence in those service sectors.[70] We believe that such initiatives would be better off as part of a legal regime which assured consumers of a degree of protection through general principles.

However, in the near future any EC initiatives are likely to favour a sectoral approach to service regulation. The problem with this is that many service sectors are also powerful political lobbies and so the process of adopting sector specific directives is likely to be slow and the outcomes unlikely to be of great benefit to consumers. In time the need for horizontal legislation of services is likely to become apparent, mirroring the experience with goods. With respect to consumer service regulation there is still a steep learning curve which the EC (and many national) legislators have to negotiate. However, as noted in Chap. 2 section 2D, some Member States have begun to apply general rules on safety to services as well as products. It is to be hoped that in time this will give the EC the confidence to propose horizontal EC rules on service quality and safety.

---

[69]   N. Hunter, 'Changing the Face of Consumer Protection' (1996) 104 *Trading Standards Review* Issue 9, 8 at 9.

[70]   Incidentally many of these initiatives involve the use of 'soft law' (see next section).

6. LEGAL TECHNIQUES

A. Soft Law[71]

(i) The Concept

'Soft law' refers to non–binding norms. In the EC context it is necessary to distinguish two levels at which the concept is used. It can be used to describe the non–binding EC legislative acts – recommendations and opinions – which might be used to encourage action at the national level (possibly even involving legislation). Alternatively it can describe situations where the EC legislator declines to impose rules on industry in favour of the development of voluntary self–regulatory standards. These standards are generally produced by the industry sector itself often after a period of concertation with regulators and social groups affected (including consumer groups). It is with this latter use of the term 'soft law' which we are primarily concerned in this section, although this policy is often associated with the adoption of non–binding EC legislative acts.

Our general instinct is to be sceptical about the motivations for introducing 'soft law'. However, we will suggest that it might have a constructive role to play if seen as part of a legislative package which sets out the basic principles of consumer protection in legal regulation, but leaves 'soft law' to find the best means of achieving these goals. A precondition should, however, be the effective involvement of consumers in the development of any voluntary rules or standards.

(ii) EC Consumer 'Soft' Law

Our scepticism about soft law as a means of consumer protection is based, in part, on the fact that it is often raised in the context of deregulation. This is supported by the evidence that the EC seemed to be converted to the principle of 'soft law' in its Second Programme for a consumer protection and information policy.[72] This was introduced in recessionary times when the emphasis was on light regulation. Whilst accepting that legislation would continue to be needed in many areas it suggested 'the application of certain principles might also be sought by other means, such as the establishment of

---

71 This section is based on the ideas contained in G. Howells, '"Soft Law" in EC Consumer Law' in P. Craig and C. Harlow (eds), *Law–making in the European Union*, (Sweet & Maxwell Ireland, forthcoming).

72 OJ 1981 C 133/1.

specific agreements between the various interests held'.[73] This statement is, however, best viewed in the light of the earlier hope expressed in the same document 'that while continuing to voice its proper concerns, the consumer movement will progressively take into account the economic and social implications of the decisions on which it might wish to be consulted'.[74]

Soft law has gained a poor image amongst consumerists as it has been introduced as a second best alternative to legal regulation, rather than being promoted as a positive complement to legislation. This is also apparent at present as the Commission seeks to diffuse confrontation about its competence by proposing non–binding instruments rather than directives.[75]

The most widespread use of soft law has been in the new approach to technical harmonisation (see Chap. 2 section 4C). Although we noted some problems in the operation of the new approach, nevertheless in theory this could be viewed as a workable model for the use of soft law. Legislation continues to fix the basic principles of consumer protection – in the form of essential safety requirements – whilst standardisation ensures these are given effect to in a way which is both acceptable to consumers and causes least inconvenience to industry.

The use of soft law has also been to the fore in EC regulation of payment systems (see Chap. 6 section 3), but experience in this area does little to encourage consumers to value soft law. In fact in the area of cross–border transfers the Commission has had to accept that soft law has failed and has proposed a directive. The lesson from this area is that for soft law to work industry must be committed to it, either because it genuinely believes in its objectives or at least through fear of stricter legislation. There is also a need for consumers to be involved in the process of standard setting.

Soft law plays a slightly different function in the Misleading Advertising Directive (see Chap. 4 section 3). Here EC law adopts a legislative solution, but tolerates national self–regulatory solutions so long as legal redress is possible should those systems fail adequately to protect the consumer. We welcome this respect for national traditions, but are even more heartened to see that where it exists self–regulation is strengthened by being integrated into a legislative scheme. In fact our criticism is, if anything, that the EC has missed a trick in the advertising area. The concept 'misleading' could be fleshed out in soft law and the EC could ensure adequate consumer involvement in the process. This would give the resulting 'soft law' rules greater authority than the industry sponsored International Chamber of

---

73   *Ibid.*, item 6.

74   *Ibid.*, item 4.

75   See criticism of the Commission for this policy by the Economic and Social Committee, *Opinion of the Economic and Social Committee on the Single Market and Consumer Protection: Opportunities and Obstacles*, CES 1309/95.

Commerce Code of Advertising Practice. This model could then be used to allow the Community to develop rules of unfair advertising.

(iii) Role and Value of Soft Law

Much of the pressure for soft law has come from industry and the political right, who are opposed to and/or cynical about legislative attempts to reconstruct the market order. Political objections to intervention in the market[76] should not really be relevant. Soft law rules – just as much as traditional legal regulation – can have the objective of altering market behaviour; although admittedly they are often seen as simply codifying current best practice. The choice of soft law over traditional regulation could be seen simply as an attempt to adopt more effective means of changing trader behaviour. However, one suspects that many who favour soft law do so because they believe its content will be less severe than legal regulation and because in the final analysis it allows the trader the freedom to ignore it.

Nevertheless, much of the discussion of the advantages of soft law over traditional regulation has been rather technical. The slow process of adopting and amending laws is emphasised. It is suggested that requirements of legal certainty produce laws whose content is rather narrowly drawn and cumbersomely worded. The resulting difficulties of enforcing such laws are highlighted.

By contrast, soft law is portrayed as a flexible easily amendable form of regulation. Its rules are drafted by specialists and therefore deal with the real issues in an effective manner and can contain norms on matters such as taste and performance which could not easily be included in legislation. Moreover it is suggested that industry will have a greater commitment to abide by soft law rules which it has helped to generate and which it will police itself through trade associations. As an additional bonus, the cost of producing rules is transferred from Government to industry.

One might, however, question whether traditional legislation is as bad as its detractors would portray it (use of secondary legislation can speed up the legislative process and the modern technique of using broad concepts make it more flexible); or if soft law has all the advantages some would claim for it (soft law can take a long time to adopt or amend as interest groups negotiate and industry has not been prepared to meet the costs of European standardisation). In fact the process of adopting soft law has some very real dangers for consumers.[77] Industry, because of its greater resources, and also

---

76   See for example, R. Nozick, *Anarchy, State and Utopia*, (Blackwell, 1975).

77   See European Consumer Law Group, 'Non–legislative Means of Consumer Protection' (1983) 6 *J.C.P.* 209.

because in the final analysis it must consent to abide by the results, can dominate the self–regulatory process. Moreover, even if responsible sections of a trade sector agree to soft law rules which offer a high level of consumer protection, there is always the danger that rogue traders do not follow these principles and are either not members of trade associations or the trade association is unable/unwilling to control and sanction them effectively.

The support for soft law from industry is perhaps understandable. It is perhaps more surprising that some commentators from the 'left' favour soft law. Rather than being concerned to roll back the interventionary norms associated with the welfare state, these commentators are dissatisfied because the rules of the welfare state have failed to bring about a material change. For these commentators soft law is not deregulatory, but rather an alternative to deregulation.[78] It has also been suggested that it is a technique for extending the reach of the welfare state into new areas of regulation.[79] However, we doubt whether it would be wise to jettison entirely the rights which legislation grants consumers in favour of a new proceduralism within which consumer rights would have to result from a process of dialogue with industry. As Norbert Reich has written 'The struggle for procedure becomes a struggle for law. The power problem is relocated, but not solved'.[80] The political process may not have produced great fruits for the consumer movement, but we hesitate at the thought of consumers having to do battle face to face with industry. Indeed the main proponent of this new form of 'reflexive law', Gunther Teubner himself concedes that consumer law would be 'a shaky example of reflexive law at work because the social asymmetries of power and information are resistant to institutional attempts at equalisation'.[81]

Our favoured solution would stress that the goal of improving consumer protection should still be retained in the legislation, but within this framework there may be a role for soft law to be used as an instrument for promoting participation and encouraging a critical assessment of the protection afforded consumers.[82] It is important that soft law is viewed as an element of a legal regime which seeks to provide consumers with adequate and effective protection and not as mere window dressing and a license for industry to further its own interests. To achieve these goals soft law rules

---

[78]   Teubner, *op. cit.*, at 274

[79]   E. Blankenburg, 'The Poverty of Evolutionism' (1984) 18 *Law & Soc. Rev.* 273, who is critical of these developments.

[80]   'Reflexive Law and Reflexive Legal Theory: Reflexions on Postmodernism in Legal Theory' in ΕΝΘΥΜΗΜΑ ΑΛΚΗ ΑΡΓΥΡΙΑΔΗ (ΑΘΗΝΑ, 1995).

[81]   *Ibid.*, at 277

[82]   A similar approach can perhaps be discerned in P. Nonet and P. Selznick, *Law and Society in Transition: Toward Responsive Law*, (Harper, 1978).

and standards should be part of a legal framework which sets out the legal principles of consumer protection and also assures consumers effective participation in the procedures through which soft law norms are developed, as well as providing efficient remedies when soft law does not work properly.

B. Remedies

Those provisions of EC consumer law which require the establishment of agencies to enforce consumer protection rules may come to be seen as having provided some of the greatest practical benefit for consumers derived from EC law, at least in those countries with little previous history of consumer protection. The General Product Safety Directive is probably the best example of a directive requiring an administrative structure to be put in place (Chap. 2 section 4E(vi)). It also specifies the powers which the authority should have to be able to perform its duties. The Consumer Credit Directive also has a similar requirement, but is more flexible as to how enforcement can be secured (Chap. 6 section 2J).

Nevertheless, criticism can be levied at the public law controls for failing to specify sanctions. This criticism works at two levels. First, it is not clear that there have to be any sanctions for breach of some EC consumer law principles. For instance, it is possible to read the General Safety Directive as not requiring any specific sanction for marketing unsafe products. Indeed this is the approach France has taken in continuing the approach of its domestic law which sees the general safety obligation as simply an organising concept which can trigger other action under the product safety regime. Second, EC law fails as a general rule to specify which public law sanctions should be available. Of course there is a natural hesitancy to interfere in national traditions. In some countries infraction of consumer protection statutes is treated as criminal, whilst in others it is subject to sanctions of an administrative character. These national traditions could be respected, however, even if the directives (i) made it clear that there should be a sanction, and (ii) specified the nature of that sanction in general terms without classifying its precise legal characterisation (e.g. fine, imprisonment, publication of notice etc.). Some agreement on maximum and minimum penalties would also help ensure the law had equal force throughout Europe.

Trading conditions will differ throughout the Community even if the same rule applies so long as the chances of infractions being detected and prosecuted differ and the sanctions imposed vary. It is not sufficient to rely on the general principle of effective remedies in this context, not in the least because it requires someone to invoke that principle. The trader or state imposing the sanction is unlikely to claim it is inadequate; whilst few third parties, even if they had standing, would be able to detect the inadequacy as each individual case would be relatively insignificant.

One remedy which is being developed under the influence of EC consumer law is the injunction (see Chap. 8 section 3C). The impact of this approach will be great in those countries where it was not previously possible to obtain an injunction of this nature to protect the collective interest of consumers. In some Member States, such as the United Kingdom, it could bolster the consumer movement if it eventually leads to consumer organisations being given what would be for them a new right of action. It is, however, far from clear that Member States will be required to give consumer groups a right of action. In fact the legislation introducing injunction procedures is facilitative in character. Persons and organisations with a legitimate interest in consumer protection are entitled to seek injunctions, but are not required to. Paradoxically the United Kingdom approach of giving the power to a public official, who must investigate complaints and is subject to public law controls of his exercise of that power, may actually provide a more certain guarantee of protection than those countries which grant standing to consumer organisations, but whose consumer groups are not able to take advantage of the powers. Obviously the best solution would be a combination of both public authority and consumer organisation control.

We noted in relation to public law controls that the impact of legal rules depended upon a combination of their content, their enforcement and sanctions. This is also true of civil liability rules. A clear example of this is product liability. Europe and the USA now have similar liability rules, but the impact differs because in the USA it is easier to bring cases and damage awards are far higher than in Europe. However, even within Europe we have noted significant differences in damage levels (see Chap. 2 section 3G). The Product Liability Directive does little to reduce these disparities, indeed if anything it accentuates the problem by allowing Member States to decide whether there should be a cap of not less than 70M ECU for personal injury damages. It leaves the question of non–material damages to Member States and so in Germany such damages are not recoverable at all under the strict product liability regime, whereas in other countries, like the United Kingdom, they can form a sizeable portion of the damages recovered. There are many other instances of EC Directives introducing substantive rights, but leaving the consequences to national law. For example, the Doorstep Selling Directive and the draft Distant Selling Directive both introduce the principle of cancellation, but leave the consequences to national law.

By contrast the draft Directive on consumer sales is fairly precise about the remedies available under it – repair, replacement, price reduction, rescission. However, again there is no indication of how the price reduction should be calculated or what the consequences of rescission should be (for instance which account is to be taken of any enjoyment obtained from the goods). Consequential damages are also not mentioned.

There is an understandable desire to leave national rules on remedies untouched if at all possible. They lie at the heart of the national legal system and any alteration is bound to cause consternation among lawyers who fear the knock–on effects of tampering with the traditional structure of their law. This may be particularly true in the common law system which is based around actions for remedies rather than a system of rights, but in any system remedies are central to its functioning. However, it is because of the importance of remedies to a legal system and legal culture that they need to be included more comprehensively within the *acquis communautaire* if harmonisation is to be meaningful. Consumers need harmonised legal rights, equal access to justice and comparable remedies throughout the Community. This is necessary both to provide consumers with security and to ensure the burden of legal rules is equal across the Community.

C. Consumer Code

In Chap. 3 section 1 we mentioned the attempt to develop general principles of European contract law. These will be clearly influenced to some extent by EC consumer law principles. However, in the immediate future the value of this work is likely to be pedagogic, although there may be hopes that arbitrators and the ECJ will be influenced by it. Certainly, the idea of a general European Civil Code looks a distant prospect.[83]

However, the codification of consumer law is a more discrete and manageable project. It is a relatively modern subject which has seen the proliferation of legislation, that has not always been well co–ordinated or consistent. It could be considered as an area ripe for the thorough review and systematisation which would be part of the codification process. Recent years have seen a national codification of consumer law in France[84] and a formal proposal for a consumer code in Belgium.[85] One of the present authors has even argued that the United Kingdom would benefit from such a codification.[86]

---

83   See A. Hartkamp, M. Heeselink, E. Hondius, C. du Perron and J. Vranken (eds), *Towards a European Civil Code*, (Ars Aequi Libri/Martinus Nijhoff, 1994).

84   See J. Calais–Auloy, *Propositions Pour un Code de la Consommation*, (La Documentation Française, 1990) which resulted in *Code de la Consommation*, (Journal Officiel, 1993).

85   See Th. Bourgoignie, *Propositions Pour une Loi Générale sur la Protection des Consommateurs*, (Ministère des Affaires Economiques, 1995).

86   G. Howells, 'A Consumer Code for the United Kingdom?' [1995] *Consum.L.J.* 201.

It could be argued that a codification at the European level would be superfluous as the bulk of EC consumer law is found in directives which become law through national implementing legislation. However, three reasons might suggest that a codification of EC consumer law would be a worthwhile endeavour. First, the legislative process is even more complicated at the EC than the national level. This is reflected in the poor quality of the drafting of some EC laws[87] and the inconsistencies which are sometimes evident between pieces of EC legislation. A codification would ensure that terms were used consistently, that legislation fitted together as a coherent package and overall the quality of draftmanship could be reviewed. Second, access to EC law will continue to be important, both for purposes of interpreting national law, as part of the ongoing process of review and reform of EC law and to educate consumers and their advisers. Codification would both raise the profile of EC consumer law and make it more transparent and accessible. Third, the codification process would highlight lacunae's in the present EC regulation of consumer problems and provide an opportunity to deal with problems in areas such as service quality and safety and unfair advertising and marketing practices which have not yet been addressed at the EC level.

On the other hand several arguments raised against the codification of European civil law and contract law in general are relevant in this context.[88] A codification of European consumer law would suffer from the same lack of democratic legitimation as a General Civil Code, although this argument would have less force if it was mainly restricted to systematising rules which were already part of national law through legislation implementing directives. However, it might be objected that such a codification would make more definitive the shift in legislative power in this area away from the Member States to the European Union. There might be legitimate concern if this meant that this would reduce the power of Member States to react to socio–economic changes and to develop consumer protection creatively. The development of such a Code at the Community level would of course be a complicated task to achieve given the EC's cumbersome legislative procedures.

Whether or not a Consumer Code is needed is perhaps a side debate to the more central question of the need to improve the quality of EC consumer legislation. There is a clear need to achieve more consistency and systematic homogeneity in EC consumer legislation than is presently the case.

---

[87]   See T. Burns, 'Better Lawmaking? An evaluation of the Law reform in the European community', paper presented at the 1996 W.G. Hart Workshop, proceedings to be published in P. Craig and C. Harlow (eds), *op. cit.*

[88]   See in more detail, Wilhelmsson (1995), *op. cit.*, at 111 *et seq.*

10 Epilogue

Epilogues are normally found at the end of long rambling literary works. Although we would not wish to claim our work possesses any particular literary value, we do believe that the reader who has remained with us thus far in our ramble through EC consumer law deserves our brief reflections on how we perceive the role of EC consumer law and our suggestions for how it should develop in the future.

It is, perhaps, easiest to start by stating what we do not believe EC consumer law should be about. It should not simply seek to regulate the specific problems associated with the single market, i.e. cross–border disputes. Leaving to one side issues of social justice, there are practical reasons for rejecting such a limited role for EC law. The scale of cross–border disputes is so small – and in our view will never be so large – that of itself the problems it gives rise to do not justify the enormous efforts involved in EC regulation. This is not to say that it is not worthwhile addressing cross–border problems in legislation which also has a broader function. Furthermore we would resist the idea of a dual system of law, one for cross–border disputes, another for national law. This would leave consumers and businesses facing the complexity of dealing with two sets of rules and having to decide which set applied to particular transactions.

Neither should EC consumer law be seen solely as a support for the internal market. Some rules, such as those mandating particular product designs or packaging, may create a segregated market if national laws differ. However, we do not believe that most of the controls on consumer contracts, advertising, marketing and liability rules impose onerous direct costs on industry or require such significant changes in procedures and conduct that they really pose a threat to the functioning of the internal market. After all, one rarely sees industry clamouring for harmonised consumer laws; usually it is hostile to such proposals or at best concedes some modest benefits could be derived from some specific limited provisions. Indeed the trend towards minimum harmonisation seems to give the lie to suggestions that EC consumer law is based upon an internal market rationale. In fact we have seen that even the earliest consumer law directives cited consumer protection as one of their motivations. The various Community programmes and action plans certainly evidence aspirations towards an autonomous Community consumer policy. This seems to be encapsulated in the Maastricht Treaty which includes consumer protection as an independent objective of the Community and makes it a distinct basis for Community jurisdiction.

In short we believe that the EC should be interested in consumer protection laws for their own inherent worth and not simply view them as part of an internal market strategy. We will suggest that one of the problems with EC law has been that the continual interplay between consumer protection and internal market justifications has obscured any clear conception of Community consumer policy from developing. Further we shall suggest that creating an appropriate ideological framework for the development of a sound consumer policy is just as important as the specific laws enacted at the Community level, although the quality of both are doubtless inter–related.

There are several reasons why the EC should be involved in consumer law and policy. Consumers in the 15 Member States are now citizens of the European Union. However, the Union started off as an economic community, and remains predominantly so. Thus the main relationship the average citizen has with Europe is as an economic agent, i.e. a consumer. If the citizens are to feel empathy for Europe they must see benefits accruing to them from membership of the Union. In part this means that competition laws must ensure that consumers derive a fair share of the benefits of the internal market,[1] but also they must feel that Europe ensures that all the goods and services circulating in the Community are safe, properly marketed and that they are able to secure redress should things go wrong. In countries with well developed consumer laws and enforcement structures this may mean that for the most part Europe simply supports their existing levels of protection, whilst in countries with less developed consumer laws it means providing legal rules and ensuring structures exist to protect consumers. Community policy should both counter the new risks which the internal market exposes consumers to and provide a set of common consumer rights to be enjoyed throughout the Community. Consumer protection should be seen as one of the rights attaching to citizenship of a developed economic and political union.

One of the advantages the EC has over national governments is that it can create a level playing field and thereby help prevent a 'race to the bottom', whereby industries locate in countries with lax consumer laws. The Product Liability Directive is a good example of an area of law in which reform had been resisted at the national level because of arguments based on competitiveness, but was adopted at the European level because the level playing provided by a harmonising measure removed from industry the competitiveness argument. However, the competitive argument is double edged. Consumer law rules may in the short term be seen as burdens on

---

[1]   Competition law is of course outside the scope of the present work, for a discussion of competition policy and the consumer interest, see G. Howells and S. Weatherill, *Consumer Protection Law*, (Dartmouth, 1995) Ch. 15.

businesses. However, if one takes a longer term view and seeks to place Europe in a global context a different picture emerges. World trade is likely to increase and Europe will face many challenges, particularly from the 'tiger' economies of the Far East. The implications of this have not yet been fully realised. Assuming that a retreat to protectionism does not ensue, Europe will have to find a way of competing with the emerging economies. They will not be able to do this on price as our labour costs are likely to be far in excess of theirs. In this global competition, in the final analysis, it will be those countries which provide high quality goods and services that will eventually prosper.[2] Consumer protection laws are a guarantee of that quality and hence an effective guarantee of Europe's long term competitiveness and prosperity. Consumer protection is a long term not a short term strategy. In this light it is also possible to see the need for consumer protection to be integrated into other policies in relation to the environment and social equality.

EC consumer law and policy showed signs of developing an autonomous content – through the Community's consumer protection and information programmes and the directives adopted – at a time when the Treaty of Rome gave very little encouragement to such developments. Ironically, now that consumer protection has a firmer position in the Treaty and consumer policy has its own Directorate–General there are signs that the internal market ideology is becoming dominant. Of course, internal market ideas have always been a brake on the development of a truly autonomous consumer policy – witness the lack of activity in relation to services – but now under the influence of the subsidiarity principle the need for EC regulation outside cross–border matters is being challenged and 'soft law' is being increasingly looked to as an alternative to traditional regulation. Of course this picture is uneven. For instance the proposals on access to justice focus mainly on the problems associated with resolving cross–border disputes;[3] whereas the draft Directive on consumer sales has surprisingly few provisions tackling the particular problems of consumers purchasing across borders.[4] What is missing is a clear vision of what EC consumer policy should aspire to. In part, we shall suggest that this is because the relationship between EC and national laws has not yet developed into the symbiotic nature required by the Maastricht Treaty which sits the subsidiarity principle alongside the objective of achieving a high level of consumer protection.

It is true that EC consumer law has brought about improvements in the legal position of consumers, even if there is a need to shore up these advances by improving access to justice and the performance of enforcement

---

2   M. Porter, *The Competitive Advantage of Nations*, (MacMillan, 1990).
3   See COM(95) 712 and COM(96) 13.
4   See COM(95) 520.

authorities. In some countries, particularly in Southern Europe, these improvements have been significant. Even in the Nordic countries which have a tradition of consumer protection some improvements can be detected. Also the existence of EC laws has acted as a brake on deregulation movements, for the EC rules represent a guaranteed minimum level of protection which Member States must provide.

Admittedly, EC involvement in consumer policy has the potential to have a negative impact. The fact the EC is discussing an idea can put national reforms on hold. The modest solutions adopted at the EC level may be taken as a signal for Member States to resist progressive ideas or even repeal more protective national laws. Thankfully, however, there are few concrete examples of the EC having such a negative effect. In the long run, however, the EC focus on an information and transparency strategy favouring the strong active internal–market consumers may have negative effects on the ideas prevailing in those Member States more inclined to protect weak consumers by substantive measures. In a purely legal perspective, the trend to favour minimal harmonisation has of course helped to ensure that membership of the EC does not prevent the development of more progressive national consumer policies. However, in some areas – such as the new approach to technical harmonisation and global approach to conformity assessment – vigilance is still needed to ensure consumer protection is not sacrificed on the altar of free trade.

On the whole, however, EC law seems to provide for harmonisation at a fairly low level. Principles which are already common to the majority of Member States provide the content of most EC directives. Except in those states which have not developed a domestic consumer protection policy, most directives require only minor changes to national law. In fact one sees an increasing tendency for some Member States to claim that their domestic law is simply equivalent to the EC rules and that therefore no implementation is required.

One can detect a pattern of the Commission proposing an ambitious draft for a directive, only for this to be watered down during negotiations to a rather bland final text. The policy of increased transparency by the Commission seems to be encouraging this process. In relation to consumer sales, for instance, many of the interesting ideas floated in the Green Paper[5] are not to be found in the draft Directive on consumer sales.[6]

Sometimes the resulting EC legislation grants such insignificant improvements to consumers (at least in those states with existing consumer laws), that consumerists might almost join with industrialists in questioning whether the efforts are worthwhile. However, one might refer to the political

---

5   *Guarantees for Consumer Goods and After–sales Services*, COM(93) 509.
6   COM(95) 520.

reality to argue that in the first instance it is important to gain acceptance by the Member States of the Community's competence to legislate on a particular topic. Many contentious directives have a review process built into them. We see it as important that the Commission uses these reviews to attempt to reintroduce new ways of thinking into the EC legislation and national debates. The review of the Consumer Credit Directives is a good example of how such reports can stimulate a debate, so that in time the EC law can be refined in the light of national experiences.[7] In contrast the one page assessment of the Product Liability Directive can be viewed as disappointing.[8]

At its best the relationship between national and EC law can be seen as being an evolving one. The EC puts topics on the Community agenda. A discussion ensues which results in a modest harmonisation of laws. The implementation leads to improvements in the position of consumers in those states with little existing consumer protection. In those states which already had regulations on the topic, the discussions preceding the adoption of the directive may encourage national legislators to adopt some of the more ambitious proposals which did not find their way into the final text of the directive. The review process can point to these national experiments and argue that they show the wisdom of adopting them at the Community level. Over time EC laws can become more and more refined and a higher level of consumer protection can be achieved across the Community. In line with the subsidiarity principle EC regulation does not impose Community solutions, but aims at achieving a high level of protection within the Community through the co-ordination of national experiences.

Therefore our provisional conclusion must be that it is too early to say whether the EC will enhance consumer protection for its citizens. With the notable exception of services, it has managed to adopt some legislation on most of the major areas of consumer protection. This legislation is without doubt far from perfect and is incomplete; but according to our theory this is almost inevitable and what is important is that there are procedures to develop these rules.

Given that consumer protection has only been an express aim of the Community since the Maastricht Treaty the amount of EC legislation might be seen as a sign of the EC's commitment to consumer protection. Indeed, there is no doubt that some of the legislation does represents the fruits of hard negotiations by commission officials. Nevertheless legislation on a topic is easier to achieve – Governments like to be seen to be doing something to help consumers – than ensuring that it is good legislation which meets the real needs of consumers. Herein lies our main criticism of the EC's role in

---

7   COM (95) 117.
8   COM(95) 617.

consumer protection. It lays down no coherent strategy for the development of consumer law and policy.

At various points in the text we have suggested that EC consumer law is based on an information strategy, which essentially seeks to protect the rational information seeking consumer. That impression derives from judgments of the ECJ and the content of the EC legislation. Some elements of both, however, point towards a more protective attitude. Equally, some of the elements left out of draft directives or mentioned in Green Papers or reviews of the operation of directives also indicate a more radical line of thought. Does this mean that the information strategy has to continue as the EC's preferred approach or could a more radical policy evolve?

Part of the problem may be that the Commission has not thoroughly thought through its consumer protection strategy in the light of the evolution of the single market and its new competence under the Maastricht Treaty. The Community first Preliminary Programme for a consumer protection and information strategy showed signs of clear thinking about consumer rights and how they could be achieved.[9] Recently the Commission has moved to adopting action plans. These are more pragmatic, but specific worthwhile actions become lost on the wider canvas. There is a need for the Community to rethink its consumer policy. In doing so we would suggest that the role of the Community should be seen as much to promote internal debate and reforms within the Member States as to impose legal norms on the Member States. The base level for harmonised laws is likely to be fixed at a level which reflects the evolution of laws within the Member States. The more protective Member States laws are the easier it will be to argue for a fairly high harmonised level of protection.

We hope the Community will develop a policy which does provide consumers with adequate information to make effective choices in the market, but which also appreciates that information needs to be given in a way which is meaningful to the consumer. This may involve an active information strategy involving, *inter alia*, duties to counsel the consumer and the provision of cancellation rights. Moreover, it must be accepted that there is a duty to protect vulnerable consumers. This is particularly true as the frontiers of the Welfare State are being rolled back throughout Europe and vulnerable consumers are less able to look to social insurance for support. Indeed an effective consumer protection strategy must also recognise that even for average consumers information may not always be an adequate form of protection. For reasons of time and expertise consumers must be allowed to leave some decisions to the collective, by means such as minimum quality and safety standards, and to allow their interest to be protected by collective actions. We hope this work has convinced the reader of the merit

---

9   OJ 1975 C 92/1.

of some of these ideas and hope that the Community and Member States will open up their policy debate so that consumer law and policy can develop within a well thought out framework.

Appendix 1

Council Directive 85/374/EEC of 25 July 1985 on the Approximation of the Laws, Regulations and Administrative Provisions of the Member States Concerning Liability for Defective Products (footnotes omitted).

THE COUNCIL OF THE EUROPEAN COMMUNITIES,

Having regard to the treaty establishing the European Economic Community, and in particular Article 100 thereof,

Having regard to the proposal from the Commission,

Having regard to the opinion of the European Parliament,

Having regard to the opinion of the Economic and Social Committee,

Whereas approximation of the laws of the Member States concerning the liability of the producer for damage caused by the defectiveness of his products is necessary because the existing divergences may distort competition and affect the movement of goods within the common market and entail a differing degree of protection of the consumer against damage caused by a defective product to his health or property;

Whereas liability without fault on the part of the producer is the sole means of adequately solving the problem, peculiar to our age of increasing technicality, of a fair apportionment of the risks inherent in modern technological production;

Whereas liability without fault should apply only to movables which have been industrially produced; whereas, as a result, it is appropriate to exclude liability for agricultural products and game, except where they have undergone a processing of an industrial nature which could cause a defect in these products; whereas the liability provided for in this Directive should also apply to movables which are used in the construction of immovables or are installed in immovables;

Whereas protection of the consumer requires that all producers involved in the production process should be made liable, in so far as their finished product, component part or any raw material supplied by them was defective; whereas, for the same reason, liability should extend to importers of products into the community and to persons who present themselves as producers by affixing their name, trade mark or other distinguishing feature or who supply a product the producer of which cannot be identified;

Whereas, in situations where several persons are liable for the same damage, the protection of the consumer requires that the injured person should be able to claim full compensation for the damage from any one of them;

Whereas, to protect the physical well–being and property of the consumer, the defectiveness of the product should be determined by reference not to its fitness for use but to the lack of safety which the public at large is entitled to expect; whereas the safety is assessed by excluding any misuse of the product not reasonable under the circumstances;

Whereas a fair apportionment of risk between the injured person and the producer implies that the producer should be able to free himself from liability if he furnishes proof as to the existence of certain exonerating circumstances;

Whereas the protection of the consumer requires that the liability of the producer remain unaffected by acts or omissions of other persons having contributed to cause the damage; whereas however, the contributory negligence of the injured person may be taken into account to reduce or disallow such liability;

Whereas the protection of the consumer requires compensation for death and personal injury as well as compensation for damage to property; whereas the latter should nevertheless be limited to goods for private use or consumption and be subject to a deduction of a lower threshold of a fixed amount in order to avoid litigation in an excessive number of cases; whereas this directive should not prejudice compensation for pain and suffering and other non–material damages payable, where appropriate, under the law applicable to the case;

Whereas a uniform period of limitation for the bringing of action for compensation is in the interests both of the injured person and of the producer;

Whereas products age in the course of time, higher safety standards are developed and the state of science and technology progresses; whereas, therefore, it would not be reasonable to make the producer liable for an unlimited period for the defectiveness of his product; whereas, therefore, liability should expire after a reasonable length of time, without prejudice to claims pending at law;

Whereas, to achieve effective protection of consumers, no contractual derogation should be permitted as regards the liability of the producer in relation to the injured person;

Whereas under the legal systems of the Member States an injured party may have a claim for damages based on grounds of contractual liability or on grounds of non–contractual liability other than that provided for in this directive; in so far as these provisions also serve to attain the objective of effective protection of consumers, they should remain unaffected by this Directive; whereas, in so far as effective protection of consumers in the sector of pharmaceutical products is already also attained in a Member State under a special liability system, claims based on this system should similarly remain possible;

Whereas, to the extent that liability for nuclear injury or damage is already covered in all Member States by adequate special rules, it has been possible to exclude damage of this type from the scope of this Directive;

Whereas, since the exclusion of primary agricultural products and game from the scope of this Directive may be felt, in certain Member States, in view of what is expected for the protection of consumers, to restrict unduly such protection, it should be possible for a Member State to extend liability to such products;

Whereas, for similar reasons, the possibility offered to a producer to free himself from liability if he proves that the state of scientific and technical knowledge at the time when he put the product into circulation was not such as to enable the existence of a defect to be discovered may be felt in certain Member States to restrict unduly the protection of the consumer; whereas it should therefore be possible for a Member State to maintain in its legislation or to provide by new legislation that this exonerating circumstance is not admitted; whereas, in the case of new legislation, making use of this derogation should, however, be subject to a Community stand–still procedure in order to raise, if possible, the level of protection in a uniform manner throughout the community;

Whereas, taking into account the legal traditions in most of the Member States, it is inappropriate to set any financial ceiling on the producer's liability without fault; whereas, in so far as there are, however, differing traditions, it seems possible to admit that a Member State may derogate from the principle of unlimited liability by providing a limit for the total liability of the producer for damage resulting from a death or personal injury and caused by identical items with the same defect, provided that this limit is established at a level sufficiently high to guarantee adequate protection of the consumer and the correct functioning of the common market;

Whereas the harmonisation resulting from this cannot be total at the present stage, but opens the way towards greater harmonisation; whereas it is therefore necessary that the Council receive at regular intervals, reports from the Commission on the application of this Directive, accompanied, as the case may be, by appropriate proposals;

Whereas it is particularly important in this respect that a re–examination be carried out of those parts of the Directive relating to the derogations open to the Member States, at the expiry of a period of sufficient length to gather practical experience on the effects of these derogations on the protection of consumers and on the functioning of the common market,

HAD ADOPTED THIS DIRECTIVE;

Article 1

The producer shall be liable for damage caused by a defect in his product.

Article 2

For the purpose of this Directive 'product' means all movables, with the exception of primary agricultural products and game, even though incorporated into another movable or into an immovable. 'Primary agricultural products' means the products of the soil, of stock–farming and of fisheries, excluding products which have undergone initial processing. 'Product' includes electricity.

Article 3

1. 'Producer' means the manufacturer of a finished product, the producer of any raw material or the manufacturer of a component part and any person who, by putting his name, trade mark or other distinguishing feature on the product presents himself as its producer.

2. Without prejudice to the liability of the producer, any person who imports into the Community a product for sale, hire, leasing or any form of distribution in the course of his business shall be deemed to be a producer within the meaning of this Directive and shall be responsible as a producer.

3. Where the producer of the product cannot be identified, each supplier of the product shall be treated as its producer unless he informs the injured person, within a reasonable time, of the identity of the producer or of the person who supplied him with the product. The same shall apply, in the case of an imported product, if this product does not indicate the identity of the importer referred to in paragraph 2, even if the name of the producer is indicated.

Article 4

The injured person shall be required to prove the damage, the defect and the causal relationship between defect and damage.

Article 5

Where, as a result of the provisions of this Directive, two or more persons are liable for the same damage, they shall be liable jointly and severally, without prejudice to the provision of national law concerning the rights of contribution or recourse.

Article 6

1. A product is defective when it does not provide the safety which a person is entitled to expect, taking all circumstances into account, including:
(a) the presentation of the product;
(b) the use to which it could reasonably be expected that the product would be put;
(c) the time when the product was put into circulation.

2. A product shall not be considered defective for the sole reason that a better product is subsequently put into circulation.

Article 7

The producer shall not be liable as a result of this Directive if he proves:
(a) that he did not put the product into circulation; or

(b)   that, having regard to the circumstances, it is probable that the defect which caused the damage did not exist at the time when the product was put into circulation by him or that this defect came into being afterwards; or

(c)   that the product was neither manufactured by him for sale or any form of distribution for economic purpose nor manufactured or distributed by him in the course of his business; or

(d)   that the defect is due to compliance of the product with mandatory regulations issued by the public authorities; or

(e)   that the state of scientific and technical knowledge at the time when he put the product into circulation was not such as to enable the existence of the defect to be discovered; or

(f)   in the case of a manufacturer of a component, that the defect is attributable to the design of the product in which the component has been fitted or to the instructions given by the manufacturer of the product.

Article 8

1. Without prejudice to the provisions of national law concerning the right of contribution or recourse, the liability of the producer shall not be reduced when the damage is caused both by a defect in product and by the act or omission of a third party.

2. The liability of the producer may be reduced or disallowed when, having regard to all the circumstances, the damage is caused both by a defect in the product and by the fault of the injured person or any person for whom the injured person is responsible.

Article 9

For the purpose of Article 1, 'damage' means:

(a)   damage caused by death or by personal injuries:

(b)   damage to, or destruction of, any item of property other than the defective product itself, with a lower threshold of 500 ECU, provided that the item of property:

(i) is of a type ordinarily intended for private use or consumption, and

(ii) was used by the injured person mainly for his own private use or consumption.

This Article shall be without prejudice to national provisions relating to non–material damage.

Article 10

1. Member States shall provide in their legislation that a limitation period of three years shall apply to proceedings for the recovery of damages as provided for in this Directive. The limitation period shall begin to run from the day on which the plaintiff became aware, or should reasonably have become aware, of the damage, the defect and the identity of the producer.
2. The laws of Member States regulating suspension or interruption of the limitation period shall not be affected by the Directive.

Article 11

Member States shall provide in their legislation that the rights conferred upon the injured person pursuant to this Directive shall be extinguished upon the expiry of a period of 10 years from the date on which the producer put into circulation the actual product which caused the damage, unless the injured person has in the meantime instituted proceedings against the producer.

Article 12

The liability of the producer arising from this Directive may not, in relation to the injured person, be limited or excluded by a provision limiting his liability or exempting him from liability.

Article 13

This Directive shall not affect any rights which an injured person may have according to the rules of the law of contractual or non–contractual liability or a special liability system existing at the moment when this Directive is notified.

Article 14

This Directive shall not apply to injury or damage arising from nuclear accidents and covered by international conventions ratified by the Member States.

Article 15

1. Each Member State may:
(a) by way of derogation from Article 2, provide in its legislation that within the meaning of Article 1 of this Directive 'product' also means primary agricultural products and game;
(b) by way of derogation from Article 7(e), maintain or, subject to the procedure set out in paragraph 2 of this Article, provide in this legislation that the producer shall be liable even if he proves that the state of scientific and technical knowledge at the time when he put the product into circulation was not such as to enable the existence of a defect to be discovered.
2. A Member State wishing to introduce the measure specified in paragraph 1(b) shall communicate the test of the proposed measure to the Commission. The Commission shall inform the other Member States thereof.
The Member State concerned shall hold the proposed measure in abeyance for nine months after the Commission is informed and provided that in the meantime the Commission has not submitted to the Council a proposal amending this Directive on the relevant matter. However, if within three months of receiving the said information, the Commission does not advise the Member State concerned that it intends submitting such a proposal to the Council, the Member State may take the proposed measure immediately.
If the Commission does submit to the Council such a proposal amending this Directive within the aforementioned nine months, the Member State concerned shall hold the proposed measure in abeyance for a further period of 18 months from the date on which the proposal is submitted.
3. Ten years after the date of notification of this Directive, the Commission shall submit to the Council a report on the effect that rulings by the courts as to the application of Article 7(e) and of paragraph 1(b) of this Article have on consumer protection and the functioning of the common market. In the light of this report the Council, acting on a proposal from the Commission and pursuant to the terms of Article 100 of the Treaty, shall decide whether to repeal Article 7(e).

Article 16

1. Any Member State may provide that a producer's total liability for damage resulting from a death or personal injury and caused by identical items with the same defect shall be limited to an amount which may not be less than 70 million ECU.
2. Ten years after the date of notification of this Directive, the Commission shall submit to the Council a report on the effect on consumer protection and

the functioning of the common market of the implementation of the financial limit on liability by those Member States which have used the option provided for in paragraph 1. In the light of this report the Council, acting on a proposal from the Commission and pursuant to the terms of Article 100 of the Treaty, shall decide whether to repeal paragraph 1.

Article 17

This Directive shall not apply to products put into circulation before the date on which the provisions referred to in Article 19 enter into force.

Article 18

1. For the purposes of this Directive, the ECU shall be that defined by Regulation (EEC) No 3180/78, as amended by Regulation (EEC) No 2626/84. The equivalent in national currency shall initially be calculated at the rate obtaining on the date of adoption of this Directive.
2. Every five years the Council, acting on a proposal from the Commission, shall examine and, if need be, revise the amounts in this Directive, in the light of economic and monetary trends in the Community.

Article 19

1. Member States shall bring into force, not later than three years from the date of notification of this Directive, the laws, regulations and administrative provisions necessary to comply with this Directive. They shall forthwith inform the Commission thereof.
2. The procedure set out in Article 15(2) shall apply from the date of notification of this Directive.

Article 20

Member States shall communicate to the Commission the texts of the main provisions of national law which they subsequently adopt in the field governed by this Directive.

Article 21

Every five years the Commission shall present a report to the Council on the application of this Directive and, if necessary, shall submit appropriate proposals to it.

Article 22

This Directive is addressed to the Member States.

Done at Brussels, 25 July 1985.

Appendix 2

Council Directive 92/59/EEC of 29 June 1992 on General Product Safety (footnotes omitted).

THE COUNCIL OF THE EUROPEAN COMMUNITIES,

Having regard to the Treaty establishing the European Economic Community, and in particular Article 100a thereof,

Having regard to the proposal from the Commission,

In co–operation with the European Parliament,

Having regard to the opinion of the Economic and Social Committee,

Whereas it is important to adopt measures with the aim of progressively establishing the internal market over a period expiring on 31 December 1992; whereas the internal market is to comprise an area without internal frontiers in which the free movement of goods, persons, services and capital is ensured;

Whereas some Member States have adopted horizontal legislation on product safety, imposing, in particular, a general obligation on economic operators to market only safe products; whereas those legislations differ in the level of protection afforded to persons; whereas such disparities and the absence of horizontal legislation in other Member States are liable to create barriers to trade and distortions of competition within the internal market;

Whereas it is very difficult to adopt Community legislation for every product which exists or may be developed; whereas there is a need for a broadly based, legislative framework of a horizontal nature to deal with those products, and also to cover lacunae in existing or forthcoming specific legislation, in particular with a view to ensuring a high level of protection of safety and health of persons, as required by Article 100a(3) of the Treaty;

Whereas it is therefore necessary to establish on a Community level a general safety requirement for any product placed on the market that is intended for consumers or likely to be used by consumers; whereas certain second–hand goods should nevertheless be excluded by their nature;

Whereas production equipment, capital goods and other products used exclusively in the context of a trade or business are not covered by this Directive;

Whereas, in the absence of more specific safety provisions, within the framework of Community regulations, covering the products concerned, the provisions of this Directive are to apply;

Whereas when there are specific rules of Community law, of the total harmonisation type, and in particular rules adopted on the basis of the new approach, which lay down obligations regarding product safety, further obligations should not be imposed on economic operators as regards the placing on the market of products covered by such rules;

Whereas, when the provisions of specific Community regulations cover only certain aspects of safety or categories of risks in respect of the product concerned, the obligations of economic operators in respect of such aspects are determined solely by those provisions;

Whereas it is appropriate to supplement the duty to observe the general safety requirement by an obligation on economic operators to supply consumers with relevant information and adopt measures commensurate with the characteristics of the products, enabling them to be informed of the risks that these products might present;

Whereas in the absence of specific regulations, criteria should be defined whereby product safety can be assessed;

Whereas Member States must establish authorities responsible for monitoring product safety and with powers to take the appropriate measures;

Whereas it is necessary in particular for the appropriate measures to include the power for Member States to organise, immediately and efficiently, the withdrawal of dangerous products already placed on the market;

Whereas it is necessary for the preservation of the unity of the market to inform the Commission of any measure restricting the placing on the market of a product or requiring its withdrawal from the market except for those relating to an event which is local in effect and in any case limited to the territory of the Member State concerned; whereas such measures can be taken only in compliance with the provisions of the Treaty, and in particular Articles 30 to 36;

Whereas this Directive applies without prejudice to the notification procedures in Council Directive 83/189/EEC of 28 March 1983 laying down a procedure for the provision of information in the field of technical standards and regulations and in Commission Decision 88/383/EEC of 24 February 1988 providing for the improvement of information on safety, hygiene and health at work;

Whereas effective supervision of product safety requires the setting-up at national and Community levels of a system of rapid exchange of information in emergency situations in respect of the safety of a product and whereas the procedure laid down by Council Decision 89/45/EEC of 21 December 1988 on a Community system for the rapid exchange of information on dangers arising from the use of consumer products should therefore be incorporated into this Directive and the above Decision should be repealed; whereas it is also advisable for this Directive to take over the detailed procedures adopted under the above Decision and to give the Commission, assisted by a committee, power to adapt them;

Whereas, moreover, equivalent notification procedures already exist for pharmaceuticals, which come under Directives 75/319/EEC and 81/851/EEC concerning animal diseases referred to in Directive 82/894/EEC, for products of animal origin covered by Directive 89/662/EEC, and in the form of the system for the rapid exchange of information in radiological emergencies under Decision 87/600/Euratom;

Whereas it is primarily for Member States, in compliance with the Treaty and in particular with Articles 30 to 36 thereof, to take appropriate measures with regard to dangerous products located within their territory;

Whereas in such a situation the decision taken on a particular product could differ from one Member State to another; whereas such a difference may entail unacceptable disparities in consumer protection and constitute a barrier to intra-Community trade;

Whereas it may be necessary to cope with serious product-safety problems which affect or could affect, in the immediate future, all or a large part of the Community and which, in view of the nature of the safety problem posed by the product cannot be dealt with effectively in a manner commensurate with the urgency of the problem under the procedures laid down in the specific rules of Community law applicable to the products or category of products in question;

Whereas it is therefore necessary to provide for an adequate mechanism allowing, in the last resort, for the adoption of measures applicable throughout the Community, in the form of a decision addressed to the Member States, in order to cope with emergency situations as mentioned above; whereas such a decision is not of direct application to economic operators and must be incorporated into a national instrument; whereas measures adopted under such a procedure can be no more than interim measures that have to be taken by the Commission assisted by a committee of representatives of the Member States; whereas, for reasons of co-operation with the Member States, it is appropriate to provide for a regulatory committee according to procedure III (b) of Decision 87/373/EEC;

Whereas this Directive does not affect victims' rights within the meaning of Council Directive 85/374/EEC of 25 July 1985 on the approximation of the laws, regulations and administrative provisions of the Member States concerning liability for defective products;

Whereas it is necessary that Member States provide for appropriate means of redress before the competent courts in respect of measures taken by the competent authorities which restrict the placing on the market of a product or require its withdrawal;

Whereas it is appropriate to consider, in the light of experience, possible adaptation of this Directive, particularly as regards extension of its scope and provisions on emergency situations and intervention at Community level;

Whereas, in addition, the adoption of measures concerning imported products with a view to preventing risks to the safety and health of persons must comply with the Community's internal obligations,

HAS ADOPTED THIS DIRECTIVE:

Title I
Objective - Scope - Definitions

Article 1

1. The purpose of the provisions of this Directive is to ensure that products placed on the market are safe.

2. The provisions of this Directive shall apply in so far as there are no specific provisions in rules of Community law governing the safety of the products concerned.

In particular, where specific rules of Community law contain provisions imposing safety requirements on the products which they govern, the provisions of Articles 2 to 4 of this Directive shall not, in any event, apply to those products.

Where specific rules of Community law contain provisions governing only certain aspects of product safety or categories of risks for the products concerned, those are the provisions which shall apply to the products concerned with regard to the relevant safety aspects or risks.

Article 2

For the purposes of this Directive:

(a) *product* shall mean any product intended for consumers or likely to be used by consumers, supplied whether for consideration or not in the course of a commercial activity and whether new, used or reconditioned. However, this Directive shall not apply to second-hand products supplied as antiques or as products to be repaired or reconditioned prior to being used, provided that the supplier clearly informs the person to whom he supplies the product to that effect;

(b) *safe product* shall mean any product which, under normal or reasonably foreseeable conditions of use, including duration, does not present any risk or only the minimum risks compatible with the product's use, considered as acceptable and consistent with a high level of protection for the safety and health of persons, taking into account the following points in particular;

- the characteristics of the product, including its composition, packaging, instructions for assembly and maintenance,
- the effect on other products, where it is reasonably foreseeable that it will be used with other products,
- the presentation of the product, the labelling, any instructions for its use and disposal and any other indication or information provided by the producer,

  - the categories of consumers at serious risk when using the product, in particular children.

The feasibility of obtaining higher levels of safety or the availability of other products presenting a lesser degree of risk shall not constitute grounds for considering a product to be 'unsafe' or 'dangerous';

(c) *dangerous product* shall mean any product which does not meet the definition of 'safe product' according to point (b) hereof;

(d) *producer shall* mean:
  - the manufacturer of the product, when he is established in the Community, and any other person presenting himself as the manufacturer by affixing to the product his name, trade mark or other distinctive mark, or the person who reconditions the product,
  - the manufacturer's representative, when the manufacturer is not established in the Community or, if there is no representative established in the community, the importer of the product,
  - other professionals in the supply chain, insofar as their activities may affect the safety properties of a product placed on the market.

(e) *distributor* shall mean any professional in the supply chain whose activity does not affect the safety properties of a product.

Title II
General safety requirement

Article 3

1. Producers shall be obliged to place only safe products on the market.
2. Within the limits of their respective activities, producers shall:
-     provide consumers with the relevant information to enable them to assess the risks inherent in a product throughout the normal or reasonably foreseeable period of its use, where such risks are not immediately obvious without adequate warnings, and to take precautions against those risks.
      Provision of such warnings does not, however, exempt any person from compliance with the other requirements laid down in this Directive,
-     adopt measures commensurate with the characteristics of the products which they supply, to enable them to be informed of risks which these products might present and to take appropriate action including, if necessary, withdrawing the product in question from the market to avoid these risks.
      The above measures shall for example include, whenever appropriate, marking of the products or product batches in such a way that they can

be identified, sample testing of marketed products, investigating complaints made and keeping distributors informed of such monitoring.

3. Distributors shall be required to act with due care in order to help to ensure compliance with the general safety requirement, in particular by not supplying products which they know or should have presumed, on the basis of the information in their possession and as professionals, do not comply with this requirement. In particular, within the limits of their respective activities, they shall participate in monitoring the safety of products placed on the market, especially by passing on information on product risks and co-operating in the action taken to avoid these risks.

Article 4

1. Where there are no specific Community provisions governing the safety of the products in question, a product shall be deemed safe when it conforms to the specific rules of national law of the Member State in whose territory the product is in circulation, such rules being drawn up in conformity with the Treaty, and in particular Articles 30 and 36 thereof, and laying down the health and safety requirements which the product must satisfy in order to be marketed.

2. In the absence of specific rules as referred to in paragraph 1, the conformity of a product to the general safety requirement shall be assessed having regard to voluntary national standards giving effect to a European standard or, where they exist, to Community technical specifications or, failing these, to standards drawn up in the Member State in which the product is in circulation, or to the codes of good practice in respect of health and safety in the sector concerned or to the state of the art and technology and to the safety which consumers may reasonably expect.

3. Conformity of a product which the provisions mentioned in paragraphs 1 or 2 shall not bar the competent authorities of the Member States from taking appropriate measures to impose restrictions on its being placed on the market or to require its withdrawal from the market where there is evidence that, despite such conformity, it is dangerous to the health and safety of consumers.

Title III
Obligations and powers of the Member States

Article 5

Member States shall adopt the necessary laws, regulations and administrative provisions to make producers and distributors comply with their obligations under this Directive in such a way that products placed on the market are safe.

In particular, Member States shall establish or nominate authorities to monitor the compliance of products with the obligation to place only safe products on the market and arrange for such authorities to have the necessary powers to take the appropriate measures incumbent upon them under this Directive, including the possibility of imposing suitable penalties in the event of failure to comply with the obligations deriving from this Directive. They shall notify the Commission of the said authorities; the Commission shall pass on the information to the other Member States.

Article 6

1. For the purposes of Article 5, Member States shall have the necessary powers, acting in accordance with the degree of risk and in conformity with the Treaty, and in particular Articles 30 and 36 thereof, to adopt appropriate measures with a view, *inter alia, to:*

(a) organising appropriate checks on the safety properties of products, even after their being placed on the market as being safe, on an adequate scale, up to the final stage of use of consumption;

(b) requiring all necessary information from the parties concerned;

(c) taking samples of a product or a product line and subjecting them to safety checks;

(d) subjecting product marketing to prior conditions designed to ensure product safety and requiring that suitable warnings be affixed regarding the risks which the product may present;

(e) making arrangements to ensure that persons who might be exposed to a risk from a product are informed in good time and in a suitable manner of the said risk by, *inter alia,* the publication of special warnings;

(f) temporarily prohibiting, for the period required to carry out the various checks, anyone from supplying, offering to supply or exhibiting a product or product batch, whenever there are precise and consistent indications that they are dangerous;

(g) prohibiting the placing on the market of a product or product batch which has proved dangerous and establishing the accompanying measures needed to ensure that the ban is complied with;

(h) organising the effective and immediate withdrawal of a dangerous product or product batch already on the market and, if necessary, its destruction under appropriate conditions.

2. The measures to be taken by the competent authorities of the Member States under this Article shall be addressed, as appropriate, to:

(a) the producer;

(b) within the limits of their respective activities, distributors and in particular the party responsible for the first stage of distribution on the national market;

(c) any other person, where necessary, with regard to co–operation in action taken to avoid risks arising from a product.

Title IV
Notification and Exchanges of Information

Article 7

1. Where a Member State takes measures which restrict the placing of a product or a product batch on the market or require its withdrawal from the market, such as provided for in Article 6(1)(d) to (h), the Member State shall, to the extent that such notification is not required under any specific Community legislation, inform the Commission of the said measures, specifying its reasons for adopting them. This obligation shall not apply where the measures relate to an event which is local in effect and in any case limited to the territory of the Member State concerned.

2. The Commission shall enter into consultations with the parties concerned as quickly as possible. Where the Commission concludes, after such consultations, that the measure is justified, it shall immediately inform the Member State which initiated the action and the other Member States. Where the Commission concludes, after such consultations, that the measure is not justified, it shall immediately inform the Member State which initiated the action.

Title V
Emergency situations and action at Community level

Article 8

1. Where a Member State adopts or decides to adopt emergency measures to prevent, restrict or impose specific conditions on the possible marketing or use, within its own territory, of a product or product batch by reason of a serious and immediate risk presented by the said product or product batch to the health and safety of consumers, it shall forthwith inform the Commission thereof, unless provision is made for this obligation in procedures of a similar nature in the context of other Community instruments.

This obligation shall not apply if the effects of the risk do not, or cannot, go beyond the territory of the Member State concerned.

Without prejudice to the provisions of the first subparagraph, Member States may pass on to the Commission any information in their possession regarding the existence of a serious and immediate risk before deciding to adopt the measures in question.

2. On receiving this information, the Commission shall check to see whether it complies with the provisions of this Directive and shall forward it to the other Member States, which, in turn, shall immediately inform the Commission of any measures adopted.

3. Detailed procedures for the Community information system described in this Article are set out in the Annex. They shall be adapted by the Commission in accordance with the procedure laid down in Article 11.

Article 9

If the Commission becomes aware through notification given by the Member States or through information provided by them, in particular under Article 7 or Article 8, of the existence of a serious and immediate risk from a product to the health and safety of consumers in various Member States and if:

(a) one of more Member States have adopted measures entailing restrictions on the marketing of the product or requiring its withdrawal from the market, such as those provided for in Article 6(1)(d) to (h);

(b) Member States differ on the adoption of measures to deal with the risk in question;

(c) the risk cannot be dealt with, in view of the nature of the safety issue posed by the urgency of the case under the other procedures laid down by the specific Community legislation applicable to the product or category of products concerned; and

(d) the risk can be eliminated effectively only by adopting appropriate measures applicable at Community level, in order to ensure the protection of the health and safety of consumers and the proper functioning of the common market,

the Commission, after consulting the Member States and at the request of at least one of them, may adopt a decision, in accordance with the procedure laid down in Article 11, requiring Member States to take temporary measures from among those listed in Article 6(1)(d) to (h).

Article 10

1. The Commission shall be assisted by a Committee on Product Safety Emergencies, hereinafter referred to as 'the Committee', composed of the representatives of the Member States and chaired by a representative of the Commission.

2. Without prejudice to Article 9(c), there shall be close co-operation between the Committee referred to in paragraph 1 and the other Committees established by specific rules of Community law to assist the Commission as regards the health and safety aspects of the product concerned.

Article 11

1. The Commission representative shall submit to the Committee a draft of the measures to be taken. The Committee, having verified that the conditions listed in Article 9 are fulfilled, shall deliver its opinion on the draft within a time limit which the Chairman may lay down according to the urgency of the matter but which may not exceed one month. The opinion shall be delivered by the majority laid down in Article 148(2) of the Treaty for adoption of decisions by the Council on a proposal from the Commission. The votes of the representatives of the Member States within the Committee shall be weighted in the manner set out in that Article. The Chairman shall not vote.

The Commission shall adopt the measures in question, if they are in accordance with the opinion of the Committee. If the measures proposed are not in accordance with the Committee's opinion, or in the absence of an opinion, the Commission shall forthwith submit to the Council a proposal regarding the measures to be taken. The Council shall act by a qualified majority.

If the Council has not acted within 15 days of the date on which the proposal was submitted to it, the measures proposed shall be adopted by the Commission unless the Council has decided against them by a simple majority.

2. Any measure adopted under this procedure shall be valid for no longer than three months. That period may be prolonged under the same procedure.
3. Member States shall take all necessary measures to implement the decisions adopted under this procedures within less than 10 days.
4. The competent authorities of the Member States responsible for carrying out measures adopted under this procedure shall, within one month, give the parties concerned an opportunity to submit their view and shall inform the Commission accordingly.

Article 12

The Member States and the Commission shall take the steps necessary to ensure that their officials and agents are required not to disclose information obtained for the purposes of this Directive which, by its nature, is covered by professional secrecy, except for information relating to the safety properties of a given product which must be made public if circumstances so require, in order to protect the health and safety of persons.

Title VI
Miscellaneous and final provisions

Article 13

This Directive shall be without prejudice to Directive 85/374/EEC.

Article 14

1. Any decision adopted under this Directive and involving restrictions on the placing of a product on the market, or requiring its withdrawal from the market, must state the appropriate reasons on which it is based. It shall be notified as soon as possible to the party concerned and shall indicate the remedies available under the provisions in force in the Member State in question and the time limits applying to such remedies

The parties concerned shall, whenever feasible, be given an opportunity to submit their views before the adoption of the measure. If this has not been done in advance because of the urgency of the measures to be taken, such opportunity shall be given in due course after the measure has been implemented.

Measures requiring the withdrawal of a product from the market shall take into consideration the need to encourage distributors, users and consumers to contribute to the implementation of such measures.

2. Member States shall ensure that any measure taken by the competent authorities involving restrictions on the placing of a product on the market or requiring its withdrawal from the market can be challenged before the competent courts.

3. Any decision taken by virtue of this Directive and involving restrictions on the placing of a product on the market or requiring its withdrawal from the market shall be entirely without prejudice to assessment of the liability of the party concerned, in the light of the national criminal law applying in the case in question.

Article 15

Every two years following the date of adoption, the Commission shall submit a report on the implementation of this Directive to the European Parliament and the Council.

Article 16

Four years from the date referred to in Article 17(1), on the basis of a Commission report on the experience acquired, together with appropriate proposals, the Council shall decide whether to adjust this Directive, in particular with a view to extending its scope as laid down in Article 1(1) and Article 2(a), and whether the provisions of Title V should be amended.

Article 17

1. Member States shall adopt the laws, regulations and administrative provisions necessary to comply with this Directive by 29 June 1994 at the latest. They shall forthwith inform the Commission thereof. The provisions adopted shall apply with effect from 29 June 1994.

2. When these measures are adopted by the Member States, they shall contain a reference to this Directive or be accompanied by such a reference on the occasion of their official publication. The methods of making such a reference shall be laid down by the Member States.

3. Member States shall communicate to the Commission the text of the provisions of national law which they adopt in the area covered by this Directive.

Article 18

Decision 89/45/EEC is hereby repealed on the date referred to in Article 17(1).

Article 19

This Directive is addressed to the Member States.

Done at Luxembourg, 29 June 1992.

Annex

Detailed procedures for the Application of the Community System for the Rapid Exchange of Information provided for in Article 8

1. The system covers products placed on the market as defined in Article 2 (a) of this Directive.
Pharmaceuticals, which come under Directive 75/319/EEC and 81/851/EEC, and animals, to which Directive 82/894/EEC applies and products of animal origin, as far as they are covered by Directive 89/662/EEC, and the system for radiological emergencies which covers widespread contamination of products (Decision 87/600/ Euratom), are excluded, since they are covered by equivalent notification procedures.
2. The system is essentially aimed at a rapid exchange of information in the event of a serious and immediate risk to the health and safety of consumers. It is impossible to lay down specific criteria as to what, precisely, constitutes an immediate and serious risk; in this regard, the national authorities will therefore judge each individual case on its merits. It should be noted that, as Article 8 of this Directive relates to immediate threats posed by a product to consumers, products involving possible long-term risks, which call for a study of possible technical changes by means of directives or standards are not concerned.
3. As soon as a serious and immediate risk is detected, the national authority shall consult, in so far as possible and appropriate, the producer or distributor of the product concerned. Their point of view and the details which they supply may be useful both to the administrations of the Member States and to the Commission in determining what action should be taken to ensure that the consumer is protected with a minimum of commercial disruption. To these ends the Member States should endeavour to obtain the

maximum of information on the products and the nature of the danger, without compromising the need for rapidity.

4. As soon as a Member State has detected a serious and immediate risk, the effects of which extend or could extend beyond its territory, and measures have been taken or decided on, it shall immediately inform the Commission. The Member State shall indicate that it is notifying the Commission under Article 8 of this Directive. All available details shall be given, in particular on:

(a) information to identify the product;
(b) the danger involved, including the results of any tests/analyses which are relevant to assessing the level of risk;
(c) the nature of the measures taken or decided on;
(d) information on supply chains where such information is possible.

Such information must be transmitted in writing, preferably by telex or fax, but may be preceded by a telephone call to the Commission. It should be remembered that the speed with which the information is communicated is crucial.

5. Without prejudice to point 4, Member States may, where appropriate, pass information to the Commission at the stage preceding the decision on the measures to be taken. Immediate contact, as soon as a risk is discovered or suspected, can in fact facilitate preventive action.

6. If the Member State considers certain information to be confidential, it should specify this and justify its request for confidentiality, bearing in mind that the need to take effective measures to protect consumers normally outweighs considerations of confidentiality. It should also be remembered that precautions are taken in all cases, both by the Commission and by the members of the network responsible in the various Member States, to avoid any unnecessary disclosure of information likely to harm the reputation of a product or series of products.

7. The Commission shall verify the conformity of the information received with Article 8 of this Directive, contact the notifying country, if necessary, and forward the information immediately by telex or fax to the relevant authorities in the other Member States with a copy to each permanent representation; these authorities may, at the same time as the transmission of the telex, be contacted by telephone. The Commission may also contact the Member State presumed to be the country of origin of the product to carry out the necessary verifications.

8. At the same time the Commission, when it considers it to be necessary, and in order to supplement the information received, can in exceptional circumstances institute an investigation of its own motion and/or convene the Committee on Emergencies provided for in Article 10(1) of this Directive.

In the case of such an investigation Member States shall supply the commission with the requested information to the best of their ability.

9. The other Member States are requested, wherever possible, to inform the Commission without delay of the following:

(a)   whether the product has been marketed in its territory;

(b)   supplementary information it has obtained on the danger involved, including the results of any tests/analyses carried out to assess the level of risk,

and in any case they must inform the Commission as soon as possible of the following:

(c)   the measures taken or decided on, of the type mentioned in Article 8(1) of this Directive;

(d)   when the product mentioned in this information has been found within their territory but no measures have been taken or decided on and the reasons why no measures are to be taken.

10. The Commission may, in the light of the evolution of a case and the information received from Member States under point 9 above, convene the above Committee on Emergencies in order to exchange views on the results obtained and to evaluate the measures taken. The Committee on Emergencies may also be convened at the request of a representative of a Member State.

11. The Commission shall, by means of its internal co-ordination procedures, endeavour to:

(a)   avoid unnecessary duplication in dealing with notifications;

(b)   make full use of the expertise available within the Commission;

(c)   keep the other services concerned fully informed;

(d)   ensure that discussions in the various relevant committees are held in accordance with Article 10 of this Directive.

12. When a Member State intends, apart from any specific measures taken because of serious and immediate risks, to modify its legislation by adopting technical specifications, the latter must be notified to the Commission at the draft stage, in accordance with Directive 83/189/EEC, if necessary, quoting the urgent reasons set out in Article 9(3) of that Directive.

13. To allow it to have an overview of the situation, the Committee on Emergencies shall be periodically informed of all the notifications received and of the follow-up. With regard to points 8 and 10 above, and in those cases which fall within the scope of procedures and/or committees provided for by Community legislation governing specific products or product sectors, those committees shall be involved. In cases where the Committee on Emergencies is not involved and no provisions are made under 11(d), the contact points shall be informed of any exchange of views within other committees.

14. At present there are two networks of contact points: the food products network and the non-food products network. The list of contact points and officials responsible for the networks with telephone, telex and fax numbers and addresses is confidential and distributed to the members of the network

only. This list enables contact to be established with the Commission and between Member States in order to facilitate clarification of points of detail. When such contacts between Member States give rise to new information of general interest, the Member States which initiated the bilateral contact shall inform the Commission. Only information received or confirmed through contact points in Member States may be considered as received through the rapid exchange of information procedure.

Every year the Commission shall carry out a review of the effectiveness of the network, of any necessary improvements and of the progress made in the communications technology between the authorities responsible for its operation.

Appendix 3

Council Directive 93/13/EEC of 5 April 1993 on Unfair Terms in Consumer Contracts (footnotes omitted).

THE COUNCIL OF THE EUROPEAN COMMUNITIES,

Having regard to the Treaty establishing the European Economic Community, and in particular Article 100 A therefore,

Having regard to the proposal from the Commission,

In co–operation with the European Parliament,

Having regard to the opinion of the Economic and Social Committee,

Whereas it is necessary to adopt measures with the aim of progressively establishing the internal market before 31 December 1992; whereas the internal market comprises an area without internal frontiers in which goods, persons, services and capital move freely;

Whereas the laws of Member States relating to the terms of contract between the seller of goods or supplier of services, on the one hand, and the consumer of them, on the other hand, show many disparities, with the result that the national markets for the sale of goods and services to consumers differ from each other and that distortions of competition may arise amongst the sellers and suppliers, notably when they sell and supply in other Member States;

Whereas, in particular, the laws of Member States relating to unfair terms in consumer contracts show marked divergences;

Whereas it is the responsibility of the Member States to ensure that contracts concluded with consumers do not contain unfair terms;

Whereas, generally speaking, consumers do not know the rules of law which, in Member States other than their own, govern contracts for the sale of goods or services; whereas this lack of awareness may deter them from direct transactions for the purchase of goods or services in another Member State;

Whereas, in order to facilitate the establishment of the internal market and to safeguard the citizen in his role as consumer when acquiring goods and services under contracts which are governed by the laws of Member States other than his own, it is essential to remove unfair terms from those contracts;

Whereas sellers of goods and suppliers of services will thereby be helped in their task of selling goods and supplying services, both at home and throughout the internal market; whereas competition will thus be stimulated, so contributing to increased choice for Community citizens as consumers;

Whereas the two Community programmes for a consumer protection and information policy underlined the importance of safeguarding consumers in the matter of unfair terms of contract; whereas this protection ought to be provided by laws and regulations which are either harmonised at Community level or adopted directly at that level;

Whereas in accordance with the principle laid down under the heading 'Protection of the economic interests of the consumers', as stated in those programmes: 'acquirers of goods and services should be protected against the abuse of power by the seller or supplier, in particular against one–sided standard contracts and the unfair exclusion of essential rights in contracts';

Whereas more effective protection of the consumer can be achieved by adopting uniform rules of law in the matter of unfair terms; whereas those rules should apply to all contracts concluded between sellers or suppliers and consumers; whereas as a result *inter alia* contracts relating to employment, contracts relating to succession rights, contracts relating to rights under family law and contracts relating to the incorporation and organisation of companies or partnership agreements must be excluded from this Directive;

Whereas the consumer must receive equal protection under contracts concluded by word of mouth and written contracts regardless, in the latter case, of whether the terms of the contract are contained in one or more documents;

Whereas, however, as they now stand, national laws allow only partial harmonisation to be envisaged: whereas, in particular, only contractual terms which have not been individually negotiated are covered by this Directive; whereas Member States should have the option, with due regard for the Treaty, to afford consumers a higher level of protection through national provisions that are more stringent than those of this Directive;

Whereas the statutory or regulatory provisions of the Member States which directly or indirectly determine the terms of consumer contracts are presumed not to contain unfair terms; whereas, therefore, it does not appear to be necessary to subject the terms which reflect mandatory statutory or regulatory provisions and the principles or provisions of international conventions to which the Member States or the Community are party; whereas in that respect the wording 'mandatory statutory or regulatory provisions' in Article 1(2) also covers rules which, according to the law, shall apply between the contracting parties provided that no other arrangements have been established;

Whereas Member States must however ensure that unfair terms are not included, particularly because this Directive also applies to trades, business or professions of a public nature;

Whereas it is necessary to fix in a general way the criteria for assessing the unfair character of contract terms;

Whereas the assessment, according to the general criteria chosen, of the unfair character of terms, in particular in sale or supply activities of a public nature providing collective services which take account of solidarity among users, must be supplemented by a means of making an overall evaluation of the different interests involved; whereas this constitutes the requirement of good faith; whereas, in making an assessment of good faith, particular regard shall be had to the strength of the bargaining positions of the parties, whether the consumer had an inducement to agree to the term and whether the goods or services were sold or supplied to the special order of the consumer; whereas the requirement of good faith may be satisfied by the seller or supplier where he deals fairly and equitably with the other party whose legitimate interests he has to take into account;

Whereas, for the purposes of this Directive, the annexed list of terms can be of indicative value only and, because of the cause of the minimal character of the Directive, the scope of these terms may be the subject of amplification or more restrictive editing by the Member States in their national laws;

Whereas the nature of goods or services should have an influence on assessing the unfairness of contractual terms;

Whereas, for the purposes of this Directive, assessment of unfair character shall not be made of terms which describe the main subject matter of the contract nor the quality/price ratio of the goods or services supplied; whereas the main subject matter of the contract and the price/quality ratio may nevertheless be taken into account in assessing the fairness of other terms; whereas it follows, *inter alia,* that in insurance contracts, the terms which clearly define or circumscribe the insured risk and the insurer's liability shall not be subject to such assessment since these restrictions are taken into account in calculating the premium paid by the consumer;

Whereas contracts should be drafted in plain, intelligible language, the consumer should actually be given an opportunity to examine all the terms and, if in doubt, the interpretation most favourable to the consumer should prevail;

Whereas Member States should ensure that unfair terms are not used in contracts concluded with consumers by a seller or supplier and that if, nevertheless, such terms are so used, they will not bind the consumer, and the contract will continue to bind the parties upon those terms if it is capable of continuing in existence without the unfair provisions;

Whereas there is a risk that, in certain cases, the consumer may be deprived of protection under this Directive by designating the law of a non–Member country as the law applicable to the contract; whereas provisions should therefore be included in this Directive designed to avert this risk;

Whereas persons or organisations, if regarded under the law of a Member State as having a legitimate interest in the matter, must have facilities for initiating proceedings concerning terms of contract drawn up for general use in contracts concluded with consumers, and in particular unfair terms, either before a court or before an administrative authority competent to decide upon complaints or to initiate appropriate legal proceedings; whereas this possibility does not, however, entail prior verification of the general conditions obtaining in individual economic sectors;

Whereas the courts or administrative authorities of the Member States must have at their disposal adequate and effective means of preventing the continued application of unfair terms in consumer contracts,

HAS ADOPTED THIS DIRECTIVE:

Article 1

1. The purpose of this Directive is to approximate the laws, regulations and administrative provisions of the Member States relating to unfair terms in contracts concluded between a seller or supplier and a consumer.

2. The contractual terms which reflect mandatory statutory or regulatory provisions and the provisions or principles of international conventions to which the Member States or the Community are party, particularly in the transport area, shall not be subject to the provisions of this Directive.

Article 2

For the purposes of this Directive:
(a) 'unfair terms' means the contractual terms defined in Article 3;
(b) 'consumer' means any natural person who, in contracts covered by this Directive, is acting for purposes which are outside his trade, business or profession;
(c) 'seller or supplier' means any natural or legal person who, in contracts covered by this Directive, is acting for purposes relating to his trade, business or profession. whether publicly owned or privately owned.

Article 3

1. A contractual term which has not been individually negotiated shall be regarded as unfair if, contrary to the requirement of good faith, it causes a significant imbalance in the parties' rights and obligations arising under the contract, to the detriment of the consumer.

2. A term shall always be regarded as not individually negotiated where it has been drafted in advance and the consumer has therefore not been able to influence the substance of the term, particularly in the context of a pre-formulated standard contract.

The fact that certain aspects of a term or one specific term have been individually negotiated shall not exclude the application of this Article to the rest of a contract if an overall assessment of the contract indicates that it is nevertheless a pre-formulated standard contract.

Where any seller or supplier claims that a standard term has been individually negotiated, the burden of proof in this respect shall be incumbent on him.

3. The Annex shall contain an indicative and non-exhaustive list of the terms which may be regarded as unfair.

Article 4

1. Without prejudice to Article 7, the unfairness of a contractual term shall be assessed, taking into account the nature of the goods or services for which the contract was concluded and by referring, at the time of conclusion of the contract, to all the circumstances attending the conclusion of the contract and to all the other terms of the contract or of another contract on which it is dependent.
2. Assessment of the unfair nature of the terms shall relate neither to the definition of the main subject matter of the contract nor to the adequacy of the price and remuneration, on the one hand, as against the services or goods supplied in exchange, on the other, in so far as these terms are in plain intelligible language.

Article 5

In the case of contracts where all or certain terms offered to the consumer are in writing, these terms must always be drafted in plain, intelligible language. Where there is doubt about the meaning of a term, the interpretation most favourable to the consumer shall prevail. This rule on interpretation shall not apply in the context of the procedures laid down in Article 7(2).

Article 6

1. Member States shall lay down that unfair terms used in a contract concluded with a consumer by a seller or supplier shall, as provided for under their national law, not be binding on the consumer and that the contract shall continue to bind the parties upon those terms if it is capable of continuing in existence without the unfair terms
2. Member States shall take the necessary measures to ensure that the consumer does not lose the protection granted by this Directive by virtue of the choice of the law of a non–Member country as the law applicable to the contract if the latter has a close connection with the territory of the Member States.

Article 7

1. Member States shall ensure that, in the interests of consumers and of competitors, adequate and effective means exist to prevent the continued use

of unfair terms in contracts concluded with consumers by sellers or suppliers.

2. The means referred to in paragraph 1 shall include provisions whereby persons or organisations, having a legitimate interest under national law in protecting consumers, may take action according to the national law concerned before the courts or before competent administrative bodies for a decision as to whether contractual terms drawn up for general use are unfair, so that they can apply appropriate and effective means to prevent the continued use of such terms.

3. With due regard for national laws, the legal remedies referred to in paragraph 2 may be directed separately or jointly against a number of sellers or suppliers from the same economic sector or their associations which use or recommend the use of the same general contractual terms or similar terms.

Article 8

Member States may adopt or retain the most stringent provisions compatible with the Treaty in the area covered by this Directive, to ensure a maximum degree of protection for the consumer.

Article 9

The Commission shall present a report to the European Parliament and to the Council concerning the application of this Directive five years at the latest after the date in Article 10(1).

Article 10

1. Member States shall bring into force the laws, regulations and administrative provisions necessary to comply with this Directive no later than 31 December 1994. They shall forthwith inform the Commission thereof.

These provisions shall be applicable to all contracts concluded after 31 December 1994.

2. When Member States adopt these measures, they shall contain a reference to this Directive or shall be accompanied by such reference on the occasion of their official publication. The methods of making such a reference shall be laid down by the Member States.

3. Member States shall communicate the main provisions of national law which they adopt in the field covered by this Directive to the Commission.

Article 11

This Directive is addressed to the Member States.

Done at Luxembourg, 5 April 1993

Annex

Terms referred to in Article 3(3)

1. Terms which have the object or effect of:
(a) excluding or limiting the legal liability of a seller or supplier in the event of the death of a consumer or personal injury to the latter resulting from an act or omission of that seller or supplier;
(b) inappropriately excluding or limiting the legal rights of the consumer *vis–à–vis* the seller or supplier or another party in the event of total or partial non–performance or inadequate performance by the seller or supplier of any of the contractual obligations, including the option of offsetting a debt owed to the seller or supplier against any claim which the consumer may have against him;
(c) making an agreement binding on the consumer whereas provision of services by the seller or supplier is subject to a condition whose realisation depends on his own will alone;
(d) permitting the seller or supplier to retain sums paid by the consumer where the latter decides not to conclude or perform the contract, without providing for the consumer to receive compensation of an equivalent amount from the seller or supplier where the latter is the parry cancelling the contract;
(e) requiring any consumer who fails to fulfil his obligation to pay a disproportionately high sum in compensation;
(f) authorising the seller or supplier to dissolve the contract on a discretionary basis where the same facility is not granted to the consumer, or permitting the seller or supplier to retain the sums paid for services not yet supplied by him where it is the seller or supplier himself who dissolves the contract;
(g) enabling the seller or supplier to terminate a contract of indeterminate duration without reasonable notice except where there are serious grounds for doing so;
(h) automatically extending a contract of fixed duration where the consumer does not indicate otherwise, when the deadline fixed for the consumer to express this desire not to extend the contract is unreasonably early;

(i) irrevocably binding the consumer to terms with which he had no real opportunity of becoming acquainted before the conclusion of the contract;

(j) enabling the seller or supplier to alter the terms of the contract unilaterally without a valid reason which is specified in the contract;

(k) enabling the seller or supplier to alter unilaterally without a valid reason any characteristics of the product or service to be provided;

(l) providing for the price of goods to be determined at the time of delivery of allowing a seller of goods or supplier of services to increase their price without in both cases giving the consumer the corresponding right to cancel the contract if the final price is too high in relation to the price agreed when the contract was concluded;

(m) giving the seller or supplier the right to determine whether the goods or services supplied are in conformity with the contract, or giving him the exclusive right to interpret any term of the contract;

(n) limiting the seller's or supplier's obligation to respect commitments undertaken by his agents or making his commitments subject to compliance with a particular formality;

(o) obliging the consumer to fulfil all his obligations where the seller or supplier does not perform his;

(p) giving the seller or supplier the possibility of transferring his rights and obligations under the contract, where this may serve to reduce the guarantees for the consumer, without the latter's agreement;

(q) excluding or hindering the consumer's right to take legal action or exercise any other legal remedy, particularly by requiring the consumer to take disputes exclusively to arbitration not covered by legal provisions, unduly restricting the evidence available to him or imposing on him a burden of proof which, according to the applicable law, should lie with another party to the contract.

2. Scope of subparagraphs (g), (j) and (l)

(a) Subparagraph (g) is without hindrance to terms by which a supplier of financial services reserves the right to terminate unilaterally a contract of indeterminate duration without notice where there is a valid reason, provided that the supplier is required to inform the other contracting party or parties thereof immediately.

(b) Subparagraph (j) is without hindrance to terms under which a supplier of financial services reserves the right to alter the rate of interest payable by the consumer or due to the latter, or the amount of other charges for financial services without notice where there is a valid reason, provided that the supplier is required to inform the other contracting party or parties thereof at the earliest opportunity and that the latter are free to dissolve the contract immediately.

Subparagraph (j) is also without hindrance to terms under which a seller or supplier reserves the right to alter unilaterally the conditions of a contract of indeterminate duration, provided that he is required to inform the consumer with reasonable notice and that the consumer is free to dissolve the contract.

(c) Subparagraphs (g), (j) and (l) do not apply to:
  - transactions in transferable securities, financial instruments and other products or services where the price is linked to fluctuations in a stock exchange quotation or index or a financial market rate that the seller or supplier does not control;
  - contracts for the purchase or sale of foreign currency, traveller's cheques or international money orders denominated in foreign currency;

(d) Subparagraph (l) is without hindrance to price–indexation clauses, where lawful, provided that the method by which prices vary is explicitly described.

Appendix 4

Council Directive 84/450/EEC of 10 September 1984 relating to the Approximation of the Laws, Regulations and Administrative Provisions of the Member States Concerning Misleading Advertising (footnotes omitted).

THE COUNCIL OF THE EUROPEAN COMMUNITIES

Having regard to the Treaty establishing the European Economic Community, and in particular Article 100 thereof,

Having regard to the proposal from the Commission,

Having regard to the opinion of the European Parliament,

Having regard to the opinion of the Economic and Social Committee,

Whereas the laws against misleading advertising now in force in the Member States differ widely; whereas, since advertising reaches beyond the frontiers of individual Member States, it has a direct effect on the establishment and the functioning of the common market;

Whereas misleading advertising can lead to distortion of competition within the common market;

Whereas advertising, whether or not it induces a contract, affects the economic welfare of consumers;

Whereas misleading advertising may cause a consumer to take decisions prejudicial to him when acquiring goods or other property, or using services, and the differences between the laws of the Member States not only lead, in many cases, to inadequate levels of consumer protection, but also hinder the execution of advertising campaigns beyond national boundaries and thus affect the free circulation of goods and provisions of services;

Whereas the second programme of the European Economic Community for a consumer protection and information policy provides for appropriate action for the protection of consumers against misleading and unfair advertising;

Whereas it is in the interest of the public in general, as well as that of consumers and all those who, in competition with one another, carry on a trade, business, craft or profession, in the common market, to harmonise in the first instance national provisions against misleading advertising and that, at a second stage, unfair advertising and, as far as necessary, comparative advertising should be dealt with, on the basis of appropriate Commission proposals;

Whereas minimum and objective criteria for determining whether advertising is misleading should be established for this purpose;

Whereas the laws to be adopted by Member States against misleading advertising must be adequate and effective;

Whereas persons or organisations regarded under national law as having a legitimate interest in the matter must have facilities for initiating proceedings against misleading advertising, either before a court or before an administrative authority which is competent to decide upon complaints or to initiate appropriate legal proceedings;

Whereas it should be for each Member State to decide whether to enable the courts or administrative authorities to require prior recourse to other established means of dealing with the complaint;

Whereas the courts or administrative authorities must have powers enabling them to order or obtain the cessation of misleading advertising;

Whereas in certain cases it may be desirable to prohibit misleading advertising even before it is published; whereas, however, this in no way implies that Member States are under an obligation to introduce rules requiring the systematic prior vetting of advertising;

Whereas provision should be made for accelerated procedures under which measures with interim or definitive effect can be taken;

Whereas it may be desirable to order the publication of decisions made by courts or administrative authorities or of corrective statements in order to eliminate any continuing effects of misleading advertising;

Whereas administrative authorities must be impartial and the exercise of their powers must be subject to judicial review;

Whereas the voluntary control exercised by self–regulatory bodies to eliminate misleading advertising may avoid recourse to administrative or judicial action and ought therefore to be encouraged;

Whereas the advertiser should be able to prove by appropriate means, the material accuracy of the factual claims he makes in his advertising, and may in appropriate cases be required to do so by the court or administrative authority;

Whereas this Directive must not preclude Member States from retaining or adopting provisions with a view to ensuring more extensive protection of consumers, persons carrying on a trade, business, craft or profession, and the general public,

HAS ADOPTED THIS DIRECTIVE:

Article 1

The purpose of this Directive is to protect consumers, persons carrying on a trade or business or practising a craft or profession and the interests of the public in general against misleading advertising and the unfair consequences thereof.

Article 2

For the purpose of this Directive:
1. 'advertising' means the making of a representation in any form in connection with a trade, business, craft or profession in order to promote the supply of goods or services, including immovable property, rights and obligations;
2. 'misleading advertising' means any advertising which in any way, including its presentation, deceives or is likely to deceive the persons to whom it is addressed or whom it reaches and which, by reason of its deceptive nature, is likely to affect their economic behaviour or which, for those reasons, injures or is likely to injure a competitor;
3. 'person' means any natural or legal person.

Article 3

In determining whether advertising is misleading, account shall be taken of all its features, and in particular of any information it contains concerning:

(a) the characteristics of goods or services, such as their availability, nature, execution, composition, method and date of manufacture or provision, fitness for purpose, uses, quantity, specification, geographical or commercial origin or the results to be expected from their use, or the results and material features of tests or checks carried out on the goods or services;

(b) the price or the manner in which the price is calculated, and the conditions on which the goods are supplied or the services provided;

(c) the nature, attributes and rights of the advertiser, such as his identity and assets, his qualifications and ownership of industrial, commercial or intellectual property rights or his awards and distinctions.

Article 4

1. Member States shall ensure that adequate and effective means exist for the control of misleading advertising in the interests of consumers as well as competitors and the general public.

Such means shall include legal provisions under which persons or organisations regarded under national law as having a legitimate interest in prohibiting misleading advertising may–

(a) take legal action against such advertising; and/or

(b) bring such advertising before an administrative authority competent either to decide on complaints or to initiate appropriate legal proceedings.

It shall be for each Member State to decide which of these facilities shall be available and whether to enable the courts or administrative authorities to require prior recourse to other established means of dealing with complaints, including those referred to in Article 5.

2. Under the legal provisions referred to in paragraph 1, Member States shall confer upon the courts or administrative authorities powers enabling them, in cases where they deem such measures to be necessary taking into account all the interests involved and in particular the public interest:

– to order the cessation of, or to institute appropriate legal proceedings for an order for the cessation of, misleading advertising, or

– if misleading advertising has not yet been published but publication is imminent, to order the prohibition of, or to institute appropriate legal proceedings for an order for the prohibition of, such publication, even without proof of actual loss or damage or of intention or negligence on the part of the advertiser.

Member States shall also make provision for the measures referred to in the first subparagraph to be taken under an accelerated procedure–

– either with interim effect, or
– with definitive effect,

on the understanding that it is for each Member State to decide which of the two options to select.

Furthermore, Member States may confer upon the courts or administrative authorities powers enabling them, with a view to eliminating the continuing effects of misleading advertising the cessation of which has been ordered by a final decision–

– to require publication of that decision in full or in part and in such form as they deem adequate,
– to require in addition the publication of a corrective statement.

3. The administrative authorities referred to in paragraph 1 must:

(a) be composed so as not to cast doubt on their impartiality;
(b) have adequate powers, where they decide on complaints, to monitor and enforce the observance of their decisions effectively;
(c) normally give reasons for their decisions.

Where the powers referred to in paragraph 2 are exercised exclusively by an administrative authority, reasons for its decisions shall always be given. Furthermore in this case, provision must be made for procedures whereby improper or unreasonable exercise of its powers by the administrative authority or improper or unreasonable failure to exercise the said powers can be the subject of judicial review.

Article 5

This Directive does not exclude the voluntary control of misleading advertising by self–regulatory bodies and recourse to such bodies by the persons or organisations referred to in Article 4 if proceedings before such bodies are in addition to the court or administrative proceedings referred to in that Article.

Article 6

Member States shall confer upon the courts or administrative authorities powers enabling them in the civil or administrative proceedings provided for Article 4–

(a) to require the advertiser to furnish evidence as to the accuracy of factual claims in advertising if, taking into account the legitimate interests of the advertiser and any other party to the proceedings, such a requirement appears appropriate on the basis of the circumstances of the particular case; and

(b) to consider factual claims as inaccurate if the evidence demanded in accordance with (a) is not furnished or is deemed insufficient by the court or administrative authority.

Article 7

This Directive shall not preclude Member States from retaining or adopting provisions with a view to ensuring more extensive protection for consumers, persons carrying on a trade, business, craft or profession, and the general public.

Article 8

Member States shall bring into force the measures necessary to comply with this Directive by 1 October 1986 at the latest. They shall forthwith inform the Commission thereof.

Member States shall communicate to the Commission the text of all provisions of national law which they adopt in the field covered by this Directive.

Article 9

This Directive is addressed to the Member States.

Done at Brussels, 10 September 1984.

Appendix 5

Council Directive 79/581/EEC of 19 June 1979 on Consumer Protection in the Indication of the Prices of Foodstuffs (as amended, footnotes omitted).

THE COUNCIL OF THE EUROPEAN COMMUNITIES,

Having regard to the Treaty establishing the European Economic Community, and in particular Article 235 thereof,

Having regard to the proposal from the Commission,

Having regard to the opinion of the European Parliament,

Having regard to the opinion of the Economic and Social Committee,

Whereas the preliminary programme of the European Economic Community for a consumer protection and information policy provides for the establishment of common principles for indicating prices;

Whereas the indication of the selling price and the unit of foodstuffs will make it easier for consumers to compare prices at the place of sale; whereas this would thereby increase market transparency and ensure greater protection for consumers;

Whereas the obligation to indicate these prices must apply in principle to all foodstuffs offered to the final consumer, irrespective of whether they are marketed in bulk or in pre–packaged form; whereas this obligation must also apply to written or printed advertising and to catalogues wherever these mention the selling price of foodstuffs;

Whereas the selling price and the unit price must be indicated in accordance with the specific procedures for each category of foodstuffs, so as not to place an undue burden on the retailer as regards labelling;

Whereas the obligation to indicate the unit price should be waived for foodstuffs sold in bulk or pre–packaged for which such indication would be meaningless;

Whereas the obligation to indicate the unit price should, wherever possible, be replaced by standardisation of quantities of pre–packaged foodstuffs; whereas, in order to enable standardisation to progress at national and Community level, provision should be made for a delay in the application of this obligation to pre–packaged foodstuffs in pre–established quantities;

Whereas the rules laid down in this Directive are needed for the purposes of consumer information and protection and further the attainment of one of the objectives of the Community by contributing to the improvement of living conditions and the harmonious development of economic activities throughout the Community; whereas the Treaty has not provided the necessary powers,

HAS ADOPTED THIS DIRECTIVE:

Article 1

1. This Directive relates to the indication of the selling price and the price per unit of measurement of foodstuffs which are to be supplied to the final consumer, or which are advertised with their prices stated, whether they are sold in bulk or pre–packaged in pre–established or variable quantities.
2. This Directive shall not apply to foodstuffs sold in hotels, restaurants, cafes, public houses, hospitals, canteens and similar establishments and consumed on the premises, to foodstuffs bought for the purpose of a trade or commercial activity, nor to foodstuffs supplied in the course of the provision of a service,
3. Member States may provide that this Directive shall not apply to foodstuffs sold on the farm or to private sales.

Article 2

For the purposes of this Directive:
(a) 'foodstuffs sold in bulk (or not packaged)' means foodstuffs which are not pre–packaged and/or are not measured or weighted for sale except in the presence of the final consumer;
(b) 'pre–packaged foodstuffs' means foodstuffs packaged other than in the consumers' presence whether such packaging encloses the foodstuffs completely or only partially;
(c) 'foodstuffs pre–packaged in pre–established quantities' means foodstuffs pre–packaged in such a way that the quantity in the package corresponds to a previously selected value;

(d) 'foodstuffs pre–packaged in variable quantities' means foodstuffs pre–packaged in such a way that the quantity contained in the package does not correspond to a previously selected value;

(e) 'selling price' means the price for a given quantity of the foodstuff;

(f) 'unit price' means the price for a quantity of one kilogram or one litre of the foodstuffs, subject to Article 6(2) and the second subparagraph of Article 10.

Article 3

1. The foodstuffs referred to in Article 1 shall bear an indication of the selling price under the conditions laid down in Article 4.
2. The foodstuffs pre–packaged in pre–established quantities listed in the Annex and the foodstuffs pre–packaged in variable quantities shall also bear an indication of the unit price, subject to Articles 7 to 10.
3. The unit price of foodstuffs marketed in bulk must be indicated. However the Member States may specify the conditions under which the selling price per piece may be indicated for certain categories of these foodstuffs.
4. The selling price and the unit price shall relate to the final price of the foodstuff under the conditions laid down by the Member States.

Article 4

The selling price and the unit price must be unambiguous, easily identifiable and clearly legible. Each Member State may lay down the specific rules for such indication of prices, e.g. by means of posters, labels on shelves or on packaging.

Article 5

Any written or printed advertisement or catalogue which mentions the selling price of foodstuffs referred to in Article 1 shall indicate the unit price, subject to Article 3(2).

Article 6

1. The unit price shall be expressed as a price per litre for foodstuffs sold by volume and as a price per kilogram for foodstuffs sold by weight.

2. Member States may, however, authorise that, for foodstuffs marketed by volume, the unit price shall refer to a quantity of 100 millilitres, 10 centilitres, one decilitre or 0.1 litre and, for those marketed by weight, to a quantity of 100 grams.

3. The unit price of pre–packaged foodstuffs shall refer to the quantity declared, in accordance with national and Community provisions. Where two or more quantities are declared on the packaging, the Member States may determine which one is to be used to calculate the unit price.

Article 7

1. Member States may waive the obligation to indicate the unit price of foodstuffs marketed in bulk or pre–packaged for which such indication would be meaningless.

2. The foodstuffs referred to in paragraph 1 include in particular:
   (a) foodstuffs exempt from the obligation to indicate weight or volume (in particular foodstuffs sold by the piece);
   (b) different foodstuffs sold in a single package;
   (c) foodstuffs sold from automatic dispensers;
   (d) prepared dishes or dishes of preparation contained in a single package;
   (e) fancy products;
   (f) multipacks referred to in the first subparagraph of Article 4 of Directive 80/232 where they are made up of individual items corresponding to one of the values appearing in a Community quantity range.

3. Highly perishable foodstuffs may, if sold at reduced prices on account of the danger of their deteriorating, be exempted by the Member States from the requirement to indicate the new unit price.

4. Member States may exempt from the requirement to indicate the unit price foodstuffs of less than fifty grams or 50 millilitres and those exceeding 10 kilograms or 10 litres.

Article 8

1. The obligation to indicate the unit price shall not apply to:
   – foodstuffs pre–packaged in pre–established quantities referred to in Article 6(1) of Directive 73/241,
   – foodstuffs pre–packaged in pre–established quantities referred to in Article 6(2) of Directive 73/241,
   – foodstuffs pre–packaged in pre–established quantities referred to in Article 1 (points 1, 2 and 3) of Directive 73/437,

- foodstuffs pre–packaged in pre–established quantities referred to in Article 4 of Directive 77/436,
- foodstuffs pre–packaged in pre–established quantities listed in Annex III points 1, 2, 4, 5 and 6 to Directive 75/106, where they are sold in the ranges of nominal volumes given in columns I and II of the said Annex,
- foodstuffs pre–packaged in pre–established quantities referred to in Annex I (except for points 1.2, 1.5.4, 1.8, 2 and 3) to Directive 80/232, where they are sold in the ranges of nominal quantities of contents given in the said Annex.

2. The obligation to indicate the unit price may be waived by the Member States for:

- foodstuffs pre–packaged in pre–established quantities referred to in Annex III, points 3, 7, 8 and 9 to Directive 75/106, where they are sold in the nominal volumes given in columns I and II of the said Annex,
- foodstuffs pre–packaged in pre–established quantities referred to in Annex III to Directive 75/106, where they are sold in re–usable bottles in nominal volumes of 0.70 litre, and foodstuffs pre–packaged in pre–established quantities referred to in points l(c), 2(b), 3 and 7 in Annex III to Directive 75/106, where they are sold in re–usable bottles in nominal volumes of 0.5 pint, 1.0 pint, 1¹/₃ pint and 2.0 pints,
- foodstuffs pre–packaged in pre–established quantities listed in Annex I, points 1.2, 1.5.4, 1.8, 2 and 3, and in Annex II, points 1 and 2 to Directive 80/232, where they are sold in the ranges of nominal quantities given in the said Annexes, and foodstuffs pre–packaged in pre–established quantities listed in Annex I to Directive 80/232 where they are sold in the ranges of nominal quantities of contents given in Annex III to the said Directive.

3. The obligation to indicate the unit price may be waived by the Member States for pre–packaged foodstuffs listed in paragraphs 1 and 2, where they are sold in quantities which are smaller than the lowest or larger than the highest values in the Community ranges.

Article 9

When Community measures are adopted concerning the harmonisation of ranges of nominal quantities relating to foodstuffs pre–packaged in pre–established quantities or the ranges of quantities previously adopted are revised, the Council, acting on a proposal from the Commission, shall amend Article 8.

Article 10

As a transitional measure, Member States shall be allowed a period of seven years from the date of adoption of Directive 88/314/EEC to apply the provisions of this Directive relating to the foodstuffs pre–packaged in pre–established quantities referred to in the Annex. During this transitional period, any national measures or practices existing at the date of adoption of Directive 88/314 relating to these foodstuffs may be maintained in force.

Until the expiry of the transitional period during which use of the imperial system of units of measurement if authorised by Community provisions relating to units of measurement, the competent national authorities in Ireland and the United Kingdom shall determine, for each foodstuff or each category of foodstuffs, the units of mass or volume of international system or the imperial system in which indication of the unit price is compulsory.

Article 11

1. Member States may exempt pre–packaged foodstuffs which are sold by certain small retail businesses and handed directly by the seller to the purchaser from the obligation to indicate the unit price, where the indication of unit prices:
   – is likely to constitute an excessive burden for such businesses, or
   – appears to be impracticable owing to the number of foodstuffs offered for sale, the sales area, its layout or the conditions peculiar to certain forms of trading, such as particular types of itinerant trading.

2. The exemptions referred to in paragraph 1 shall be without prejudice to more stringent obligations to indicate prices existing under national provisions at the time of the notification of Directive 88/314.

Article 12

1. Member States shall bring into force the laws, regulations and administrative provisions necessary to comply with this Directive within 24 months of the date of its notification. They shall forthwith inform the Commission thereof.

2. Member States shall communicate to the Commission the texts of the provisions of national law which they adopt in the field covered by this Directive.

3. The Commission shall submit to the Council by 1 July 1983, a report on the exemptions granted by the Member States pursuant to Articles 1(3) and 7(1) and (2), accompanied by a proposal for revision in the light of

experience. On the basis of this report and the proposal for revision the Council shall decide to maintain or amend or to delete all or part of the provisions relating to the aforesaid exemptions.

Article 13

This Directive is addressed to the Member States.

Done at Luxembourg, 19 June 1979.

Annex omitted.

Appendix 6

Council Directive 88/314/EEC of 7 June 1988 on Consumer Protection in the Indication of the Prices of Non–Food Products (footnotes omitted).

THE COUNCIL OF THE EUROPEAN COMMUNITIES,

Having regard to the Treaty establishing the European Economic Community, and in particular Article 100a thereof,

Having regard to the proposal from the Commission,

In co–operation with the European Parliament,

Having regard to the opinion of the Economic and Social Committee,

Whereas the programmes of the Community for a consumer protection and information policy provide for the establishment of common principles for indicating prices;

Whereas Council Directive 79/581 of 19 June 1979 on consumer protection in the indication of the prices of foodstuffs makes it compulsory to indicate the prices of foodstuffs; whereas the Council resolution of 19 June 1979 on the indication of the prices of foodstuffs and non–food household products pre–packaged in pre–established quantities invites the Commission to submit a proposal concerning the indication of the selling price and the unit price for non–food household products;

Whereas it is important to adopt measures with the aim of progressively establishing the internal market over a period expiring on 31 December 1992 at the latest;

Whereas indication of the selling price and the unit price of non–food products makes it easier for consumers to compare prices at places of sale; whereas it accordingly increases market transparency and ensures greater protection for consumers;

Whereas the obligation to indicate these prices must apply in principle to all non–food products offered to the final consumer; whereas this obligation must also apply to written or printed advertising and catalogues wherever these give the selling prices of the products;

Whereas the selling price and the unit price must be indicated in accordance with specific procedures for each category of products so as not to place an undue burden on the retailer as regards labelling;

Whereas the obligation to indicate the unit price may be waived by Member States for products in respect of which such indication would be meaningless;

Whereas, in the case of pre–packaged products, the obligation to indicate the unit price should, wherever possible, be replaced by standardisation of quantities; whereas account should be taken of the progress made as regards the standardisation at Community level of quantity ranges for products pre–packaged in pre–established quantities and provision should therefore be made for the exemption of ranges of quantities so standardised;

Whereas Council Directive 80/232, as last amended by Directive 87/356, lays down the ranges of nominal quantities and nominal capacities permitted for certain pre–packaged products;

Whereas the rules laid down in this Directive are aimed at informing and protecting consumers.

HAS ADOPTED THIS DIRECTIVE:

Article 1

1. This Directive relates to the indication of the selling price and the price per unit of measurement of non–food products offered to the final consumer or advertised indicating the price, whether they are sold in bulk or pre–packaged in pre–established or variable quantities.
2. This Directive shall not apply to:
–   products bought for the purpose of a trade or commercial activity,
–   products supplied in the course of the provision of a service,
–   private sales,
–   sales by auction and sales of works of art and antiques.

Article 2

For the purposes of this Directive:
(a) 'products sold in bulk' means products which are not pre–packaged and/or are not measured or weighed except in the presence of the final consumer;
(b) 'products sold by individual item' means products which cannot be broken down without changing their nature or properties;
(c) 'pre–packaged products' means products packaged other than in the consumer's presence, whether the packaging encloses the product completely or only partially;
(d) 'products pre–packaged in pre–established quantities' means products pre–packaged in such a way that the quantity in the package corresponds to a previously selected value;
(e) 'products pre–packaged in variable quantities' means products pre–packaged in such a way that the quantity in the package does not correspond to a previously selected value;
(f) 'selling price' means the price for a given quantity of the product;
(g) 'unit price' means the price for one kilogram, one litre, one metre or one square metre of the product, subject to Article 6(2) and the second subparagraph of Article 10.

Article 3

1. The products referred to in Article 1 shall bear an indication of the selling price under the conditions laid down in Article 4.
2. The products pre–packaged in pre–established quantities listed in the Annex and the products pre–packaged in variable quantities shall also bear an indication of the unit price, subject to Articles 7 to 10.
3. The unit price of products sold in bulk must be indicated. However, Member States may specify the conditions under which the selling price per piece may be indicated for certain categories of these products.
4. The selling price and the unit price shall relate to the final price of the product under the conditions laid down by the Member States.

Article 4

The selling price and the unit price must be unambiguous, easily identifiable and clearly legible. Each Member State may 'lay down the specific rules for such indication of prices', e.g. by means of posters, labels on shelves or on packaging.

Article 5

Any written or printed advertisement and any catalogue which mentions the selling price of products referred to in Article 1 shall indicate the unit price, subject to Article 3(2).

Article 6

1. The unit price shall be expressed as a price per litre or per cubic metre for products sold by volume, as a price per kilogram or per tonne for products sold by weight, as a price per metre for products sold by length and as a price per square metre for products sold by area.
2. Member States may, however, allow the unit price to be expressed in relation to decimal multiples or fractions of the units referred to in paragraph 1, in order to take account of the quantities in which certain products are normally sold.
3. The unit price of pre–packaged products shall refer to the quantity declared, in accordance with national and Community provisions.

Article 7

1. Member States may waive the obligation to indicate the unit price of products sold in bulk or pre–packaged for which such indication would be meaningless.
2. The products referred to in paragraph 1 include in particular:
   (a) products exempted from the obligation to indicate weight or volume (in particular products sold by individual item);
   (b) different products sold in a single package;
   (c) products sold from automatic dispensers;
   (d) products contained in a single package from which a mixture is to be prepared;
   (e) multipacks referred to in the first subparagraph of Article 4 of Directive 80/232, where they are made up of individual items corresponding to one of the values appearing in a Community quantity range.

Article 8

1. The obligation to indicate the unit price shall not apply to the products listed in Annex I, points 5, 8.2, 8.3, 8.5, 8.6, 9, 10 and 11 to Directive

80/232, where they are sold in the ranges of nominal quantities of contents given in the said Annex.

2. The obligation to indicate the unit price may be waived by the Member States for:

- the products listed in Annex I, points 4, 6, 7, 8.1 and 8.4 to Directive 80/232, where they are sold in the ranges of nominal quantities of contents given in the said Annex,
- the products referred to in Annex II, point 3 to Directive 80/232, where they are sold in rigid containers in capacity ranges given in the said Annex and are not listed in Annex I to the said Directive,
- the products referred to in Annex I to the Directive 80/232, where they are sold in rigid containers in capacity ranges given in Annex III to the said Directive.

3. The obligation to indicate the unit price may be waived by the Member States for the pre–packaged products listed in paragraphs 1 and 2, where they are sold in quantities which are smaller than the lowest or larger than the highest values in the Community ranges.

Article 9

When Community measures are adopted concerning the harmonisation of ranges of quantities relating to products pre–packaged in pre–established quantities or when the ranges of quantities previously adopted are revised, the Council, acting on a proposal from the Commission, shall amend Article 8.

Article 10

As a transitional measure, Member States shall be allowed a period of seven years from the date of adoption of this Directive to apply the provisions of this Directive relating to the products pre–packaged in pre–established quantities referred to in the Annex. During this transitional period, any national measures or practices existing at the date of adoption of this Directive and relating to these products may be maintained in force.

Until the expiry of the transitional period during which use of the imperial system of units of measurement is authorised by Community provisions relating to units of measurement, the competent national authorities in Ireland and the United Kingdom shall determine, for each product or each category of product, the units of mass, volume, length or area of the international system or the imperial system in which indication of the unit price is compulsory.

Article 11

1. Member States may exempt pre–packaged products which are sold by certain small retail businesses and handed directly by the seller to the purchaser from the obligation to indicate the unit price, where the indication of unit prices:
-   is likely to constitute an excessive burden for such businesses, or
-   appears to be impracticable owing to the number of products offered for sale, the sales area, its layout or the conditions peculiar to certain forms of trading, such as particular types of itinerant trading.

2. The exemptions referred to in paragraph 1 shall be without prejudice to more stringent obligations to indicate prices existing under national provisions at the time of adoption of this Directive.

Article 12

1. Member States shall bring into force the laws, regulations and administrative provisions necessary to comply with this Directive within two years of its adoption. They shall forthwith inform the Commission thereof.

2. Member States shall communicate to the Commission the texts of the provisions of national law which they adopt in the field governed by this Directive.

Article 13

This Directive is addressed to the Member States.

Done at Luxembourg, 7 June 1988.

Annex omitted.

Appendix 7

Council Directive 85/577/EEC of 20 December 1985 to Protect the Consumer in respect of Contracts Negotiated Away from Business Premises (footnotes omitted).

THE COUNCIL OF THE EUROPEAN COMMUNITIES,

Having regard to the Treaty establishing the European Economic Community, and in particular Article 100 thereof,

Having regard to the proposal from the Commission,

Having regard to the opinion of the European Parliament,

Having regard to the opinion of the Economic and Social Committee,

Whereas it is a common form of commercial practice in the Member States for the conclusion of a contract or a unilateral engagement between a trader and consumer to be made away from the business premises of the trader, and whereas such contracts and engagements are the subject of legislation which differs from one Member State to another;

Whereas any disparity between such legislation may directly affect the functioning of the common market; whereas it is therefore necessary to approximate laws in this field;

Whereas the preliminary programme of the European Economic Community for a consumer protection and information policy provides *inter alia*, under paragraphs 24 and 25, that appropriate measures be taken to protect consumers against unfair commercial practices in respect of doorstep selling; whereas the second programme of the European Economic Community for a consumer protection and information policy confirmed that the action and priorities defined in the preliminary programme would be pursued;

Whereas the special feature of contracts concluded away from the business premises of the trader is that as a rule it is the trader who initiates the contract negotiations, for which the consumer is unprepared or which he does not accept; whereas the consumer is often unable to compare the quality and price of the offer with other offers; whereas this surprise element generally exists not only in contracts made at the doorstep but also in other forms of contract concluded by the trader away from his business premises;

Whereas the consumer should be given a right of cancellation over a period of at least seven days in order to enable him to assess the obligations arising under the contract;

Whereas appropriate measures should be taken to ensure that the consumer is informed in writing of this period for reflection;

Whereas the freedom of Member States to maintain or introduce a total or partial prohibition on the conclusion of contracts away from business premises, inasmuch as they consider this to be in the interest of consumers, must not be affected;

HAS ADOPTED THIS DIRECTIVE:

Article 1

1. This Directive shall apply to contracts under which a trader supplies goods or services to a consumer and which are concluded:
–   during an excursion organised by the trader away from his business premises, or
–   during a visit by a trader
    (i) to the consumer's home or to that of another consumer;
    (ii) to the consumer's place of work;
where the visit does not take place at the express request of the consumer.
2. This Directive shall also apply to contracts for the supply of goods or services other than those concerning which the consumer requested the visit of the trader, provided that when he requested the visit the consumer did not know, or could not reasonably have known, that the supply of those other goods or services formed part of the trader's commercial or professional activities.
3. This Directive shall also apply to contracts in respect of which an offer was made by the consumer under conditions similar to those described in paragraph 1 or paragraph 2 although the consumer was not bound by that offer before its acceptance by the trader.
4. This Directive shall also apply to offers made contractually by the consumer under conditions similar to those described in paragraph 1 or paragraph 2 where the consumer is bound by his offer.

Article 2

For the purposes of this Directive:

'consumer' means a natural person who, in transactions covered by this Directive, is acting for purposes which can be regarded as outside his trade or profession;

'trader' means a natural or legal person who, for the transaction in question, acts in his commercial or professional capacity, and anyone acting in the name or on behalf of a trader.

Article 3

1. The Member States may decide that this Directive shall apply only to contracts for which the payment to be made by the consumer exceeds a specified amount. This amount may not exceed 60 ECU.

The Council, acting on a proposal from the Commission, shall examine and, if necessary, revise this amount for the first time no later than four years after notification of the Directive and thereafter every two years, taking into account economic and monetary developments in the Community.

2. This Directive shall not apply to:

(a) contracts for the construction, sale and rental of immovable property or contracts concerning other rights relating to immovable property.

Contracts for the supply of goods and for their incorporation in immovable property or contracts for repairing immovable property shall fall within the scope of this Directive;

(b) contracts for the supply of foodstuffs or beverages or other goods intended for current consumption in the household and supplied by regular roundsmen;

(c) contracts for the supply of goods or services, provided that all three of the following conditions are met:

(i) the contract is concluded on the basis of a trader's catalogue which the consumer has a proper opportunity of reading in the absence of the trader's representative,

(ii) there is intended to be continuity of contact between the trader's representative and the consumer in relation to that or any subsequent transaction,

(iii) both the catalogue and the contract clearly inform the consumer of his right to return goods to the supplier within a period of not less than seven days of receipt or otherwise to cancel the contract within that period without obligation of any kind other than to take reasonable care of the goods;

(d) insurance contracts;

(e)   contracts for securities.

3. By way of derogation from Article 1(2), Member States may refrain from applying this Directive to contracts for the supply of goods or services having a direct connection with the goods or services concerning which the consumer requested the visit of the trader.

Article 4

In the case of transactions within the scope of Article 1, traders shall be required to give consumers written notice of their right of cancellation within the period laid down in Article 5, together with the name and address of a person against whom that right may be exercised.

Such notice shall be dated and shall state particulars enabling the contract to be identified. It shall be given to the consumer:

(a)   in the case of Article 1(1), at the time of conclusion of the contract;

(b)   in the case of Article 1(2), not later than the time of conclusion of the contract;

(c)   in the case of Articles 1(3) and 1(4), when the offer is made by the consumer.

Member States shall ensure that their national legislation lays down appropriate consumer protection measures in cases where the information referred to in this Article is not supplied.

Article 5

1. The consumer shall have the right to renounce the effects of his undertaking by sending notice within a period of not less than seven days from receipt by the consumer of the notice referred to in Article 4, in accordance with the procedure laid down by national law. It shall be sufficient if the notice is dispatched before the end of such period.

2. The giving of the notice shall have the effect of releasing the consumer from any obligations under the cancelled contract.

Article 6

The consumer may not waive the rights conferred on him by this Directive.

Article 7

If the consumer exercises his right of renunciation, the legal effects of such renunciation shall be governed by national laws, particularly regarding the reimbursement of payments for goods or services provided and the return of goods received.

Article 8

This Directive shall not prevent Member States from adopting or maintaining more favourable provisions to protect consumers in the field which it covers.

Article 9

1. Member States shall take the measures necessary to comply with this Directive within 24 months of its notification. They shall forthwith inform the Commission thereof.
2. Member States shall ensure that the texts of the main provisions of national law which they adopt in the field covered by this Directive are communicated to the Commission.

Article 10

This Directive is addressed to the Member States.

Done at Brussels, 20 December 1985.

Appendix 8

Council Directive 87/102/EEC of 22 December 1986 for the Approximation of the Laws, Regulations and Administrative Provisions of the Member States Concerning Consumer Credit (as amended, footnotes omitted).

THE COUNCIL OF THE EUROPEAN COMMUNITIES,

Having regard to the Treaty establishing the European Economic Community, and in particular Article 100 thereof,

Having regard to the proposal from the Commission,

Having regard to the opinion of the European Parliament,

Having regard to the opinion of the Economic and Social Committee,

Whereas wide differences exist in the laws of the Member States in the field of consumer credit;

Whereas these differences of law can lead to distortions of competition between grantors of credit in the common market;

Whereas these differences limit the opportunities the consumer has to obtain credit in other Member States; whereas they affect the volume and the nature of the credit sought, and also the purchase of goods and services;

Whereas, as a result, these differences have an influence on the free movement of goods and services obtainable by consumers on credit and thus directly affect the functioning of the common market;

Whereas, given the increasing volume of credit granted in the Community to consumers, the establishment of a common market in consumer credit would benefit alike consumers, grantors of credit, manufacturers, wholesalers and retailers of goods and providers of services;

Whereas the programmes of the European Economic Community for a consumer protection and information policy provide, *inter alia*, that the consumer should be protected against unfair credit terms and that a harmonisation of the general conditions governing consumer credit should be undertaken as a priority;

Whereas differences of law and practice result in unequal consumer protection in the field of consumer credit from one Member State to another;

Whereas there has been much change in recent years in the types of credit available to and used by consumers; whereas new forms of consumer credit have emerged and continue to develop;

Whereas the consumer should receive adequate information on the conditions and cost of credit and on his obligations; whereas this information should include, *inter alia,* the annual percentage rate of charge for credit, or, failing that, the total amount that the consumer must pay for credit; whereas, pending a decision on a Community method or methods of calculating the annual percentage rate of charge, Member States should be able to retain existing methods or practices for calculating this rate, or failing that, should establish provisions for indicating the total cost of the credit to the consumer;

Whereas the terms of credit may be disadvantageous to the consumer; whereas better protection of consumers can be achieved by adopting certain requirements which are to apply to all forms of credit;

Whereas, having regard to the character of certain credit agreements or types of transaction, these agreements or transactions should be partially or entirely excluded from the field of application of this Directive;

Whereas it should be possible for Member States, in consultation with the Commission, to exempt from the Directive certain forms of credit of a non–commercial character granted under particular conditions;

Whereas the practices existing in some Member States in respect of authentic acts drawn up before a notary or judge are such as to render the application of certain provisions of this Directive unnecessary in the case of such acts; whereas it should therefore be possible for Member States to exempt such acts from those provisions;

Whereas credit agreements for very large financial amounts tend to differ from the usual consumer credit agreements; whereas the application of the provisions of this Directive to agreements for very small amounts could create unnecessary burdens both for consumers and grantors of credit; whereas therefore, agreements above or below specified financial limits should be excluded from the Directive;

Whereas the provision of information on the cost of credit in advertising and at the business premises of the creditor or credit broker can make it easier for the consumer to compare different offers;

Whereas consumer protection is further improved if credit agreements are made in writing and contain certain minimum particulars concerning the contractual terms;

Whereas, in the case of credit granted for the acquisition of goods, Member States should lay down the conditions in which goods may be repossessed, particularly if the consumer has not given his consent; whereas the account between the parties should upon repossession be made up in such manner as to ensure that the repossession does not entail any unjustified enrichment;

Whereas the consumer should be allowed to discharge his obligations before the due date; whereas the consumer should then be entitled to an equitable reduction in the total cost of the credit;

Whereas the assignment of the creditor's rights arising under a credit agreement should not be allowed to weaken the position of the consumer;

Whereas those Member States which permit consumers to use bills of exchange, promissory note or cheques in connection with credit agreement should ensure that the consumer is suitably protected when so using such instruments;

Whereas, as regards goods or services which the consumer has contracted to acquire on credit, the consumer should, at least in the circumstances defined below, have rights *vis-à-vis* the grantor of credit which are in addition to his normal contractual rights against him and against the supplier of the goods or services; whereas the circumstances referred to above are those where the grantor of credit and the supplier of goods or services have a pre–existing agreement whereunder credit is made available exclusively by that grantor of credit to customers of the supplier for the purpose of enabling the consumer to acquire goods or services from the latter;

Whereas the ECU is as defined in Council Regulation (EEC) 3180/78, as last amended by Regulation (EEC) 2626/84; whereas Member States should to a limited extent be at liberty to round off the amounts in national currency resulting from the conversion of amounts of this Directive expressed in ECU; whereas the amounts in this Directive should be periodically re–examined in the light of economic and monetary trends in the Community, and, if need be revised;

Whereas suitable measures should be adopted by Member States for authorising persons offering credit or offering to arrange credit agreements or for inspecting or monitoring the activities of persons granting credit or arranging for credit to be granted or for enabling consumers to complain about credit agreements or credit conditions;

Whereas credit agreements should not derogate, to the detriment of the consumer, from the provisions adopted in implementation of this Directive or corresponding to its provisions; whereas those provisions should not be circumvented as a result of the way in which agreements are formulated;

Whereas, since this Directive provides for a certain degree of approximation of the laws, regulations and administrative provisions of the Member States concerning consumer credit and for a certain level of consumer protection, Member States should not be prevented from retaining or adopting more stringent measures to protect the consumer, with due regard for their obligations under the Treaty;

Whereas not later than 1 January 1995, the Commission should present to the Council a report concerning the operation of this Directive,

HAS ADOPTED THIS DIRECTIVE:

Article 1

1. This Directive applies to credit agreements.
2. For the purpose of this Directive:
   (a) 'consumer' means a natural person who, in transactions covered by this Directive, is acting for purposes which can be regarded as outside his trade or profession;
   (b) 'creditor' means a natural or legal person who grants credit in the course of his trade, business or profession or a group of such persons;
   (c) 'credit agreement' means an agreement whereby a creditor grants or promises to grant to a consumer a credit in the form of a deferred payment, a loan or other similar financial accommodation.
   Agreements for the provision on a continuing basis of a service or a utility, where the consumer has the right to pay for them, for the duration of their provision, by means of instalments, are not deemed to be credit agreements for the purpose of this Directive;
   (d) 'total cost of the credit to the consumer' means all the costs, including interest and other charges, which the consumer has to pay for the credit';

(e) 'annual percentage rate of charge' means the total cost of the credit to the consumer expressed as an annual percentage of the amount of the credit granted and calculated in accordance with Article 1a.

Article 1a

1. (a) The annual percentage rate of charge, which shall be that equivalent, on an annual basis, to the present value of all commitments (loans, repayments and charges), future or existing, agreed by the creditor and the borrower, shall be calculated in accordance with the mathematical formula set out in Annex II.
    (b) Four examples of the method of calculation are given in Annex III, by way of illustration.

2. For the purposes of calculating the annual percentage rate of charge, the 'total cost of the credit to the consumer' as defined in Article 1(2)(d) shall be determined, with the exception of the following charges:

(i) charges payable by the borrower for non–compliance with any of his commitments laid down in the credit agreement;

(ii) charges other than the purchase price which in purchases of goods or services, the consumer is obliged to pay whether the transaction is paid in cash or by credit;

(iii) charges for the transfer of funds and charges for keeping an account intended to receive payments towards the reimbursement of the credit the payment of interest and other charges except where the consumer does not have reasonable freedom of choice in the matter and where such charges are abnormally high; this provision shall not, however, apply to charges for collection of such reimbursements or payments, whether made in cash or otherwise;

(iv) membership subscriptions to associations or groups and arising from agreements separate from the credit agreement, even though such subscriptions have an effect on the credit terms;

(v) charges for insurance or guarantees; included are, however those designed to ensure payment to the creditor, in the event of the death, invalidity, illness or unemployment of the consumer, of a sum equal to or less than the total amount of the credit together with relevant interest and other charges which have to be imposed by the creditor as a condition for credit being granted.

3. (a) Where credit transactions referred to in this Directive are subject to the provisions of national laws in force on 1 March 1990 which impose maximum limits on the annual percentage rate of charge of such transactions and, where such provisions permit standard costs other than those described in paragraph 2(i) to (v)

not to be included in those maximum limits, Member States may, solely in respect of such transactions, not include the aforementioned costs when calculating the annual percentage rate of charge, as stipulated in this Directive, provided that there is a requirement, in the cases mentioned in Article 3 and in the credit agreement, that the consumer be informed of the amount and inclusion thereof in the payments to be made.

(b)   Member States may no longer apply point (a) from the date of entry into force of the single mathematical formula for calculating the annual percentage rate of charge in the Community, pursuant to the provisions of paragraph 5(c).

4.   (a)   The annual percentage rate of charge shall be calculated at the time the credit contract is concluded, without prejudice to the provisions of Article 3 concerning advertisements and special offers.

(b)   The calculation shall be made on the assumption that the credit contract is valid for the period agreed and that the creditor and the consumer fulfil their obligations under the terms and by the dates agreed.

5.   (a)   As a transitional measure, notwithstanding the provisions of paragraph 1(a), Member States which, prior to 1 March 1990, applied legal provisions whereby a mathematical formula different from that given in Annex II could be used for calculating the annual percentage rate of charge, may continue applying that formula within their territory for a period of three years starting from 1 January 1993.

Member States shall take the appropriate measures to ensure that only one mathematical formula for calculating the annual percentage rate of charge is used within their territory.

(b)   Six months before the expiry of the time limit laid down in point (a) the Commission shall submit to the Council a report, accompanied by a proposal, which will make it possible in the light of experience, to apply a single Community mathematical formula for calculating the annual percentage rate of charge.

(c)   The Council shall, acting by a qualified majority on the basis of the proposal from the Commission, take a decision before 1 January 1996.

6. In the case of credit contracts containing clauses allowing variations in the rate of interest and the amount or level of other charges contained in the annual percentage rate of charge but unquantifiable at the time when it is calculated, the annual percentage rate of charge shall be calculated on the assumption that interest and other charges remain fixed and will apply until the end of the credit contract.

7. Where necessary, the following assumptions may be made in calculating the annual percentage rate of charge:
- if the contract does not specify a credit limit, the amount of credit granted shall be equal to the amount fixed by the relevant Member State, without exceeding a figure equivalent to ECU 2,000;
- if there is no fixed timetable for repayment, and one cannot be deduced from the terms of the agreement and the means for repaying the credit granted, the duration of the credit shall be deemed to be one year;
- unless otherwise specified, where the contract provides for more than one repayment date, the credit will be made available and the repayments made at the earliest time provided for in the agreement.

Article 2

1. This Directive shall not apply to:
(a) credit agreements or agreements promising to grant credit:
- intended primarily for the purpose of acquiring or retaining property rights in land or in an existing or projected building,
- intended for the purpose of renovating or improving a building as such;
(b) hiring agreements except where these provide that the title will pass ultimately to the hirer;
(c) credit granted or made available without payment of interest or any other charge;
(d) credit agreements under which no interest is charged provided the consumer agrees to repay the credit in a single payment;
(e) credit in the form of advances on a current account granted by a credit institution or financial institution other than on credit card accounts. Nevertheless, the provisions of Article 6 shall apply to such credits;
(f) credit agreements involving amounts less than 200 ECU or more than 20,000 ECU;
(g) credit agreements under which the consumer is required to repay the credit:
- either, within a period not exceeding three months,
- or, by a maximum number of four payments within a period not exceeding 12 months.
2. A Member State may, in consultation with the Commission, exempt from the application of this Directive certain types of credit which fulfil the following conditions:
- they are granted at rates of charge below those prevailing in the market, and
- they are not offered to the public generally.

3. The provisions of Article 1a and of Articles 4 to 12 shall not apply to credit agreements or agreements promising to grant credit, secured by mortgage on immovable property, insofar as these are not already excluded from the Directive under paragraph 1(a).

4. Member States may exempt from the provisions of Article 6 to 12 credit agreements in the form of an authentic act signed before a notary or judge.

Article 3

Without prejudice to Council Directive 84/450 of 10 September 1984, relating to the approximation of the laws, regulations and administrative provisions of the Member States concerning misleading advertising, and to the rules and principles applicable to unfair advertising, any advertisement, or any offer which is displayed at business premises, in which a person offers credit or offers to arrange a credit agreement and in which a rate of interest or any figures relating to the cost of the credit are indicated, shall also include a statement of the annual percentage rate of charge, by means of a representative example if no other means is practicable.

Article 4

1. Credit agreements shall be made in writing. The consumer shall receive a copy of the written agreement.

2. The written agreement shall include:
   (a) a statement of the annual percentage rate of charge;
   (b) a statement of the conditions under which the annual percentage rate of charge may be amended.
   In cases where it is not possible to state the annual percentage rate of charge, the consumer shall be provided with adequate information in the written agreement. This information shall at least include the information provided for in the second indent of Article 6(1).
   (c) a statement of the amount, number and frequency or dates of the payments which the consumer must make to repay the credit, as well as of the payments for interest and other charges; the total amount of these payments should also be indicated where possible;
   (d) a statement of the cost items referred to in Article 1a(2) with the exception of expenditure related to the breach of contractual obligations which were not included in the calculation of the annual percentage rate of charge but which have to be paid by the consumer in given circumstances, together with a statement identifying such circumstances. Where the exact amount of those items is known, that

sum is to be indicated; if that is not the case, either a method of calculation or as accurate an estimate as possible is to be provided where possible.

3. The written agreement shall further include the other essential terms of the contract.

By way of illustration, the Annex to this Directive contains a list of terms which Member States may require to be included in the written agreement as being essential.

Article 5

(Deleted)

Article 6

1. Notwithstanding the exclusion provided for in Article 2(1)(e), where there is an agreement between a credit institution or financial institution and a consumer for the granting of credit in the form of an advance on a current account, other than on credit card accounts, the consumer shall be informed at the time or before the agreement is concluded–
- of the credit limit, if any,
- of the annual rate of interest and the charges applicable from the time the agreement is concluded and the conditions under which these may be amended,
- of the procedure for terminating the agreement.
  This information shall be confirmed in writing.

2. Furthermore, during the period of the agreement, the consumer shall be informed of any change in the annual rate of interest or in the relevant charges at the time it occurs. Such information may be given in a statement of account or in any other manner acceptable to Member States.

3. In Member States where tacitly accepted overdrafts are permissible, the Member States concerned shall ensure that the consumer is informed of the annual rate of interest and the charges applicable, and of any amendment thereof, where the overdraft extends beyond a period of three months.

Article 7

In the case of credit granted for the acquisition of goods, Member States shall lay down the conditions under which goods may be repossessed, in particular if the consumer has not given his consent. They shall further ensure that where the creditor recovers possession of the goods the account between the parties shall be made up so as to ensure that the repossession does not entail any unjustified enrichment.

Article 8

The consumer shall be entitled to discharge his obligations under a credit agreement before the time fixed by the agreement. In this event, in accordance with the rules laid down by the Member States, the consumer shall be entitled to an equitable reduction in the total cost of the credit.

Article 9

Where the creditor's rights under a credit agreement are assigned to a third person, the consumer shall be entitled to plead against the third person any defence which was available to him against the original creditor, including set–off where the latter is permitted in the Member State concerned.

Article 10

The Member States which, in connection with credit agreements, permit the consumer:
(a) to make payment by means of bills of exchange including promissory notes
(b) to give security by means of bills of exchange including promissory notes and cheques, shall ensure that the consumer is suitably protected when using these instruments in those ways.

Article 11

1. Member States shall ensure that the existence of a credit agreement shall not in any way affect the rights of the consumer against the supplier of goods or services purchased by means of such an agreement in cases where the goods or services are not supplied or are otherwise not in conformity with the contract for their supply.
2. Where:
(a) in order to buy goods or obtain services the consumer enters into a credit agreement with a person other than the supplier of them; and

(b) the grantor of the credit and the supplier of the goods or services have a pre–existing agreement whereunder credit is made available exclusively by that grantor of credit customers of that supplier for the acquisition of goods or services from that supplier; and

(c) the consumer referred to in subparagraph (a) obtains his credit pursuant to that pre–existing agreement; and

(d) the goods or services covered by the credit agreement are not supplied, or are supplied only in part, or are not in conformity with the contract for supply of them; and

(e) the consumer has pursued his remedies against the supplier but has failed to obtain the satisfaction to which he is entitled,

the consumer shall have the right to pursue remedies against the grantor of credit. Member States shall determine to what extent and under what conditions these remedies shall be exercisable.

3. Paragraph 2 shall not apply where the individual transaction in question is for an amount less than the equivalent of 200 ECU.

Article 12

1. Member States shall:

(a) ensure that persons offering credit or offering to arrange credit agreements shall obtain official authorisation to do so, either specifically or as suppliers of goods and services; or

(b) ensure that persons granting credit or arranging for credit to be granted shall be subject to inspection or monitoring of their activities by an institution or official body; or

(c) promote the establishment of appropriate bodies to receive complaints concerning credit agreements or credit conditions and to provide relevant information or advice to consumers regarding them.

2. Member States may provide that the authorisation referred to in paragraph 1(a) shall not be required where persons offering to conclude or arrange credit agreements satisfy the definition in Article 1 of the first Council Directive of 12 December 1977 on the co–ordination of laws, regulations and administrative provisions relating to the taking up and pursuit of the business of credit institutions and are authorised in accordance with the provisions of that Directive.

Where persons granting credit or arranging for credit to be granted have been authorised both specifically, under the provisions of paragraph 1(a) and also under the provisions of the aforementioned Directive, but the latter authorisation is subsequently withdrawn, the competent authority responsible for issuing the specific authorisation to grant credit under paragraph 1(a) shall be informed and shall decide whether the persons concerned may continue to grant credit, or arrange for credit to be granted, or whether the specific authorisation granted under paragraph 1(a) should be withdrawn.

Article 13

1. For the purposes of this Directive, the ECU shall be that defined by Regulation (EEC) No 3180/78, as amended by Regulation (EEC) No 2626/84. The equivalent in national currency shall initially be calculated at the rate obtaining on the date of adoption of this Directive.

Member States may round off the amounts in national currency resulting from the conversion of the amounts in ECU provided such rounding off does not exceed 10 ECU.

2. Every five years, and for the first time in 1995, the Council, acting on a proposal from the Commission, shall examine and, if need be, revise the amounts in this Directive, in the light of the economic and monetary trends in the Community.

Article 14

1. Member States shall ensure that credit agreements shall not derogate, to the detriment of the consumer, from the provisions of national law implementing or corresponding to this Directive.

2. Member States shall further ensure that the provisions which they adopt in implementation of this directive are not circumvented as a result of the way in which agreements are formulated, in particular by the device of distributing the amount of credit over several agreements.

Article 15

This Directive shall not preclude Member States from retaining or adopting more stringent provisions to protect consumers consistent with their obligations under the Treaty.

Article 16

1. Member States shall bring into force the measures necessary to comply with this Directive not later than 1 January 1990 and shall forthwith inform the Commission thereof.

2. Member States shall communicate to the Commission the texts of the main provisions of national law which they adopt in the field covered by this Directive.

Article 17

Not later than 1 January 1995 the Commission shall present a report to the Council concerning the operation of this Directive.

Article 18

This Directive is addressed to the Member States.

Done at Brussels, 22 December 1986.

Annex I

List of terms referred to Article 4(3)

1. Credit agreements for financing the supply of particular goods or services:
(i)   a description of the goods or services covered by the agreement;
(ii)   the cash price and the price payable under the credit agreement;
(iii) the amount of the deposit, if any, the number and amount of instalments and the dates on which they fall due, or the method of ascertaining any of the same if unknown at the time the agreement is concluded;
(iv)   an indication that the consumer will be entitled, as provided in Article 8, to a reduction if he repays early;
(v)   who owns the goods (if ownership does not pass immediately to the consumer) and the terms on which the consumer becomes the owner of them;
(vi)   a description of the security required, if any;
(vii) the cooling off period, if any;
(viii) an indication of the insurance(s) required, if any, and, when the choice of insurer is not left to the consumer, an indication of the cost thereof.
(ix)   the obligation on the consumer to save a certain amount of money which must be placed in a special account.
2. Credit agreements operated by credit cards:
(i)   the amount of the credit limit, if any;
(ii)   the terms of repayment or the means of determining them;
(iii) the cooling–off period, if any.

3. Credit agreements operated by running account which are not otherwise covered by the Directive:
(i)   the amount of the credit limit, if any, or the method of determining it;
(ii) the terms of use and repayment;
(iii) the cooling–off period, if any.
4. Other credit agreements covered by the Directive:
(i)   the amount of the credit limit, if any;
(ii) an indication of the security required, if any;
(iii) the terms of repayment:
(iv) the cooling–off period, if any;
(v)   an indication that the consumer will be entitled, as provided in Article 8, to a reduction if he repays early.

Annex II

The basic equation expressing the equivalence of loans on the one hand, and repayments and charges on the other:

$$\sum_{K=1}^{K=m} \frac{A_K}{(1+i)^{t_K}} = \sum_{K'=1}^{K'=m'} \frac{A'_{K'}}{(1+i)^{t_{K'}}}$$

Meaning of letters and symbols:

K   is the number of a loan
K'   is the number of a repayment or a payment of charges
A_K is the amount of loan number K
$A'_{K'}$ is the amount of repayment number K'
Σ represents a sum
m   is the number of the last loan
m'   is the number of the last repayment or payment of charges
t_K is the interval, expressed in years and fractions of a year, between the date of loan No 1 and those of subsequent loans Nos. 2 to m
$t_{K'}$ is the interval expressed in years and fractions of a year between the date of loan No 1 and those of repayments or payments of charges Nos 1 to m'

i   is the percentage rate that can be calculated (either by algebra, by successive approximations, or by a computer programme) where the other terms in the equation are known from the contract or otherwise.

Remarks

(a) The amounts paid by both parties at different times shall not necessarily be equal and shall not necessarily be paid at equal intervals.
(b) The starting date shall be that of the first loan.
(c) Intervals between dates used in the calculations shall be expressed in years or in fractions of a year.

Annex III

Examples of calculations

First example
Sum loaned S=ECU 1,000.
It is repaid in a single payment of ECU 12,000 made 18 months, i.e. 1.5 years, after the date of the loan.

The equation becomes $1{,}000 = \dfrac{1{,}200}{(1 + i)^{1.5}}$

$$\text{or } (1 + i)^{1.5} = 1.2$$
$$1 + i = 1.129243\ldots$$
$$i = 0.129243\ldots$$

This amount will be rounded down to 12.9 per cent or 12.92 per cent depending on whether the State or habitual practice allows the percentage to be rounded off to the first or second decimal.

Second example

The sum agreed is S=1,000 but the creditor retains ECU 50 for enquiry and administrative expenses, so that the loan is in fact ECU 950; the repayment of ECU 1,200, as in the first example, is made 18 months after the date of the loan.

$$\text{The equation becomes } 950 = \frac{1{,}200}{(1+i)^{1.5}}$$

$$\text{or } (1+i)^{1.5} = 1{,}200$$

$$\frac{}{950} = 1.263157\ldots$$

$$1+i = 1.16851\ldots$$

$$I = 0.16851\ldots$$

rounded off to 16.9% or 16.85%.

Third example

The sum lent is ECU 1,000, repayable in two amounts each of ECU 600, paid after one and two years respectively.

$$\text{The equation becomes } 1{,}000 = \frac{600}{1+i} + \frac{600}{(1+i)^2};$$

it is solved by algebra and produces i=0.1306623, rounded off to 13.1% or 13.07%.

Fourth example

The sum lent is ECU 1,000 and the amounts to be paid by the borrower are:

After three months	(0.25 years)	ECU 272
After six months	(0.50 years)	ECU 272
After twelve months	(1 year)	ECU 544
Total		ECU 1,088

The equation becomes:

$$1{,}000 = \frac{272}{(1+i)^{0.25}} + \frac{272}{(1+o)^{0.50}} + \frac{544}{1+i}$$

This equation allows i to be calculated by successive approximations, which can be programmed on a pocket computer.

i=0.1321 rounded off to 13.2 or 13.21%.

Appendix 9

Council Directive 90/314/EEC of 13 June 1990 on package travel, package holidays and package tours (footnotes omitted).

THE COUNCIL OF THE EUROPEAN COMMUNITIES,

Having regard to the Treaty establishing the European Economic Community, and in particular Article 100a thereof,

Having regard to the proposal from the Commission,

In co–operation with the European Parliament,

Having regard to the opinion of the Economic and Social Committee,

Whereas one of the main objectives of the Community is to complete the internal market, of which the tourist sector is an essential part;

Whereas the national laws of Member States concerning package travel, package holidays and package tours, hereinafter referred to as 'packages', show many disparities and national practices in this field are markedly different, which gives rise to obstacles to the freedom to provide services in respect of packages and distortions of competition amongst operators established in different Member States;

Whereas the establishment of common rules on packages will contribute to the elimination of these obstacles and thereby to the achievement of a common market in services, thus enabling operators established in one Member State to offer their services in other Member States and Community consumers to benefit from comparable conditions when buying a package in any Member State;

Whereas paragraph 36(b) of the Annex to the Council resolution of 19 May 1981 on a second programme of the European Economic Community for a consumer protection and information policy invites the Commission to study, *inter alia,* tourism and, if appropriate, to put forward suitable proposals, with due regard for their significance for consumer protection and the effects of differences in Member States' legislation on the proper functioning of the common market;

Whereas in the resolution on a Community policy on tourism on 10 April 1984 the Council welcomed the Commission's initiative in drawing attention to the importance of tourism and took note of the Commission's initial guidelines for a Community policy on tourism;

Whereas the Commission communication to the Council entitled 'A New Impetus for Consumer Protection Policy', which was approved by resolution of the Council on 6 May 1986, lists in paragraph 37, among the measures proposed by the Commission, the harmonisation of legislation on packages;

Whereas tourism plays an increasingly important role in the economies of the Member States; whereas the package system is a fundamental part of tourism; whereas the package travel industry in Member States would be stimulated to greater growth and productivity if at least a minimum of common rules were adopted in order to give it a Community dimension; whereas this would not only produce benefits for Community citizens buying packages organised on the basis of those rules, but would attract tourists from outside the Community seeking the advantages of guaranteed standards in packages;

Whereas disparities in the rules protecting consumers in different Member States are a disincentive to consumers in one Member State from buying packages in another Member State;

Whereas this disincentive is particularly effective in deterring consumers from buying packages outside their own Member State, and more effective than it would be in relation to the acquisition of other services, having regard to the special nature of the services supplied in a package which generally involve the expenditure of substantial amounts of money in advance and the supply of the services in a State other than that in which the consumer is resident;

Whereas the consumer should have the benefit of the protection introduced by this Directive irrespective of whether he is a direct contracting party, a transferee or a member of a group on whose behalf another person has concluded a contract in respect of a package;

Whereas the organiser of the package and/or the retailer of it should be under obligation to ensure that in descriptive matter relating to packages which they respectively organise and sell, the information which is given is not misleading and brochures made available to consumers contain information which is comprehensible and accurate;

Whereas the consumer needs to have a record of the terms of contract applicable to the package; whereas this can conveniently be achieved by requiring that all the terms of the contract be stated in writing or such other documentary form as shall be comprehensible and accessible to him, and that he be given a copy thereof;

Whereas the consumer should be at liberty in certain circumstances to transfer to a willing third person a booking made by him for a package;

Whereas the price established under the contract should not in principle be subject to revision except where the possibility of upward or downward revision is expressly provided for in the contract; whereas that possibility should nonetheless be subject to certain conditions;

Whereas the consumer should in certain circumstances be free to withdraw before departure from a package travel contract;

Whereas there should be a clear definition of the rights available to the consumer in circumstances where the organiser of the package cancels it before the agreed date of departure;

Whereas if, after the consumer has departed, there occurs a significant failure of performance of the services for which he has contracted or the organiser perceives that he will be unable to procure a significant part of the services to be provided; the organiser should have certain obligations towards the consumer;

Whereas the organiser and/or retailer party to the contract should be liable to the consumer for the proper performance of the obligations arising from the contract; whereas moreover, the organiser and/or retailer should be liable for the damage resulting for the consumer from failure to perform or improper performance of the contract unless the defects in the performance of the contract are attributable neither to any fault of theirs nor to that of another supplier of services;

Whereas in cases where the organiser and/or retailer is liable for failure to perform or improper performance of the services involved in the package, such liability should be limited in accordance with the international conventions governing such services, in particular the Warsaw Convention of 1929 in International Carriage by Air, the Berne Convention of 1961 on Carriage by Rail, the Athens Convention of 1974 on Carriage by Sea and the Paris Convention of 1962 on the Liability of Hotel–keepers; whereas, moreover, with regard to damage other than personal injury, it should be possible for liability also to be limited under the package contract provided, however, that such limits are not unreasonable;

Whereas certain arrangements should be made for the information of consumers and the handling of complaints;

Whereas both the consumer and the package travel industry would benefit if organisers and/or retailers were placed under an obligation to provide sufficient evidence of security in the event of insolvency;

Whereas Member States should be at liberty to adopt, or retain, more stringent provisions relating to package travel for the purpose of protecting the consumer.

HAS ADOPTED THIS DIRECTIVE:

Article 1

The purpose of this Directive is to approximate the laws, regulations and administrative provisions of the Member States relating to packages sold or offered for sale in the territory of the Community.

Article 2

For the purposes of this Directive:
1.   'package' means the pre–arranged combination of not fewer than two of the following when sold or offered for sale at an inclusive price and when the service covers a period of more than twenty–four hours or includes overnight accommodation:
(a)   transport;
(b)   accommodation;
(c)   other tourist services not ancillary to transport or accommodation and accounting for a significant proportion of the package.
The separate billing of various components of the same package shall not absolve the organiser or retailer from the obligations under this Directive;
2.   'organiser' means the person who, other than occasionally, organises packages and sells or offers them for sale, whether directly or through a retailer;
3.   'retailer' means the person who sells or offers for sale the package put together by the organiser;

4.   'consumer' means the person who takes or agrees to take the package ('the principal contractor'), or any person on whose behalf the principal contractor agrees to purchase the package ('the other beneficiaries') or any person to whom the principal contractor or any of the other beneficiaries transfers the package ('the transferee');

5.   'contract' means the agreement linking the consumer to the organiser and/or the retailer.

Article 3

1. Any descriptive matter concerning a package and supplied by the organiser or the retailer to the consumer, the price of the package and any other conditions applying to the contract must not contain any misleading information.

2. When a brochure is made available to the consumer, it shall indicate in a legible, comprehensible and accurate manner both the price and adequate information concerning:

(a)   the destination and the means, characteristics and categories of transport used;

(b)   the type of accommodation, its location, category or degree of comfort and its main features, its approval and tourist classification under the rules of the host Member State concerned;

(c)   the meal plan;

(d)   the itinerary;

(e)   general information on passport and visa requirements for nationals of the Member State or States concerned and health formalities required for the journey and the stay;

(f)   either the monetary amount or the percentage of the price which is to be paid on account, and the timetable for payment of the balance;

(g)   whether a minimum number of persons is required for the package to take place and, if so, the deadline for informing the consumer in the event of cancellation.

The particulars contained in the brochure are binding on the organiser or retailer, unless:

–   changes in such particulars have been clearly communicated to the consumer before conclusion of the contract, in which case the brochure shall expressly state so,

–   changes are made later following an agreement between the parties to the contract.

Article 4

1. (a)   The organiser and/or the retailer shall provide the consumer, in writing or any other appropriate form, before the contract is concluded, with general information on passport and visa requirements applicable to nationals of the Member State or States concerned and in particular on the periods for obtaining them, as well as with information on the health formalities required for the journey and the stay;

    (b)   The organiser and/or retailer shall also provide the consumer, in writing or any other appropriate form, with the following information in good time before the start of the journey:

        (i)   the times and places of intermediate stops and transport connections as well as details of the place to be occupied by the traveller, e.g. cabin or berth on ship, sleeper compartment on train;

        (ii)   the name, address and telephone number of the organiser's and/or retailer's local representative or, failing that, of local agencies on whose assistance a consumer in difficulty could call.

           Where no such representatives or agencies exist, the consumer must in any case be provided with an emergency telephone number or any other information that will enable him to contact the organiser and/or the retailer;

        (iii)   in the case of journeys or stays abroad by minors, information enabling direct contact to be established with the child or the person responsible at the child's place of stay;

        (iv)   information on the optional conclusion of an insurance policy to cover the cost of cancellation by the consumer or the cost of assistance, including repatriation, in the event of accident or illness.

2. Member States shall ensure that in relation to the contract the following principles apply:

(a)   depending on the particular package, the contract shall contain at least the elements listed in the Annex;

(b)   all the terms of the contract are set out in writing or such other form as is comprehensible and accessible to the consumer and must be communicated to him before the conclusion of the contract; the consumer is given a copy of these terms;

(c)   the provision under (b) shall not preclude the belated conclusion of last–minute reservations or contracts.

3. Where the consumer is prevented from proceeding with the package, he may transfer his booking, having first given the organiser or the retailer reasonable notice of his intention before departure, to a person who satisfies all the conditions applicable to the package. The transferor of the package and the transferee shall be jointly and severally liable to the organiser or retailer party to the contract for payment of the balance due and for any additional costs arising from such transfer.

4. (a) The prices laid down in the contract shall not be subject to revision unless the contract expressly provides for the possibility of upward or downward revision and states precisely how the revised price is to be calculated, and solely to allow for variations in:
  – transportation costs, including the cost of fuel,
  – dues, taxes or fees chargeable for certain services, such as landing taxes or embarkation or disembarkation fees at ports and airports,
  – the exchange rates applied to the particular package.

(b) During the twenty days prior to the departure date stipulated, the price stated in the contract shall not be increased.

5. If the organiser finds that before the departure he is constrained to alter significantly any of the essential terms, such as the price, he shall notify the consumer as quickly as possible in order to enable him to take appropriate decisions and in particular:
  – either to withdraw from the contract without penalty,
  – or to accept a rider to the contract specifying the alterations made and their impact on the price.

The consumer shall inform the organiser or the retailer of his decision as soon as possible.

6. If the consumer withdraws from the contract pursuant to paragraph 5, or if, for whatever cause, other than the fault of the consumer, the organiser cancels the package before the agreed date of departure, the consumer shall be entitled:

(a) either to take a substitute package of equivalent or higher quality where the organiser and/or retailer is able to offer him such a substitute. If the replacement package offered is of lower quality, the organiser shall refund the difference in price to the consumer;

(b) or to be repaid as soon as possible all sums paid by him under the contract.

In such a case, he shall be entitled, if appropriate, to be compensated by either the organiser or the retailer, whichever the relevant Member State's law requires, for non–performance of the contract, except where:

(i) cancellation is on the grounds that the number of persons enrolled for the package is less than the minimum number required and the consumer is informed of the cancellation, in writing, within the period indicated in the package description; or

(ii) cancellation, excluding overbooking, is for reasons of *force majeure*, i.e. unusual and unforeseeable circumstances beyond the control of the party by whom it is pleaded, the consequences of which could not have been avoided even if all due care had been exercised.

7. Where, after departure, a significant proportion of the services contracted for is not provided or the organiser perceives that he will be unable to procure a significant proportion of the services to be provided, the organiser shall make suitable alternative arrangements, at no extra cost to the consumer, for the continuation of the package, and where appropriate compensate the consumer for the difference between the services offered and those supplied.

If it is impossible to make such arrangements or these are not accepted by the consumer for good reasons, the organiser shall, where appropriate, provide the consumer, at no extra cost, with equivalent transport back to the place of departure, or to another return–point to which the consumer has agreed and shall, where appropriate, compensate the consumer.

Article 5

1. Member States shall take the necessary steps to ensure that the organiser and/or retailer party to the contract is liable to the consumer for the proper performance of the obligations arising from the contract, irrespective of whether such obligations are to be performed by that organiser and/or retailer or by other suppliers of services without prejudice to the right of the organiser and/or retailer to pursue those other suppliers of services.

2. With regard to the damage resulting for the consumer from the failure to perform or the improper performance of the contract, Member States shall take the necessary steps to ensure that the organiser and/or retailer is/are liable unless such failure to perform or improper performance is attributable neither to any fault of theirs nor to that of another supplier of services, because:

– the failures which occur in the performance of the contract are attributable to the consumer,
– such failures are attributable to a third party unconnected with the provision of the services contracted for, and are unforeseeable or unavoidable,
– such failures are due to a case of *force majeure* such as that defined in Article 4(6), second subparagraph (ii), or to an event which the organiser and/or retailer or the supplier of services, even with all due care, could not foresee or forestall.

In the cases referred to in the second and third indents, the organiser and/or retailer party to the contract shall be required to give prompt assistance to a consumer in difficulty.

In the matter of damages arising from the non–performance or improper performance of the services involved in the package, the Member States may allow compensation to be limited in accordance with the international conventions governing such services.

In the matter of damage other than personal injury resulting from the non–performance or improper performance of the services involved in the package, the Member States may allow compensation to be limited under the contract. Such limitation shall not be unreasonable.

3. Without prejudice to the fourth subparagraph of paragraph 2, there may be no exclusion by means of a contractual clause from the provisions of paragraphs 1 and 2.

4. The consumer must communicate any failure in the performance of a contract which he perceives on the spot to the supplier of the services concerned and to the organiser and/or retailer in writing or any other appropriate form at the earliest opportunity.

This obligation must be stated clearly and explicitly in the contract.

Article 6

In cases of complaint, the organiser and/or retailer or his local representative, if there is one, must make prompt efforts to find appropriate solutions.

Article 7

The organiser and/or retailer party to the contract shall provide sufficient evidence of security for the refund of money paid over and for the repatriation of the consumer in the event of insolvency.

Article 8

Member States may adopt or return more stringent provisions in the field covered by this Directive to protect the consumer.

Article 9

1. Member States shall bring into force the measures necessary to comply with this Directive before 31 December 1992. They shall forthwith inform the Commission thereof.
2. Member States shall communicate to the Commission the texts of the main provisions of national law which they adopt in the field governed by this Directive. The Commission shall inform the other Member States thereof.

Article 10

This Directive is addressed to the Member States.

Done at Luxembourg, 13 June 1990.

Annex

Elements to be included in the contract if relevant to the particular package;
(a) the travel destination(s) and, where periods of stay are involved, the relevant periods, with dates;
(b) the means, characteristics and categories of transport to be used, the dates, times and points of departure and return;
(c) where the package includes accommodation, its location, its tourist category or degree of comfort, its main features, its compliance with the rules of the host Member State concerned and the meal plan;
(d) whether a minimum number of persons is required for the package to take place and, if so, the deadline for informing the consumer in the event of cancellation;
(e) the itinerary;
(f) visits, excursions or other services which are included in the total price agreed for the package;
(g) the name and address of the organiser, the retailer and, where appropriate, the insurer;
(h) the price of the package, an indication of the possibility of price revisions under Article 4(4) and an indication of any dues, taxes or fees chargeable for certain services (landing, embarkation or disembarkation fees at ports and airports, tourist taxes) where such costs are not included in the package;
(i) the payment schedule and method of payment;

(j) special requirements which the consumer has communicated to the organiser or retailer when making the booking, and which both have accepted;

(k) periods within which the consumer must make any complaint concerning failure to perform or improper performance of the contract.

Appendix 10

Council Directive 94/47/EC of the European Parliament and the Council of 26 October 1994 on the protection of purchasers in respect of certain aspects of contracts relating to the purchase of the right to use immovable properties on a timeshare basis (footnotes omitted).

THE EUROPEAN PARLIAMENT AND THE COUNCIL OF THE EUROPEAN UNION,

Having regard to the Treaty establishing the European Community, and in particular Article 100a thereof,

Having regard to the proposal from the Commission,

Having regard to the opinion of the Economic and Social Committee,

Acting in accordance with the procedure laid down in Article 189b of the Treaty.

1. Whereas the disparities between national legislations on contracts relating to the purchase of the right to use one or more immovable properties on a time–share basis are likely to create barriers to the proper operation of the internal market and distortions of competition and lead to the compartmentalisation of national markets;

2. Whereas the aim of this Directive is to establish a minimum basis of common rules on such matters which will make it possible to ensure that the internal market operates properly and will thereby protect purchasers; whereas it is sufficient for those rules to cover contractual transactions only with regard to those aspects that relate to information on the constituent parts of contracts, the arrangements for communicating such information and the procedures and arrangements for cancellation and withdrawal; whereas the appropriate instrument to achieve that aim is a Directive; whereas this Directive is therefore consistent with the principle of subsidiarity.

3. Whereas the legal nature of the rights which are the subject of the contracts covered by this Directive varies considerably from one Member State to another, whereas reference should therefore be made in

summary form to those variations, giving a sufficiently broad definition of such contracts, without thereby implying harmonisation within the Community of the legal nature of the rights in question;

4.   Whereas this Directive is not designed to regulate the extent to which contracts for the use of one or more immovable properties on a timeshare basis may be concluded in Member States or the legal basis for such contracts;

5.   Whereas, in practice, contracts relating to the purchase of the right to use one or more immovable properties on a timeshare basis differ from tenancy agreements; whereas that difference can be seen from, *inter alia*, the means of payment;

6.   Whereas it may be seen from the market that hotels, residential hotels and other similar residential tourist premises are involved in contractual transactions similar to those which have made this Directive necessary;

7.   Whereas it is necessary to avoid any misleading or incomplete details in information concerned specifically with the sale of the rights to use one or more immovable properties on a timeshare basis; whereas such information should be supplemented by a document which must be made available to anyone who requests it; whereas the information therein must constitute part of the contract for the purchase of the right to use one or more immovable properties on a timeshare basis;

8.   Whereas, in order to give purchasers a high level of protection and in view of the specific characteristics of systems for using immovable properties on a timeshare basis, contracts for the purchase of the right to use one or more immovable properties on a timeshare basis must include certain minimal items;

9.   Whereas, with a view to establishing effective protection for purchasers in this field, it is necessary to stipulate minimum obligations with which vendors must comply *vis–à–vis* purchasers;

10.   Whereas the contract for the purchase of the right to use one or more immovable properties on a timeshare basis must be drawn up in the official language or one of the official languages of the Member State in which the purchaser is resident or in the official language or one of the official languages of the Member State of which he is a national which must be one of the official languages of the Community; whereas, however, the Member State in which the purchaser is resident may

require that the contract be drawn up in its language or its languages which must be an official language or official languages of the Community; whereas provision should be made for a certified translation of each contract for the purpose of the formalities to be completed in the Member State in which the relevant property is situated;

11. Whereas to give the purchaser the chance to realise more fully what his obligations and rights under the contract are he should be allowed a period during which he may withdraw from the contract without giving reasons since the property in question is often situated in a State and subject to legislation which are different from his own;

12. Whereas the requirement on the vendor's part that advance payments be made before the end of the period during which the purchaser may withdraw without giving reasons may reduce the purchaser's protection; whereas, therefore, advance payments before the end of that period should be prohibited;

13. Whereas in the event of cancellation of or withdrawal from a contract for the purchase of the right to use one or more immovable properties on a timeshare basis the price of which is entirely or partly covered by credit granted to the purchaser by the vendor or by a third party on the basis of an agreement concluded between that third party and the vendor, it should be provided that the credit agreement should be cancelled without penalty;

14. Whereas there is a risk, in certain cases, that the consumer may be deprived of the protection provided for in this Directive if the law of a non–Member State is specified as the law applicable to the contract; whereas this Directive should therefore include provisions intended to obviate that risk;

15. Whereas it is for the Member States to adopt measures to ensure that the vendor fulfils his obligations,

HAVE ADOPTED THIS DIRECTIVE:

Article 1

The purpose of this Directive shall be to approximate the laws, regulations and administrative provisions of the Member States on the protection of purchasers in respect of certain aspects of contracts relating directly or indirectly to the purchase of the right to use one or more immovable properties on a timeshare basis.

This Directive shall cover only those aspects of the above provisions concerning contractual transactions that relate to:

– information on the constituent parts of a contract and the arrangements for the communication of that information,

– the procedures and arrangements for cancellation and withdrawal.

With due regard to the general rules of the Treaty, the Member States shall remain competent for other matters, *inter alia* determination of the legal nature of the rights which are the subject of the contracts covered by this Directive.

Article 2

For the purposes of this Directive:

– 'contract relating directly or indirectly to the purchase of the right to use one or more immovable properties on a timeshare basis', hereinafter referred to as 'contract', shall mean any contract or group of contracts concluded for at least three years under which, directly or indirectly, on payment of a certain global price, a real property right or any other right relating to the use of one or more immovable properties for a specified or specifiable period of the year which may not be less than one week, is established or is the subject of a transfer or an undertaking to transfer,

– 'immovable property' shall mean any building or part of a building for use as accommodation to which that right which is the subject of the contract relates,

– 'vendor' shall mean any natural or legal person who, acting in transactions covered by this Directive and in his professional capacity, establishes, transfers or undertakes to transfer the right which is the subject of the contract,

– 'purchaser' shall mean any natural person who, acting in transactions covered by this Directive, for purposes which may be regarded as being outwith his professional capacity, has the right which is the subject of the contract transferred to him or for whom the right which is the subject of the contract is established.

Article 3

1. The Member States shall make provision in the legislation for measures to ensure that the vendor is required to provide any person requesting information of the immovable property or properties with a document which, in addition to a general description of the property or properties, shall provide at least brief and accurate information on the particulars referred to in points (a), (g), (i) and (1) of the Annex and on how further information may be obtained.

2. The Member States shall make provision in the legislation to ensure that all the information referred to in paragraph 1 which must be provided in the document referred to in paragraph 1 forms an integral part of the contract.

Unless the parties expressly agree otherwise, only changes resulting from circumstances beyond the vendor's control may be made to the information provided in the document referred to in paragraph 1.

Any changes to that information shall be communicated to the purchasers before the contract is concluded. The contract shall expressly mention any such changes.

3. Any advertising referred to in the immovable property concerned shall indicate the possibility of obtaining the document referred to in paragraph 1 and where it may be obtained.

Article 4

The Member States shall make provision in their legislation to ensure that:

– the contract, which shall be in writing, includes at least the items referred to in the Annex,

– the contract and the document referred to in Article 3(1) are drawn up in the language or one of the languages of the Member State in which the purchaser is resident or in the language or one of the languages of the Member State of which he is national which shall be an official language or official languages of the Community, at the purchaser's option. The Member State in which the purchaser is resident may, however, require that the contract be drawn up in all cases in at least its language or languages which must be an official language or official languages of the Community, and

– the vendor provides the purchaser with a certified translation of the contract in the language or one of the languages of the Member State in which the immovable property is situated which shall be an official language or official languages of the Community.

Article 5

The Member States shall make provision in their legislation to ensure that:

1. in addition to the possibilities available to the purchaser, under national laws on the nullity of contracts, the purchaser shall have the right:

   – to withdraw without giving any reason within 10 calendar days of both parties' signing the contract or of both parties' signing a binding preliminary contract. If the 10th day is a public holiday, the period shall be extended to the first working day thereafter,

   – if the contract does not include the information referred to in points (a), (b), (c), (d)(1), (d)(2), (h), (i), (k), (l) and (m) of the Annex, at the time of both parties' signing the contract or of both parties' signing a binding preliminary contract, to cancel the contract within three months thereof. If the information in question is provided within those three months, the purchaser's withdrawal period provided for in the first indent, shall then start,

   – if by the end of the three–month period provided for in the second indent the purchaser has not exercised the right to cancel and the contract does not include the information referred to in points (a), (b), (c), (d)(1), (d)(2), (h), (i), (k), (l) and (m) of the Annex, to the withdrawal period provided for in the first indent from the day after the end of that three–month period;

2. if the purchaser intends to exercise the rights provided for in paragraph 1 he shall, before the expiry of the relevant deadline, notify the person whose name and address appear in the contract for that purpose by a means which can be proved in accordance with national law in accordance with the procedures specified in the contract pursuant to

point (1) of the Annex. The deadline shall be deemed to have been observed if the notification, if it is in writing, is dispatched before the deadline expires;

3. where the purchaser exercises the right provided for in the first indent of paragraph 1, he may be required to defray, where appropriate, only those expenses which, in accordance with national law, are incurred as a result of the conclusion of and withdrawal from the contract and which, correspond to legal formalities which must be completed before the end of the period referred to in the first indent of paragraph 1. Such expenses shall be expressly mentioned in the contract;

4. where the purchaser exercises the right of cancellation provided for in the second indent of paragraph 1 he shall not be required to make any defrayal.

Article 6

The Member States shall make provision in their legislation to prohibit any advance payment by a purchaser before the end of the period during which he may exercise the right of withdrawal.

Article 7

The Member States shall make provision in their legislation to ensure that:

–   if the price is fully or partly covered by credit granted by the vendor, or

–   if the price is fully or partly covered by credit granted to the purchaser by a third party on the basis of an agreement between the third party and the vendor,

the credit agreement shall be cancelled, without any penalty, if the purchaser exercises his right to cancel or withdraw from the contract as provided for in Article 5.

The Member States shall lay down detailed arrangements to govern the cancellation of credit agreements.

Article 8

The Member States shall make provision in their legislation to ensure that any clause whereby a purchaser renounces the enjoyment of rights under this Directive or whereby a vendor is freed from the responsibilities arising from this Directive shall not be binding on the purchaser, under conditions laid down by national law.

Article 9

The Member States shall take the measures necessary to ensure that, whatever the law applicable may be, the purchaser is not deprived of the protection afforded by this Directive, if the immovable property concerned is situated within the territory of a Member State.

Article 10

The Member States shall make provision in their legislation for the consequences of non–compliance with this Directive.

Article 11

This Directive shall not prevent Member States from adopting or maintaining provisions which are more favourable as regards the protection of purchasers in the field in question, without prejudice to their obligations under the Treaty.

Article 12

1. Member States shall bring into force the laws, regulations and administrative provisions necessary for them to comply with this Directive no later than 30 months after its publication in the Official *Journal of the European Communities*. They shall immediately inform the Commission thereof.

When Member States adopt those measures, they shall include references to this Directive or shall accompany them with such references on their official publications. The Member States shall lay down the manner in which such references shall be made.

2.	The Member States shall communicate to the Commission the texts of the provisions of national law which they adopt in the field governed by this Directive.

Article 13

This Directive is addressed to the Member States.

Done at Strasbourg, 26 October 1994.

Annex

Minimum list of items to be included in the contract referred to in Article 4

(a)	The identities and domiciles of the parties, including specific information on the vendor's legal status at the time of the conclusion of the contract and the identity and domicile of the owner.

(b)	The exact nature of the right which is the subject of the contract and a clause setting out the conditions governing the exercise of that right within the territory of the Member State(s) in which the property or properties concerned relates is or are situated and if those conditions have been fulfilled or, if they have not, what conditions remain to be fulfilled.

(c)	When the property has been determined, an accurate description of that property and its location.

(d)	Where the immovable property is under construction:

(1) the state of completion;

(2) a reasonable estimate of the deadline for completion of the immovable property;

(3) where it concerns a specific immovable property, the number of the building permit and the name(s) and full address(es) of the competent authority or authorities;

(4) the state of completion of the services rendering the immovable property fully operational (gas, electricity, water and telephone connections);

(5) a guarantee regarding completion of the immovable property or a guarantee regarding reimbursement of any payment made if the property is not completed and, where appropriate, the conditions governing the operation of those guarantees.

(e) The services (lighting, water, maintenance, refuse collection) to which the purchaser has or will have access and on what conditions.

(f) The common facilities, such as swimming pool, sauna, etc., to which the purchaser has or may have access, and, where appropriate, on what conditions.

(g) The principles on the basis of which the maintenance of and repairs to the immovable property and its administration and management will be arranged.

(h) The exact period within which the right which is the subject of the contract may be exercised and, if necessary, its duration; the date on which the purchaser may start to exercise the contractual right.

(i) The price to be paid by the purchaser to exercise the contractual right; and estimate of the amount to be paid by the purchaser for the use of common facilities and services; the basis for the calculation of the amount of charges relating to occupation of the property, the mandatory statutory charges (for example, taxes and fees) and the administrative overheads (for example, management, maintenance and repairs).

(j) A clause stating that acquisition will not result in costs, charges or obligations other than those specified in the contract.

(k) Whether or not it is possible to join a scheme for the exchange or resale of the contractual rights, and any costs involved should an exchange and/or resale scheme be organised by the vendor or by a third party designated by him in the contract.

(l) Information on the right to cancel or withdraw from the contract and indication of the person to whom any letter of cancellation or withdrawal should be sent, specifying also the arrangements under which such letters may be sent; precise indication of the nature and amount of the costs which the purchaser will be required to defray pursuant to Article 5(3) if he exercises his right to withdraw; where appropriate, information on the arrangements for the cancellation of the credit agreement linked to the contract in the event of cancellation of the contract or withdrawal from it.

(m) The date and place of each party's signing of the contract.

Subject Index

Index of Authors Cited

Index of Cases Cited